The Mindbrain and Dreams

In *The Mindbrain and Dreams: An Exploration of Dreaming, Thinking, and Artistic Creation*, Mark J. Blechner argues that the mind and brain should be understood as a single unit – the "mindbrain" – that manipulates our raw perceptions of the world and reshapes that world through dreams, thoughts, and artistic creation.

This book explores how dreams are key to understanding mental processes, and how working with dreams clinically with individuals and groups provides an essential route toward achieving transformation within the psychoanalytic process. Covering such key topics as knowledge, emotion, metaphor, and memory, this book sets out a radical new agenda for understanding the importance of dreams in human thought and their clinical importance in psychoanalysis. Blechner builds on his previous work and takes it much farther, drawing on the latest neuroscientific findings to set out a new way of how the mindbrain constructs reality, while providing guidance on how best to help people understand their dreams.

The Mindbrain and Dreams: An Exploration of Dreaming, Thinking, and Artistic Creation will appeal to psychologists, psychoanalysts, philosophers, and cognitive neuroscientists who want new ways to explore how people think and understand the world.

Mark J. Blechner, Ph.D., is a psychologist and psychoanalyst in New York City. He is a training and supervising psychoanalyst at William Alanson White Institute. He has taught at Columbia University, Yale University, and New York University.

Psychoanalysis in a New Key Book Series

Donnel B. Stern
Series Editor

When music is played in a new key, the melody does not change, but the notes that make up the composition do: change in the context of continuity, continuity that perseveres through change. Psychoanalysis in a New Key publishes books that share the aims psychoanalysts have always had, but that approach them differently. The books in the series are not expected to advance any particular theoretical agenda, although to this date most have been written by analysts from the Interpersonal and Relational orientations.

The most important contribution of a psychoanalytic book is the communication of something that nudges the reader's grasp of clinical theory and practice in an unexpected direction. Psychoanalysis in a New Key creates a deliberate focus on innovative and unsettling clinical thinking. Because that kind of thinking is encouraged by exploration of the sometimes surprising contributions to psychoanalysis of ideas and findings from other fields, Psychoanalysis in a New Key particularly encourages interdisciplinary studies. Books in the series have married psychoanalysis with dissociation, trauma theory, sociology, and criminology. The series is open to the consideration of studies examining the relationship between psychoanalysis and any other field – for instance, biology, literary and art criticism, philosophy, systems theory, anthropology, and political theory.

But innovation also takes place within the boundaries of psychoanalysis, and Psychoanalysis in a New Key therefore also presents work that reformulates thought and practice without leaving the precincts of the field. Books in the series focus, for example, on the significance of personal values in psychoanalytic practice, on the complex interrelationship between the analyst's clinical work and personal life, on the consequences for the clinical situation when patient and analyst are from different cultures, and on the need for psychoanalysts to accept the degree to which they knowingly satisfy their own wishes during treatment hours, often to the patient's detriment. A full list of all titles in this series is available at: www.routledge.com/series/LEAPNKBS

TITLES IN THIS SERIES INCLUDE:

Vol. 43 The Mindbrain and Dreams
An Exploration of Dreaming, Thinking, and Artistic Creation
Mark J. Blechner

Vol. 42 Further Developments in Interpersonal Psychoanalysis, 1980s–2010s
Evolving Interest in the Analyst's Subjectivity
Edited by Donnel B. Stern and Irwin Hirsch

Vol. 41 Understanding the Sexual Betrayal of Boys and Men
The Trauma of Sexual Abuse
Edited by Richard B. Gartner

Vol. 40 Healing Sexually Betrayed Men and Boys
Treatment for Sexual Abuse, Assault, and Trauma
Edited by Richard B. Gartner

Vol. 39 The Voice of the Analyst
Narratives on Developing a Psychoanalytic Identity
Edited by Linda Hillman and Therese Rosenblatt

Vol. 38 Interpersonal Psychoanalysis and the Enigma of Consciousness
Edgar A. Levenson and edited by Alan Slomowitz

The Mindbrain and Dreams

An Exploration of Dreaming, Thinking, and Artistic Creation

Mark J. Blechner

LONDON AND NEW YORK

First published 2018
by Routledge
2 Park Square, Milton Park, Abingdon, Oxon OX14 4RN

and by Routledge
711 Third Avenue, New York, NY 10017

Routledge is an imprint of the Taylor and Francis Group, an informa business

© 2018 Mark J. Blechner

The right of Mark J. Blechner to be identified as author of this work has been asserted by him in accordance with sections 77 and 78 of the Copyright, Designs and Patents Act 1988.

All rights reserved. No part of this book may be reprinted or reproduced or utilized in any form or by any electronic, mechanical, or other means, now known or hereafter invented, including photocopying and recording, or in any information storage or retrieval system, without permission in writing from the publishers.

Trademark notice: Product or corporate names may be trademarks or registered trademarks, and are used only for identification and explanation without intent to infringe.

British Library Cataloguing-in-Publication Data
A catalogue record for this book is available from the British Library

Library of Congress Cataloging-in-Publication Data
Names: Blechner, Mark J., author.
Title: The mindbrain and dreams: an exploration of dreaming, thinking, and artistic creation / Mark J. Blechner.
Description: New York: Routledge, 2018. | Series: Psychoanalysis in a new key book series; 43 | Includes bibliographical references and index.
Identifiers: LCCN 2017052166 (print) | LCCN 2017054664 (ebook) | ISBN 9781351185677 (Master) | ISBN 9781351185653 (ePUB) | ISBN 9781351185660 (Web PDF) | ISBN 9781351185646 (Mobi/Kindle) | ISBN 9780815394563 (hardback: alk. paper) | ISBN 9780815394570 (pbk.: alk. paper)
Subjects: LCSH: Dreams. | Thought and thinking. | Creative ability. | Psychoanalysis.
Classification: LCC BF1078 (ebook) | LCC BF1078.B564 2018 (print) | DDC 154.6/3–dc23
LC record available at https://lccn.loc.gov/2017052166

ISBN: 978-0-8153-9456-3 (hbk)
ISBN: 978-0-8153-9457-0 (pbk)
ISBN: 978-1-351-18567-7 (ebk)

Typeset in Times New Roman
by Wearset Ltd, Boldon, Tyne and Wear

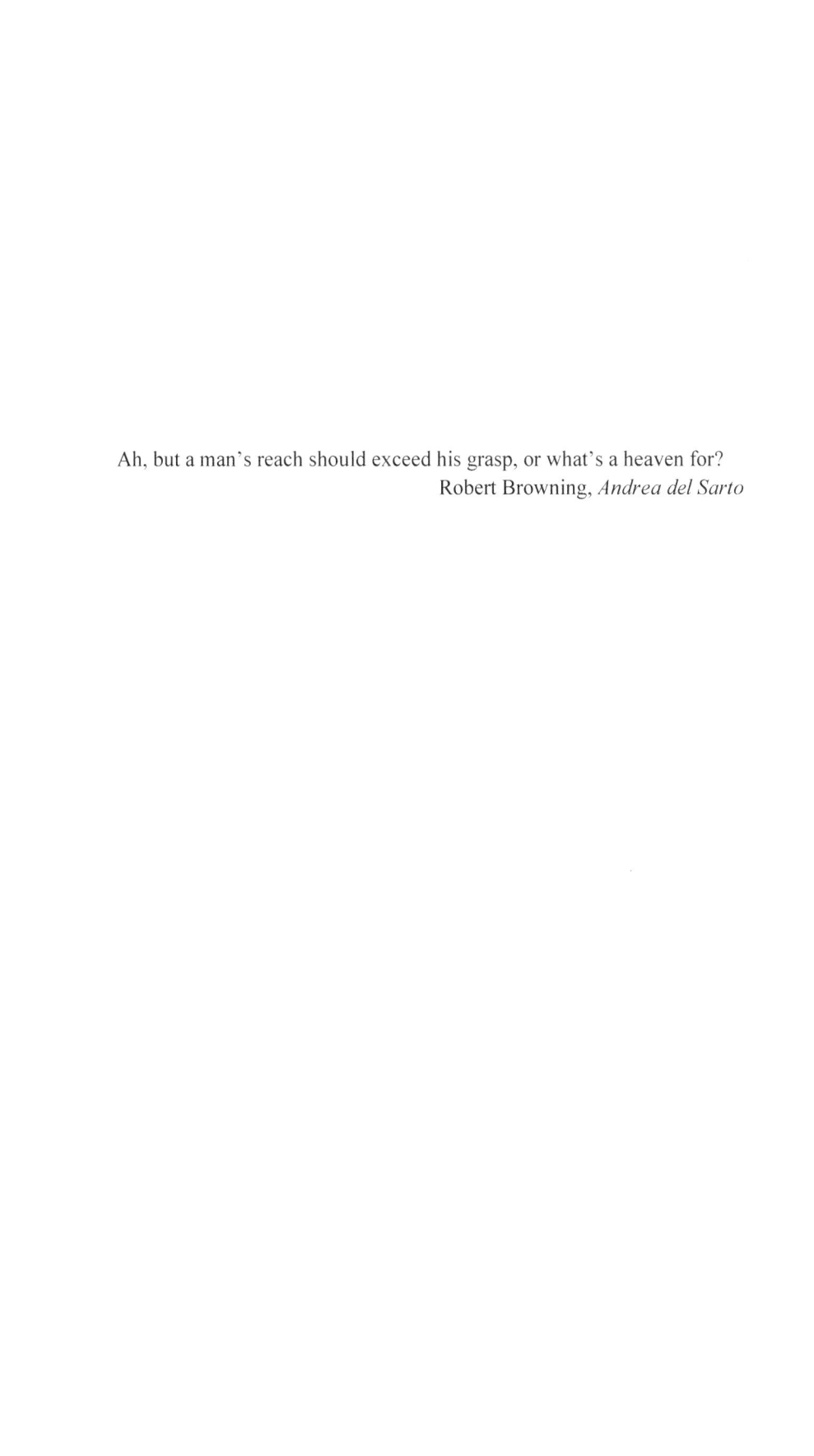

Ah, but a man's reach should exceed his grasp, or what's a heaven for?
Robert Browning, *Andrea del Sarto*

Contents

List of figures xi
Acknowledgments xii

1 Introduction 1

PART I
How the mindbrain transforms the world 13

2 The mindbrain creates its own version of the world 15

3 Condensation, interobjects, and categories 25

4 Displacement 42

5 Metaphor 45

6 Puns – linguistic and nonlinguistic 100

7 Homoforms and homomelodies 107

8 Metonymy 111

9 Symbols 120

10 Dreams and the mindbrain's structuring of experience 134

11 Psychological defenses and dreams 146

x Contents

PART II
Working with dreams clinically   183

12 New ways of conceptualizing and working with dreams   185

13 The dream guides its own analysis: how to work with dreams over time   196

14 Group dream interpretation   220

PART III
Dreams, knowledge, memory, emotion, and the mindbrain   235

15 How neuropsychoanalysis and clinical psychoanalysis can learn from each other   237

16 Elusive illusions: reality judgment and reality assignment in dreams and waking life   252

17 When your mindbrain knows things that you don't   265

18 Memory, knowledge, and dreams   280

19 The language of thought and the wakingwork   294

List of dreams in The Mindbrain and Dreams   305
References   309
Index   334

Figures

3.1	Pablo Picasso, *Baboon and Her Young*	36
5.1	Caspar David Friedrich, *Solitary Tree*, 1821	70
5.2	René Magritte, *The Rape*	71
5.3	White Diamonds Perfume Advertisement	72
5.4	Which is kiki and which is bouba?	74
5.5	Colorado River Aqueduct at Hayfield, February 2012	79
5.6	Swimming Pool	79
5.7	Seal	80
5.8	Boat	80
5.9	Lock	81
5.10	Hinge	81
5.11	Cellphone-baby	82
5.12	Rebus 1	86
5.13	Rebus 2	87
6.1	Face-vase	105
6.2	Wife-mother-in-law	105
7.1	Figurative transposition	110
8.1	René Magritte, *Memory*	114
8.2	Joan Miró, *This Is the Color of My Dreams*, 1925	115
8.3	Pablo Picasso, *Pipe Rack and Still Life on Table*	116
17.1a	Brahms Clarinet Sonata, Op. 120, #2, first movement, clarinet part, theme 1	267
17.1b	Theme 2	267
17.2	The Müller-Lyer optical illusion with arrows (1889)	275

Acknowledgments

I have been fortunate to have been supported throughout my life by teachers, colleagues, family, and friends who nurtured and supported my multifarious intellectual pursuits and never boxed me in. Writing this book has brought me back into contact with teachers from nearly 50 years ago, including musicologists Robert Marshall and Ann B. Scott, and the brilliant researchers at Haskins Laboratories and Bell Laboratories. My peer supervision group, the Viceroys – Sandra Buechler, Richard Gartner, John O'Leary, Allison Rosen, and Robert Watson, all precious to me – have collaborated enthusiastically with me in experiments about dreams and clinical work. Fred Stern was especially creative in suggesting experiments for our private dream group.

I am immensely grateful to Barbara Sevde and Daniel Kozloff, who carefully read the entire text and gave me excellent suggestions. In addition, portions of the text benefited from astute comments by Nanette Auerhahn, Marianne Goldberger, and Sue Shapiro. My ideas were also enhanced by many friends and colleagues, including Robert Bartlett, Easley Blackwood, Jr., Robert Bosnak, Grant Brenner, Jane Bressler, Lee Bressler, Richard Brockman, Ellen Cassedy, Amy Cooney, James Cutting, Ruth Day, William Domhoff, Kate Dunn, Susan Fabrick, Debra Farbman, Han Feng, Leonard Ferrante, Motoni Fong Hodges, Helen Fronshtein, William Hirst, J. Allan Hobson, Stephen Isaacson, Zela Khan, Susan Klebanoff, Susan Kolod, Emily Kuriloff, Lauren Levine, Paul Lippmann, Raul Ludmer, Lisa Lyons, Jennifer McCarroll, David Olds, Aaron Painter, Alexander Petruska, Melissa Ritter, Alan Schwartz, Mark Solms, Johannes Somary, Fred Stern, Ruth Szmarag, Vivien Tartter, Christopher Warnke, Robin Young, and Polly Young-Eisendrath. My nephew, Scott Bressler, has expertly designed and managed my website and set up the links in the book to musical passages. I regret that my parents, Hannah and Norbert Blechner, and my oldest sister, Jane Bressler, who supported my work enthusiastically, did not live to see the publication of this book.

Sue Littleford professionally edited the entire manuscript with wit and insight and corrected my understanding of the attributes of snakes. I am immensely grateful to her, as well as to Donnel Stern, who shepherded the project with encouragement and determination, to Matt Deacon who sped along the print production, and to the expert management team at Taylor and Francis, Kate Hawes and Charles Bath. Conrad Cummings transcribed the Brahms examples expertly.

My patients, who must remain unnamed, deserve the greatest thanks for allowing me the chance to understand their psychological processes and explore their dreams.

Every effort has been made to contact the copyright holders for their permission to reprint selections in this book. Routledge would be grateful to hear from any copyright holder who is not here acknowledged and will undertake to rectify any errors or omissions in future editions of this book. Credit for the images featured is given underneath each in their respective chapters.

Portions of Chapters 3, 9, and 19 were first published in Blechner, M. (2001). *The Dream Frontier*. New York: Routledge. Reprinted by permission of Taylor and Francis, LLC.

An earlier version of Chapter 12, "New ways of conceptualizing and working with dreams" was published in *Contemporary Psychoanalysis*, 2013, 49: 259–275. Reprinted by permission of Taylor and Francis, LLC.

An earlier version of Chapter 14, "Group dream interpretation" was published in *Contemporary Psychoanalysis*, 2011, 47: 406–419. Reprinted by permission of Taylor and Francis, LLC.

An earlier version of Chapter 15, "How neuropsychoanalysis and clinical psychoanalysis can learn from each other" was published in *The Annual of Psychoanalysis*, 2014, 38–39: 142–155. Reprinted by kind permission of the journal Editor, James W. Anderson.

An earlier version of Chapter 16, "Elusive illusions: Reality judgment and reality assignment in dreams and waking life" was published in *Neuropsychoanalysis*, 2005, 7: 95–101. Reprinted by permission of Taylor and Francis, LLC.

Chapter 1

Introduction

> It is worthy of remark that a belief constantly inculcated during the early years of life, while the brain is impressible, appears to acquire almost the nature of an instinct; and the very essence of an instinct is that it is followed independently of reason.
>
> Charles Darwin, *The Descent of Man*

Let us start with the word "mindbrain." I made it up, but not out of whole cloth. It is a word that has been gestating for a long time. When we say "mind," we mean the collection of mental processes and faculties. When we say "brain," we mean the bodily organ located in our cranium which most scientists think is responsible for the processes we call mind. We hear that distinction from our earliest years, and so it evolves into a conceptual distinction that is hard to shake.

Descartes argued that mind was separate from brain, and we have been wrangling with Descartes's dualism for 400 years. Modern neuroscientists find it incompatible with scientific evidence; we are quite sure today that Descartes was wrong that the mind or soul was located in the pineal gland. We have been moving ever closer to viewing the unity of the mind and brain. Linguistically, it has become quite common to write about the "mind/brain."[1] But that forward slash retained the trace of dualism. Since the words "mind" and "brain" continually force us into Descartes's dualism, no matter how much we try to escape from it, we must take linguistic action and create a new word that will enable us to think new thoughts.

In my book *The Dream Frontier* (2001), I wrote:

> The aim of modern neuroscience, as well as Freud's aim in his *Project for a Scientific Psychology*, is to be able to account for mental events in terms of neurobiological processes, and vice versa, so that ultimately

we will understand them as unitary phenomena. And so, many of us have come to talk about the "mind/brain." This compound term is the closest we can get in English these days to bypass Cartesian dualism. Maybe someday we will have a single word for the mind/brain. Perhaps we will say "mind/brain" often enough, and it will be slurred into a new word like "mibron." Or maybe a completely new word will be coined. Maybe someone will create such a new word in a dream.

I will no longer wait for "someone." I have decided to take the linguistic bull by the horns, coin the new word, and use it over and over. You may ask, "How far is mindbrain from mind/brain?" My answer is,

Very far. Get rid of the forward slash, and you may free human thought from the semantic trap of dualism. By the time you reach the end of this book, see whether you have gotten used to "mindbrain" and have found your thinking about the mind and brain restructured.

Semantic liberation is conceptual liberation.

"Mindbrain" is not just a new word. It is what Foucault called an episteme. Foucault wrote (1972, p. 197): "I would define the episteme retrospectively as the strategic apparatus which permits of separating out from among all the statements which are possible those that will be acceptable within." New epistemes allow or restrict new thoughts and new statements; this is the case with "mindbrain."

The *Stanford Encyclopedia of Philosophy* tells us (Smart, 2017):

Idiomatically we do use "She has a good mind" and "She has a good brain" interchangeably, but we would hardly say "Her mind weighs fifty ounces".

But consider this: we can say "She has a good mindbrain" and we can say "Her mindbrain weighs fifty ounces." As stated above, the lack of a unifying term propagates the dualism of mind and brain, and my hope is that my neologism of "mindbrain" will allow us to think in new ways.[2]

I would like in this book also to outline new ways of understanding dreams and what they can tell us about the operation of the mindbrain. Dreams are given short shrift or neglected completely by most cognitive neuroscientists. Why is dreaming so ignored?

One reason is that it is hard to study people while they are asleep. No one has reported the content of a dream while it is happening. Part of the dreaming mindbrain is set up to inhibit motor action while we are dreaming; this is a good thing, for it prevents us from acting out our dreams while they are happening. But so far, we only have reports of dreams after the fact. Sometimes, if we are awakened in the middle of a dream, there is virtually no time lag between dream and report; but even then, we do not know how close the dream report is to the actual dream experience. Therefore, research psychologists have been skittish about studying dreams and incorporating observations about dreams into general psychological theories; their rationale is that the data may not be very reliable. We have access to memories of dreams, they claimed, but not the dreams themselves as they are happening.

This may no longer be true. I wrote in *The Dream Frontier* (Blechner, 2001) that we only had access to memories of dreams. No one had been able to observe another person's dream as it is happening, except in the science-fiction film *Brainstorm*. Since then, however, a group of Japanese neuroscientists (Horikawa *et al.*, 2013) have been able to record magnetic resonance images (MRI) while someone is asleep and determine from the brain scans some of the content that the person is dreaming. The prospect of being able to track the actual narrative of a person's dream in real time seems a possibility in the not-too-distant future.

In the meantime, if the content and structure of dreams are subject to uncertainty, they are nevertheless important. About one third of our lives is spent asleep, and much of that time is spent dreaming. It is risky to exclude all that mental activity from our psychological theories. I would like in this book to address some of the essential characteristics of dreams and dream thinking. In my view, they are essential to our theories of thinking, experiencing, consciousness, emotion, metaphor, defenses, and problem solving. I will try to address some of the ways that dreams expand our understanding of all these subfields in psychology and cognitive neuroscience.

How the mindbrain transforms the world

Freud believed that the dream starts with the latent dream thought, which can often be an unacceptable wish that emerges during the night while we are sleeping. In order to stay asleep, the mindbrain disguises the latent dream thought by transforming it through what Freud called "the mechanisms of the dreamwork." These mechanisms include condensation, displacement, symbolization, and pictorialization.

Yet many dreams are not very disguised. People who work with dreams clinically day after day are astonished at how little disguise is applied to some of the themes that are important to the dreamer and would be expected to be taboo. Freud did not know, as we do today, that we dream regularly through the night, much more often than we consciously realize. Dreaming occurs during most REM periods and also occurs during non-REM periods. Since dreams are such a regular occurrence during the night, it seems less sensible to look for a unitary cause of dreaming. If we keep asking "Why do we dream?" then we shall have to ask also "Why do we think?" In neither case can we expect a single answer. We know that disguise occurs in some waking thought, through ego defenses (A. Freud, 1936; McWilliams, 1994) and what Sullivan (1953) called "selective inattention," but we do not assume a high level of disguise and censorship in all waking thoughts. The same may well be true of dreams.

The main source of the difficulty we have in understanding dreams is that dreams are not concerned with communicability (Blechner, 2001). This view of dreams shifts our view of the unconscious; it is not only a place of churning drives that are kept out of awareness by repression. That may be a part of it, but not the main part of it. The bulk of our thinking is unconscious, and part of what keeps it unconscious, besides dynamic repression, is that it has meaning without communicability.

If we do not agree with Freud that the mechanisms of the dreamwork serve to disguise a hidden wish, we nevertheless can appreciate Freud's extraordinary documentation and analysis of the mechanisms of the dreamwork, which laid the groundwork for our understanding how the mindbrain can register and transform reality. In dreams, we see the mindbrain reconstructing the world – in condensation, different objects can be chunked together. In displacement, important things are minimized, and small details are put in the foreground. Things, body parts, emotions, and almost anything else can be symbolized in a different form. Words, their homonyms, and pictures are interchanged. Freud (1900a) listed many ways these processes appear in dreams.

In this book, I will extend Freud's observations of how the mindbrain perceives, distorts, and transforms the world. In doing so, I will review and update Freud's mechanisms of the dreamwork, such as condensation, displacement, rebus,[3] and symbolization, but add mechanisms that Freud did not address by name, such as the many forms of metaphor and metonymy. How does the mindbrain, especially in dreams, represent meaning metaphorically? How does the mindbrain create new metaphors and compound metaphors? How is the dreaming mindbrain a natural punster?

Dreams are connected with all the arts, especially literary, musical, and visual arts. The kinds of transformations that come naturally to artists often appear in dreams, even the dreams of people who have no inclination in waking life toward artistic creation. As the poet Jean Paul Richter observed, when we dream, we are "involuntary artists" (Darwin, 1902).

In the latter half of the twentieth century, the human mindbrain was called an information processor – it is that, but the mindbrain is also an *information transformer that re-represents the world* (Dror, 2005). These processes are vividly seen in dreams and artworks.

Linguistic and nonlinguistic thoughts and transformations of the world

There is a tendency in many models of intellectual development to see the first years of mental life as preverbal or prelinguistic, that is, involving images and emotions before we have the words to describe them. When humans develop the capacity for language, the preverbal is thought to give way to the predominance of linguistic thoughts and communication of those thoughts with words.

In my view, nonlinguistic thought is not superseded by linguistic thought (Blechner *et al.*, 1976; Gardner, 1983, 1985). Instead, nonlinguistic thought continues to evolve well into adulthood, and the mindbrain becomes increasingly adept at representing the world, making calculations, and developing ideas without the intervention of language. These nonlinguistic mechanisms of thought evolve into high levels of complexity and sophistication. They are most easily seen in our dreams and in artworks, but they permeate all our mental activity. Musicians are especially attuned to the mindbrain's ability for complex thoughts without words. As composer Ned Rorem wrote:

> Dreams are dreams, with their own integrity, not symbols designed to keep us asleep. Like music, whose sense and strength and very

reason-for-being can never be explained by mere intelligence, the meaning of dreams forever evades us, not because that meaning is too vague for words but because it is too precise for words.

(Rorem, 1994, p. 517)

One of the aims of this book is to document and analyze many forms of nonlinguistic thought. In *The Dream Frontier* (Blechner, 2001), I made the claim that dreams can produce ideas that are "extralinguistic." Dreams can be reflective not just of early modes of thought (prelinguistic), but of fully developed, advanced kinds of thinking that are not constrained by language (extralinguistic) and may be difficult or impossible to express in words.

Dreams can be extralinguistic in several ways. They can create objects for which we have no name. They can also be extralinguistic in that they can step beyond the bounds of conventional metaphor. They can create entirely new metaphors, and they can also extend and combine commonly used metaphors in brand new ways. These complex compound metaphors can be represented in a dream without any words, but packed together into a single image (see Chapter 5, p. 61 for a dream that combines four metaphors).

Metaphors and puns are usually thought to be linguistic, but in dreams and artworks, we also see the mindbrain creating nonlinguistic metaphors and puns, including what I call homoforms (in the visual realm) and homomelodies (in the musical realm). There can also be metaphors from one sensory modality to another, "cross-modal" metaphors. We will look into synesthesia and synkinesia, which may be the mindbrain's wired-in mechanisms of cross-modal metaphor.

Psychological defenses

Psychological defenses transform the world through many mental processes, including hiding information, separating emotions and thoughts, transforming an emotion into its opposite, and many other processes. The defenses may look like a different subject matter from the dreamwork, but the dreamwork and defenses may be part of a larger group of mental mechanisms that transform the world and our experience of it. Erik Erikson (1954) led the way on this subject, as I show in Chapter 10. Erikson taught us how to chart dreams according to several precise dimensions (population, affect, time, and space), a very valuable approach to exploring a person's unique way of organizing the world in dreams and waking life.

Erikson's approach leads logically into a consideration of the operation of psychological defenses in dreams. Anna Freud, who wrote a classic text on psychological defenses, thought that most defenses could not be observed in dreams, except for the mechanisms of the dreamwork described by her father, Sigmund Freud. I think she was wrong, and I explore how the mindbrain represents defensive operations three ways in dreams (see Chapter 11).

Dream translators, dream immersers, and dream doubters

This book also has a clinical side, and the second section of the book addresses clinical matters. Freud and Jung were the twentieth century's pioneers in exploring how dreams are important in human psychology. Together, they led us to wonder about what dreams mean and how best to discover that meaning.

Freud was a dream translator. He said that dreams were meant to hide their meaning. One needed a procedure to decode them, and he thought that the waking thoughts that we associated to each of the dream elements would lead us to that meaning.

Jung was a dream immerser. He moved away from Freud's view that dreams needed to be translated and interpreted. Instead Jung immersed himself directly into the dream's images and feelings. We will examine different approaches to working with dreams, translating them, immersing ourselves in them, or other approaches.

I take a more concrete approach to dreams. I have suggested (Blechner, 2001) that the understanding of dreams requires first an assumption that something true is represented in the dream. If you start with that assumption, then analysis of dreams asks: Not, *is* this true? But rather, *how* is this true? This led to my proposing that the analysis of dreams may, in some cases, be like the television show *Jeopardy!*, in which you are provided with the answer, and you must discover the correct question that corresponds to that answer. With many dreams, if you provide the correct question, the dream itself will be the answer.[4]

In the late twentieth century, there came a period of dream doubters. Hobson and McCarley (1977) wrote a paper (which was the most cited paper in the history of the *American Journal of Psychiatry*) in which they presented their Activation-Synthesis Hypothesis. They suggested that Freud was wrong, that dream formation did not start with a taboo wish which was then disguised by the mind. Instead, they suggested that the basic stimulus of the dream is an image produced during REM sleep by firing of the pons, a structure in the brainstem. Such images, which Hobson and McCarley believed to be random, are then synthesized by the higher levels of the brain into an ongoing narrative.

The process suggested by the Activation-Synthesis Hypothesis is very much like the mindbrain administering to itself a TAT (Thematic Apperception Test), showing itself an image that could be interpreted in many ways and then elaborating a story based on that image.

Many people began to wonder whether dreams were as important to psychology as previously thought; some wondered whether dreams were meaningful at all. And yet, there never was any proof of Hobson and McCarley's hypothesis. And even if it were correct, it suggests only a difference with Freud about how dreams are *instigated* in the mindbrain. It really says nothing about the meaningfulness of dreams. How the mindbrain makes up a story about a random picture tells you much about your psychology, whether it is in a dream or a TAT test.

Not so well known is the fact that Hobson, despite his aggressive stance against the psychoanalytic approach to dreams, is a great lover of dreams and is enthralled with their meaning. He kept a diary of all his dreams starting when he was 40.

It was especially poignant when, decades after challenging the psychoanalytic understanding of dreams, Hobson (2005) published a book, *Thirteen Dreams that Freud Never Had*. It is one of the most forthright and painful records of how dreams reflect the central psychological concerns of the dreamer. Hobson had a stroke in 2001 that nearly killed him. His subsequent book presents and discusses dreams that show his dread of losing bodily functions because of his stroke, his sadness about sexual impotence, his urinary problems, and his fear that his wife will be unfaithful to him. I know of no book that conveys more convincingly how dreams portray our most fundamental concerns.

Hobson's analyses of his dreams are in accord with my contemporary psychoanalytic view of dreams – the view that dreams are not created to disguise, but show the dreamer's primary concerns condensed together, without concern for communicability. Hobson's dreams are alive with lust, ambition, and wishes for eternal youth. Intense erotic liaisons are suggested or actually begun. Competition with colleagues is engaged often and with vigor. Older people appear unchanged from their younger selves.

Hobson's dreams are also filled with symbols of his concerns about his body and mortality. In one dream, he and his son are carrying a very heavy and peculiar fence post consisting of a cedar log with a plastic tubular bottom. He realizes in the dream the purpose of this bizarre object is to have strength above the ground and resistance to rotting below – a symbol of potency and strength with protection from decay.

In another dream, Hobson considers going down a waterfall. He descended it in the past, and now he considers going down the same waterfall inside a fragile glass box from the Tiffany period. He realizes the danger of the glass breaking and the impossibility of the whole situation. In this way, he symbolizes the loss of an ability he once had; the wish for help and protection to do things he could once do; and his sense of vulnerability to shattering and foreboding about what will happen next.

Mortality shows up even more bluntly in a dream in which Hobson is to meet an old friend to play squash. The friend does not show up, and a valet announces that he has died.

Loss of effectiveness and sexual potency are symbolized in another dream; his wife has given or sold a drill bit that is one of Hobson's precious tools. The penis symbolism is obvious enough, but then, more bluntly, his wife states in the dream that she needs to be free to have an affair with the man to whom she transferred the drill bit.

Hobson reports a dream in which he has an erotic kiss with an unidentified woman. He connects this dream with erotic experiences in his past, a six-year extramarital affair, and extreme sexual excitement and spontaneous ejaculation when watching naked showgirls in Paris when he was 18. He tells us:

> Is this the disguise and censorship of forbidden desire? Not at all. It is the revelation of rekindled desire that never quits, even though the conscious mind and the body are not up for it! ... This realization confirms the power of instinct over volition, which we must credit Freud for recognizing and emphasizing.
>
> (Hobson, 2005, p. 167)

He is right. Dreams are not very disguised, but they show the power of our desires, even when they can no longer be satisfied.

The same durability in dreamlife of our desires can be seen in the following dream of a woman with Stage IV metastatic breast cancer a week before she died:

> *I'm in a ballroom. There were all these women in there, only one man. The man is taking one woman at a time, and dancing with her and spinning with her. I was the last one, and we twirled and twirled and danced more than anyone else. And then I went into a very long sleep.*

When she had the dream, she consciously wanted to die as soon as possible, since her quality of life had plummeted. Yet the dream condenses two wishes – for one last "dance" and then sleep. Her dream supports Hobson's observation: Desire never quits.

In Part II of this book, "Working with dreams clinically," I build on the clinical insights of *The Dream Frontier*, often pushed by students who have asked me to address clinical issues that were not covered in that book. For example, a student asked me to discuss how the analysis of a dream played out during the time span of a psychoanalytic therapy, and so I have written Chapter 13 "The dream guides its own analysis: How to work with dreams over time." I also address other questions: What is the difference, in a psychotherapy session, between doing a thorough analysis of a dream, as opposed to focusing on a single aspect of the dream that will have a powerful effect in the moment?

How do dreams reflect how the dreamer in psychotherapy is experiencing the treatment, and how can the clinician learn from the patient's dreams and rectify certain problems in the treatment?

I compare patients' dreams from the beginning and end of treatment. How are the psychological issues the same? How do the dreams show how the psychotherapy has allowed the patient to deal with the same psychological issues in a different way?

How much do patients hide from their analysts (and themselves) while working on dreams? I give the example of a patient who, at the end of treatment, showed me his notes from the beginning of treatment, which revealed that he had avoided telling me some parts of a dream that we had been working on for nine years.

When a patient comes for "reanalysis," how can a dream clarify what he or she is looking for in treatment and did not achieve in the prior treatment?

When working on a dream, how can a patient's physical behavior and actions tell you things about the dream? How do the dream's story line and the patient's actual interactions with the psychotherapist become intertwined?

Does the dream always precede the interpretation, or can the interpretation precede the dream? Sometimes in a session, the psychotherapist makes a comment, and the patient suddenly remembers a dream, and the comment that spurred the memory is the interpretation of the dream.

In Chapter 14, I discuss a method of analyzing dreams in groups, derived from the pioneering work of Montague Ullman. Having worked this way for 20 years, it has influenced my work with dreams enormously. What can we learn from group dream interpretation? How does it change the classical psychoanalytic view that the dreamer's associations are crucial for dream understanding? How do those experiences change the way a clinician works with dreams one-on-one? We will consider how dreams are disguised to the dreamer but less so to other people. I also compare Ullman's group dream approach with a way of working with dreams that concentrates on the dreamer's emotions, Bosnak's (2003) "embodied imagination."

In my view, the clinical and the scientific are not separate domains. In the third and last part of the book, "Dreams, knowledge, memory, emotion, and the mindbrain," I integrate the findings from clinical work and from laboratory and introspective studies. The name given to the intersection of psychoanalysis and neurology is *neuropsychoanalysis*. In Chapter 15 "How neuropsychoanalysis and clinical psychoanalysis can learn from each other," I consider the ways we learn from dreams about how the mindbrain works, and how scientific study of the mindbrain can improve clinical psychoanalytic treatment. In Chapter 16, "Elusive illusions" I examine how we know that a dream is "not real" and how some dreams can give the illusion of being "really real." I examine the connection of this phenomenon to pathological delusions and hallucinations, as well as the "normal hallucination" of a dead close relative.

In Chapter 17, "When your mindbrain knows things that you don't," I examine situations in which our mindbrain has solved a problem or achieved an insight, but our conscious selves don't have access to that solution, which Albert Einstein said was his experience in working out the theory of relativity. In Chapter 18, "Memory, knowledge, and dreams," I consider further how we can make calculations and solve problems in our dreams without realizing we have done so, starting with an experiment of dream researcher William Dement, which I have replicated many times.

I then explore what dreams tell us about the language of thought (Fodor, 1975; Schneider, 2011), which I started to explore in *The Dream Frontier*, but which I take further in this book (Chapter 19). Freud (1900a, p. 534) thought that the "mechanisms of the dreamwork" transform our waking verbal thoughts into a pictorial form. I propose that the opposite may be true: that dreams are themselves the language of thought (or, as I would prefer to call it, the "substrate of thought"), and that there may be a mental process called the "wakingwork" that transforms our imagistic-emotional dream thoughts into verbal, communicable form.

Notes

1 The compound word was also sometimes written with a hyphen, i.e., "mind-brain."
2 Ursula K. Le Guin wrote (2004): "Words are events, they do things, change things. They transform both speaker and hearer."
3 A rebus is a series of images that, on first examination, do not seem to have much to do with one another. If, however, you transform each image into an equivalent word, *or its homonym*, you will get a sentence that is grammatical and meaningful. I will discuss the rebus further on p. 85 ff.
4 I thought this was a new idea when I first published it (Blechner, 2001). In the meantime, I have found a precursor in Rollo May (1961, p. 19), who wrote: "The dream is an 'answer' from unconscious levels to a 'question' posed by the patient's immediate existence."

Part I
How the mindbrain transforms the world

Chapter 2

The mindbrain creates its own version of the world

> My friend, it is precisely the poet's task
> to interpret and record his dreamings.
> Believe me, man's truest madness
> is disclosed to him in dreams:
> all poetry and versification
> is nothing but true dream interpretation.
>   Hans Sachs in Richard Wagner's
>   *The Mastersingers of Nuremberg*

I have in my library many books on the mindbrain – books on emotion, memory, thinking, psychological defenses, consciousness, and unconscious processes. Very few of them mention dreams, and even fewer of them consider the phenomena of dreams necessary to get a complete picture of the mindbrain.

It is risky to ignore such a major aspect of our mentation. We spend nearly a third of our lives asleep, and during much of that sleep-time, we are dreaming. Would such an intricate form of mental activity have evolved if it were not important and useful? I believe dreams to be critical to understanding our thought processes. In this chapter, I hope to demonstrate how an understanding of mentation in dreams may help us understand all mentation. I will summarize the different mental operations we will examine. Then, in subsequent chapters, we will look at each mental operation in more detail.

In dreams, we see evidence of how the mindbrain transforms the world during the time that it mostly does not have to deal directly with the world. It changes things, combines things, organizes things into categories, and alters the significance of things. It also suppresses things that are disturbing or conflicted. With all these transformations, the mindbrain creates meaning and alters meaning. The dreaming mindbrain also is able to make calculations and solve problems, although it may be difficult for the waking mindbrain to get access to these solutions.

In dreams, we see the mindbrain creating meaning in many forms and shifting meaning from one form to another. We see the intersection of words, images, sounds, tastes, smells, ideas, and emotions. There are many ways that the mindbrain represents, transforms, and connects meaning: condensation, displacement, metaphor, metonym, rebus, pun, homoform, and symbol.

The mindbrain is always on the lookout for similarities and concordances in the world. Once it finds them, it is ready to express the intersection of one realm of knowledge in terms of the other (metaphor). It also finds similarities and concordances in nonverbal materials (homoforms); once it finds them, one specimen can stand in for another, creating a visual symbol. The mindbrain is also ready to represent a concept or object by referring to just a part of it (synecdoche). And the mindbrain keeps track of things that go together, by actual physical contiguity or association (metonymy). When it does this with words, it finds homonyms; when it laces homonyms with surprising humor, it creates puns. These transformations occur not only with words and verbal thoughts, but without words, in music, visual arts, and other media. We will consider each of these phenomena on their own terms, as well as how they operate in dreams.

We will consider how abstract ideas, such as purely logical relationships, are portrayed by the mindbrain in pictures. And then we will go back to reexamine this sentence. We said that logical relationships are *portrayed* in pictures. That sentence implied that logical relationships are the main thing, and that in dreams they are portrayed pictorially, because dreams deal mainly in visual images, not in ideas expressed in words. But is that sentence misleading? Is the portrayal of logical relations and other abstract ideas in pictures or sensory form not secondary, but primary? Are images and sensory representations what has been called by cognitive scientists and philosophers "the language of thought," or what I would prefer to call "the substrate of thought"? Is spatial and pictorial representation a transformation of verbal thought? Or is verbal thought a transformation of pictorial thought? Is one primary to the other, or are they equally and symmetrically interchangeable (Gardner, 1983)?[1]

We will take a new look at symbols, long considered an essence of dreaming. Symbols are varied and can partake of any and all of the transformational processes – including metaphor, metonymy, rebus, and homoform. Symbols are usually arbitrarily small units, yet symbolic processes can be extended in dreams to whole story lines, even to the entire dream.

All these mental operations are imbued with emotion and shaped by emotion. Dreams are filled with emotion; is that a special property of dreamlife, or does it reveal to us that most of our waking thought is also embedded in emotion, only we are less aware of it?

We will look at mental operations gone awry, slightly, as in mixed metaphor, or significantly, as in contamination and other forms of pathological thought disorder.

We will also look at special crossovers between different modes of perception in synesthesia (such as a link between musical notes and colors) and between different modes of motoric control in synkinesia (such as when cutting something with a pair of scissors, we clench and unclench our jaw). Is synesthesia a sensory analogue of metaphor, and synkinesia a motor analogue of metaphor?

In Chapter 5, we will consider oxymoronic speech acts, where words and action collide. Are these a quirk of psychopathology, or do oxymoronic speech acts reveal the normal compartmentalization of the mindbrain that allows such disjunctures to pass unnoticed? We will expand this view of the mindbrain to explore more compartmentalization, between waking and sleeping, between multiple self-states, and other divisions. Along the way, we will construct sentences that sound bizarre, but accurately describe psychological experience.

By examining all these phenomena, we will see how "normal" mental functioning can be quite strange, and how the mindbrain creates its own version of the world. It transforms, expands, vivifies, and hides meaning, in a continual interplay between the verbal and nonverbal, image, idea, emotions, and the crossroads of mental and bodily experience. Is the way the mindbrain works while we are sleeping qualitatively different and separate from when we are awake, or are there underlying connections between the two? We will also examine how the processes involved in artistic creation and appreciation of artworks, in all forms, are related to the mindbrain processes we observe in dreaming.

How the mindbrain transforms reality

Like all great scientists, Freud was a meticulous observer. In his description of what he called the dreamwork, he observed the many ways that the mindbrain changes, manipulates, and combines aspects of reality. In condensation, the mindbrain mixes two or more things together. For example, two people can be "morphed" into one, or two words can be joined together, creating a new word. In displacement, the mindbrain transforms the significance of different parts of reality: A small detail can become the main thing that we notice, while a prominent aspect of reality can be reduced to a small detail, barely noticed. This sort of displacement was also observed by Jesus (Matthew 7:3): "Why do you see the speck that is in your brother's eye, but do not notice the log that is in your own eye?"[2]

In "symbolization," one thing is used to stand for another. A snake can symbolize a penis; or more rarely (at least in Western culture), a penis can symbolize a snake. A cross can symbolize the Christian religion. It can also symbolize "a burden" (the cross that I bear). People can develop idiosyncratic symbols, too, based on their personal history. For a man whose wife was wearing a green dress when she told him she wanted a divorce, the color green symbolized[3] pain and loss. A fireplace, which for many people can symbolize the warmth of family life, can symbolize the Holocaust for a survivor of a concentration camp.

Freud's observations of how the mindbrain transforms reality are impressive and timeless. This is so, even if his theory of why those transformations occur is wrong, as I believe it is. Freud believed that the dreamwork occurs in order to disguise unacceptable thoughts and wishes that were part of underlying "dream thoughts."

I think that dreams are not crafted to disguise, nor are they crafted to communicate. They show the mindbrain creating meaning without needing for the meaning to be communicable. The mindbrain's pictures are assembled without many of the rules that we usually impose on waking thought. Imagine you have several pictures: one, a picture of something that happened to you yesterday; another picture of something that happened to you long ago; and the third, a picture of a serious concern that has been preoccupying you during the last weeks. If you take those three pictures and superimpose them, what will the single picture look like?

Some details will be obscured. Some objects will be blended with others. Some areas may be highlighted. This is like the mindbrain putting together multiple aspects of reality in a dream.

Because of the rules of sanity that we usually obey in waking thought, certain things can be expressed in dreams that we would reject in waking life. One example is disjunctive cognitions. People commonly dream "I knew it was my mother, even though she didn't look like my mother." In waking life, if we said such things, we would be diagnosed as psychotic. But we all seem to know that this is "normal" in dreams. I call it a "commonplace bizarreness of dreamlife."

We also dream of what I call "interobjects," another commonplace bizarreness of dreamlife. A child dreamt "he and his friends were crossing a channel, got into trouble, but were saved by a seal-boat." In waking life, adults probably would not speak so easily about a "seal-boat"; indeed, the child's father, trying to train his son in the rules of reality, said, "So really, it was a big, safe boat." The boy held fast to the integrity of his dream and said, "It was a boat, but it was still a big, friendly seal." He had not yet learned to regularize his perception to fit the way the world works.[4]

The dreamwork or the wakingwork?

Freud's model was that the mindbrain starts with "dream thoughts" which can be formulated as sentences, and the dreaming mindbrain transforms and disguises the dream thoughts into the language of dreams, of images and emotions. I think that what Freud called "dream thoughts" may not be the primary material upon which the dreamwork exercises its transformations. I would propose that *the language of dreams, composed mostly of images and emotions, could be the primary substrate of thinking*. It takes what we could call the "wakingwork" to transform these imagistic-emotional thoughts into sentences that can be communicated in words.

I think that dreams show the mindbrain working on material without such material being formulated in words. The mindbrain's "language of thought" is not a language of words only. It is a language composed of sensory material, images and emotions. It might be more accurate to call it the "substrate of thought," not a language, since language connotes words for most of us. It is possible that Freud, while compiling brilliant observations, explained them with a theory that might be exactly the opposite of the case.

If dreams show the mindbrain thinking without needing to be communicable, it is possible that the mindbrain often or always works that way. Even while we are awake and conscious, our mindbrains are whirring away with thought processes we are never aware of. There are thought processes that go on that we can understand or get access to only with a great deal of difficulty. Freud said this happens because the ideas or feelings are in some way unacceptable or anxiety-provoking. The thesis of this book is that this may also happen not because the ideas or feelings are threatening, but because the mindbrain works that way behind the scene of consciousness. Many thoughts and feelings are unconscious and not available to conscious thought. Most thinking may not be done with words; it may be done with affects and images and perhaps some be other more fundamental thought material. *Formulation of thinking in words may be done after the thinking already has happened.*

Dreams as stories that we tell ourselves

The questions of agency and experience are complicated when it comes to our dreams. We experience dreams as if they are a story that is authored by someone else. By whom? The ancients thought that they were messages from the gods. Freud told us that they were messages from our unconscious. If Freud is right, it leaves us with an astonishing experience. The dream is told to us by our own mindbrain, and yet it feels interpersonal. It feels as if we are experiencing the dream without awareness of its source and, usually, without any control about how the dream goes. It feels as if it is authored by someone else, but it is ours. The dream becomes a prime example of an experience in which our own mindbrain is experienced as if it is another person.

Dreaming is an involuntary creative activity. In our dreams, all of us are bards, storytellers, weavers of new experience. We know that "we" do it, but we feel that the "I" that we experience, as our intentional conscious willful self, is usually not involved in the dream's creation. Instead, some other I, our night-I, or our unconscious I, with an intelligence and inspiration at least as good as our waking life and maybe better, takes over.[5] This aspect of experience is made explicit in certain languages like Greek, in which one says, literally, "I saw a dream."

The neurologist V. S. Ramachandran, who directs the Center for Brain and Cognition in San Diego, reports having a dream in which someone was telling him a very funny joke that made him laugh heartily in the dream. This dream suggested to Ramachandran (Ramachandran *et al.*, 1996, p. 44) that:

> *there must have been at least two mutually amnesic personalities inside me during the dream – the experience of laughing heartily at a joke requires an element of surprise. Who told the joke in the dream and who laughed at it?*

Ramachandran asserts that his dream proves the plausibility of multiple personalities. But in another way, *most* dreams suggest the experience of multiple personalities, since the personality that creates the dream scenario and the personality that experiences it usually seem separate to us, and our dreams can surprise us in many ways, besides jokes. It is very common, in dream reports, to find the word "suddenly." We often experience sudden surprising shifts in dreams that may frighten us, delight us, or intrigue us. But the experience of something happening in a dream that seems "out of the blue" increases our sense of some strong independent force directing the dream narrative. If we were conscious of concocting the dream ourselves, those sudden shifts would not feel so surprising.

This poses a basic conundrum. If our dreams surprise us, who is their author? We must conclude that our mindbrains produce dreams without our conscious involvement. And yet, our mindbrain is also the dream's audience. There may be a division between the part of my mindbrain that experiences my dreams, and the part of my mindbrain that produces them. The mindbrain is not a single unit, but an assemblage of sub-mindbrains that operate with varying degrees of connection or disconnection.

Thus, dreams make us realize vividly that our mindbrain is composed of multiple subsystems, and that our mindbrain is active in many ways that do not involve our conscious activity or will. Our mindbrains do a lot more thinking, feeling, and creating than we are aware of. Our mindbrains have many parts, which can operate simultaneously and more or less independently. Instead of saying "my mindbrain," we probably should say, more accurately, "my mindbrains."

How can we best describe the segmentation of our mindbrains? And to what degree are each of those segments connected with independent selves? This is one of the fundamental questions of contemporary neurobiology and psychoanalysis, which we will consider in Chapter 17, "When your mindbrain knows things that you don't."

We need new ways of speaking about dreams, but they have not yet evolved or been invented. I say, "I dreamt." If I say, "I had a dream but I don't remember it," the implication is that at one point I was conscious of the dream, but now I have forgotten it. We don't usually say, referring to a dream that was *never* conscious, "I had a dream but I don't remember it. I never remembered it, or at least I don't remember ever remembering it." This statement, however, is often the true state of our dreamlife. In 1953, Aserinsky and Kleitman discovered that we dream regularly throughout the night, at least once every 90 minutes, although we do not remember having had most of those dreams. Since the discovery of Aserinsky and Kleitman, it would also be correct to say, "I had more than five dreams last night, and I don't remember any of them." In this case, the conviction of having had dreams is based on the knowledge of the regularity of dreaming, rather than on the first-hand conscious experience of dreaming.

Libet *et al.* (1983) discovered that our mindbrains often make a decision before we feel aware of that decision, so that we may inaccurately feel we have made the decision consciously. Someone who knows Libet's research might say, "I decided to do it before I realized that I decided to do it," but in our world, so far, such a sentence would sound strange. Richard Restak (1991) crystallized this problem with his clever book title: *The Brain Has a Mind of Its Own*. The different "I's" in the sentence have different referents. We do not yet have different words in our language to refer to those different I's; we do not have nouns to discriminate the "I-ness" of our unconscious mindbrain activity that precedes the more familiar "I-ness" of the conscious sense of willing.

In 1911, the French neurologist Claparède invented the term "moïté" which David Rapaport translated in 1951 as "me-ness," but this word has not entered common usage. (This is discussed further in Chapter 18, "Memory, knowledge, and dreams.")

Me-ness can undergo remarkable transformations in dreams. Most dreamers do not question whether a remembered dream was "my dream." In about 90 percent of dreams, the dreamer's self appears in the dream, experiencing things or observing the action from a first-person viewpoint.

In about 10 percent of dreams, however, the dream-self is totally absent from the dream (Strauch and Meier, 1996), yet even in those dreams, the dreamer does not usually doubt that the dream was "my dream."

Remembered dream experience has "me-ness." This is so, even when the "I" of the dream undergoes remarkable transformations, such as changing sex. For example, an American man told me:

I dreamt I had made the decision, because I was being mistreated or harassed, to disappear. I did, for 12 years, or 15, or 17. No one knew where I was. I was watching myself in the dream. The person I was watching was a female. Then I was trying to locate Bruce (my partner of 30 years). I was upset I hadn't seen him in so long. His telephone number had changed. I couldn't locate him.[6]

Similarly, a 25-year-old blond Finnish female student dreamt:

It's the Second World War and I am a dark-haired, strongly built Finnish male soldier. The enemies are probably German ... [Later in the same dream]: I could see myself in a mirror. Now I was a blond, strongly built woman.

(Revonsuo, 2005, p. 213)

In rare cases, a dreamer can even experience herself as an animal in a dream, while still retaining a sense of "me-ness": A 22-year-old female student described a dream in which she was "a dog or some other animal. She was running in a dark forest with another animal, hunting for prey. Eventually she caught a rabbit, but something larger than herself took it away from her" (Revonsuo, 2005, p. 214).

Notes

1 The question of whether the mindbrain's transformations are unidirectional or bidirectional is important, concerning metaphor, synesthesia, symbolization, and other processes.
2 This was Freud's original use of the term *displacement*, which he later called "displacement of accent." Later, he added other kinds of displacement (see Chapter 4, p. 42).
3 Franz Schubert, in his song "The Evil Color (*Die böse Farbe*)," showed how a color could symbolize an emotion through such a personal connection.

4 For a more detailed discussion of disjunctive cognitions, see pp. 240–244.
5 An exception to this is the "lucid dream," in which the dreamer can feel a certain level of awareness that he is dreaming and sometimes an ability to control the progress of events in the dream (van Eeden, 1913; LaBerge, 1985).
6 This dream is discussed further on p. 218.

Chapter 3

Condensation, interobjects, and categories

> The human mind is so constituted that it will insist on finding a resemblance between any two objects or forms presented for its inspection; and the more unlike the two objects, the more enjoyable is the challenge to discover the secret likeness.
>
> Goethe, *Wilhelm Meister*

In *The Interpretation of Dreams* (1900a), Freud's chapter on condensation is itself highly condensed. It is a treasure trove of observations on how the mindbrain perceives things in the world but also combines them through condensation. Freud's observations can be categorized and reorganized according to the kinds of condensation and the materials that are condensed – a kind of "anatomy of condensation."

There are several kinds of condensation. They all have in common the fact that they combine several ideas or objects into a single dream element. Condensations can be distinguished both by *what* is condensed and *how* it is condensed. What is condensed can be words, natural objects of the world (including people), and ideas. These three kinds of condensation can be classified as follows:

1   **LEXICAL condensation** – which combine words or word fragments; e.g., Freud's (1900a, p. 296) "Norekdal," which condenses Ibsen's characters Nora and Ekdal. A woman dreamt of a man who was "staunchy" – staunch and paunchy.

    Some lexical condensations may at first be mistaken for an error. A woman had a dream in which one horse bit another horse in the "tracula" – she pointed to an area between her neck and chest. The dreamer was not a native English speaker, so I first thought she must be erring in her English, and "really" meant trachea. But she confirmed that "tracula" was a condensation of Dracula and trachea. A man dreamt of seeing someone who was suffering, and said that in the dream he felt "Sangfreud"; he was enjoying the other people's suffering. It sounded at first as if he was mispronouncing *Schadenfreude*, the German word for enjoyment of another person's sufferings. But he said the word was a combination of *Schadenfreude* with the French word *sangfroid*, which means "coolness of mind; calmness; or composure."[1] But sangfroid literally means "cold blood" and the dreamer had once witnessed a relative commit suicide. "Sangfreud" could combine all three meanings – enjoying another person's suffering, coolness of mind, and murder in "cold blood" (and there could be further meanings, involving Freud's name).

2 **FORMAL condensation** – involves the melding of two images into one, by combining their physical characteristics – in the manner of Galton's composite photographs, or, we would say today, computer morphing of images. Formal condensation usually involves visual features, but it can involve other sense modalities (for example, melodies – see pp. 108–110).

 The mindbrain can even condense stimuli that individually have no apparent meaning. Kubovy *et al.* (1974) fed sounds into the left and right ear that individually were heard as noise. But when the mindbrain combined the two inputs, the melody "Daisy" was heard. Julesz (1971) achieved a similar phenomenon of feeding separate inputs into the eyes that each seemed like noise individually, but yielded a meaningful image when fused by the mindbrain.

3 **IDEATIONAL condensation** – involves the mixing of two or more ideas into one dream formation. This can include all aspects, including linguistic, visual, and other aspects. Since it is in the nature of dreams to be sensory, primarily visual, most ideational condensation partakes of sensory representation. Nevertheless, the condensation is ideational when the combination achieved by the dreamwork is not of the word or the image, but of the idea represented by the image. Identifying ideational condensation often requires the interpretation of symbols. It may not be apparent in the manifest dream itself, and hence one could argue that it is not a category equivalent to the other two.

Ideational condensation has led to several important inventions and scientific discoveries, such as Elias Howe's perfection of the sewing machine (Kaempffert, 1924), August Kekulé's (1890) discovery of the structure of the benzene ring, and Dimitri Mendeleyev's discovery of the periodic table (Strathern, 2000).

In addition, condensations can be classified according to their *outcome*. They differ in terms of the nature of the product of the condensation – whether it is (1) an object that exists in waking life; (2) a new object never before seen in waking life, but which could exist in waking life; and (3) a new object never before seen in waking life, which could not exist in the waking world as we know it. I call these three kinds of condensation *simple overdetermined condensation*, *creative condensation*, and *partial condensation*, for reasons that I will now explain.

Simple overdetermined condensation

In simple overdetermined condensation, the dreamwork condenses several ideas into one object. No new object or concept is created by the dreamer, but a single element may represent the convergence of several different things. That object is familiar to us from our waking life, but it signifies several underlying ideas, through the principle of overdetermination.

We see the object in the dream and have no evidence on the surface that it is a condensation. But when we ask the dreamer for associations, we begin to unravel the condensation. The evidence of the condensation comes from the various strands of associations that reveal the multiple sources of the manifest dream content. Thus, condensation occurs when multiple thoughts converge on a single object, much as in language, when multiple meanings can converge on a single word. For example, "bread" can mean a kind of food. Colloquially, bread also means "money." More figuratively, "bread" can also stand for any basic necessity. These multiple meanings of any word may converge on a single dream element. This may also occur with homonyms, where the written version of the word may differ while the spoken version is the same. "Read," as in "he has read a book" may be the past participle of reading. "Red," which has the same sound, can mean the color red. It can also imply coarseness ("redneck"), the emotion of embarrassment (to redden, i.e., blush), or communism ("Red China"). The record of such condensation can be found in the radiations of meaning that emanate from the dreamer's associations.

In this way, every element of a dream may be the product of condensation. If we ask for associations, we will find the sources of condensation. The problem here, though, is that we cannot tell if the associations tell us the true sources of the dream element, or if they provide an after-the-fact elaboration of the dream element.

One of my patients dreamt that she was addicted to heroin and had been put on methadone maintenance. She analyzed the dream in terms of her addiction to analysis and her erotic feelings toward me. In a subsequent session, she spoke of her need to accomplish great things to win people's love. She said, "I need to be a heroine" (mispronouncing the word with a long "i" sound). She then talked of needing to be a "hero." It emerged that she had connected her thoughts of being a heroine with her addiction in the dream to the drug, heroin, and tried to cover up this association by her mispronunciation of "heroine" (which became a sure giveaway that something was going on) and then switching to the masculine "hero." Thus, her "heroin" addiction in the dream was overdetermined. It condensed her erotic addiction to analysis and her addiction to being a heroine.

We can see in this example that condensation often relies on homonyms and puns. The mindbrain freely brings together things whose words sound alike. We know from the studies of Swinney (1979) that when we hear a word, all the meanings of the word are simultaneously activated in the mindbrain, and we then pick the meaning that most fits the context.[2] One of Swinney's examples was the word "bug" for which the meaning "insect" and "spy device" are both activated at first. Rather than select one of several meanings, the dreaming mindbrain may do the opposite – exploit the multiple meanings of a word to condense more than one idea.

A telling sign of condensation is unusual or redundant use of words in a dream. For example, a woman dreamt:

> *I was taking a bath and the water was really black. Later, someone poured milk into the tub.*

Note that the word "really" is not necessary; its redundancy may indicate that it is overdetermined. The woman was of mixed race. As she told the dream, she had no awareness of the dream's reference to mixed race and her concerns about whether she herself was really black. The liquid in the bath may have condensed the issues of race, cleanliness, and nurturance.

Creative condensation

In creative condensation, features of two different objects are combined to create a new object. The manifest dream content contains a new person, or object, or concept that is not part of the dreamer's waking world. The new creation of the dream is fully formed, yet the evidence that condensation has occurred is discernible in the manifest dream content. Associations may reveal the source of the condensation, but even without associations, we know that it has occurred.

The combined features may come from the same modality, such as two visual elements. In the nineteenth century, Francis Galton was known for merging two photographs together into one composite image. In the twentieth century, this process was achieved with computers and came to be known as "composite portraiture" or "morphing." One example of such condensation is Freud's dream (1900a, p. 137) in which "*My friend R. was my uncle. [He was not in reality.] I saw before me his face, somewhat changed. It was as though it had been drawn out lengthways. A yellow beard that surrounded it stood out especially clearly.*" The features of various people are drawn together by Freud's dream into one new person, never seen before this dream. The assembled physical characteristics radiate out in meaning to people with different personal characteristics, but Freud's analysis of the dream showed the two men were related to one another by the question, "How guilty of crime are they?" – Freud's yellow-bearded Uncle Joseph, who had been convicted of illegal financial transactions, is combined with R., whose unblemished character is marred by one small crime.

The work of condensation can be apparent in some cases from the manifest content without any associations, although associations may clarify the source of condensation. If someone dreams of a woman who looks like Judy Garland, but is blond and tall, you know that there is condensation at work, although you may need the dreamer's associations to know what blondness and tallness mean to the dreamer and how they combine with the dreamer's associations to Judy Garland.

The condensation of two identities in a single dream figure can be especially useful to clinicians. Sometimes such dreams help the dreamer become aware of unconscious connections between people that help clarify mysteriously strong feelings. For example, a woman was having trouble in her marriage. Her husband's sexual advances left her cold or repulsed her. While trying to decide whether to divorce, she had a scary dream. She was in the house in which she grew up, and Saddam Hussein was living in the house. Another man was there, either David (her husband) or Bruce (her brother). Then they are in an apartment, and they try to escape. The dream continued with their escape maneuvers.

In thinking about the dream, the patient was surprised by the male figure who was "either David or Bruce." They do not look alike and she wasn't sure how a person could be either, but that was her experience in the dream. It led her to wonder if they were connected psychologically for her. I noted that she seemed terrified in the dream. She started crying and recalled being persistently physically abused by her brother during her childhood. Most people who knew her then had no idea of the abuse and assumed that she and her brother were perfectly close (just as in her adulthood, most people thought her marriage to be a good one). The dream raised the fundamental question of which ways, rationally or not, her husband seemed similar to her brother (as well as to Saddam Hussein) and how that connection could be frightening her and contributing to her marital difficulties.

Partial condensation – "interobjects"

Sometimes condensation occurs differently. Instead of the dream thoughts converging on a single element in the manifest dream, they converge and create a new object that does not occur in waking life and could not occur in waking life. The condensation may be incomplete; it may have a vague structure that is described as "something between an X and a Y." Hobson dreamt of "a piece of hardware, something like the lock of a door or perhaps a pair of paint-frozen hinges." In dreams we accept these sorts of intermediate structures. Hobson called them "incomplete cognitions" and Freud called them "intermediate and composite structures." I prefer to call them *interobjects*. Rather than focus on what they are not (not complete condensations), I prefer to focus on what they are (new creations derived from blends of other objects).

The combination is not fully formed into a new object with a complete gestalt but rather remains incompletely fused. With interobjects, the evidence of condensation is much more obvious from the manifest content than in the other two types. The created object is not easily describable in the terms of the waking world of objects. The dreamer may say, "It was something between a phonograph and a balance" (Meltzer, 1984, p. 45). It is unclear whether, in the dream itself, the object's characteristics were vague, or merely hard to describe. An artist could probably draw a single object that was something between a phonograph and a balance, perhaps incorporating familiar parts from each object. But it is also possible that in the dream experience, the object so described was either a stable double image, or an image that shifted between two objects, or something else. An inquiry into the dreamer's experience may clarify this. Can the dreamer elaborate on how the object in the dream was "between" two objects?

In conducting such an inquiry, the interpreter should tread carefully. Secondary revision and the reality principle are always ready to smooth out incongruous perceptions that are unacceptable in the waking world. For this reason, *it is important, in studying dreams, to transcribe verbatim the wording first used by the dreamer to describe the dream.* Otherwise, the details are easily glossed over or "regularized."

Some interobjects are symbolic of a question being unconsciously considered by the dreamer: Is it X or Y? There is a fine example of this in Ferenczi's *Clinical Diary* (1933/1988, p. 90):

> Patient B.:
> 26 April 1932
> *Dream, with an almost certain pre-history of infantile-genital violence: She sees a row of soldiers or gymnasts all without heads, lined up stiffly; on the left side (shoulder) of each one there is an upright, fleshy appendage sticking up. The association shifts to a bowling alley (ninepins). The single thrusts are signified by individual soldiers; the idea of orgasm, perhaps, by all nine. Simultaneously their headlessness represents pure emotionality, all intellectual control being absent: L'amour est un taureau acéphale. [Love is a headless bull.] But at the same time the patient's psychic state is also represented: it occurs to her that it must be difficult for the ninepins to keep their balance, since they are weighted down unilaterally on their left side.*

The interobject is the "soldiers or gymnasts," and the dreamer provides associations necessary to clarify the meaning.[3] Both the soldiers and gymnasts are headless; their main function is bodily, not mental. The dreamer, having experienced infantile-genital violence, identifies sexuality, at least that of her abuse history, with mindlessness. The focal question of the dream may be: What are men like for me – soldiers or gymnasts? Is their physicality and aggression dangerous or merely sport?

Sometimes interobjects are created from words. A patient of Erikson (1954) reported a dream with such a lexical interobject, in which she saw a novel word S[E]INE, which turned out to be a condensation of the words *seine* ("his" in German), *sine* ("without" in Latin), Seine (the French river), and the letter "E" which was the initial of Erikson's name.[4]

Freud (1900a, p. 602) seemed not to think highly of interobjects. He wrote:

> But it is obvious that condensations of ideas, as well as intermediate and compromise structures, must obstruct the attainment of the identity aimed at. Since they substitute one idea for another, they cause a deviation from the path which would have led on from the first idea. Processes of this kind are therefore scrupulously avoided in secondary thinking.

Freud is right that in communicating waking thoughts, we avoid intermediate and compromise structures, lest we be thought psychotic. Yet if they are socially unacceptable, that does not mean that they have no use. These intermediate and compromise structures, these interobjects, may have an elementary function in human thought that has barely been explored. There are constructive aspects of extralinguistic formations, like interobjects, that can be crucial in the formation of really new ideas. They also may reveal how the mindbrain creates metaphors or how metaphors are a fundamental process of thinking.

With interobjects, the mindbrain also creates mental categories. Soldiers and gymnasts together form the category of "men focused on the physical." A phonograph and a balance scale form the category "man-made objects with a circular platter and an elongated metal bar." A paint-frozen hinge and a lock form the category of "man-made metal objects that allow or restrict a door's movement." An aqueduct and a swimming pool form the category of "man-made objects that contain large amounts of water."

Such categories may or may not be useful to the individual dreamer. They may not be of much interest to other people or to our culture at large. When I talk about these interobjects, usually people listen politely, until I mention a "cellphone-baby." That interobject usually evokes delight in my audience; they seem to have an "aha" experience. The category created is small objects that we hold close to our bodies. We speak softly to them and, at times completely to our surprise, they make loud noises (ringing or crying) that disturb other people. This group of interobjects reveal the principle of Oneiric Darwinism (Blechner, 2001). Dreams create thought mutations and new categories, some of which have little general interest and may not be particularly useful to the dreamer. These are discarded and forgotten. But some dream creations have "survival value." They are of use to the dreamer and sometimes to the culture at large. Those survive and are remembered.

Condensation and categories

Which are the most salient dimensions by which we classify our environment, and which ones can be condensed? When I teach a course on dreams, I introduce my students to the "Condensation Game." I ask them: "Let us try deliberately to simulate dream condensation. Imagine, for instance: What is between a tree and a horse?" When I ask my students this question, I am always astonished at the range of answers they produce; each answer highlights a different dimension of "horse-ness" and "tree-ness."

One answer is "a wooden horse." Another answer is "a tree with short hair and the texture and warmth of a horse's body." Both of these are a condensation of materials and form. In the first, the wood of the tree has been combined with the shape of the horse (perhaps this answer was inspired by the Trojan example). In the second, the materials of the horse's body have been reshaped into a tree.

Another strategy of condensation is to combine features. Thus, we could get a horse with branches coming out of it. Or a tree trunk that culminates in a horse's head. Or a tree with a mane.

One can also combine actions: hence, a tree that neighs. Or a horse that sheds in winter.

Another condensation is a giraffe. Here, the height of a tree is grafted onto the neck of the horse.

Another strategy is to combine words, a lexical condensation. In this manner, we arrive at a tree-house (a loose distortion of tree and horse) or a "sawhorse" (this one is more complex in origin, perhaps, combining the conception of woodwork with horse) or the German actor, Horst Buchholz. Here the condensation plays with the similarity in sound of "horse" and "Horst" and *Holz*, which is the German word for "wood."

And one fellow, answering the question "what is between a tree and a horse," responded "grass." That, too, involves a kind of dreamwork; it takes the word "between" and focuses on its spatial meaning rather than its conceptual meaning – it involves imagining a horse and a tree in a real location, and between them is grass.

In summary, the many possible condensations make us aware of how we categorize our world (Epstein, 1994). We can create condensations using the materials, forms, or features of objects, or we can use words themselves as objects to condense. The Condensation Game makes us very aware of how we think about any one object or person, and how differently other people may encode the same object or person.

Category transgressions

The Condensation Game also invites us to relax our normal sense of categories, as we do in our dreams. Category transgressions are unacceptable in daytime communication, except perhaps to poets and madmen, but they are acceptable to most of us in our dreams.

Dreams can transgress category boundaries with impunity. Suzanne Langer (1967, p. 121) wrote: "When new unexploited possibilities of thought crowd in upon the human mind, the poverty of everyday language becomes acute." And so we dream. As Ullman (1969, p. 699) has noted,

> The task before the dreamer is to express relations he has never before experienced. The sensory effects streaming down to the arousal center employ the visual mode predominantly and as these generate further arousal new and relevant motivational systems or feelings are tapped.

Freud (1900a, pp. 302–303) reported a dream in which he transgressed linguistic boundaries. His dream included the word "erzefilich," which does not exist in German. He analyzed that it was a condensation of several words, including *erzieherisch* (educational) and "syphilis."

I (Blechner, 1997) reported a dream which contained the words "prestyl dolby." While I thought of Dolby noise-reduction systems, the dreamer's associations revealed a different condensation. He began tapping his fingers on the couch (a nonverbal association). I asked him what he was doing; he replied that he was playing the piano. "Playing the piano" had another meaning for him; his father owned a store with an old-style cash register. "Playing the piano" was an expression that meant hitting the cash-register keys so that the drawer would open and you could steal some cash. Thus, Prestyl Dolby meant "Press [the] till, dough'll be yours" – which meant "Open the cash register and steal the money inside it."[5]

Psychologists such as Eleanor Rosch (1977) have studied the "natural categories" of our waking consciousness, but in dreams, myths, and art, we can be freed from these categories. It is not that they stop existing for us, but that they become "transgressable"; we can violate them without necessarily being considered mad.

Artists have been notorious for transgressing categories: Da Vinci's painting of John the Baptist in the Louvre is of a person who is between man and woman, or both man and woman. (The theory that the Mona Lisa is actually da Vinci's self-portrait as a woman works along similar lines, but the portrait of John the Baptist combines the genders even more smoothly.) We saw above (p. 23) that people can change their sex in dreams and sometimes change their sex back.

Picasso produced a sculpture, *Baboon and Her Young*, that is a car-monkey (Figure 3.1). He took a model car and showed how it could also be seen as a monkey face.

Category transgression occurs in music, too. Musical form creates its own categories, and then great composers write compositions that defy those categories, both falling within them and lying outside them. For example, Viennese classical composers established a relatively expectable sonata form, in which there usually was an exposition section with a first melodic theme in the tonic key, and a second melodic theme in the dominant key. Beethoven took this sonata form, and in some of his late work, created a musical structure that left the key structure of sonata form intact, but had the change in keys occur within a unitary melodic element, blurring the distinction between first and second themes.

Figure 3.1 Pablo Picasso, *Baboon and Her Young*.

Source: © 2017 Estate of Pablo Picasso/Artists Rights Society (ARS), New York, RMN-Grand Palais/Art Resource, NY/ARS, NY.

Arnold Schönberg did something similar, creating waltzes that are not danceable. He also created the new category of speech/song, that, when performed correctly, is not like anything heard before from the human voice. The very word "speech/song (*Sprechgesang*)" sounds like a dream creation.

Category transgressions are familiar from mythology, and many have their counterparts there. The man who becomes a woman is incorporated into the story of Tiresias. There are many instances in which the human/animal distinction is transgressed: The Minotaur, for example, was half-man, half bull. Snakes grew from the head of Medusa. Zeus transfigured himself into a swan, and as a swan, ravished the human Leda. And we saw above how a human dreamer can experience herself as a nonhuman animal in her dreams (p. 23). The human/plant distinction is also transgressed in the story of Daphne, a woman who is transformed into a tree.

The Old Testament, too, has bushes that speak (the Burning Bush), animals that speak (Balaam's ass), and time that stops (the sun and moon stop for Joshua). Our familiar parameters of dividing and organizing the world are up for grabs.

Transgressions of species, so common in mythology, are common in children's dreams. In the famous childhood dream of Freud's patient, the "Wolf-Man," the wolves in the dream were "white and looked more like foxes or sheep-dogs, for they had big tails like foxes and they had their ears pricked like dogs when they pay attention to something" (Freud, 1914/1918, p. 29). Children are much more tolerant of interobjects than adults.

Psychotics also show freedom to transgress boundaries and categories, and the link between psychosis and dreams has long been noticed. Psychotics are fond of neologisms that transgress linguistic boundaries. When one of my patients told me I was "consaring," he was, I discovered, combining "concerned" and "caring." Our waking sane consciousness might ask, "Why not say concerned and caring?" but he might ask, "Why not join them?" In doing so, he made his communication harder to fathom but avoided the humiliation that he feared from explicit statements of affection.

Limits of category transgression

There is a subtle form of boundary transgression that occurs in language, where words that ordinarily occur in one category transmigrate into another category. In late twentieth century North America, for example, it became a relatively common process to force nouns into verbs by using them so. People came to accept "impact" as a verb, such as in the sentence, "How does the president's decision impact the economy?" But we do not yet accept all nouns as verbs. In our waking linguistic usage, we cannot yet say, "The heavy rains greened the field" – although poets can say such things and be understood.

By this principle, all colors could become verbs, yet some have done so to a greater degree than others. We speak of the "graying" of America, meaning the increase in the proportion of the population who are elderly. "Yellowing" is the process by which objects become yellow, that is, stale. This happens enough to white clothing in a natural process so that we have created the verb "to yellow." The color red has received a special treatment. When things become red, we do not say that they have redded; we have a new verb form: to redden. The same form has been used for white – to whiten. We also whiten clothes, although white can also be used in a verb form: If we make a mistake in typing, we can "white it out." (That verb form may already be nearly as obsolete as the mechanical typewriter, although we still retain "whiteout" as a weather situation where thick snow severely limits visibility.) We also have brown-outs (partial loss of electric power). But as far as I know, we do not yet have verb forms of orange or purple.

The Condensation Game shows how, given the right instructions, people can more freely transgress boundaries while awake. But there are limits. *The two objects to be condensed must have similarity along some dimension.* If you ask, what is halfway between a turkey and a theorem, or a banana and a theorem, you have a much harder time accomplishing any condensation. As Hillman (1979) has pointed out (p. 84):

> only *similars can be opposites*. Only those pairs having something material, essential in common can be sensibly opposed. A turkey cannot be opposed to a theorem, unless we can discover in what way they are like each other. Our psychological view is able to save the phenomenon of opposites by regarding opposition as an *extreme metaphor*, a radical way of saying one thing as though it were two violently differing things in sharp war with itself (Heraclitus again), which the valiant ego must imagine literally and meet as a challenge.

What is halfway between a banana and a theorem? That is a tough riddle. They don't even have any letters in common. If you work on them long enough, of course you will find something. For instance, they both have three syllables.

I have never actually heard a dream in which there was an object halfway between a banana and a theorem, and I would think it very unlikely (unless you are dreaming after reading this chapter). Even in the splendid chaos of dreaming, there are probably rules for creating interobjects. What those rules are has not been specified. To address this question adequately, we need to consider some of the findings and theories of modern cognitive neuroscience.

It would seem from the present discussion that novel pairings can occur only between objects already linked in the mindbrain along some dimension. One model of the mind, known as Parallel Distributed Processing or Connectionism (McClelland, Rumelhart, and the PDP Research Group, 1986), proposed that each object may be represented in several places in the mindbrain, not in a single neuron, but in neuronal fields. Adopting this model of the mind, we might say that there are weighted links between the representations of objects in our neurons. When we are awake, certain rule systems, like day-logic, grammar, etc. govern those linkages. At night some of those rule systems give way.

However, other neurological studies suggest that different regions of the mindbrain may be more specialized intrinsically for different categories of objects. One of the earliest such studies showed that people with aphasia (language disorder) may lose the ability to name only a certain category of objects. For example, a patient who was globally aphasic after a left-hemisphere stroke retained the ability to identify food, animal, and flower items, but could not identify inanimate objects. In contrast, patients with herpes simplex encephalitis could identify inanimate objects, but not living things and foods (Warrington and McCarthy, 1983). Since then, scientists have discovered other language defects that are specialized for particular kinds of things (Mahon and Caramazza, 2009) – animals (Blundo *et al.*, 2006), fruits and vegetables (Hart *et al.*, 1985; Samson and Pillon, 2003), humans (Miceli *et al.*, 2000) and non-living things (Laiacona and Capitani, 2001). We may propose a continuum of inanimate objects, vegetables and fruit, animals, and humans, with each group processed in a different part of the mindbrain (Devlin *et al.*, 2002). One could hypothesize that the mindbrain, in creating dream interobjects, tends to compare things within each of these four groups, and that it sometimes conjoins objects that are one category apart from each other.

However, some interobjects do not obey these rules. A cellphone/baby violates the animate/inanimate divide. We might infer two things from such examples: (1) the divisions in the mindbrain that we see in brain damage do not apply to dream interobjects; (2) when such divisions are violated, we can see that the mindbrain has brought about a metaphoric transfer between categories, such as the assignment of human characteristics to an inanimate object. The cellphone/baby interobject could be taken as evidence that people experience their cellphones as human. We would not be too startled by the sentence: "My cellphone and I are very close." Such sentences show our intuitive grasp of certain metaphoric relationships.

Similarly, in some brain-damaged patients, there is a loss of ability to name body parts and musical instruments, which does not respect the living-thing/nonliving-thing divide (Warrington and McCarthy, 1987). Musical instruments are played close to the body (especially instruments like the cello) and may be experienced as extensions of the body. Thus, there may be "category blurring" or a "metaphoric transfer of meaning" for inanimate objects that are held close to the body or experienced as extensions of the body, things that are experienced as "somewhat animate" and "somewhat human" even though they are technically inanimate. We would probably not be startled by the sentence "I played him like a cello."

In this way, the interobjects produced in dreams may tell us something about the organization of the mindbrain. In dreams, when the mindbrain is *generating* stimuli rather than perceiving them, these internal organizational factors, of which we are usually unaware, can make their existence known. When the mindbrain is producing percepts during dreaming, patterns of neural firing may bring together representations that are stored adjacent to one another, which allows the creation of new objects. Although aqueducts have very different functions from swimming pools, we may ignore that in dreaming. Instead, the dreaming mindbrain "notices" the similarity of aqueducts and swimming pools – they are both man-made objects containing large amounts of water – and can condense them into "something between a swimming pool and an aqueduct," or an "aque-pool," as occurred in the dream of Bert States (1995).

If we could amass a large catalogue of interobjects, we might be better able to generalize about these guidelines. It may be relevant, also, to consider the kinds of interobjects that have appeared in mythology, in modern fiction (such as children's cartoons), and in the products of computer "morphing" programs (e.g., Goldenberg *et al.*, 1999).

Notes

1 Taken from: www.dictionary.com/browse/sangfroid?s=t, accessed December 8, 2017.
2 It would be useful to determine whether nonlinguistic multiple meanings are also activated simultaneously in the mindbrain. If one presented an abstract

form that could look like a penis or a cigar or a building, are all those meanings simultaneously activated? (See section on "homoforms" p. 107.) The dreaming mindbrain might also perform the reverse operation, transforming homoforms into symbols, using nonlinguistic puns. We also do not know whether the Swinney effect applies to complex homonyms, like "cantaloupe = can't elope" (see p. 92).
3 It may be questioned whether "soldiers or gymnasts" is a true interobject. Further inquiry (which is no longer possible with Ferenczi's patient) might clarify whether the dreamer's percept involved something between soldiers and gymnasts, or whether the dreamer simply couldn't tell which they were.
4 For a more extensive discussion of this dream and its meaning, see p. 118.
5 For a more extensive discussion of this dream, see p. 207.

Chapter 4
Displacement

The concept of displacement has a complex history in psychoanalysis. Freud's original idea was clear (Freud, 1900a). Displacement is a shift in emphasis and salience; little things are made to stand out and big things are obscured. As Freud (1933, p. 21) put it:

> Something that played only a minor part in the dream-thoughts seems to be pushed into the foreground in the dream as the main thing, while, on the contrary, what was the essence of the dream-thoughts finds only passing and indistinct representation in the dream.

He also connected displacement with what Nietzsche called a transvaluation of psychical values.

Freud (1916) later referred to this form of displacement as "displacement of accent,"[1] to differentiate it from the many other meanings that displacement was accruing. In publications on topics other than dreams, Freud developed quite different meanings of displacement. Displacement came to include situations in which some aspect of psychic life was shifted, and many different such shifts were identified by Freud.

There is "displacement of object": feelings that are connected with one person are displaced onto another person. A common example is the man who has had a bad day at the office, comes home and yells at his wife and children. Freud (1913) thought that childhood animal phobias could result from the displacement of fear of the parents onto animals. Displacement of object is the essence of transference; feelings toward parents or other significant figures of early life are displaced onto the psychoanalyst or another person in one's adult life.

Displacement of object can also involve turning one's feeling toward others back onto oneself. For example, Freud said that a person who is uncomfortable with his own aggression toward other people may become aggressive toward himself. "The more a man controls his aggressiveness, the more intense becomes his ideal's inclination to aggressiveness against his ego. It is like a displacement, a turning round upon his own ego" (Freud, 1923, p. 54).[2] This can happen with disparaging terms of prejudice: Some Blacks refer to themselves with the "N-word," some Native Americans call themselves Indians, and some Mexicans call themselves "beaners."

There is "displacement of emotion" in which an emotion is transformed. Freud (1925, p. 254) argued that women, after seeming to relinquish their penis-envy, sometimes displace those feelings into a general character trait of jealousy.

Freud (1901) spoke about "displacement of time period." "An indifferent impression of recent date establishes itself in the memory as a screen memory, although it owes that privilege merely to its connection with an earlier experience which resistances prevent from being reproduced directly" (Freud, 1901, p. 44). Freud (1931, p. 242) referred to Melanie Klein's timing of the Oedipus complex to the second year of life as a "displacement backwards" which he rejected.

There is also displacement of attribution. A characteristic that one perceives in oneself but seems unacceptable is instead attributed to another person. This is essentially the mechanism of projection; an aspect of the self is projected (displaced) onto someone else (see pp. 161–162). Freud (1927) thought that people commonly displace their own desires onto God. I have argued that people also displace their disgust and other emotions onto God (Blechner, in press).

There are bodily displacements. A genital sensation may be experienced in the mouth (displacement upward) or an oral sensation may be experienced genitally (displacement downward). Novelist John Cleland (1749) referred to the vagina as "the nethermouth." Freud thought such displacements of feeling could occur more generally in sexuality. Sexual attraction toward a human body is displaced, sometimes onto a particular body part, like feet, or sometimes onto an inanimate fetish object. A feeling of constriction around the mouth could be displaced vaginismus (Freud, 1908b, p. 33). Anal preoccupations could be displaced upwards into obsessional acts of talking and eating (Freud, 1909b).

Sometimes, bodily displacement is combined with a displacement of affect, from pleasurable to unpleasurable.[3] Freud (1905b) considered this to be the case with his patient, Dora. She had been kissed by Herr K., and Dora displaced her unacceptable genital pleasure into an unpleasant throat catarrh.

In summary, Freud's usage of the term "displacement" expanded from a shift of accent in dreams to a much more general and variegated process of shifting affects, objects, body parts, and innervation. Subsequent psychoanalysts expanded the range of displacements even further. The many "displacements" eventually eclipsed Freud's original usage of displacement of accent in dreams. Neubauer (1994) wrote an entire paper on displacement in psychoanalysis without mentioning Freud's original idea of displacement of accent.

The multiple meanings of displacement in Freud is relevant to the well-known analogy that Lacan (2006) made between displacement and metonymy. Without specifying, Lacan seems to have had in mind Freud's later uses of displacement. The original usage of "displacement of accent" does not make much sense as an analogue of metonymy. While I consider Lacan's formulation to be problematic,[4] it leads us to be precise about the different kinds of displacement. Bodily displacements are usually metaphoric, such as the fantasy of the female genital as a mouth that can ingest things or that can harm with teeth. Displacements of object are usually metonymic.

Notes

1 Alfred Hitchcock adapted the "displacement of accent" in his films, as noted by French film director Olivier Assayas: "[In Hitchcock's films], like in a dream, there is a sort of hyper-perception of objects. Suddenly, minor details take a preeminent place and the essential details are left in the background. And that is really what a dream is" (Jones, 2015). Lionel Trilling (1950) asserted that "displacement of accent" was adapted by James Joyce in *Finnegan's Wake*.
2 This mechanism may be seen as underlying the defense of "turning against the self" (S. Freud, 1915a; A. Freud, 1936). Displacement underlies a number of psychological defenses.
3 This seems to be intimately tied to "reaction formation" (see p. 157).
4 Lyotard (1983) ably critiques Lacan's formulation.

Chapter 5

Metaphor

Introduction

Many people think of metaphor as a linguistic device, used by writers and poets, in which one thing is described in terms of another. Shakespeare's Romeo says: "It is the East and Juliet is the sun." He does not mean that Juliet is a ball of fire in the sky. He means that Juliet has characteristics of the sun: warm, radiant, and nurturing, and she illuminates his life. The metaphor instantaneously makes us think of Juliet in terms of all of the sun's attributes – its warmth, brightness, and goodness (unless you live in the desert), so we understand this metaphor. A good metaphor needs us to have familiarity with the elements of the metaphor – otherwise it may sound capricious or crazy. If Romeo said: "It is the East and Juliet is Philadelphia," his intended meaning would be less clear.

The word "metaphor" derives from the Greek verb *metaphora* (μεταφορά) – to transport or transfer. The old definition of metaphor is: "A figure of speech in which one object is likened to another by asserting it to be that other or speaking of it as if it were the other" (*Funk and Wagnalls' New Standard Dictionary of the English Language*, 1928). However, over the years, philosophers and psycholinguists have observed that metaphor is not just a device for literary artists. It is, instead, an integral part of human language and thought (Jakobson, 1956/1995; Lakoff and Johnson, 1980). Metaphor is one way the mindbrain connects and transforms different ideas, casting one into the shape of the other.

It is hard, perhaps impossible, for people to speak without using metaphors, although most of us are not conscious of most metaphors that we use. For example, when a woman says to her boyfriend, "We are spinning our wheels," he knows that she is not saying that their car is stuck in the mud; she means that the relationship is not progressing, not "moving forward." The nature of the relationship is expressed in terms of car travel, mobility, and progress, or lack of progress, in this case.

If we say "He is moving up in the world" we don't usually mean he is driving to a higher altitude; we mean the he is achieving increased status. We are applying the domain of physical altitude to status. Along the same lines, we also say "his career is on the rise" or "his career is going downhill." In general, the metaphor is "height is goodness." We can say "Her beauty is at its peak," "His political speech hit a new low."

We know that "hot babe" does not refer to an infant with fever caused by illness. The metaphors are that "heat is sexual attractiveness" and "a beloved person is an infant." Are metaphors a uniquely human capacity? Ramachandran said: "Any monkey can reach for a peanut, but only a human can reach for the stars or even understand what that means" (quoted in von Bubnoff, 2005).

Metaphor is not just a means of poignant, intense expression devised by poets; it is basic to most of our speech, and by extension, to most of our thinking. Many metaphors are so overused that we no longer recognize them as metaphors. Nietzsche (1873/1976, pp. 46–47) observed this: "truths are illusions about which one has forgotten that this is what they are; metaphors which are worn out and without sensuous power; coins which have lost their pictures and now matter only as metal, no longer as coins."[1] When we hear "He is moving up in the world," we don't think "A metaphor!" Some of those metaphors are like old coins, so overused that their identity as metaphors is barely perceptible.

One way to make us aware of commonplace metaphors is to depict them as being heard literally. The television show *Get Smart* had a character, Hymie the robot, who made these errors. Secret agent Maxwell Smart's boss said to Hymie, "Hymie, knock that stuff off" and Hymie knocks all of his papers off the desk. Smart says, "Hymie, shake a leg," and Hymie shakes his leg. These scenes are humorous, but they demonstrate how much we take common metaphors for granted.[2] If a man went up a mountain on a funicular and said, "I am moving up in the world," most people would find it comic or even startling. We are more used to the metaphoric meaning than the literal one.

It is impossible to get away from metaphor, no matter how hard one may try. Some notable philosophers have indeed tried (Hofstadter and Sander, 2013). Thomas Hobbes, in *Leviathan*, wrote: "The light of human minds is perspicuous words, but by exact definitions first snuffed and purged from ambiguity; ... metaphors, and senseless and ambiguous words, are like *ignes fatui*; and reasoning upon them is wandering amongst innumerable absurdities" (1651/1966, pp. 116–117).

This passage is a good example of what I call an "oxymoronic speech act" (Blechner, 2007b),[3] where the intended meaning of a statement clashes with the interpersonal action implied by the utterance of the statement. Hobbes is seeking to get rid of metaphors, yet oxymoronically his condemnation of metaphors contains metaphors. Does the mindbrain contain light? Is our thought "wandering"? Can you actually cleanse a definition, and if you could, are metaphors dirt? *Ignes fatui* are will-o'-the-wisps, mysterious lights that are thought to flicker above marshes, which may be ominous or dangerous (Mills, 2000; Bostridge, 2015). Is the characterization of metaphors in this way not indeed metaphoric? Hobbes is condemning metaphor while using metaphors to condemn them.

It would seem that no matter how much we might try, we cannot rid our language of metaphor, because metaphor is not just a figure of speech. According to Cognitive Metaphor Theory, metaphor is core to our processes of thinking and speaking. This has been pointed out by Lakoff and Johnson (1980); our mindbrains swim in a sea of metaphor as a fish in water, and we are so immersed in metaphors we often do not notice them.[4]

Lakoff and Turner (1989) wrote about the grounding of much metaphor in the human body. They had some notable predecessors in this line of thinking. In 1744, the Italian philosopher Giambattista Vico pointed out the ubiquity of bodily metaphor in our thought. Vico wrote (1744/2001, pp. 159–160):

> Noteworthy too is the fact that in all languages most expressions for inanimate objects employ metaphors derived from the human body and its parts, or from human senses and emotions. Thus we say *head* for top or beginning; *front* or *brow*, and *shoulders* or *back*, for before and behind; ... *mouth* for any opening; *lip* for the rim of a pitcher or other container. We speak of the *tooth* of a plough, rake, saw, or comb; ... the *throat* of rivers and mountains [French *gorge*]. We speak of the *coast*[5] [Italian *costiera*, rib] of the sea.... Similarly, the sky or sea *smiles* on us; the wind whistles; the waves *murmur*; and a body *groans* under a great weight.

But whereas modern psycholinguists see metaphor as an inevitable and essential aspect of human thought, Vico saws the human tendency to anthropomorphize the world as reflecting a limitation of human intellect:

> Man has reduced the entire world to his own body. Now, rational metaphysics teaches us that man becomes all things through understanding, *homo intelligendo fit omnia*. But with perhaps greater truth, this imaginative metaphysics shows that man becomes all things by not understanding, *homo non intelligendo fit omnia*. For when man understands, he extends his mind to comprehend things; when he does not understand, he makes them out of himself and, by transforming himself, becomes them.
>
> (Vico, 1744/2001, p. 160)

It is an open question whether our experience of the world in terms of our bodies is inevitable or shows a limitation of human thought that could be overcome. So far, no one has done it, and it is possible that most human thought, if not all of it, is inevitably linked with our bodies (Varela *et al.*, 1991).

Metaphor and bodily experience

Thought is rooted in the body often, if not always. That was one of the great insights of psychoanalysis – bodily experience is the template on which all other experience is mapped. Forceville wrote (2009, p. 20): "Human beings find phenomena they can see, hear, feel, taste, and/or smell easier to understand and categorize than phenomena they cannot."

The early psychoanalysts discussed this extensively, noting how particular kinds of bodily interaction with the world led to certain kinds of personality characteristics (e.g., Freud, 1908a; Abraham, 1925, 1949; Reich, 1933). All infants start their lives with early feeding experiences, and these shape the adult personality and thinking, during what psychoanalysts call the oral stage. The rhythm of frustration and satiety that the infant experiences with his or her mother sets the pattern for what one expects from life and how one handles the good times and the bad. The oral metaphor is common in our speech. We say, "He can never get enough." "He is sucking me dry." "He bites the hand that feeds him."

"She has a thirst for knowledge." "He is hungry for love." "I have no appetite for this kind of theater."

All infants also evacuate their urine and feces. They have many experiences, good and bad, as they learn to regulate these bodily excretions, with corresponding reactions from caregivers (Freud, 1908a; Abraham, 1923). These experiences, during what is called the anal stage, often form characteristics of self-control, independence, rigidity, and cleanliness or their opposites. We say, "He is emotionally constipated." "She is pissed off." "I don't give a shit." "He shit on my best efforts." "He has a stick up his ass."

Ella Freeman Sharpe widened the psychoanalytic approach to metaphor and the body. She emphasized how bodily experience forms the template not only for personality, but for the very details and structure of how we think and speak. She argued that the traces of these early experiences are evident in the metaphors that saturate our speech.

Sharpe wrote:

> Metaphor is as ultimate as speech itself, and speech as ultimate as thought.... My theory is that metaphor can only evolve in language or in the arts when the bodily orifices become controlled. Then only can the angers, pleasures, desires of the infantile life find metaphorical expression and the immaterial express itself in terms of the material. *A subterranean passage between mind and body underlies all analogy.*
>
> (1940, p. 202, italics mine)

For example, her British patient would make reference to some "bloody" thing, and Sharpe would look beyond "bloody" being an expletive in the UK, and find that there was a reference in the dream to blood and menstruation.

Margaret Schlauch (1956) suggested that one of the most basic types of metaphorical transfer is the naming of a new object through its resemblance to the part of the body. We speak of "the face of a watch," "blind alleys," headlands, and foothills. In all these instances, meaning is transferred from a bodily part to other objects. In a similar vein (note yet another bodily metaphor), we also say: "She is my right arm." "He wants to bring me to my knees." "Don't wave your finger at me." "He went for the jugular."

The foundation of our language and thought in bodily experience has been studied further by today's cognitive metaphor theorists, most especially in two seminal[6] works: Mark Johnson (1987) in his book *The Body in the Mind*, and in the book co-authored with George Lakoff, *Philosophy in the Flesh* (Lakoff and Johnson, 1999). Lakoff and Johnson, like psychoanalysts, argue that our mental experience has its roots in early bodily experience. They focus on other early bodily experiences, not necessarily centered on oral, anal, and genital zones with other people. They do not mention psychoanalysis.

Johnson (1987) discusses how all infants learn about force, both as it is applied to them and can apply to people and things. As infants, we learn about force, not only with other people, but also with nonhuman physical forces that exist in our world, such as gravity, light, heat, and wind. We learn that physical objects may stand in our way, and that we can sometimes apply force to get past them. We acquire a sense of how force works, long before we have a word to describe it, and this preverbal concept of force stays with us for the rest of our lives.[7]

Melanie Klein (1946) went further and proposed that the early mix of frustration and satisfaction lead us to imagine dramatic conflicts, destruction, and reparation. When we, as adults, say, "I could kill her!" the metaphor is that anger is potential murder.

Our adult experiences of satiety and frustration and how we deal with them relate back to early feeding: How do you experience hunger? How do you get fed? How much do you trust that feeding snags will be worked out?

The study of human attachment brings out a similar issue – all experience of human closeness and distance are mapped onto early experiences of attachment. How much closeness is optimal for you (both bodily closeness and empathic closeness)? How much distance? How much can you depend on the other person? How much can you enjoy freedom from the other person? How much can you assume that somebody who disappears will come back? Does being left feel like you have lost the person forever, or does it just feel like a temporary separation?

Physical closeness has also entered the metaphors of our everyday speech. We say, "He left me in the lurch." "I need space." "She left me high and dry" (a nautical metaphor, meaning that she left me in a situation in which I was immobile and could not budge).

Freud also developed the notion of castration anxiety, which was sometimes but not always meant as metaphoric. Sometimes it seemed that Freud meant literally that the infant or adult fears castration itself, the removal of the penis or testicles. Castration is irreversible; it can be a metaphor of bodily loss or damage, either specifically of the sex organs or of other body parts or capacities.

There is debate about whether literal castration anxiety is indeed universal. Nevertheless, fear of "bodily damage" in general is an issue for most people. We all have specific experiences of bodily wounding and healing that shape our thought and character – a cut that heals; a black-and-blue mark that disappears; a burn that leaves a permanent scar; an injury that leaves us disabled; an accident that leaves us crippled. All of these experiences shape our understanding of our ability to bounce back from injury or not.

The interaction of damage and healing, which we experience with our bodies, can also be experienced in our interpersonal relations. If I offend my wife, does she forgive me? Or do I stay in the doghouse? If someone offends me, do I hold a grudge forever? Do I turn the other cheek? Do I seek revenge? The experience starts with the body, but later in life it applies metaphorically to other kinds of personal damage and the potential to recover from them or not.

Bodily damage and bodily reinforcement have found their way into our speech as metaphors of psychological well-being or disruption. We are "struck down" by illness. We "catch" a cold. We "get back to normal." She is a "ball-buster." He "cut me down to size." She "built up" my confidence.

Self-esteem is a metaphor, too. Self-esteem is often portrayed metaphorically as a container that can be filled or depleted. It can be filled by reflections and feedback from another person (Sullivan, 1940). Statements that convey the feeling of "You are good" fill me up with the sense of "I am good." How much of the time do we get those good feelings versus feelings of "I am bad"? How does our view of ourselves become modified by such feedback?

The metaphor of the container has been a part of most psychological theories of the self and approaches to treating disorders of the self: Harry Stack Sullivan (reflected appraisals), Carl Rogers (unconditional personal regard), Kohut (empathic reflection), and Eric Berne (I'm OK, you're OK). Many psychotherapists seek to "fill" the patient with positive self-esteem by pouring good evaluations into the container of the self. Pouring in bad evaluations and harsh judgments will "deplete" the person of self-esteem. We say, "He filled me with pride." "He is so draining." We also say, "He is full of himself" to mean that he has too much self-regard and, by implication perhaps, not enough regard for other people. We also say, "He is full of shit" implying that he is foolish or misguided; his self is full but with detritus.

The capacity for metaphor in dreams can develop early. At the age of three years and nine months, my nephew was singing in the hallway of a hotel early in the morning. A woman came out of her room and yelled at him for making noise. He was upset by her reproaches. That night he dreamt that "*a giant bee was buzzing around my head, scaring me.*" Although my nephew made no connection to his daytime experience, the metaphor was apparent: "A lady who attacks you with her mean words is a bumblebee who threatens and scares you."[8] This dream along with others (such as those reported in Resnick *et al.*, 1994; Sandor *et al.*, 2014; and Anzieu-Premmereur, 2016) challenge Freud's idea that in children's dreams, all wishes are represented as fulfilled without disguise. In at least this dream, the fear was represented, not the wish; and the object of fear was disguised, or, one could say, transformed; the threatening human was represented metaphorically as a bumblebee.[9]

Animal-human metaphors are common in cartoons made for children – such as Bambi, Mickey Mouse, Road Runner, and Babar. In literature for adults, we have Orwell's *Animal Farm* and Kafka's *Metamorphosis*. Anthropomorphism of animals is common in childhood. Some say it is one of the prime ways of developing children's imagination (Daston and Mitman, 2005). Anthropomorphism continues into adulthood, especially among pet owners. Many ostensibly sane people believe or fantasize into adulthood that their pets have human characteristics. The journalist Barbara Walters made news when she announced that her dog, Cha-Cha, spoke to her and said, "I love you." Hotel-heiress Leona Helmsley bequeathed 12 million dollars to her dog, Trouble.

How metaphor helps us understand dreams

Metaphor allows us to see how the dreaming mindbrain can portray one issue in terms of another. Individual elements of a dream can portray ideas metaphorically. The entire story line of a dream can be a metaphor.

There is no limit to the metaphors that dreams can invoke. However, in the history of psychoanalytic dream interpretation, six primary metaphors have been prominent in interpreting dreams.

Six primary metaphors in dream interpretation

1. Metaphor of the body
2. Metaphor of the mindbrain
3. Metaphor of sex
4. Metaphor of emotion
5. Metaphor of the dreamer's situation in life
6. Metaphor of an interpersonal relationship

The six primary metaphors

1 Metaphor of the body

Objects in a dream can stand metaphorically for body parts. The objects have shapes or topologies analogous to body parts.[10] A sword, snake, or anything elongated can be a penis; apples can be breasts; a bag or pocketbook can be a vagina or womb. Balconies on the upper stories of houses can be metaphors of the breasts, and the entire structure can stand for a woman. Water can be a symbol of birth through metonymy – when we were in our mother's womb, we were submerged in liquid, and delivery is preceded by the "water breaking." (I will say more about these bodily symbols in Chapter 9.)

Bodily traumas are often represented metaphorically in a dream. A man had been seriously injured as a child when his mother threw a pair of scissors at him that lodged in his leg. As an adult, he dreamt that his "car had been smashed in the front." His car, like his legs, allowed him to get from one place to another, and so the car damage is a metaphor for his leg damage.

Another man who, as a child, had been beaten down violently by his father, dreamt that a rooster (which is normally "cocky") is hobbling across the street, partially crippled, a metaphor for his self-confidence damaged by the trauma. Notice the similarity of the two patients' experiences, both having been traumatized by a parent's sudden anger, yet their choices of metaphor are very different. Dreams are very precise in their creation of metaphors. Each dream metaphor captures the particularity of the early trauma and its effect on the person's current life.

2 Metaphor of the mindbrain

The structure of the dream is a metaphor for the structure of the mindbrain. Walking through an apartment and finding a new room can be a metaphor for finding new areas of your mindbrain that you did not know about before, or new kinds of thinking.[11] A dream that contains three people – a young person acting impulsively, an older man giving sage advice on how one should behave, and a third man moderating the discussion can be metaphors of the id, superego, and the ego.

3 Metaphor of sex

A dream with a "key opening a lock" can be a metaphor of sexual intercourse (in this case, as in many metaphors of sex, there is overlap with metaphor of the body parts, key=penis, opened lock=penetrated vagina). Certain activities can also be metaphors of sexual intercourse, such as climbing stairs, which mimics the rhythmic movement of intercourse. And yet sex itself, in a dream, can be seen to be a metaphor for other aspects of human relatedness – such as cooperation, dominance, love, hatred, tenderness, and fertility.

4 Metaphor of emotion

Aspects of the dream can be metaphors of emotions. A dream that contained a short fuse from an automobile can be a metaphor of being quick to anger. "Cold feet" in a dream can be a metaphor for fearful hesitancy. Painful bowel movements can be metaphors of painful feelings that must be evacuated.

5 Metaphor of the dreamer's situation in life

A 30-year-old man dreamt of a broken-down rocket ship that will not take off; this was a metaphor for his "failure to launch" in life, his inability to get his career and personal life "off the ground." A woman hospitalized for depression dreamt that she was sinking to the bottom of the ocean; this was a metaphor for falling back into a deep depression and functioned as a communication to her psychiatrist that she was not ready to be discharged from the hospital (note again the overlap with metaphor of emotion).

6 Metaphor of an interpersonal relationship

A dream can be a metaphor of an intensely personal relationship, such as (a) a romantic relationship or (b) a psychotherapeutic relationship. Here are two examples:

a   A woman whose boyfriend wanted to break up wrote him an email, begging him to keep the door open. That night, she dreamt literally of "a door left open," which was a metaphor of allowing the possibility that their broken-up relationship might be reinstated, although the cold wind that came through the door signified that she was not very hopeful about the future.[12]

b   A psychoanalyst, in supervision with me, had been working with a patient for more than ten years. The patient had made a great deal of progress, and, in my view, was nearing the time for termination. The analyst saw it differently, but acknowledged that she had a very strong attachment to the patient and might not want him to terminate for her own reasons. The patient had the following dream:

> *I kept having a dream last night. I was trying to graduate from high school. I couldn't graduate because I hadn't taken an American History course and I was supposed to take the final exam or do the final paper. One of the people who went to R's wedding, she was a friend of mine there (high school), and she was in the dream and she had already taken the exam and she had failed it.*
>
> *Now I think it's a dream about therapy – wanting to graduate from therapy and not knowing what in the world I could do to do that. Which means you're the evil horrible history teacher who wouldn't let me graduate.*
>
> *In the dream, I kept putting it off until the last possible time you could take the test. And then I didn't show up. And I just kept hoping that the teacher would let me graduate anyway because it was only one course and I had been there long enough – I was there for ten years.*

Taken as a whole, the dream story is a metaphor of the psychotherapy, which is symbolized as a history course (which captures both that the patient felt he learned things in psychotherapy and that he particularly learned things about his history). The psychotherapist is symbolized as a teacher, who has expertise and power; her abuse of that power is felt as evil. Graduation is a symbol of bringing the psychotherapy to a close, and the patient finishing his work with the psychotherapist. All these unitary elements of the dream are symbolic. Taken together, the totality of the dream story is an allegory: being prevented by an evil teacher from graduating is a metaphor of being prevented by the psychotherapist from ending the therapy.

The relationship between the psychotherapist and patient has become a primary metaphor in dream interpretation. I wrote a paper (Blechner, 1995b) that showed how dreams of people in analysis could be a comment on the analyst's countertransference, so that dreams could be used as supervision.[13] I think it is a very useful way to think about dreams, but it should not squeeze out other meanings of dreams, such as portraying the dreamer's personality, state of body, and psychological defenses.

Dream as allegory

Dreams show the tendency of the mindbrain to represent our life situation in metaphoric terms. The story of any dream can be seen as an allegory, as a metaphoric transfer of one situation onto another. This was the view of Montague Ullman, who considered the dream to be metaphoric of the dreamer's total life situation or a part of it: "The dream in its totality is a metaphorical explication of a circumstance of living explored in its fullest implications for the current scene" (Ullman, 1969, p. 700).

A dream often is structured like an allegory; the entire story of the dream suggests a metaphor-like transfer of meaning. This was true of the very first recorded dream, the dream of Gilgamesh 5,000 years ago (Thompson, 1930). Gilgamesh dreamt that *an ax fell from the sky. The people gathered around it in admiration and worship. Gilgamesh threw the ax in front of his mother and then he embraced it like a wife.*

Gilgamesh told the dream to his mother, Ninsun, and she told him what it meant. She said that someone powerful would soon appear. Gilgamesh would struggle with him and try to overpower him, but he would not succeed. Eventually they would become close friends and accomplish great things. She said (Oppenheim, 1956, p. 247), "That you embraced him like a wife means: he will never forsake you! Thus your dream is solved!"

The same was true of Pharaoh's dream in the Old Testament that was interpreted by Joseph. Pharaoh dreamed:

He was standing by the Nile, and behold, there came up out of the Nile seven cows, attractive and plump, and they fed in the reed grass. And behold, seven other cows, ugly and thin, came up out of the Nile after them, and stood by the other cows on the bank of the Nile. And the ugly, thin cows ate up the seven attractive, plump cows. And Pharaoh awoke. And he fell asleep and dreamed a second time. And behold, seven ears of grain, plump and good, were growing on one stalk. And behold, after them sprouted seven ears, thin and blighted by the east wind. And the thin ears swallowed up the seven plump, full ears. And Pharaoh awoke, and behold, it was a dream.[14]

Joseph interpreted the dream as an allegory of Egypt's economic future.

> The dreams of Pharaoh are one; God has revealed to Pharaoh what he is about to do. The seven good cows are seven years, and the seven good ears are seven years; the dreams are one. The seven lean and ugly cows that came up after them are seven years, and the seven empty ears blighted by the east wind are also seven years of famine. It is as I told Pharaoh; God has shown to Pharaoh what he is about to do. There will come seven years of great plenty throughout all the land of Egypt, but after them there will arise seven years of famine, and all the plenty will be forgotten in the land of Egypt. The famine will consume the land, and the plenty will be unknown in the land by reason of the famine that will follow, for it will be very severe. And the doubling of Pharaoh's dream means that the thing is fixed by God, and God will shortly bring it about. Now therefore let Pharaoh select a discerning and wise man, and set him over the land of Egypt. Let Pharaoh proceed to appoint overseers over the land and take one-fifth of the produce of the land of Egypt during the seven plentiful years. And let them gather all the food of these good years that are coming and store up grain under the authority of Pharaoh for food in the cities, and let them keep it. That food shall be a reserve for the

land against the seven years of famine that are to occur in the land of Egypt, so that the land may not perish through the famine.[15]

Seven cows are symbols of the productivity of seven years; when the lean cows eat the fat cows, that is an allegory of seven years of famine succeeding seven years of prosperity. Freud (1900a) established this as a principle; contiguity in time in a dream can symbolize a logical or sequential relationship; in Pharaoh's dream, it is "first this, then that."[16]

How do you decide what the dream allegorizes? It can depend on what is the primary question in the dreamer's mind. For a leader of a country, the question is likely to be about the success and survival of the nation. For Gilgamesh, the dream question was: "Who shall invade and how shall I handle him?" For Pharaoh, the dream question was: "What will be the prosperity or poverty of my nation, and how shall I prepare for it?" To people who are not leaders of a country, the primary question may be on a smaller scale.

A man in a dream group reported a dream in which *he was at his country home. A foreign-born man and woman and their two children had gotten into the house and changed the lock. The dreamer said, "I need a key to that lock." The woman said she would get it to him. The dreamer said angrily, "Give it to me right now. Just give me the one that's on your key ring."* He realized that his partner had a new job that required him to live out of town during the week. His new boss was foreign-born, as was the boss's wife, and they had two children. He said,

> They have taken over my partner's life so much. He works with them, socializes with them, and at times it feels like he is more interested in them than in me. It feels like they have invaded my home and locked me out of my own life.

The dream was very specific about the family constellation of the intruders and alerted the dreamer to a very real danger of people who made him feel locked out of his own house. While in real life, he had been rather accepting of his new life with his bicoastal partner, in the dream, especially when he spoke to the others with a harsh and peremptory tone, he could feel his anger and the urgent need to change things and assert his rights – he needed to regain control of his own house.

In the *Jeopardy!* approach to dreams (Blechner, 2001), if you ask the right question, the dream itself is the answer. If we take the *Jeopardy!* approach to this dream, the dream question is: "Who is invading my home, and how shall I handle it?" The dream answer is: "Your partner's boss and family are invading your home life, and you must vigorously take back possession of your life."

Dreams pictorialize metaphors

Prominent themes, events, or conflicts in the dreamer's life are portrayed in dreams in a metaphoric way. However, a metaphor that in waking life might be expressed in words is more likely to be portrayed in a dream through a wordless picture or a wordless story. It is not hard to see how the following metaphors can be portrayed with images in a dream: "you hit the nail on the head"; "you are beating a dead horse"; "I really got into it"; "he screwed it up." Bodily metaphors are often portrayed literally: we are flying, we are stuck, we are dragging our feet, we are swimming against the current, we are sinking, we make great strides, and we break through barriers.

A man dreamt he was a steward on an airplane and offered to do laundry for people on the plane. Laundry is part of the metaphor, "Dirt is embarrassing and shameful facts." We "get the dirt on someone" meaning we find out someone's unsavory secrets. We "wash our dirty linen in public," meaning we expose shameful, personal things to others publicly. The dream pictorialized these metaphors (portrayed them in pictures); it was an attempt by the dreamer to expose secrets, to break the facade of seamless propriety that was part of his family's general manner. Since his father was a pilot, there was the question of whether he was going to air the dirty linen of his father, but since he offers laundry service to the entire plane, it seems possible that it is the dirty linen of the entire family. Here we see the metaphor, "crowd equals family" – although Freud thought that a crowd in a dream symbolized a secret. The dream also raised the question of what it felt like to talk about family secrets with the psychotherapist. In the dream, he felt very happy, although when he awoke, the idea of doing laundry on an airplane felt bizarre.

Combined metaphors, modified metaphors, and mixed metaphors

In *The Dream Frontier*, I wrote:

> Dreams ... step beyond the bounds of conventional metaphor. They create entirely new metaphors, and they also extend and combine commonly-used metaphors in brand new ways.... The understanding of dreams requires us to open our minds to unconventional metaphors, or metaphors expanded into new ranges of detail.
>
> (Blechner, 2001, p. 29)

I would like to describe some of the ways that dreams combine metaphors, create unconventional metaphors, or extend commonly used metaphors in new ways.

To start, let us be clear that a combined metaphor is not a mixed metaphor. A mixed metaphor is one that leaps from one metaphoric mapping to a second mapping inconsistent with the first. Consider the saying: "Once the toothpaste is out of the tube, it's hard to get it back in." This means that "once something is exposed and publicized, it cannot be reversed and hidden." This was said by H. R. Haldeman, referring to President Nixon's attempts to obstruct justice and cover up the crimes of Watergate. There is a similar saying: "Closing the stable door once the horse has bolted." This saying means: "Trying to stop something bad from happening when it has already happened and it is too late." In the first saying the metaphor is "irreversible event is toothpaste that has come out of the tube." In the second saying, "irreversible event is a horse that has run away before you close the barn door."

A mixed metaphor would be the following: "Once the toothpaste is out of the tube, it's too late to close the barn door." In mixed metaphors, it is as if the person cannot stick to the mapping long enough to keep a consistency to the metaphor. When we hear "Once the toothpaste is out of the tube," we are already intuiting the property of toothpaste tubes – easy to get stuff out, almost impossible to get stuff in. Then, when we hear: "it's too late to close the barn door," we recognize the suffix as *a futile attempt to have headed off an unfortunate event*. But the irreversible unfortunate event has changed: It started as keeping the toothpaste coming out of the tube, and ended as the horse getting out of the barn.

By a few mental gymnastics, we can recognize the connection of toothpaste tube and barn door, via their link to the underlying thought. But if we don't know the underlying mappings of both metaphors, the sentence would seem like nonsense.

Another example of a mixed metaphor, with four components, is:

> If we can hit that bullseye then the rest of the dominoes will fall like a house of cards. Checkmate.
>
> (*Futurama*, 1999)

The combination of so many metaphors becomes comic.[17] To understand this grouping, we must discern that all four metaphors refer to attack and victory. The metaphors of archery, dominoes, house of cards, and chess all mix (barely) into a statement that "If we handle it right, we will win completely and precipitously."

Mixed metaphors are usually seen as problematic and a deficit. But on the positive side, they show the ability of the mindbrain to find commonalities between different metaphors, to group together different mappings of the same meaning. The fact that we can understand how a person came to create a mixed metaphor shows our ability to uncover the multiple mappings necessary to produce the mixed metaphor.

Whereas single, well-constructed metaphors make meaning clearer, more vivid, and quickly understood (Aristotle, 350 BCE/2000), a mixed metaphor is confusing, vague, difficult to comprehend, and requires effort. The combined metaphors of dreams, by contrast, show the ingenuity and creativity of the unconscious mindbrain. Instead of one underlying idea and multiple mappings that we find in mixed metaphors, in combined metaphors we find multiple metaphors condensed into a single dream image.

Here is an example: Edward, a man in his mid-50s, after a divorce, married a younger woman who was pushing him to live in new and adventurous ways. Edward dreamt:

> *I am in the South of France. First, it was in Long Island. There was a very strong wind. There were fish flying in the air, not really flying, but suspended in the air, struggling in the air against a wind over dry land. I said to someone, "We could just go and take them and eat them right away."*

Edward's first wife and he used to travel often to the South of France; he and his new wife often vacation in Long Island. The dream, by creating the interobject (inter-geographic location) of South of France and Long Island poses the comparison: what was it like to be married to my first wife, and how does that compare to my marriage to my second wife? Are they the same or similar? I think my two wives are very different. Am I different in the two marriages?

Edward analyzed the image of the fish, flying in the air or suspended in the air, as a combination of several metaphors. It pictorialized the metaphor of "a fish out of water" (a person in unfamiliar and perhaps hazardous circumstances). The dream occurred around the 200th anniversary of Darwin's birth. Edward had seen a cartoon in *The New Yorker* of fish coming on land. The dream image also functioned as a metaphor of evolution. Edward said,

> I am evolving into new and difficult circumstances. Instead of going from the sea onto land, in the dream I am jumping ahead of myself, going from the sea into the air. It may be too difficult a transition to take, and I am suspended in the situation, but very alive in it. Although I might get eaten alive (another metaphor), if I am not careful.

Ironically, in the dream, the dreamer suggests that he could eat the fish right away, i.e., eat them alive. There is also the question of his voraciousness, aggression, and cannibalism. He associates to the phrase, "Eat or be eaten." He also associates to oral sex, and whether it is enlivening, aggressive, or both.

Edward also associated to an article he had read about the Russian thinker, Alexander Herzen. Herzen ridiculed Rousseau's statement: "Man is born free, yet everywhere he is in chains." Herzen said that Rousseau's statement was as silly as saying, "Fish are born to fly, yet everywhere they swim" (Berlin, 1978, p. 94). Yet in the dream, fish are flying, or at least hovering. Edward connected his dream image with the idea that he is venturing into doing things that are quite out of his nature, unusual, daring things, living in a different medium. It is requiring him to evolve: Can he change and adapt quickly enough? Is he doing things that are not in his nature? Is it a ridiculous attempt to be something that one is not, or to do something for which one is not properly equipped? Or is it adventurous to venture out of the expectable? Right now, he feels "in suspension" as he is in the dream: not making headway, not going back in the water, very alive, "struggling against a headwind" (another metaphor, which can mean fighting against opposing forces that push you in another direction, or push you back). The dream pictorializes a combination of at least three metaphors: "fish out of water," "evolution and survival of the fittest," and "struggling against a headwind."

If we put together the metaphors combined in the dream image into a single sentence, we get:

> I feel like a fish out of water, struggling against a headwind, trying to evolve and survive, but still very alive. I am also exposed and vulnerable, and someone (it could be me) could eat me alive. Or perhaps my current, second wife will eat me alive. She makes me feel exposed. She puts me in situations in which "I am out of my element." Will this lead to my evolution, or will it kill me? Can I adapt, or will I be destroyed?

All these thoughts are encoded in the dream.

The combined metaphors of dreams are quite different from mixed metaphors. They do not switch from one metaphoric mapping to another, but instead combine several metaphors into a single image. Thus, in this dream, the fish is both out of water and facing a headwind. *The two mappings do not conflict and are not alternatives to one another. They conjoin and, in doing so, enrich each other.*

The fish in Edward's dream is not thrashing or panicking, as a real fish out of water would do. The fish, instead, is calm and steadfast. He is like a fish out of water who has evolved, at least somewhat, to be in his new environment.

I also asked Edward to try to bring back the feeling of being that fish. This procedure (Bosnak, 2003), of embodied imagination and feeling oneself back into the dream, yielded surprising results, as it often does. He said that the feeling of being suspended in air with a strong wind coming against him reminded him of a childhood experience. He would be riding in the car with the window open, and he would let his arm and hand stretch forward out the window, pick up the feeling of the wind blowing by, pressing his arm up or down, depending on the angle of his fingers. He did this for hours on long car trips. It felt like his arm was flying, yet it was stationary. By shifting the angle of his fingers, the wind force would push his arm up or down. It was a very vivid, lively feeling. He remembers that the eyes of the fish in the dream were bright.

All thinking is bodily (Varela *et al.*, 1991). In waking, we usually don't notice this – but *in our dreams, the bodily aspect of thought is highlighted*. Thus, in Edward's dream, there are several bodily feeling states: flying, fighting resistance, defying gravity, exertion, lack of movement, and being stuck.

Our situation in life is not just conceptual – it is affective and bodily. Lakoff and Johnson (1980) highlight the way bodily experience is encoded in our language. When we say, metaphorically, "I am *stuck*," we mean that my life is not progressing. The overarching metaphor is "life is a journey." And I am not moving. But when we say "Now I am really flying" we mean "I am making a lot of progress, I feel elated (high), and am moving fast." The core metaphor is still "life is a journey," but the journey has different sensory, emotional, and kinesthetic properties.

When we talk about a dream image, it sounds like a picture described objectively. But when we dream the dream, the dream is usually not something we watch objectively – we *live* it. Edward could feel the dream vividly – the feeling of suspension in the air, the feeling of the wind opposing his forward movement, the excitement and the stasis that also were prominent feelings in his current life.

Thus, it is more accurate to say that the dream does not just pictorialize a metaphor; it actualizes a metaphor in lived experience, *emotionally and kinesthetically*. Edward's dream demonstrates the representation of the mental as physical, which Johnson (1987) argues is always the case in thought. The dream portrays mental experience as physical experience.

Herbert Silberer (cited in Freud, 1900a, pp. 344–345) forced himself when very tired to think of intellectual problems. Silberer observed that as he was falling asleep, his intellectual thoughts were turned into visual images.

For example, "I thought about having to revise an uneven passage in an essay" became "I saw myself planing a piece of wood."

"Thinking about metaphysical aim of working one's way through ever higher forms of consciousness and layers of existence, in one's search for the basis of existence" became "I was pushing a long knife under a cake as though to lift out a slice." (Note how the "layers of existence" was portrayed by a "layer cake."[18])

I noted a similar transformation of verbal idea into image, when I was writing a chapter on dream condensation (Blechner, 2001, Chapter 6). I dreamt that I was using a locker in a gymnasium, but that I didn't know the combination for the locker. I realized on awakening that the "combination" in the dream was a condensation. The word "combination" is a synonym for condensation, although in the manifest content of the dream, its other meaning was apparent: combination being a set of numbers used to open a lock. The dream portrayed how I was looking for the right combination of meanings of combination (condensation), i.e., how I was seeking a solution to the problem of condensation and was unraveling its many meanings. And the goods were locked up, and I couldn't get to them, and I was getting a workout.

Here is another example that combines several metaphors that enrich each other.[19] Before going to sleep, a woman emails her boyfriend, Ted, about "leaving the door open, even if we are not ready to walk through it." That night she dreams:

I walk by the front door of my apartment and I see that it has been left open all night, just a crack, and very cold air is blowing in. I am afraid that Lucy, my cat, has escaped during the night.

(Fosse *et al.*, 2003, p. 3)

This is a wonderful example of a dream pictorializing a metaphor, and also expanding on it. The transformation is visual and sensory; we "see" that the door is open just a crack, and we "feel" cold air blowing through it. Cold wind is a metaphor for a bad omen or a bad event coming toward you. Is the dream an omen that Ted will break up with her? Is she resisting the bad news, by keeping the door open only a crack, but will the news get in anyway? And will she lose her cat (perhaps a beloved pet, or a symbol of her femininity)?

In her email the night before the dream, she had suggested to Ted to "leave the door open (i.e., keep open the possibility of the relationship? marriage? some other development of the relationship?) even if they are not ready to walk through it (i.e., carry it out now)."

The dream pictorializes "leaving the door open" and then expands on the "dream thought" in a pictorial way. While her email sounded mainly positive, the dream shows caution and ambivalence, and expands on the concrete implications of leaving the door open, i.e., "cold air blowing in."

Perhaps the dreamer is afraid of being "left in the cold" (i.e., abandoned). Also, she fears that the open door has led to her cat escaping, i.e., personal loss, or a symbol of losing a part of her sexuality.

She said to Ted that she wants to leave the door open, but here it is only open a crack – not enough room for Ted to come in, but enough room for the "cold wind to blow in."

Is this expanded and detailed image of "leaving the door open" a pictorial representation of verbal thoughts? Or does the dream take the picture (actually more an emotion-laden video) and elaborate it without recourse to words? *Is the thinking itself done on the image, in the image, through the image, or is the image an after-the-fact representation of a verbal "dream thought"?*

Neuroscientist Allan Hobson reported a dream with another combined metaphor. In it, he and his psychoanalyst friend, Van, play catch with a piece of hardware.

Van then begins a gentle pirouette and tosses me a piece of hardware, something like the lock of a door or perhaps a pair of paint-frozen hinges. It is as if to say, "Here, take this as recompense." Despite my scavenger nature, I think I should refuse this "gift," and so I toss it back to Van on his next choreographic spin. He insists that it is meant for me, and the scene changes without clear resolution of whether or not I will keep it.

(Hobson, 1988, p. 22)

Hobson's dream takes the metaphor, "An intellectual discussion is a sport," but he expands it. He and Van play catch, but in a very special way. While most of us would understand, "In the debate, he threw me a curve ball," we would be startled if, in waking speech, we heard someone say, "In the debate, he threw me a paint-frozen hinge," or "He threw me a lock." But these sentences create a new metaphor: An intellectual discussion is collaborative construction. Thus, Hobson's dream joins together two metaphors, "Intellectual discussion is sport" and "Intellectual discussion is collaborative construction." The crossover, a conjoint metaphor, produces a game of catch with a piece of hardware, and this hardware is itself a condensation of multiple ideas.

French poet Paul Valéry (1936, p. 13) asked: "What is a metaphor, if not a pirouette of an idea with which one brings together different images or things?" He meant that the metaphor turns an object or person around, so we may see them from different perspectives (this is a metaphor about metaphor). And that is expressed in Hobson's dream: do dreams act as scavengers, taking stuff that looks useless, but when seen from another perspective, turns out to be useful or even a treasure? Are dreams junk or invaluable experiences? It depends on how you look at them.

People often first react to their dreams as if they are useless junk. But if they let themselves look at the dream carefully, from all angles, they will discover that there is much more to the dream than they first realized. One man's garbage is another man's treasure.

Dreams with combined metaphors raise the question of how they are constructed and what is the essential material of thought. Does the mind-brain, in creating the dream, pictorialize each metaphor and then condense multiple images, each from a different metaphor, into a single, vibrant image? Or are the images and emotions there to start with, representing the thoughts without words? Is each image connected with an affect, which then condenses with other affects in the dream? Are the images and emotions themselves the "language of thought" or the "substrate of thought"? Are words involved in dream thinking, and if so, how much, or are words brought in during waking life in order to communicate the dream? We will consider this issue further in Chapter 19.

Nonlinguistic metaphor – music, visual arts, and advertising

Please note: For a complete list of hyperlinks to the relevant musical examples featured in this chapter, please visit the author's website at the following dedicated webpage when prompted to listen: www.markblechner.com/mindbrain/music

Most of us, when we think of metaphor, think of a linguistic process – a usual meaning of a word or phrase is shifted, to map one domain of meaning onto another. However, metaphoric processes do not need words. Metaphor is a mapping of meaning from one domain to another – and neither domain needs to involve words.

A close friend asked me, "Which piece of music is you?" and I discovered that I had an immediate answer: I "was" Brahms' Second String Sextet, Op. 36. It took time for me to think through how that piece "felt like me" at the time, and I realized that whatever linguistic adjectives I came up with (optimism, tenderness, gentleness) were not as precise as the music itself. The mapping of my emotional experience onto music bypassed language, but felt metaphoric, nevertheless. Similarly, one of my patients was told by her husband that their relationship reminded him of the last movement of Mozart's Piano Concerto No. 23. She felt she knew what he meant and was very flattered.

Nonlinguistic metaphor was enshrined in classical music through the "Doctrine of Affects" (*Affekten* in German), which held that certain sequences of notes had an intrinsic, metaphoric connection to certain emotions. For example, a sequence of a descending minor seconds sounded like sighing, and a rapidly rising sequence of thirds sounded euphoric. Johann Sebastian Bach was an expert at creating these effects. The "Crucifixus" of his B-minor Mass has a constant flow of descending seconds in both the bass line and the chorus that convey the suffering on the cross (listen to Musical Example #1),[20] while the "Et resurrexit" has ascending intervals that feel triumphant (listen to Musical Example #2). Much later composers used these *Affekten* too – Beethoven, in the slow movement of his String Quartet, Op. 130 has a tremendously sad descending scale, with the marking "*beklemmt* (anguished)." (Listen to Musical Example #3 for 44 seconds.)

Mussorgsky has the Holy Fool singing mournfully about the fate of Russia in the opera *Boris Godunov*, using descending minor seconds in the orchestra that sound like continual weeping. (Listen to Musical Example #4.)

A different musical metaphor occurs in Bach's Cantata #111, "*Was mein Gott will, das g'scheh allzeit* (What my God wants, may it always happen)." In the duet for alto and tenor: "So geh' ich mit beherzten Schritten, und wenn mich Gott zum Grabe führt (I go with courageous steps, even though God be leading me to the grave.)" (Listen to Musical Example #5.) The duet has a very energetic dotted-rhythm figure that is a nonlinguistic metaphor of the "courageous steps" that are described in the text. Albert Schweitzer (1911, p. 361) said the duet "is like a gladsome, stately march."

There are so many examples of nonlinguistic metaphors in music that it would take an encyclopedia to describe them all. Some are onomatopoeic, where the sound of the music matches a human utterance, like a sigh or a laugh. In some, the rhythm of the music matches a human physical movement, as in the Bach duet.

Some musical metaphors are more abstract. In *Don Quixote*, Richard Strauss' tone poem for solo cello and orchestra, Don Quixote's bizarre, mad conclusions are continually "metaphorized" by a chord progression (the cadence D to A-flat) that sounds "off" or irrational (listen to Musical Example #6). Only at the very end, when Don Quixote is about to die and his insanity fades, do we finally hear the "normal" cadence, D to A (listen to Musical Example #7 for 35 seconds).

Russian composer Dimitri Shostakovich turned this process upside down. The famous Tristan chord, from Richard Wagner's opera *Tristan and Isolde*, leaves the listener unsure where it is going, and then resolves in a way that is continually surprising (listen to Musical Example #8 for one minute, 50 seconds). Today most listeners hear the Tristan chord and expect a surprise resolution. Shostakovich, in his last symphony (#15), last movement, first quotes excerpts from Wagner's "Ring Cycle," just to make sure the listener has Wagner at the forefront of awareness. Shostakovich then quotes the set-up of the Tristan chord, but has it resolve "normally." In context of our expectations, this is hilarious. It is not easy to write a purely musical joke, using no words, but this is one of the greatest (listen to Musical Example #9 for one minute 20 seconds).

Nonlinguistic metaphors can also be found in paintings and sculptures. The original theory of empathy, as developed by art theorists Robert Vischer (1873) and Theodor Lipps (1903, 1913), proposed the operation of nonlinguistic metaphor. We look at a painting of a nonhuman or inanimate object, and we imagine our bodies in a posture that mimics what we see in the painting. (Would Vico have condemned this as one more example of man's projecting himself into everything instead of appreciating things in themselves?) For example, the painting *The Solitary Tree* by nineteenth-century German artist Caspar David Friedrich shows a tree with contorted branches (Figure 5.1). In looking at that painting, we imagine our limbs in a similarly contorted shape, and that fantasy creates a feeling in us of strain and distress. We also imagine ourselves, like the tree, isolated in a barren area and that invokes additional feelings of loneliness.

Some painters and sculptors made an artform of nonlinguistic metaphor. In René Magritte's painting *Le Viol* ("The Rape"), a human face is mapped onto a female torso – or vice versa (Figure 5.2).

Note that the metaphor occurs without words. We can describe it in words: face=torso, but we can grasp the nonlinguistic metaphor without words.

Figure 5.1 Caspar David Friedrich, *Solitary Tree*, 1821; Oil on canvas, 55 × 71 cm.

Source: National Gallery, Berlin. Courtesy of Bpk Bildagentur/Nationalgalerie, Staatliche Museum, Berlin, Germany/Joerg P. Anders/Art Resource, NY.

Advertisers are especially adept at constructing nonlinguistic metaphors and invoking the idea that their product will bring the user great benefit, maybe even change the user's identity. When Elizabeth Taylor's perfume was shown with its eponymous "White Diamonds," the metaphor was "the scent of this perfume is American female beauty, elegance, and wealth" – without the viewer of the ad knowing anything about how the perfume smelled (Figure 5.3).

Nonlinguistic metaphors are important for semiology in general, demonstrating many exceptions to "the current penchant for stuffing the whole of semiology into linguistics" (Lyotard, 1989, p. 31).

Figure 5.2 René Magritte, *The Rape*.

Source: © 2017 C. Herscovici/Artists Rights Society (ARS), New York, Banque d'Images, ADAGP/Art Resource/ARS, NY.

Figure 5.3 White Diamonds Perfume Advertisement.

Source: All intellectual property rights associated with the ELIZABETH TAYLOR® name and mark, including rights of publicity, are owned by Interplanet Productions Limited. © Interplanet Productions Limited.

Synesthesia, synkinesia, and metaphoric mappings of the body

There can also be nonlinguistic mappings between two sense modalities, known as synesthesia. The proportion of humans with synesthesia is estimated to be 4 percent (Simner *et al.*, 2006). A synesthete might see numbers in color; the number 5 looks red and the number 7 looks blue (Fechner, 1871; Galton, 1880; Marks, 1975). Or a synesthete might involuntarily "see" a color when hearing a musical tone: A-flat may evoke blue, while C-natural evokes red (Jewanski, 1999).

People who have synesthesia readily identify experiences in which objects in one sense modality automatically trigger an actual perception in a second modality (Vernon, 1937). It is an open question whether such synesthetic experiences are a sensory version of metaphor, the "source" domain being the presented stimulus, such as a musical tone, and the target domain, being the experience in another modality, such as color. Interestingly, like most metaphor, synesthetic experiences are usually unidirectional (Dixon *et al.*, 2004), but not always (Cohen Kadosh *et al.*, 2007; Goller *et al.*, 2009).

One of my friends has synesthesia. He associates individual musical pitches with colors; E-flat for him has always been blue. He was startled to find out that this connection of pitches and colors was not universal. For the Russian composer Nicolai Rimsky-Korsakov,[21] E-flat was also blue, but for Alexander Scriabin, E-flat was red-purple (von Riesemann, 1934). The violinist Fritz Kreisler once confessed how, "in a mood of irritability and ill temper," he bought a coat "in the color of C sharp minor." This caused some alarm to those who saw him, and to reassure them he had "a collar in E flat major sewn onto it" (Taylor, 1963, p. 62). Sound-color synesthesia was described by Mahling (1926), who, though German, called it by a French name, *audition colorée*. (See also Jewanski *et al.*, 2009.)

One has to consider the difference, though, between (1) describing one sense modality *in terms of* another modality (a common human ability) compared to (2) actually seeing, feeling, or hearing (perhaps hallucinating) another sense modality (true synesthesia). We all can do the former: For example, we all know what is meant by a "loud shirt" although the shirt is soundless. The auditory adjective "loud" has come to metaphorically mean "brash, brassy colors" (note how in this explanation, I have extended the sound-color mapping with the word "brassy"; as we humans try to express ourselves, we are always expanding our use of metaphor). We know what "sharp cheese" means, even though most cheese is soft to the touch. We know what bitter cold means, even though cold has no flavor. We also, to varying degrees, can experience a color as "warm" or a light as "icy" or "harsh."

With some descriptions of one sensory impression in terms of another, it is unclear if they are examples of true synesthesia or metaphor. John Locke, in his *An Essay Concerning Human Understanding*, described "a studious blind man who ... bragged one day that he now understood what 'scarlet' signified.... It was like the sound of a trumpet" (1690/1836, p. 310).

There are less familiar types of "normal" synesthesia (commonly occurring in people who are not synesthetes), which show an intrinsic capacity for nonlinguistic metaphor. For example, show people two figures such as those in Figure 5.4, and tell them that in Martian language, one shape is called "kiki" and the other is called "bouba." Some 95 percent of people will identify the shape on the right as kiki and the shape on the left as bouba (Köhler, 1929; Werner, 1948/1980). There seems to be a psychological connection made between the sharp pointed shape and the "pointed" sound of kiki. The rounded shape feels closer to the "rounded" sound of bouba and to the rounded shape we make with our lips when we say "bouba." One could say there is a metaphoric

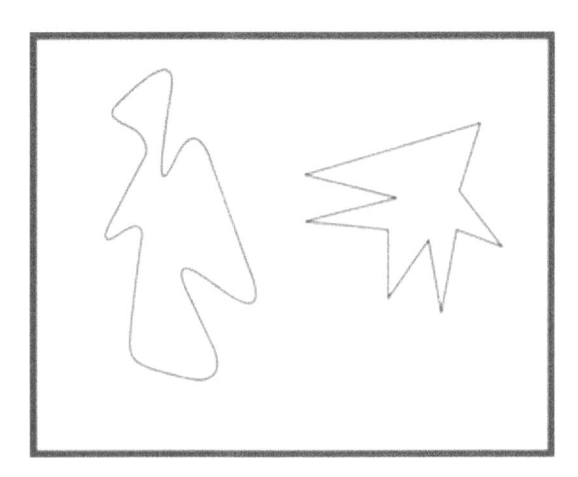

Figure 5.4 Which is kiki and which is bouba?

mapping of physical shape in the picture to the shape of the mouth in producing the sound.

Similarly, Edward Sapir (1929) studied the mapping of vowel sounds to spatial dimensions. He discovered a connection between perception of vowel "size" and the configuration of the mouth when making the vowel sound; "mal" was perceived as "larger" than "mil," which may also contribute to the kiki/bouba effect.

Some synesthetes see letters or numbers in specific colors, which is called grapheme-color synesthesia. The author Vladimir Nabokov, when looking at his initials, VN, saw the V "in a kind of pale, transparent pink, and the N in a greyish-yellowish oatmeal color." Nabokov's wife, Vera, and his son, Dimitri, also had grapheme-color synesthesia, but the mappings were not identical. The letter "M" was pink to Vladimir, blue to Vera, and purple to Dimitri. Vladimir speculated that the pink and blue of the two parents combined genetically to form a purple percept in their son, "as if genes were painting in aquarelle" (Nabokov, 1962).

Neural basis of synesthesia

One explanation of synesthesia is that there is cross-wiring in the mind-brain between different sense perception neurons. Ramachandran and Hubbard (2001) have proposed that the angular gyrus, the seat of polymodal convergence of sensory information, might be the neural locus of synesthetic experience. Damage to the angular gyrus leads to failure in the kiki/bouba effect, the loss of ability to grasp metaphors, and a tendency to be literal minded (Gardner, 1975) – suggesting that synesthesia, normal cross-modal connections, and metaphor are interrelated neurally as well as phenomenologically.

Some types of synesthesia are not graspable by ordinary humans without synesthesia, because the connections between sensory domains seems to have no inherent nonlinguistic metaphor that we can grasp, but seems due, rather, to an arbitrary neural cross-wiring. For example, in one form of synesthesia, people connect numbers with colors; the statement, "the number of boys in the room is blue" would not mean anything to most of us, but for a synesthete, the color blue may be surely and continually connected with the number 5. Ordinary mortals can find no inherent metaphoric mapping between blue and 5, as we do between the pointed sound and pointed pictorial form of "kiki."

Synkinesia

Another possibly "wired-in" form of nonlinguistic metaphor can occur between different types of muscular activity. In the phenomenon of synkinesia, when a person willfully makes one kind of movement, another body part will move involuntarily at the same time. This occurs in some pathological situations, caused by strokes or other neurological injury. For example, in Marin-Amat Syndrome, when a man opens his mouth, his eyes close (Jitendra, 2007).

But synkinesias are also found in neurologically health people (Hwang et al., 2006). Charles Darwin (1872) noticed that some people, when cutting with scissors, make an analogous up and down movement with their jaws. This might be due to the proximity of the motor maps for the mouth and hand, which are adjacent neurologically in the precentral gyrus.

I know a man who wears contact lenses; when he uses his hands to spread his upper and lower eyelids before inserting the contact lens, his mouth involuntarily opens. In both these examples, there is an involuntary movement that mimics the voluntary movement.

There might also be a sound-to-movement metaphor, which we see when people listen to music and involuntarily move their legs or fingers to the rhythm of the music. Much dancing involves transforming a musical pattern into a body movement pattern.

Metaphoric mappings between concepts and our bodies

There has been extensive research by cognitive neuroscientists that explains how much our bodies interact with our psychological perceptions, mostly unconsciously, and that certain perceptual metaphors are realized in our physical bodies. For example, we all know that when we refer to someone as "chilly," we aren't usually referring to his or her body temperature; we mean that he or she is an emotionally cold, remote person. Although this is a figure of speech, it has reality in bodily experience; the connection of physical temperature in the environment is mapped onto the experience of emotional warmth, without the need for language (Blechner, 2011).

Studies have shown that the connection between temperature and emotional experience is profound, yet out of our awareness. In one experiment, for example, half the subjects were given a warm drink, half were given a cold drink, and they were then asked to describe their relations with friends and family. Those holding warm drinks described their relationships as significantly closer emotionally than those holding cold drinks (IJzerman and Semin, 2009).

The interaction between emotions and bodily experience works in the opposite direction, too. If people are asked to describe incidents in their lives when they felt emotionally isolated, they judge the room temperature as significantly colder than if they are asked to describe times when they felt emotionally included, even though the room temperature is exactly the same in each condition (Zhong and Leonardelli, 2008). Thus, temperature affects our sense of emotional closeness, and emotional closeness affects our judgment of temperature.

Another area of study is the relationship between time and direction. We know that we usually think of time as moving forward. We say, "I see the future that lies before me," or "I want to put the past behind me." Scientists have found that these are not just figures of speech, but directions that are experienced with our bodies. If a motion sensor is placed on the body, we find that when people talk of the future, their bodies sway forward, and when they talk of the past, their bodies sway backward (Miles *et al.*, 2010).[22] Thus our bodily posture enacts the spatial metaphors of time. (See Casasanto (2017) for further examples.)

Blending theory versus cognitive metaphor theory

In the world of cognitive neuroscience, there is a fundamental debate about metaphor: whether, as in Cognitive Metaphor theory, an alignment between two conceptual domains involves a mapping of the source domain onto the target domain (Lakoff and Johnson, 1980), or whether we construct a new mental space where features from both domains are merged. The latter suggestion was proposed by the supporters of "Blending Theory" (Fauconnier and Turner, 2002). According to this theory, metaphors stimulate us to create novel conceptualizations that result from the blending of two or more interacting mental spaces. In such cases, neither domain is necessarily the source domain – rather, the mindbrain is creating a meaning-space that is equidistant between the two domains and inclusive of both of them.[23]

78 How the mindbrain transforms the world

In conceptual metaphor theory, there is a source field and a target field, such as "ideas are food;" the source field is ideas and the target field is food. When we say we have the "raw facts," the idea field, "facts" is portrayed in food terms, that is, "raw" (without cooking, without modification). When we say, "His ideas are half-baked," the source field is ideas and the target field is food once again, "half-baked" meaning not fully prepared and developed and therefore not desirable for consumption. These metaphors tend not to be reversible. We don't say, for example, "His bread is half thought-out."

In blending theory, by contrast, the two fields, "ideas" and "food" are blended. We may implicitly ask, "How are ideas and food similar?" They both must be developed by humans; they take time and effort for transformation into something that we would like to incorporate into ourselves. I will show how the two theories are not mutually exclusive, and each may apply better to different situations.

The Magritte painting, *Le Viol* (see Figure 5.2 on p. 71) is a good example of blending theory. The painting embodies a metaphor, but the metaphor seems to be reversible (which is not the case for many metaphors), i.e., the torso is seen in terms of the face, and the face is seen in terms of the torso.

Blending theory raises the question about whether a metaphoric connection is symmetric and bidirectional, or asymmetric and unidirectional. Consider the metaphor "sex is the poor man's opera." Is it also true that "opera is the rich man's sex"? Are metaphors reversible, and, if so, when (Ortony, 1993)?

Blending theory and interobjects

The blending theory of metaphor gives a theoretical underpinning to what I call dream "interobjects." It is common for people to dream of "something between an X and a Y." For example, Bert States dreamt of something between a swimming pool and an aqueduct (see Figures 5.5 and 5.6).

In most dream interobjects, we see the mindbrain identifying a connection between two objects, and creating an intermediary between them. Blending theory makes sense out of dream interobjects: the proposal of something between two objects sets up a conceptual space, or, we might say, a novel category, in which both domains are blended, without necessarily

Figure 5.5 Colorado River Aqueduct at Hayfield, February 2012.

Source: Used by kind permission of Chris "Maven" Austin.

Figure 5.6 Swimming Pool.

Source: © Elvira Kolomiytseva/Dreamstime.

80 How the mindbrain transforms the world

identifying one domain as source and another as target. The swimming pool/aqueduct finds a new category of objects – "large man-made containers of water."

A young child dreamt of something that was both a seal and a boat (see Figures 5.7 and 5.8). This interobject, the seal-boat, creates a category of "large things that are self-powered and move through the water." Neither is primary; one could say that ships are the seals of an armada, or

Figure 5.7 Seal.

Source: © Sombra12/Dreamstime.

Figure 5.8 Boat.

Source: © Iakov Filimonov/Dreamstime.

that seals are the ships of the animal kingdom, but the essence of the dream interobject is that there is a superordinate category for both.

Allan Hobson dreamt of something between a lock and a paint-frozen hinge (see Figures 5.9 and 5.10). This interobject created a superordinate category of "man-made hardware that allows or restricts the movement of doors."

Figure 5.9 Lock.

Source: © Charles Knowles/Dreamstime.

Figure 5.10 Hinge.

Source: © Nonillion/Dreamstime.

One of my patients dreamt of a "cellphone-baby" (see Figure 5.11). This interobject created the superordinate category of "small things that we hold close to our bodies, speak to them, and which make noise unpredictably."

Figure 5.11 Cellphone-baby.

Source: © Photodeti/Dreamstime.

Metaphors gone awry

One of the ways to appreciate metaphor is to study examples of thought in which the transfer of domain works badly or not at all. This can be seen in various forms of psychopathology. Psychotics often blend or combine objects, not because they can be conceptually connected, but just because they happen to appear together. This is called contamination, and can be seen on the Rorschach test (Lazar and Schwartz, 1982; Schwartz and Lazar, 1984). Two things are combined without being related, e.g., "rabbitmaidens," "rabbithand," or "lunganimals" (Kleiger, 1999; Blatt and Ford, 1994). Rabbit and hand have no underlying conceptual connection; they are put together merely because the patient had the two percepts close together in time.[24]

Metaphor and transference

The mindbrain is always involved in remappings of experiences and ideas, both in and out of dreams (Modell, 2009). The mindbrain is always asking: "This new experience – what is it like from my past?" That is the essence of transference. *Something that happens in psychoanalytic treatment is experienced in terms of related experiences from the past, and past experiences are re-remembered and revised according to current experiences.*

For example, I was away from my practice during the summer for eight weeks. Each patient experienced the break in treatment differently. What was it like for them? Here are some responses, drawn from different patients:

1 "It is like when my mother's breast was unavailable to me for too long and there was nothing I could do about it."

   In treatment, she may learn that there is something she can do about it in the present; she may also learn that smaller incidents of unavailability from the analyst, or incidents of inadequate feeding or inadequate responsiveness from the analyst, need not lead to panic or despair, but can be negotiated and regulated; also, in retrospect, she can see why her mother, with an absent father and six children to raise, might not have been optimally available.

2 "It is like when my parents sent me to 8-week summer camp at age 5 so they could travel in Asia."

The patient may discover that not all absences will lead to an overwhelming sense of abandonment; that not all absences mean a general disregard of his well-being; and, in retrospect, he can reconsider and re-evaluate the past. The parents were selfish and perhaps ill-advised; but nothing tragic happened during their absence, as it might have. The experience was nevertheless traumatic, and shaped his lifelong defenses of isolation and resistance to dependence.

3 "It is like when I could finally have some free time on my own and not have to take care of my mentally ill mother."

The patient may realize how much attachments imply the loss of freedom to him and a depressing, overbearing need from the mother; that, when faced with a needy person, he need not drop everything and forego all his own needs. He also can realize that the mother was mentally ill and could not be otherwise.

My eight-week break was experienced metaphorically as:

1 an interruption in breast feeding
2 an abandonment
3 a relief.

Each of these reactions could be encapsulated in a dream image, but it can also emerge without the intermediary of a dream. As Arlow wrote (1993, p. 1153):

> If we continue the concept of dream images representing visual metaphors, we can understand how many forms of manifest behavior represent metaphorical transformations of unconscious fantasy wishes. In analysis we have the opportunity to explore in depth the associations that the analysand may make to the metaphor. In this sense, in the psychoanalytic situation, the interaction of analyst to analysand is an exercise of mutual metaphoric stimulation, in which the analyst, in a series of approximate objectifications of the patient's unconscious thought processes, supplies the appropriate metaphors upon which the essential insights may be built.

The analyst may provide appropriate metaphors on which insights may be built. But the patient's experience of the analyst is itself an *experiential metaphor*. The experience of the past is mapped onto the present. In addition, the new experience of the present is backward-mapped (mapped retroactively) onto the memory of the past; the memory is retranscribed based on the new experience, as all of our old memories are constantly recreated (Bartlett, 1932). *The blending of old and new experiences constantly restructures our mental world.* The new experience of the present allows one to reconstruct one's way of relating to people from the past and present. The man who experienced my vacation as an abandonment could retroactively see how his parents meant him no harm, although they were insensitive to the effects of their actions. His observation of his experience gave him insight into ways that he, in his current defensive withdrawal, made others feel abandoned.

In some ways, transference may be metaphoric in the way described by "Blending Theory" (Fauconnier and Turner, 2002). According to this theory, metaphors stimulate us to create novel conceptualizations that result from the blending of two or more interacting mental spaces. In such cases, neither domain, past or present, is necessarily primary – rather, the mindbrain is creating a meaning-space that is equidistant between the two domains and inclusive of both of them.

Metaphor and rebus

The dream, Freud argued, was like a rebus (Freud, 1900a, pp. 277ff.). Many people do not know what a rebus is, and it is essential to Freud's approach to the dream. A rebus is a series of images that, on first examination, do not seem to have much to do with one another. If, however, you transform each image into an equivalent word, *or its homonym*, you will get a sentence that is grammatical and meaningful. It is important in the rebus that a thing may be represented by a picture of its homonym, a different word that sounds the same.

Here is an example of a rebus, composed of a set of five pictures (Figure 5.12). Try translating each picture into a word, so that you end up with a grammatical sentence.

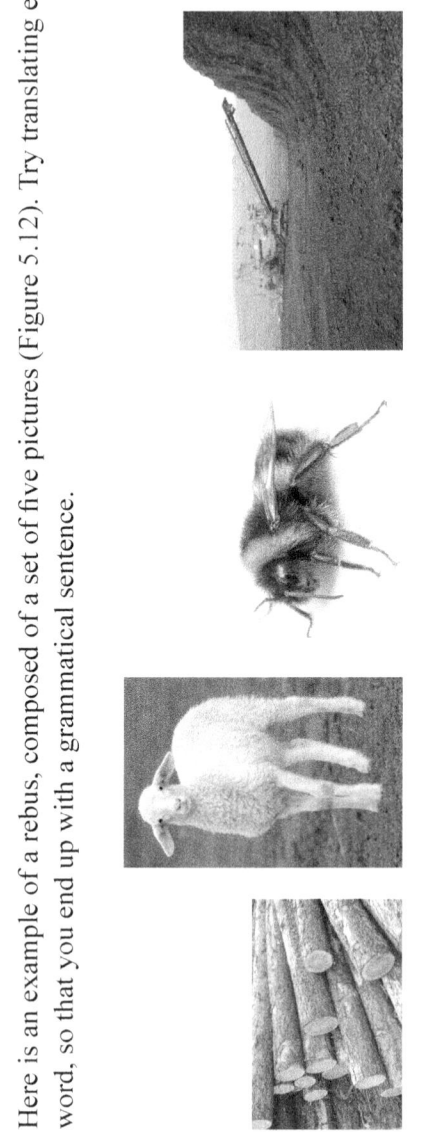

Figure 5.12 Rebus 1.

Think about what this rebus means before reading further.

Metaphor 87

Here is another rebus (Figure 5.13):

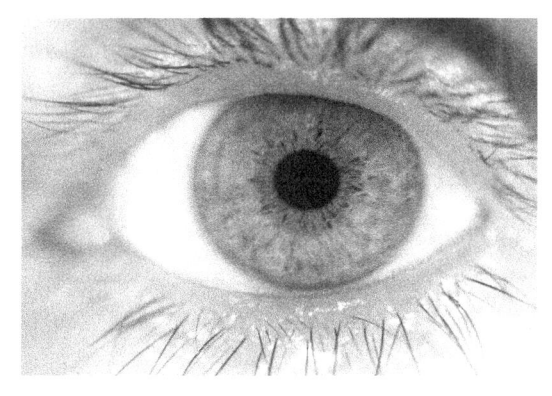

Figure 5.13 Rebus 2.

What is the message of this set of pictures? Think about it for a while before turning the page. If you do not get the message at first, try to take the rebus apart. Look at each picture, and think to yourself what the picture portrays. You should come up with two words. Then consider: What is the spatial arrangement of those two pictures? That should give you a new two-word sentence, and the rebus will be solved.

> **Rebus 1 solution:**
>
> The pictures, in order, are: wood, ewe, bee, mine, valentine.
> So the totality of the rebus is "wood ewe bee mine valentine" or "Would you be my valentine?"
> (The credits for the five pictures are: Wood © Brostock/Dreamstime. Ewe © Jose Manuel Gelpi Diaz/Dreamstime. Bee © Akilrollerowan/Dreamstime. Mine © Zbynek Burival/Dreamstime. Valentine © MINEdreamstime_xl_27413156.)

> **Rebus 2 solution:**
>
> The pictures are of a stand and an eye. The eye is underneath the stand, so the message of the rebus is "I understand."
> (The credits for the two pictures are: Stand © Josh Davis | Dreamstime. Eye © Sanja Baljkas/Dreamstime.)
> Unless you translate each picture into the word it stands for or its homonym, you will not discover the message of the group of pictures. You must translate each element of the rebus[25] and then string together the translations to understand the message. It will not help you to pay attention to the sequence of pictures themselves. You must disregard the apparent narrative, until each picture has first been translated into its verbal equivalent.[26]

Freud believed that a dream is like a rebus; you must translate each element to understand the underlying (latent) dream thought, and the way to do the translation of each element was through the dreamer's associations. When the mindbrain makes a rebus, it turns a word or its homonym into a picture.

According to Freud, you must ignore the apparent narrative of the dream, until you have translated the dream elements one by one. He wrote:

> The dream-thoughts and the dream-content are presented to us like two versions of the same subject-matter in two different languages....

A dream[27] is a picture puzzle of this sort and our predecessors in the field of dream interpretation have made the mistake of treating the rebus as a pictorial composition: and as such it has seemed to them nonsensical and worthless.

(Freud, 1900a, pp. 277–278)

My belief is that some dreams contain rebuses, but not all of them. Some people produce dreams with rebuses; one of my patients almost always had a rebus in his dream; he did an hour of word puzzles and Sudoku each morning. His practice with these puzzles may have made his mindbrain more adept at producing rebus dreams; it is also possible that the characteristic of his mindbrain that led him to produce rebus dreams also led to his attraction to puzzles.

Here is a dream with a clear rebus: A young man still in the throes of a difficult divorce has become seriously involved with another woman, and the issue of marriage has been raised. In his dream *he sees himself leaving one hotel and walking in the street toward another hotel. While in the street he tries to put on his tie but discovers he is already wearing one* (Ullman and Limmer, 1999, p. 5).

The rebus in this dream is that "in going from one place to live to another, as I try to create a new tie, I realize that I am still married (tied) to another woman." The rebus of wearing two ties involves the homonym tie (article of clothing) – tie (connection to another person).[28]

Here is another dream with a rebus. A woman dreamt: "*There were antlers in the air conditioner. In the end, I brought my boss to look at it. It seemed there was a live animal embedded in the wall.*" The woman told the dream to her boyfriend, Edward. He (no slouch in the rebus school of dream interpretation) said, "My dear needs to cool off!" They had been having relationship difficulties, and the previous week, he had suggested that they put the relationship "on cryogenic hold," i.e., take time off from seeing each other and let things cool off. The expanded interpretation of the dream might be, "My dear (deer) is Edward, who is trapped like a deer in the headlights, and I am not letting him into the house or keeping him out, but trying just to cool things down." Note how the picture of the "deer" is replaced by its homonym "dear" although the interpretation of the dream kept the meaning of *both* homonyms being frozen: my dear put on cryogenic hold and feeling frozen like a deer in the headlights.

People love rebus interpretations of dreams. They are like jokes, clever and surprising. They often contain witty puns, both verbal puns like dear and deer, and visual jokes ("How do you cool off? Get stuck in an air conditioner.")

The rebus image contains an enormous amount of information about the dreamer in a very compact form. Freud assumed that the rebus was a transformation of a verbal (word) thought into a picture. But it is also possible that the mindbrain thinks in images – it uses the rebus image as one means of representation, as useful as the word itself in some ways, more useful in a different way – because images, or really "affect-images" can be manipulated and transformed in ways that words cannot. And they are closer to experience than words themselves. The dear stuck in the air conditioner captures the experience of putting the relationship on cryogenic hold. It is as if the dreamer is saying,

> I am an animal. I am a trapped animal. Your coldness feels mechanical. (The deer is trapped in a machine, not a glacier.) Antlers only grow in the fall. Their purpose is to give the deer male power in mating. You are disabling my power with your mechanical coldness.

These are latent thoughts that the wakingwork can find in the dream image. The image is very specific; every detail matters. All aspects of it can be turned into word-thoughts, but *the image itself may be the primary substrate of thinking*. It is efficient in capturing so much, including the emotions. We can transform the image into words and call it the latent content, but that may be a process that occurs after the dream, not before.

Some rebus dreams are more complicated to translate and involve lexical similarities that are not exactly homonyms, but more complicated puns. An American visiting Moscow (Stevens, 1996, p. 41) dreamt of *a bee hovering at the entrance to a hole in a tree without going in*.

We can see in this dream a multiple transformation: The dreamer thinks of the bee as "a cagey bee." This leads him to connect the "cagey bee" with its sound-equivalent, the KGB, which was the Soviet security agency known to carefully monitor foreigners visiting the Soviet Union. It showed the dreamer's caution about entering a situation in which he would be trapped by the KGB.

The dream contains a rebus, but its meaning might be understood from the image without solving the rebus: The bee hovering at the hole of the tree – its intentions are unclear but potentially menacing. It could sting any creature trying to enter the hole in the tree. And if a creature manages to enter the hole in the tree, could it find it hard to get out?

This is often the case with a dream rebus: even if the rebus is not solved or even noticed, the imagery and emotion of the dream will express the meaning of the dream. And even if the rebus is solved, much more meaning can still be gleaned from the details of the dream image.

Sometimes the dream uses a rebus that amplifies and modifies a familiar expression. A man dreamt:

> *I was with a woman with dark curly hair. She had a tray with drugs on it, with a bowl with liquid in it. As she carried it, the drugs got wet. I took a thing – it was like a short automobile fuse with an opening in the middle – and sucked up the wet drugs.*

The dreamer associated to the small glass fuses with a central metal conductor in the electrical system of some cars. They are shaped like cylinders, and so, they resemble the glass vials and straws that some people use to snort cocaine.

But in English, a "fuse" also means the piece of string that you connect to a bomb or a firecracker to ignite it. Therefore, having "a short fuse" also means that you are easily made angry. The source of this expression is that if the fuse on a bomb is short, it will explode quickly after you light it. And the fact that it is an automobile fuse (an "auto fuse") reflects a rebus interpretation of auto ("self") – it is a fuse that ignites itself. His sucking up a combination of drugs and alcohol is igniting his anger. Thus, the dream transforms the common expression "a short fuse" into "a short auto fuse," using the homonyms "auto (car)" and "auto (self)."[29]

The dream portrays the patient's emotional struggle. Although he tries to be even-tempered, he sometimes explodes in anger. This is not always within his awareness or his conscious control.

We have a translation of the short fuse. But what about the rest of the dream? I told him I was puzzled by the bowl with liquid and the drugs that get wet. He then told me that the bowl was blue, which he associated to the color of the sleeping pill, Ambien, which he has been taking every night. Before going to sleep he drank vodka, and added to all this, he has taken cocaine. The dream shows this mixture: the blue bowl is Ambien, the liquid is vodka, and the powdered drug is cocaine.

We can translate the dream as follows: "I am mixing Ambien, vodka, and cocaine, and that mixture is giving me a short fuse, a quick temper. And I take it out on my spouse." Indeed, the night before the dream, he had said to his spouse: "If you take away my vodka, I will kill you."

The dream doesn't make clear exactly what causes what: Is he medicating his short fuse, trying to soothe, quell, and control his anger? Or is the mixture of drug and liquor *causing* him to have a short fuse, exacerbating it? Either way, the dream makes clear that the substance use and the anger are connected.

A man dreamt of a cantaloupe and analyzed its meaning to be of a fear of marrying too soon: "can't elope." This is an example of a rebus that is not a metaphor. Nevertheless, even in this example, the dream image had significance aside from its direct translation into words. The dreamer associated the cantaloupe to Edward Albee's play *Who's Afraid of Virginia Woolf?* in which George says of his wife, "Here comes Martha with her melons bobbing!"[30] Thus the cantaloupe connected to a statement of hostility to one's wife; the dreamer thought that the play portrays a hellish marriage that would scare anyone away from taking vows.

In dreams, we see the mindbrain representing its activities more in pictures and emotions than in words. Words cannot be surpassed for interpersonal communication. Although we say "A picture is worth a thousand words," most of us cannot produce pictures quickly and accurately enough for rapid and efficient communication. But in sleep, our mindbrains do not need to communicate our thoughts, so the mindbrain can generate images and emotions, which may capture our thoughts more precisely than words can, even if the result is not as communicable. It remains an open question to what degree the awake mindbrain also uses images and emotions, which can be translated into words (Horowitz, 1972; Ellman and Antrobus, 1991; Grandin, 2006). Do some dreams resemble a rebus because the sleeping mindbrain tends to rely more on images to represent thought, or is the rebus essential to a process of disguise, as Freud thought?

In the rebuses that Freud used to read in the Vienna newspaper that were intended as puzzles, the progression of images made no sense in itself. Only when each image had been translated into a word did the sequence make sense; the progression of words was seen to spell out a sentence or a verbal expression.

In dreams, however, I am not sure that the analogy holds most of the time. Even in dreams that can be solved by a rebus, the progression of dream images usually also bears some significant meaning. While my patient's "drugs and vodka" dream required some translation of the blue bowl and the short auto fuse, the elements of the rebus were connected with the message of the dream: the drugs and alcohol were there in the manifest dream and got mixed up, as they were in the dreamer's life. The auto fuse was also related to the dream message, when you realize that the glass cylinder was a way to snort cocaine. While one can translate the particular elements of the rebus, the meaning of the dream that one discovers will probably still be connected with the manifest meaning of most elements of the dream.

The same was true of the "antlers in the air conditioner" dream. The antlers were "stuck" as the dreamer was in her relationship. Her boyfriend was trying to cool things off. And antlers, as we all know, are used by deer as aggressive weapons and for self-protection, prominent aspects of the dreamer's personality that were causing her trouble in her relationship. So, once again, the elements of the rebus were connected to the primary themes of the dream.

It is rarer for the elements of the rebus not to be connected with the themes of the dream. One example is a French patient whose father had died of alcoholism and who dreamt of six roses (Malcolm, 1982). The French analyst said, "*Six roses ou cirrhose*? (pronounced: see-rose ou see-rose)" In French, the words for "six roses" and for "cirrhosis" are homonyms. Thus the dreamwork made a pictogram of a homonym of the latent content. In this case, there does not seem to be any direct relationship between the roses and the cirrhosis. However, this cannot be said definitively unless the analyst reports the patient's dream completely and verbatim.

In some dreams, the connection of the original picture and the meaning is subtle. Consider the dream of the "cagey bee" (p. 90). Like the KGB, the bee was dangerous and intrusive, and it was hard to tell what it was up to. *It is rare, if it ever happens, for a dream to have a rebus translation, where the final meaning has no connection to the actual elements in the manifest dream.* This has implications for our clinical work with dreams.

Returning to the manifest content after interpretation of a rebus

When a dream contains a rebus, and you have translated it into what you think is the latent dream thought, you ought to go back to the original elements of the dream and see how they help you further understand the meaning of the dream. The dreamer of the "antlers in the air conditioner" dream did not choose "deer" just because it is a homonym of "dear." She may also have chosen that image because it is an animal that she considered sweet-looking from a distance, but which could be vicious and dangerous close up. Was that characterization relevant to her personality? She also wondered, "Don't only male deer have antlers? Is this dream about my male identification? Or is it also about my boyfriend? Is he stuck, too? Do we both need cooling off?"

In the "drugs and vodka" dream, the whole ensemble was on a tray carried by a woman. Was the responsibility for the issue of anger and substance use "being carried by" a woman – the dreamer's mother or another woman? One would want to check that out, and, in that way, amplify the dream.

After you have interpreted the rebus, go back and consider the essential properties of the pictures in the rebus. For example, "a short auto fuse" that was a rebus for a quick temper has very specific properties: it is mechanical (and thus may feel inhuman), electrical (and thus can be shocking and sparking), and glass (which can shatter). All of these properties of the image should be considered, not ignored, in constructing the dream's meaning.

Conversely, a dream which has been understood without recourse to a rebus interpretation may, after the fact, be found to have a rebus. In some instances, a dream whose concrete meaning is uncovered by the question "Have you ever experienced what happened in the dream or something like it?" may also be solved by a rebus interpretation. For example, in the "cat-burglar dream" (Blechner, 2001) a woman dreamt she was descending an elevator shaft with a flashlight around her neck in order to steal something. I asked her if she had actually ever stolen anything. She denied it at first, but in the next session "confessed" that I had made an error in her bill, and she had avoided paying me for one month of treatment. However, her descending a shaft with a flashlight around her neck might also be a rebus. She may be trying to decide whether "to shine

Metaphor 95

light on how she is shafting the analyst." In this case, the two approaches to the dream may converge on the same meaning.

Freud cited a rebus dream interpretation from antiquity, reported by Plutarch and Artemidorus (1990, 4:24, pp. 200–201):

> Aristander also gave a most felicitous interpretation to Alexander of Macedonia when he had blockaded Tyre and was besieging it. Alexander was feeling uneasy and disturbed because of the great loss of time and dreamt that he saw a satyr dancing on his shield. Aristander was in Tyre at the time, in attendance on the king while he was waging war against the Tyrians. By dividing the word Satyros into Sa and Tyros (Tyre is yours), he encouraged the king to wage the war more zealously with the result that he took the city.

This is a striking ancient rebus interpretation; but note that the theme of someone dancing in triumph is already there. The rebus meaning does not conflict with the direct metaphor meaning, and this might be more apparent if we had the entire dream reported verbatim.

A nonlinguistic rebus?

Is there such a thing as a nonlinguistic rebus? It seems impossible, since a rebus is defined as a series of images, each of which can be translated into a word to form a message. The closest to a nonlinguistic rebus that I have found is the following:

> When I was living in the Boston area some years ago, I occasionally played chamber music with William Lipscomb, a Harvard faculty member, who was awarded the Nobel Prize in chemistry in 1976. Bill was quite an accomplished clarinetist, and we enjoyed playing chamber music at his Belmont house. Often our pianist was Stephen Morris, who also composed. Some time after our learning of Bill's having been awarded the Nobel Prize, Steve came for an evening of music, and presented Bill with the score of a recent composition of his. It was a chamber piece written for a sizable group. I don't recall the instrumentation, and I never heard it performed, but Steve made sure that we looked at the score, and he had us pay particular attention to the stave labeled "Bell." We weren't quick enough on the

uptake, and he had to point out to us that the bell part had no notes assigned, meaning that his piece was a "no bell" piece.

(Belvin, 2015)

The lack of notes in the "bell part" signified "no bell" which is a homonym of "Nobel." On reflection, this is a "musical rebus" but it is still a linguistic rebus; the "image," however, is simply the lack of notes. It was so subtle, no one figured it out without explanation from the composer.

Notes

1 Note Nietzsche's metaphor while discussing metaphor: Old metaphors are worn-out coins.
2 In more than a half-century since *Get Smart* was first aired, much progress has been made in designing robots that can understand metaphor (Sundar, 2015).
3 Oxymoronic speech acts occur in clinical psychoanalytic practice, especially when the analyst makes an observation about the patient that mobilizes the patient's defenses. For example, I once said to a patient, "Every time I make an observation about you, you point out the detail in what I have said that is wrong." The patient replied, "Not *every* time." In denying my interpretation, he lived it out and proved it correct. Oxymoronic speech acts are related to the rhetorical device of "apophasis" in which a verbal statement does the opposite of what it says. When Ronald Reagan was asked about his opponent Michael Dukakis having treatment for a psychological disorder, he replied, "Look, I'm not going to pick on an invalid." An extreme version of apophasis is prolepsis, in which the speaker spells out the details of something that he says he will not discuss. In 2016, Donald Trump said of fellow Republican presidential candidate and former Hewlett-Packard CEO Carly Fiorina,

> I promised I would not say that she ran Hewlett-Packard into the ground, that she laid off tens of thousands of people and she got viciously fired. I said I will not say it, so I will not say it.
> (*Huffington Post*, February 16, 2016, available at: www.huffingtonpost. co.uk/entry/donald-trump-rhetorical-device_ us_56c358cbe4b0c3c55052b32b, accessed December 10, 2017)

4 Linguist Roman Jakobson (1988) also asserted that metaphor and metonymy are not just figures of speech, but fundamental modes by which the mindbrain works.
5 "Coast," derived from rib, is a very old bodily metaphor; most native English speakers have no idea they are using a metaphor when they say they visited

the "seacoast." This is reminiscent of Nietzsche's discussion of "metaphors which are worn out and without sensuous power; coins which have lost their pictures and now matter only as metal, no longer as coins."
6 Once you start attending to bodily metaphors, you notice them in almost every sentence you utter. You can become quite self-conscious about this. The expression "seminal works" partakes of the metaphor "foundational generative ideas are semen."
7 This phenomenon is close to Piaget's sensorimotor stage of intelligence.
8 The dream could also be considered a rebus – that lady acting like the "Queen Bee" was bugging me. The child's grandmother (my mother) often said of entitled women, "She acts like she's the Queen Bee," but I do not know if my nephew heard her say it. Is a young child capable of constructing dreams with both a metaphor and rebus?
9 Colace (2010) has collected data that show that many children's dreams conform to Freud's theory of wish fulfillment. It would be useful if all parents wrote down their child's first dreams verbatim, along with the exact age and the circumstances surrounding it. If it is not written down immediately, it will be hard to remember accurately.
10 We could call these objects "homoforms" of body parts.
11 In New York City, however, few people would not wish that their apartment had another room, so the dream may also express a concrete wish.
12 This dream is discussed in more detail in the section on "combined metaphor" (pp. 60–67).
13 Others have also written about this, including: Kanzer (1955), Schimel (1969), Greenson (1970), Levenson (1983), and Joseph (1985).
14 Genesis, 41, 1–7, available at: www.bible.com/bible/59/GEN.41.1-38.ESV (accessed December 10, 2017).
15 Genesis, 41, 25–36, available at: www.bible.com/bible/59/GEN.41.1-38. ESV (accessed December 10, 2017).
16 Other logical relationships suggested by contiguity can be "Because of this, then that" or "Despite this, then that."
17 Shakespeare's Hamlet mixes a metaphor, too, in the famous "To be, or not to be" soliloquy: "Whether 'tis nobler in the mind to suffer / The slings and arrows of outrageous fortune, / Or to take arms against a sea of troubles" (III.1.58–610). Some critics have speculated that the mixed metaphor is intentional and shows Hamlet's troubled mind.
18 In popular language, peeling away the layers of the onion has become almost the clichéd metaphor for this idea. But for Silberer, who lived in Vienna, it is layer cake.
19 This example was discussed previously in the section on metaphors of relationship (p. 55).
20 Bach adapted this music from his earlier Cantata No. 12, whose title describes the musical effect directly: *Weinen, Klagen, Sorgen, Zagen* (Weeping, lamenting, worrying, fearing).

21 Rimsky-Korsakov used his synesthesia creatively. In his opera *Mlada* (1889), he synchronized stage lighting to fit a pattern of keys in the music and to correspond to color words in the libretto. For example, B-major corresponds to the dark blue at the start of Act 3 (Yastrebsev, 1985).
22 The relation between time and direction is not universal. In a South American Indian tribe, the Aymara, the future is considered to be behind one, and the past is in front (Núñez and Sweetser, 2006). The rationale seems to be that you cannot see the future, but you can see the past. It remains to be determined whether the Aymara move their bodies differently than Americans when discussing the past and the future.
23 Glucksberg (2008, p. 69) wrote:

> Metaphors are rarely understood via comparison. Instead, they are usually understood exactly as they appear, as class-inclusion assertions. When someone says that the surgeon was a butcher, that is what they intend: that their surgeon belongs to a category of persons who are butchers in one way or another.

24 It is virtually impossible to prove that contaminations have no superordinate sense, but in these examples of Rorschach inquiry, none could be easily found.
25 The word rebus derives from the Latin: it is the ablative and dative plural of *res* (thing), so that one might translate it as: "from the things."
26 Freud's rebus approach to dreams was treated wittily in the play *Suppressed Desires* by George Cram Cook and Susan Glasspell (1917). The heroine, Mabel, has a dream with the rebus of "step-hen-b.-rooster," which allows her to discover her suppressed romantic desire for her brother-in-law, Stephen Brewster.
27 If Freud had asserted that some dreams are picture puzzles of this sort, or some parts of some dreams, I would agree with him. Even so, as I show on p. 93, in most dreams that contain a rebus, the picture sequence itself is usually relevant to the meaning of the dream, even when each picture can be translated into a word.
28 After I had read about this dream, its symbolism sensitized me to the question of "more than one tie." I then heard the following dream from a married man:

> *I had been given some award, or come offstage or a TV show taping. I had on a navy suit, with a light blue shirt, and a green tie. Really cinnabar, an orangey green. It had dots on it. A silk tie. I had another tie in my hand.*

I said to the patient, "Are you having an affair or considering one?" I told him that I asked this because I remembered the dream in which a man was trying to put one tie on when he was already wearing a tie. My patient said there was no actual affair going on, but he was having "an affair of the mind"; he was feeling a strong attraction to a woman who reminded him of his mother. The dream was quite precise in its symbolism. Unlike Ullman's patient, who was wearing two ties, my patient was wearing one tie and holding the other in his hand, that is, keeping it as a possibility without actually wearing it yet. The tie he was actually wearing had vivid colors; he felt his wife was very beautiful and intense.

29 Freud (1900a, p. 409) identified this rebus-homonym of "automobile" in another dream:

> *[A man] dreamt that his uncle gave him a kiss in an automobile. He went on at once to give me the interpretation, which I myself would never have guessed: namely that it meant auto-erotism. The content of this dream might have been produced as a joke in waking life.*

30 He remembered the line somewhat inaccurately. The actual line in the play is: "Why, I thought you'd get all excited ... sort of heave and pant and come running at me, your melons bobbling" (p. 152).

Chapter 6

Puns – linguistic and nonlinguistic

Introduction

Because a rebus picture can stand for a word or its homonym, the rebus is inextricably linked to the pun. A pun is the humorous use of a word or phrase that has one sound but more than one meaning. In Shakespeare's *Romeo and Juliet*, Mercutio, as he is dying, says, "Ask for me tomorrow and you shall find me a grave man." A grave man most usually means a serious man, but here Mercutio, punning while dying, plays on the word to mean "a man in a grave."

Sometimes puns are set up in the form or riddles. Most people know the children's riddle: "What is black and white and red all over?" "A newspaper!"[1] This pun makes use of the homonyms "red" and "read." Or: "What do a man and an elephant have in common?" You may be expecting "They are both mammals" but the riddle's punning answer is "They both carry a trunk," punning on the two meanings of "trunk." The pun makes a joke out of the shift between two meanings, what Freud (1905a, p. 155) called the "double-dealing rascal."

While many puns use the exact same word with more than one meaning, some puns exploit similar-sounding words, almost but not quite identical, to create the humorous effect. I called these "approximate homonyms." In the "Would you be my valentine" rebus, a picture of a "mine" substituted for "my."

It is also useful to compare metaphors to puns. Puns bring together two domains, but they are not conceptually related. The two domains of meaning have to do with the fact that a single word has more than one meaning. The pun creates a sentence in which the expected meaning is forcibly shifted. For example, consider the following interchange from *Alice's Adventures in Wonderland* by Lewis Carroll:

"And how many hours a day did you do lessons?" said Alice, in a hurry to change the subject.

"Ten hours the first day," said the Mock Turtle, "nine the next, and so on."

"What a curious plan!" exclaimed Alice.

"That's the reason they're called lessons," the Gryphon remarked: "because they lessen from day to day."

(1865, p. 145)

This is funny because the two words – "lesson" and "lessen" – which sound virtually identical, are set up by the story to make it sound like their two meanings are actually connected, when they are not. Thus, in puns, the *sounds* of words are their connection, whereas in metaphor, the *meaning* of words underlies their connection. "A metaphor reveals a *deep* similarity, whereas a pun is a *superficial* similarity masquerading a deep one – hence its comic appeal" (Ramachandran and Hubbard, 2003, p. 53, original emphasis).

Some puns exploit the meanings of two words that sound virtually the same as a single word, or vice versa. For example, a patient who said: "I want to be little" could be heard by the analyst as wanting to belittle other people (Skelton, 1996, p. 174). The name "Eileen" could be a pun for "I lean" (Fosshage and Loew, 1987). A patient of Ella Freeman Sharpe (1937, p. 39) dreamt of "Iona Cathedral" which was a pun for "I own a cathedral." One of my patients troubled by guilt feelings dreamt that flying toward her was a man named "Mr. Gill Tee."

Sometimes numbers can be puns. A man dreamt that he was looking for the room that his class was in, and he thought it was 302. In waking life, he was involved in a relationship with a married woman. In the dream, he found out that his lover had previously slept with his old best friend. The combination of the real situation and the dream suggested that it might be important to him to be involved in a triangle. Consequently, he concluded, the number "302" in the dream should be pronounced "Three or two?"

A psychoanalyst was treating a woman who was trying to conceive in her 40s and had just had a miscarriage. She was considering fertility treatments in which about five fertilized eggs would be implanted in her uterus, with the likelihood that multiple births were possible, but some might not survive. The psychoanalyst dreamt that that he was supervising the delivery of five parcels from the United Parcel Service, each one packed in a different way. The "delivery" combined the meaning of bringing something home and bringing a baby into the world.

Semantic and syntactic puns

All the puns we have examined so far are what I would call "semantic puns" – they play on the fact that words and their homonyms can have multiple meanings. Semantic puns are the most common type, but some puns involve the meaning of an entire sentence rather than just a word or two. I call these "syntactic puns." They play on the fact that two sentences can have the exact same words but two different meanings, because the syntax of the sentence can be parsed in two ways. Consider the following interchange:

TEACHER: I used to teach Copernicus.
STUDENT: You're *that* old?

Here the punning involves two meanings of the sentence "I used to teach Copernicus." The intended meaning was "I used to teach students about Copernicus." The unintended meaning, heard by the student, was: "I used to teach lessons to Copernicus himself." In English, the direct object of the verb "to teach" can either mean the subject matter of the teaching or the person who is taught.[2]

Sometimes puns are quite complex. We all know the nursery rhyme that begins: "Mary had a little lamb." But consider what happens when we add: "Mary had a little lamb – and Jane a little pork." The sentence changes its meaning, and we suddenly become aware of two meanings of "had" – (1) to possess; (2) to eat (see Vendler, 1977). The effect strikes us as comic; we thought of Mary as a sweet girl with her cute little lamb, and suddenly she is eating the lamb.

The sentence makes us aware not only of the two meanings of "had," but of another peculiar aspect of our language. If the sentence had been lengthened thus: "Mary had a little lamb – and Jane a little pig," the word "had" would not have been changed. The sentence highlights that in English, we often use two versions of an animal name – the generic name versus the food label – such as pig versus pork, cow versus beef, sheep versus mutton, calf versus veal. With "lamb," the generic name and the food label are identical, which allows for the surprise effect of "Mary had a little lamb – and Jane a little pork."

Dreams show the mindbrain's abilities as a pun-maker, even when the person, in waking life, does not seem able or willing to use puns, as was the case with the woman who dreamt of "Mr. Gill Tee." One could always question, when the pun is identified by the dream interpreter rather than the dreamer, whether the pun was intended by the dreamer's mindbrain or was created by the dream interpreter.

Puns without words

Although most people connect puns with word-play, there are many sorts of nonlinguistic puns that can create double meanings without involving words – nonverbal puns. There can be two identical (or near-identical) images that have different identities. For example, the chef Michel Richard created a dessert that looked like a hard-boiled egg, but the "egg-white" was made of white chocolate, and it encased a "yolk" made of lemon pudding. It looked like an egg but tasted like dessert. The dish was a nonverbal pun, but the chef gave it a name that was a verbal pun – "Lemon Egg-ceptional" (Grimes, 2016).

There are also musical puns. By a musical pun, I do not mean word-puns on the subject of music, like the following:

"What do you call a pod of musical whales?"
"An orcastra!"

Please note: For a complete list of hyperlinks to the relevant musical examples featured in this chapter, please visit the author's website at the following dedicated webpage when prompted to listen: www.markblechner.com/mindbrain/music

Instead, in a purely musical pun, we suddenly hear that a passage of music is doing "double-duty" by referring to another passage of music. One of the most famous musical puns was produced by Beethoven, in his *Thirty-Three Variations on a Waltz by Diabelli* (listen to Musical Example #10). The *Diabelli Variations* start with a waltz, in which the bass line is a series of jumping alternating fourths, followed by a more stepwise downward descent. The melody line repeats, one step higher, while the harmony goes to the dominant. Then there is a simple ascending figure that also repeats one step higher.

Beethoven produces 21 imaginative variations of this waltz. And then, in variation 22, we suddenly hear Leporello's aria, "Nott'e giorno faticar," from the beginning of Mozart's *Don Giovanni*. And we realize that the musical elements in Diabelli's waltz – the fourths and the stepwise upward motion – latently contained the elements of the Mozart aria![3] (Listen to Musical Example #11 for one minute 32 seconds for the original aria in the original opera; and listen to Musical Example #12 for 26 seconds for a synthesized version of the aria with the musical score. Listen to Musical Example #13 for 19 seconds for Beethoven's take-off.)

This is a purely musical joke. It can be explained with words, after the fact, but the joke can be heard without any intervention of words. Beethoven pushes the comedy by ending the variation with an onomatopoeic imitation of laughter (listen to Musical Example #14 for ten seconds).

Another complex musical pun comes from Alban Berg's opera *Wozzeck*. At the start of the opera, the English horn melody in the fourth measure (bar) (listen to Musical Example #15 for five seconds) is a pun on the opening melody of Beethoven's *Pastoral Symphony* (listen to Musical Example #16 for seven seconds). This is an especially complex and witty pun, since Beethoven's symphony has many allusions to the sounds of nature: babbling brooks, thunder, rainstorm, birdcalls, etc. The pun jumps between two musical meanings and between two meanings of the word "Nature": "Nature: the joys of the outdoors," depicted in Beethoven's symphony; and human nature and the expression "When nature calls – the need to urinate."[4] All of these meanings are encoded in the musical pun, since Wozzeck is a poor man who earns money by being a subject of the doctor's experiments to show that the human will can triumph over natural needs, including withholding his urine. The musical pun on the Pastoral Symphony later is spelled out in words when Wozzeck, who has urinated against the doctor's orders, protests: "But Doctor, when *nature* calls..." (Berg, 1952).

Visual puns

There are also nonlinguistic visual puns. One example is bistable images, in which there are two different ways of seeing an entire image.

Figures 6.1 and 6.2 show two examples of bistable images.

Figure 6.1 Face-vase.

Source: © Nktwentythree/Dreamstime.com.

Figure 6.2 Wife-mother-in-law.

Source: Hill, 1915.

There are also images that are not bistable, but represents two things simultaneously, which I call combination images. For example, Magritte's painting, *Le Viol (The Rape)* (Figure 5.2, p. 71), combines the images of a face and a torso. In Picasso's sculpture, *Baboon and Her Young*, a toy car becomes a baboon head (Figure 3.1, p. 36).

You can see both images without having to shift perspective within your mindbrain to the degree you do in the classic bistable images. In bistable images, the viewer often says at first, "I can only see one of the images," then suddenly, "Oh, now I see the other image." In combination images, the viewer can see both images simultaneously, without a sudden shift from one image to the other.

Notes

1 When I was a child, I heard a riddle that capitalized on the expectations set up by this well-known riddle: "What is black and white and red all over?" "A nun falling down a staircase." However tasteless, this riddle did away with the pun "red-read" and was deemed funny by frustrating one's expectation of the pun (Blechner, 2001). A similar joke was created in musical terms by Dimitri Shostakovich in his Symphony No. 15 (see p. 69), which also breaks an expectation that he will break an expectation.
2 The essence of syntactic puns formed the basis of Chomsky's (1957) groundbreaking studies of transformational grammar. Chomsky compared the two sentences (1) "John is eager to please" and (2) "John is easy to please." Both seem on the surface to have the same grammatical structure: noun-copula-adjective-infinitive verb. "Eager" and "Easy" are both adjectives. Despite the identity of each word's part of speech in both sentences, they have very different syntax and have different rules of rewriting. You can say "It is easy to please John" and you will have not changed the meaning of sentence #2. But you cannot do the same transformation with sentence #1. If you say "It is eager to please John" the meaning of the original sentence will be lost.
3 Some listeners also hear puns on Beethoven's own Op. 111 Sonata in Variation 17 and Variation 20.
4 These double meanings work in English as well as in the original German.

Chapter 7

Homoforms and homomelodies

As discussed in Chapter 5 (p. 91), a man dreamt of an "automobile fuse" and noticed the connection with the glass straw used to snort cocaine. Both have cylindrical glass tubes. The automobile fuse is sealed on both ends with a metal cover, while the glass cocaine straw is open on both ends. The mindbrain observes resemblances between objects that have similar shapes or other properties, and in dreams can substitute one for the other. In such "homoforms," there are two (or more) objects whose physical characteristics – including shape, texture, material, and color – are similar, analogous, or identical. The homoform, like the homonym, contains a near equivalent. In homonyms, the equivalence is in the sound of the word. In homoforms the equivalence is in the shape or structure or other physical property of the objects. Many familiar Freudian symbols are homoforms: sword–penis, purse–vagina, balcony–breasts, apple–breast, for example. (See p. 121, for further discussion of the relation between homoforms and symbols.)

Interobjects can reveal more complicated homoforms: The "phonograph – balance scale" (Meltzer, 1984) is a complex homoform, with two objects that both have a round metal platter and an adjacent long straight movable metal object.

Does the Swinney effect extend to homoforms?

We know from experimental research that when words are first heard, the mindbrain activates all meanings of the words, including homonyms. This is called the "Swinney effect." Psycholinguist David Swinney (1979) played sentences like "Rumor had it that, for years, the government building had been plagued with problems. The man was not surprised when he found several spiders, roaches, and other bugs in the corner of his room." Swinney showed that both meanings of the word "bug" (an insect and a spy device) are mentally activated, at least for 200–500 milliseconds after hearing it before choosing which meaning is more appropriate to the context.

The mindbrain, in dreams, exercises this connectivity of homonyms in an active rather than a passive way. In a dream, any word may be transposed to its homonym, especially if its homonym lends itself better to visual representation. Thus, a dream might be more likely to show a "bug" (insect), which is easier to represent as a picture than a "bug" (spy device).

There may be a phenomenon, like the Swinney effect for homonyms, that occurs when we perceive nonlinguistic objects with shapes and other characteristics in common (homoforms). Perhaps when we first see an object, the shapes, textures, colors, forms, and materials are processed, and every object that could contain all or most of those features (every homoform of that object) is simultaneously activated (just as every homonym is first activated). And the different homoforms can appear together in a dream as interobjects, i.e., it was something between homoform A and homoform B, e.g., something between an apple and a breast. So far, I have not been able to find any empirical studies of the Swinney effect for nonlinguistic homoforms. It would be important to find out if it exists.

Please note: For a complete list of hyperlinks to the relevant musical examples featured in this chapter, please visit the authors website at the following dedicated webpage when prompted to listen: www.markblechner.com/mindbrain/music

Homomelodies

The most familiar homoforms occupy visual space, but we can ask, do homoforms exist in other sense modalities? Are there homoforms in the world of nonlinguistic sounds, for example, with analogies in tone sequences, which we could call "homomelodies"? Can we speak of one melody being the metaphor, pun, or transformation of another melody?[1] I would say yes. Indeed, there are so many examples of this, one would have to say it is central to serious music of many eras. Beethoven's Fifth Symphony starts with a famous four-note motif: three repeated notes, dropping to a fourth note a major third below. (Listen to Musical Example #17 for 23 seconds.)

The Scherzo of the same symphony is a homoform or "homomelody" of the first movement's main theme, with three repeated notes now followed by the same note – the rhythm is the same, but the emotion is transformed. (Listen to Musical Example #18 for one minute.)

Other homomelodies include:

1 Brahms Second Clarinet Sonata, where, in the first movement, the second theme is a transformation of the first (see Chapter 17).
2 In Beethoven's Pathétique Sonata, the second theme of the first movement (listen to Musical Example #19 for 30 seconds) and the first theme of the third movement (listen to Musical Example #20 for ten seconds).
3 In Prokofiev's Seventh Piano Sonata, a brief middle-voice passage in measures (bars) five and six (listen for 11 seconds to the beginning of the sonata, Musical Example #21, and then again for three seconds, for just the middle-voice passage, in Musical Example #22). This becomes the homomelody of the much extended, slowed-down second theme in the Andantino section (listen to Musical Example #23 for 36 seconds). Later, the slowed-down version of the theme reappears as the bass line in measure 185 (listen to Musical Example #24 for 18 seconds).

Sometimes a composer will emulate or transform a melody of another composer. These transformations often function as puns and have a comic effect the way puns do. We already have seen how Beethoven, in the *Diabelli Variations*, made a pun on the opening aria of Mozart's opera *Don Giovanni*.

Homomelodies are legion in the history of classical music. Here are three examples:

1 The first theme of the last movement of Brahms' First Symphony (listen to Musical Example #25 for 19 seconds) and the opening theme of Mahler's Third Symphony (listen to Musical Example #26 for the first 34 seconds).
2 The first movement of Beethoven's last piano sonata (Op. 111) (listen to Musical Example #27 for 18 seconds) and the fifth movement of Mahler's second symphony (listen to Musical Example #28 for 27 seconds; notice how Beethoven's trill is transposed by Mahler into the percussion section.)

110   How the mindbrain transforms the world

3   A passage in Beethoven's "Les Adieux" Sonata (listen to Musical Example #29 for 12 seconds) and from the Piano Quintet of Thomas Adès (listen to Musical Example #30 for 15 seconds). (See also Chapter 17, "When your mindbrain knows things you don't.")

These homomelodies create dramatic musical connectedness within a single composition that may or may not be consciously noticed by the listener or even the performer. In traditional musicology, these homomelodies are usually called thematic transformations, and the link to linguistic metaphor may not be apparent. But as Wittgenstein noted: "Understanding a sentence is much more akin to understanding a theme in music than one may think" (Wittgenstein, 2001, frag. 527). Massimo Schinco (2011, p. 113), musician and psychologist, writes:

> What a music composer does in waking life, and a dreamer does while sleeping, are quite similar. They arrange thoughts by following semantic and syntactic rules that have been shaped and inherited though centuries and millennia of human and pre-human experience. Eventually, they turn the enfolded material into unfolded, the unexpressed into the expressed, the virtual into the actual, and the future into a new different present.

Note

1 I also have one example of a "figurative transposition" in which a dreamer drew an image from her dream and presented it to a dream group. No one could understand the image until one group member turned the page upside down. We all immediately saw the image of a woman giving birth, and the meaning of the dream became apparent. The dreamer herself did not know (consciously) the meaning of the image she had drawn before the group member turned it upside down.

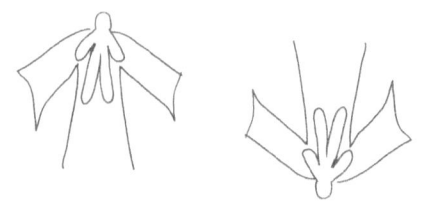

Figure 7.1 Figurative transposition.

Chapter 8

Metonymy

> WALTHER
> So it might be not dream, but poetry?
> SACHS
> The two are friends, gladly standing by each other.
> Richard Wagner, *The Mastersingers*
> *of Nuremberg*

Metonymy is the substitution of the name of an attribute or adjunct for that of the thing meant (the fundament). The *crown* is a metonym for the *king*, since the crown is worn by the king and is a symbol of his power. *Washington* is a metonym for the *United States government*, since Washington is where most of the federal government is located.

In each of these examples, the metonym is associated to the thing it stands for, but the association for each one is different – something worn by the fundament (as in *suits* for *business executives)*; the place where the fundament performs its function (*Brussels* is a metonym for the *European Union)*; a metonym which forms a part of the fundament (*my wheels* is a metonym for *my car*). When we say "The pen is mightier than the sword" we are using a double metonym, pen for written works, sword for military action.

Like metaphor, metonymy used to be considered mainly a figure of speech, but is now recognized as a fundamental method of conveying meaning.

Metonymy and synecdoche

Metonymy is often identified with another figure of speech called synecdoche.[1] Metonymy and synecdoche resemble each other but are not the same. Synecdoche refers to a thing by the name of one of its parts. For example, we can refer to a fleet of sails, by which we mean a fleet of ships. A part of the ship, the "sail" stands for the whole ship. In a metonymy, on the other hand, the word we use to describe another thing is closely linked to that particular thing, but may not be a part of it. For example, "Hollywood" often refers to the film industry. Technically, it is not a part of the film industry. It is the location of the film industry, which makes it a metonym, but not synecdoche. Perhaps this can be summarized as follows: All synecdoche is metonymy, but not all metonymy is synecdoche.

Common and idiosyncratic metonyms

Some metonyms are so common, they eventually become an accepted definition of the word. For example, the word "dish" is most literally a flat utensil on which food is served, but it became the metonym of the food itself: "She made us a delicious dish." That metonym has become so accepted that now one of the accepted definitions of "dish" is the prepared food itself.

Some metonyms come into usage from a very specific incident, and hence may not be understandable without knowing the context. Such metaphors are less likely to become incorporated into our language. For example (Fauconnier, 1985, p. 6), one waitress in a restaurant says to another: "The mushroom omelet left without paying the bill." The speaker does not mean that some cooked eggs left the restaurant. In context, it can be perfectly grammatical, if the "mushroom omelet" is a metonym for the customer who ordered the mushroom omelet.

Similarly, it may not be clear what the following sentence means (Lakoff and Johnson, 1980, p. 12): "Please sit in the apple-juice seat." While in isolation this sentence has no meaning, it did in the context of its creation. "An overnight guest came down to breakfast. There were four place settings, three with orange juice and one with apple juice. It was clear what the apple-juice seat was."

Couples who have been together for a long time often develop private metonyms. If you heard someone say, "Take the brown," you probably would not understand. But if you are a couple that owns two backpacks, one brown and one blue, you would understand "Take the brown backpack." The color without the associated noun becomes the metonym of the backpack (Blechner, 2001).

I experienced a "metonym-conflict" when writing *The Dream Frontier* (2001). Chapter 5 originally had the title, "Dreams never lie." My colleague William Hirst said to me, "Dreams can't lie. Lying is a deliberate act. The dreamer can lie, but not the dream." I changed the chapter title to "We never lie in our dreams." The instigator (or non-instigator) of the lie is the dreamer, not the dream. I have no regrets about the change, but the original title was a metonym. The dream stood for the dreamer. It is similar to when we say, "The buses are on strike." Buses cannot go on strike. Buses are inanimate objects with no will. But we know that "The buses are on strike" means that "The bus-drivers are on strike." When we hear "The Pentagon advised against a pre-emptive attack," we know that the building in Washington, DC isn't giving advice, but rather the military people who work in the Pentagon.

There is a slippery slope between vivid expression and imprecise ideas. Scientific writing may require more precision than ordinary speech. Hirst's objection to my title captures the ambivalence of scholars toward metaphor and metonymy versus an insistence on precise, literal expression. We discussed above how philosophers like Giambattista Vico and Thomas Hobbes argued in favor of direct speech, but could not avoid metaphors in their treatises. Are metonyms imprecise expressions that need correction, or are metonyms a way to make our language more vivid and concise? When Shakespeare has Brutus say, "Friends, Romans, countrymen, lend me your ears," it is surely more engaging than if he had said, "Friends, Romans, countrymen, listen to me." Lending an ear is more visceral and intimate, giving temporary ownership of a part of one's body to the speaker. A sign of the effectiveness of the metonym is the fact that over time, "lend an ear" has become a common expression in English.

Metonyms can also be wordless. For example, Jakobson (1971, p. 256) argued that cubist art relied heavily on metonyms, while surrealist art relied more on metaphors. A Picasso cubist painting of a guitar might show five parallel strings without the wood frame on which they are mounted; the strings are a metonym for the guitar. Magritte's surrealist painting *The Memory* shows a Greco-Roman sculpture of a woman's head with blood on her temple (Figure 8.1).

The precise meaning may be debated, but the painting implies the evidence of a serious injury. The bloodied head is there with no body. Next to it is a leaf with no tree. One metaphor may be that "memory of

Figure 8.1 René Magritte, *Memory*.

Source: © 2017 C. Herscovici/Artists Rights Society (ARS), New York, Herscovici/Art Resource, NY/ARS, NY.

injury" is a kind of death or separation from oneself. The implied comparison may be: My disconnection from my trauma is like the disconnection of the leaf from the tree. It looks intact now, but its disconnection will lead to death.

Words in paintings

Lakoff and Turner (1989, p. 108) have argued that all words are metonyms: "Words stand for the concepts they express." Some artists have used actual words as metonyms in their paintings. For example, Miró's 1925 painting *Photo: This Is the Color of My Dreams* has the word "photo" to represent the image of his dreams (Figure 8.2).

This painting comes from a series of paintings called *peintures-poésies* (paintings-poems) which reflect Miró's interest in dreams and the subconscious (Rowell, 1976) and the relationship of words, images, and thoughts.

Picasso, in his 1911 painting *Pipe Rack and Still Life on Table* inserts the word "Ocean" rather than painting an ocean:

These paintings by Miró and Picasso are, in a sense, *the reverse of a rebus: the word stands for the picture, instead of the picture standing for the word.*

Figure 8.2 Joan Miró, *This Is the Color of My Dreams*, 1925.

Sources: © Successió Miró/Artists Rights Society (ARS), New York/ADAGP, Paris 2017; Image © The Metropolitan Museum of Art/Art Resource, NY/ARS, NY.

Figure 8.3 Pablo Picasso, *Pipe Rack and Still Life on Table*.

Sources: © 2017 Estate of Pablo Picasso/Artists Rights Society (ARS), New York; Image © The Metropolitan Museum of Art/Art Resource, NY/ARS, NY.

There are many more examples of painters who have used words in their creations, including Marcel Duchamp, Sol LeWitt, Ed Ruscha, Christopher Wool, Mel Bochner, and Suzanne McClelland, all with different interactions between word and image.

Dreams and metonyms

Dreams can use metonyms, in which one person or object is substituted for another. A man had a dream in which he had "sex with his daughter," which was metonymy for "incest in general." He never had sex with his daughter, but when he was a teenager, he raped his cousin but never told anyone. When the cousin, as an adult, said to him, "I want to speak with you about what happened when we were teenagers and you raped me," he replied, "You are making it up. It never happened" – knowing he was lying. The dream metonym, by replacing the cousin with the daughter, had an implied message: I can try to avoid the guilt feelings toward my cousin, but if it were my daughter I had raped, it would be harder or impossible. By making the offense even more egregious (in the dreamer's view), the dream highlighted the pain he had caused his cousin.[2]

Ryan dreamt: *"I found these coins that were like Susan B. Anthony dollars and like English money – coins that can be worth more than paper money. One was worth $1. Another was worth $8."*

Most Susan B. Anthony dollars are worth $1. It was unclear why one was worth $8 in the dream. Ryan was very conflicted about money; he saw it as a symbol of male potency. He usually felt that he did not have enough money and found it difficult to be generous. Yet at the time of the dream, he had more money than his partner, Len. For the very first time in their 20-year relationship, he offered to help Len out with money. Ryan had $2,000 in the bank and offered to "excuse" $800 of Len's expenses (the eight-dollar coin in the dream). The $8 was a metonym of $800; the coin that was worth more than its face value was a symbol of Ryan's enhanced financial condition and his overall self-esteem.

When a dream uses a personal metonym, as in Ryan's dream, it helps to have the dreamer's associations to decode the metonym, especially when the psychotherapist may be unfamiliar with some of things that are commonplace for the dreamer. For example, in the dream of the blue bowl with white powder, liquid, and the short auto fuse (p. 91), I could decode the pun of the short fuse, I knew about the vodka and the cocaine, but the blue bowl was an enigma to me, until the dreamer associated to the blue sleeping pill, Ambien.[3]

Levenson wrote:

> Briefly, dreams may be interpreted along the two basic linguistic axes – that is, metaphorically and metonymically.... Metaphor is the story line of the dream, accessible to any listener's interpretation. Metonymy specifies the dream images that can be understood only by knowing the patient's associations and, to a lesser degree, the therapist's. It is the reservoir of the idiosyncratic experience of both participants. It is nonlinear and doesn't tell a story, as does the metaphoric line.
>
> (2000, p. 120)

I think the situation may be more complicated than Levenson describes. In some instances, metonyms may apply only to certain elements of the dream, but in other instances, the entire story line may be a metonym. The dream of "having sex with my daughter" may be seen either way: The dream could be a metonym of "having sex with my cousin." It could also indicate the dreamer's general relationship to incestuous wishes, so that "having sex with my daughter" might also indicate an actual incestuous wish directed toward his daughter.

Erik Erikson (1954, pp. 18–19) described a dream that is the epitome of terseness and complicates the question of metaphor and metonymy, as we first saw in Chapter 3. In the dream of Erikson's patient, there is only the image of a single word "S[E]INE," seen light against a dark background. It was dreamt by a woman whose difficulties were traced back to her seeing the painting of the *Circumcision of Christ* at the Louvre in Paris. The dreamer was multilingual, and she and Erikson analyzed the dream image as a condensation of four elements: (1) the river SEINE in Paris, where the original trauma occurred; (2) SINE, which is "without" in Latin; (3) the German "SEINE," which means "his"; and (4) the bracketed E, which is the first initial of Erikson's name. Together this is "To see E without his ... in Paris." (The ellipsis seems to be Erikson's.) According to Erikson's analysis, each aspect of the dream connected with an aspect of the patient's pathology. He tells us that the patient has a visual amnesia, and hence in the dream, there are no images, only a single word. That the dream-space is dark and completely motionless around a clear image was an inverted representation of the patient's memory of the trauma: an area with a dark spot in the center, a lacuna (the repressed picture), surrounded by bright and colorful halls. The lack of motion in the dream corresponds to the patient's symptoms: agoraphobia and immobilization.[4] There is no time dimension in the dream, just as there is now none in the patient's life.

I would say that the entirety of the dream in this case in not just one metaphor. Instead, it is a hypercondensed set of metonyms, metaphors, and rebuses, each connected with an aspect of a traumatic history and brought into the transference.

The ellipsis in Erikson's report is quite astonishing to me. What does it stand for? Erikson does not tell us, and I have not been able to find any literature that explains the ellipsis. It seems likely that the full sentence which is hidden by Erikson is either "To see Erikson without his loincloth in Paris" or "To see Erikson without his foreskin in Paris." One wonders whether the dreamer knew, consciously or unconsciously, that Erikson's mother was Jewish and raised him as a Jew, but that Erikson was diffident about acknowledging this aspect of his identity (Berman, 1975). The ellipsis is an extraordinary example of tertiary revision which parallels the dreamer's secondary revision. Just as the dreamer hides from herself what she has seen in the dream image, her analyst hides his interpretation with an ellipsis. Erikson, too, has a lacuna in his history.

Notes

1 Ella Freeman Sharpe (1937), who was an English professor before becoming a psychoanalyst, identified the way poetic devices, like synecdoche, were integral to the formation and understanding of dreams.
2 This dream raises problems for Freud's theory that dreams disguise unacceptable thoughts, wishes, and experiences. In this dream, the act portrayed was more unacceptable to the dreamer than his actual remembered act. If there was a dream censor, it was not working very well.
3 A colleague who heard this dream connected "blue bowl" with "blue-balls," a colloquial expression for male sexual frustration. Such an association might have applied as an additional "approximate homonym" in the series of rebuses, and indeed the dreamer was dissatisfied with his sexual life. But it would have to be offered as a possible idea to the dreamer to see if it felt relevant.
4 This is an example of what Lakoff and Johnson (1999) were later to call "the embodied mind," in which the bodily experience of the world is transmuted metaphorically into the dream.

Chapter 9

Symbols

> The symbol in the dream has more the value of a parable. It does not conceal, it teaches.
>
> Carl Jung, *Dreams*

Introduction

Symbol translation is the easiest part of dream interpretation, but good symbol translation is the hardest part. People often ask for formulas, and in the simplest dream interpretation, one could look up various symbols in a book or on the Internet, find out what they supposedly mean, and go on from there to construct a meaning for the entire dream. Of course, the task of the symbol-dictionary writer is never done, because there are always new things in the world. One of my patients began a session asking, "What do credit cards mean in dreams?" None of my books on dream symbols had credit cards listed, but new ones will. Credit cards can symbolize, most obviously, economic power, false financial security, and the temptation to indulge oneself beyond reasonable limits.

Dream symbolism touches on the fundamental question: how does our mindbrain organize the world? What aspects of the organization of the world are intrinsic to it (Gibson, 1966, 1979) and to what degree are they imposed on the world by our mindbrains?[1] Symbolism brings out an added aspect – how does the mindbrain, in its transformative capacity, use one object to stand for another?

In this way, the means of transformation that we have already discussed – metaphor, metonym, pun, rebus, homonym, and homoform – all can contribute to the formation of a symbol.

Our lives are drenched in symbolism. We do not necessarily think of words as symbols, so much is their usage overlearned, but language itself is nonstop symbolism. Words are used to stand for objects, usually as metonyms, but less frequently as audio homoforms, as in onomatopoeia, where the word sounds like what it stands for (such as buzz, boom, and whoosh).

Culture is built of symbols. But how? What aspects of our external world are brought into play in symbol construction? The answer is complex and multifold. We will consider some of the primary sources of relation between symbol and symbolized.

1 **Similarity of shape or form**: These symbols are homoforms. Things that look alike can stand for one another. This is the source of much of classical Freudian sexual symbolism. The penis is oblong and cylindrical, so any object with a similar shape can symbolize a penis. This includes poles, brooms, cigars, hoses, spears, etc. The vagina and womb have internal space, and so, as topology meets psychoanalysis, any object with an internal space can symbolize the vagina or the womb. This includes rooms, houses, buckets, purses, boxes, etc.

   Sometimes these symbol-homoforms are more subtle. A woman dreamt she was wearing a hat whose side-pieces hung downwards in such a way that one side was lower than the other (Freud, 1900a, p. 361). Her associations led to the similar structure of a man's testicles, with one hanging down lower than the other. Bismarck dreamt that he held a whip in his hand "which grew to an endless length." Hanns Sachs (1913) interpreted this as symbolic of masturbation (the whip is a homoform for the penis, which is held in his hand) as well as a symbol of infinite power (a penis of endless length).[2]

2 **Linguistic connection**: As we saw in Chapter 5, any object can stand for another object when their names are either homonyms or otherwise related linguistically. Thus, the bee that flew around strangely, the "cagey bee," (see p. 90) can stand for the Soviet intelligence agency (KGB). A man who was feeling conflicted about commitment to marriage dreamt about a cantaloupe, which sounded the same as "can't elope."

   Dream symbols can rely on approximate homonyms. A patient who dreamt of "violets" connected the flowers' name to "violates," which led to the idea that "defloration" (another reference to flowers) was "violent."

3 **Cultural references**: These symbols can involve any arbitrary representation of one thing by another through long-standing cultural association and hence are metonyms. Thus, anything in the shape of a cross can stand for Christianity. Stars, especially the six-pointed variety, can stand for Judaism. Stars and stripes stand for the United States. These are so commonly used and ingrained in us that when we hear them in a dream, we may not think of them as symbols, but they are. As with metaphors, some metonyms and symbols can become like worn-out coins through overuse.

4 **Similarity of associated materials**: Such symbolism involves the connection of the symbol and symbolized through a similarity of primary or accessory features (metonyms). For example, swimming dreams, which are common in enuretics, may symbolize bed-wetting. Fire may also symbolize enuresis, possibly through the unconscious connection of urination with the extinction of flames.

5 **Mythic references – the collective unconscious**: Jung posited that certain symbols may be consciously unknown to us, but are part of our collective psychological heritage. Archetypal mythic characters may symbolize certain human characteristics. Thus a clown may be connected with the mythic trickster, or a bearer of messages with the mythic messenger, Hermes. Through these mythic connections, characters in dreams can stand for many of the attributes associated with the mythic character. Any Mary-like figure can symbolize the theme of virginity or motherhood.

6 **Idiosyncratic connections**: Very personal symbols may be connected with their referents in a manner that is unique to the individual dreamer. A patient dreamt that the left side of his body was much warmer than the right side. His associations led to the strong emotional warmth that he felt from me, so that the side of him nearest to me was warmer. However, he was born prematurely and had spent the first two weeks of his life in an incubator, so the dream may have had its source in that experience. Another patient, wracked by an inordinate sense of guilt, dreamt of a man on a flying bicycle that made a buzzing sound warning of his approach. His name was "Mr. Gill Tee." She thus combined a punning name with an added wished-for feature of a warning sound that could prepare her for his guilt-laden onslaught.[3] For a man whose wife wore a green dress when she announced that she wanted a divorce, green became a symbol of loss and unhappiness.

Symbols can combine all the different modes of mental transformation that we have already examined. The person who is more familiar with the modes of mental transformation will be more skillful at understanding and interpreting symbols. When, for example, Freud said that climbing stairs was symbolic of sexual intercourse, the basis was a nonlinguistic metaphor. The rhythmic motion of climbing stairs was a metaphor of the rhythmic movement of sexual intercourse, and the increased height as one climbs stairs is metaphoric of heightened sexual excitement.

A man dreamt that he stabbed himself with a screwdriver; this action was symbolic, metaphorically, with "screwing himself" (Blechner, 2001, p. 223); the screwdriver was a rebus of the self-destructive act of screwing oneself.

Dreams show the mindbrain at work creating symbols. But what in a dream is a symbol? We decide that after the fact. Often our decision is based on the strangeness of the object. New creations in dreams are often thought of symbolically. Jung (1960) interpreted the combination crab-lizard of his patient as a symbol of the conflict between the cerebro-spinal and the sympathetic nervous system.

The decision of what constitutes a symbol may be arbitrary. Any object or action in a dream may be symbolic. Thus, the gestalt psychologists proposed a principle of clinical work with dreams – that every entity in a dream, human, animal, or *inanimate*, is a symbol of some aspect of the dreamer. The dream interpreter can therefore explore the nature of anything in the dream, even the most common object, for symbolic significance. According to this approach, if you hear a dream that begins, "I was taking a bath" the bath is a symbol, and the implied bathtub is also a symbol. The gestalt therapist might ask the dreamer to imagine being the bathtub: "What are you like? What do you feel? Are you new, shiny, clean, white, and hard? Or are you old, dull, grimy, and gray? Is the water cold, lukewarm, or hot?"

What stands for what? The fact is that the potential number of symbols, of referents, and of connections between the two, is infinite. It makes life simpler for the dream interpreter if you posit that one area of human experience is of primary importance, although that strategy may not do full justice to the dream. When Freud identified bodily and sexual experience as having special importance, his followers had an easier time with symbols. Their task became circumscribed – to find the symbols of body parts and body processes. In Chapter 6 of *The Interpretation of*

Dreams, there are lists of objects that stand for the penis, the vagina, sexual intercourse, urination, defecation, menstruation, and other bodily parts and processes. Even with such a limited focus, the lists are long (and became longer in revisions of the book). You can find other lists of symbols in other books, e.g., Stekel (1943/1967), Gutheil (1951), and Garma (1974). Yet you should always be ready to learn that the dreamer may have reason to have a quite different meaning for the symbol. For example, Freud reasoned that tall, cylindrical objects often symbolized the male phallus, and this, of course, includes trees. But when his patient, the Wolf-Man (Freud, 1914/1918), dreamt of a tree, it was also a symbol of a woman; he associated it with the legend of Tancred, whose beloved Clorinda was imprisoned in a tree; Tancred did not know this, slashed the tree with a sword, and blood flowed from the tree's wound.

The clinician's theoretical convictions about questions raised by symbols may profoundly affect the practical approach to working with them in dream interpretation. Is the best route to the symbol through the dreamer's associations, or is it better to bypass personal associations and consider accepted symbols of the culture? To what degree is the symbol acquired? Are we all born with a vocabulary of symbols? Are we born with certain innate rules of symbol formation? The clinician may decide to use the patient's associations as the guidelines for which are the important symbols. Obviously, if one is looking for sexuality, or if one has another ax to grind (notice the symbolism in that phrase), the search for symbols will be directed accordingly.

Freud saw symbolism as a process of the dreamwork by which taboo elements in a dream, mostly bodily and sexual, are represented by other objects.[4] He saw symbol interpretation originally as a process that the dream interpreter can invoke when the dreamer fails to produce any associations (Freud, 1900a, p. 372). Later, Freud (1933) considered the possibility that symbol interpretation was a viable alternative approach to working with dreams, although he continued to see it mainly as a disguise of taboo topics, such as bodily and sexual concerns, parental and sibling relationships, birth, death, and nakedness.

I consider dream symbolism not restricted to taboo or sexual topics. Instead, I assume that aspects of a dream can symbolize any dimension of living and experiencing, through the unconscious system of mental representation, including metaphor (Lakoff and Johnson, 1980; Lakoff,

1993, 1997), metonym, rebus, and all the other transformations that we have examined.

As with most aspects of dream interpretation, one need not choose a single path to understanding, but may benefit from multiple approaches. Symbols are themselves condensations of various meanings. When hearing a symbol in a dream, the interpreter should consider at least three aspects of meaning:

1. the symbol's personal meaning to the dreamer as derived from associations
2. the symbol's meaning as a universal symbol
3. the symbol's representation of itself (e.g., a cigar is a cigar).

The last principle could be restated as "Every symbol is also itself." The most telling statement of this principle is the famous line of Gertrude Stein: "A rose is a rose is a rose."

Stein's statement originated in her observation that as words get used and reused over centuries, they lose their power to evoke vivid sensory images of what they stand for. Word use leads to a kind of "meaning fatigue." By saying that a rose is a rose is a rose, Stein tried to bring back all the evocative qualities of the word rose. As she said herself:

> Now listen! Can't you see that when the language was new – as it was with Chaucer and Homer – the poet could use the name of a thing and the thing was really there? He could say "O moon," "O sea," "O love," and the moon and the sea and love were really there. And can't you see that after hundreds of years had gone by and thousands of poems had been written, he could call on those words and find that they were just worn out literary words? No listen! I'm no fool. I know that in daily life we don't go around saying "is a ... is a ... is a ..." Yes, I'm no fool; but I think that in that line the rose is red for the first time in English poetry for a hundred years.
> (Simon, 1944, p. 132)

The same thing may be said to have happened with psychoanalytic dream symbolism. For those raised in a psychoanalytic culture whose association of traditional sexual symbols is overlearned, it is a worthwhile exercise to try to consider them in nonsexual ways. When I teach dreams, I ask my students to try to hear a dream of a snake without thinking of the usual Freudian genital symbolism, which is not an easy task. It is like the old cartoon in *MAD Magazine*: A radio announcer says,

> Now boys and girls, I am going to play you a great piece of music. Most of you will associate it with *The Lone Ranger*, but it is actually the overture to *William Tell*, a great opera by Rossini, about a Swiss hero. I want you to listen to the music, and force yourselves to think about that story.

The next panel shows the children squinting their eyes, trying to concentrate on the music. And the next panel shows their unshaven father running into the room, yelling, "Hi ho Silver!" Here the music has so strongly become associated with the Lone Ranger that for many Americans, the music's original significance for the Swiss military and William Tell may feel surprising. The symbolism of the last part of the overture, at least in the United States, has become the symbol of horseback riding, with the music's rhythm and force a nonlinguistic metaphor of a galloping horse.

Equating a dream-snake with a penis (a homoform) has become almost automatic in Western, post-Freudian culture, but there are parts of the world where this symbol formula seems odd. A Chinese-born woman was rather startled by the snake-symbol equation. She told me that for her and most other Chinese, snakes are considered food and popularly are turned into soup. Perhaps culture can shape any symbol system, and presumptions of universality are possible only if you stay home with your own.

Jung also argued that so-called sexual symbols should not be the endpoints of interpretation, but that overt sexual organs should also be considered as symbolizers:

> the sexual language of dreams is not always to be interpreted in a concretistic way – that it is, in fact an archaic language which naturally uses all the analogies readiest to hand without their necessarily coinciding with a real sexual content. It is therefore unjustifiable to take the sexual language of dreams literally under all circumstances, while other contents are explained as symbolical. But as soon as you take the sexual metaphors as symbols for something unknown, your conception of the nature of dreams at once deepens.
>
> (1916–1948, pp. 49–50)

Erich Fromm (1951) cautioned us against cultural myopia and urged us to consider the context of the dreamer's life before assuming we understood his symbols. He noted that many people could agree that the sun symbolized mother, even life itself. But to the dweller in the Sahara desert, it might symbolize thirst, evil, even death. Even so-called standard sexual symbols can shift in cultures depending on the particular value system. In an ironic twist on Freudianism, for the Jivaro tribe of South America, an erect penis in a dream is thought to stand for a snake, since for the Jivaro, the subject matter of ultimate importance is hunting (Gregor, 1981). Theoretically, then, it follows that a penis could also symbolize a cigar, although I have not yet heard of such a dream.

The principle that sexuality in dreams may symbolize something non-sexual and vice versa was known to the scholars of the Talmud. According to the Talmud, if a man dreams of having sexual relations with his mother, it is seen as an indication that he will be rational; if he sleeps with his sister in a dream, he will be wise. But if he dreams of pouring oil on an olive tree, it was interpreted to indicate incestuous wishes (Berakhot, 9:56b):

> He who in a dream waters an olive tree with olive oil dreams of incest. Similarly, a man came to Rabbi Ishmael and said: "I dreamed that one of my eyes kissed the other eye." The Rabbi replied: "You should be dead; you slept with your sister."
>
> (Lorand, 1957, p. 96)

The implication is that incest is symbolized by the mingling of similar organic products.

Every symbol is also itself

Freud also was not averse to considering the symbol as itself, when he supposedly said, upon lighting a cigar, "Gentlemen, this may be the symbol of penis, but let us remember that it is also a cigar." This is often taken as an incident in which Freud was resistant to psychoanalytic interpretation applied to himself. But his statement has a much more profound implication – namely, that every object, no matter what it symbolizes, is also itself.

This may seem like a truism, unnecessary to state, but in the clinical practice of dream interpretation, it is often not given enough importance.

Because of Freud's division of manifest and latent content, psychoanalysts have tended to feel that the symbol is less important than the symbolized. The approach that I have been proposing in this book is that they are of equal importance and interrelated. The meaning of a symbol should be considered in tandem with the specific features of the symbol itself.

Thus, when a person dreams of snakes, it is not enough to translate snake into penis. Why did the person dream of snakes rather than penises? The usual idea is that the sexual meaning is taboo, and therefore symbolism is required to disguise the "true" sexual meaning. But even in our modern times, when some people seem quite at ease in discussing penises and vaginas at social events, people still dream of snakes and spears and rooms and purses. It is an error to jump to the sexual symbol without considering the significance of the dream element for the dreamer. Does the person think of snakes, for example, as dangerous? Venomous? Sneaky? Fast and treacherous? Something to be charmed? The source of beautiful leather?

Symbol interpretation requires the application of selective attention and then its renunciation. For example, to make the connection between the female genitals and its symbols, we have to focus on a particular dimension. Taking the topological point of view, we focus on the question of internal space. Anything with an internal space can symbolize the womb. But having thus achieved symbolization, we are left with the choice of symbol – why a room and not a purse? With enough attention, we start to notice other aspects of the symbol. A purse has internal space, but it also is meant to hold certain kinds of things and not others. It tends to be dry inside (unlike the female genitalia); it tends to hold money; it is portable; and so on. A room, like a purse, has internal space. But it also is larger; it has residential properties; it is not portable; and so on. When we think of these two symbols of the female genitalia, we see broad differences in their implications about the genitalia – to what degree is it capacious, portable, moist or dry, easily opened or closed, simply constructed or elaborately constructed, related to money or shelter, etc. *Symbols, then, are condensations – of the symbol with the symbolized.* After we attend to the symbolized, we must reintegrate it with the properties of the symbol itself. The specific properties of the symbol are transferred metaphorically to the symbolized.

Very often, first dreams in treatment foretell the main themes, emotional concerns, and significant early memories that will emerge in the therapy (Caligor and May, 1968). Whatever happens to the patient in the dream may be either a fear or a wish of what might happen to the patient. A patient who dreamt of having her scalp pulled off (Blechner, 2001) was afraid of damage being done to her, although it may also have been a wish to have her defenses penetrated. But even if the dream is interpreted metaphorically and symbolically, one must not lose sight of the specificity of the symbol. The woman was afraid, but she also was referring in the dream to actual physical attacks to her head that had occurred during her childhood and adulthood.

Similarly, consider a man whose first dream in analysis was that he needed surgery. It is easy to see surgery as a metaphor for psychoanalytic treatment: the patient is opened up, changes are made inside, and the hope is that he will function better after the treatment. But even as one considers such an interpretation, one has to wonder, "Why has the dreamer chosen surgery? What is the experience of the dreamer with actual surgery? Is there a trauma associated with previous surgery?" In this way, surgery is seen as symbolic of psychoanalytic treatment, and simultaneously, surgery represents itself. Surgery is psychoanalysis; surgery is surgery. Dream interpretation requires an analysis of both.

These two approaches to symbolism relate to Jung's distinction between the "causal" and the "final" approach to symbolism. The terms are a bit confusing, but the distinction is nevertheless an important one. The causal approach asks, "What does this symbol stand for?" The final approach asks, "Even if we are correct about what the symbol stands for, why did the dreamer pick this particular symbol and not another?" When dreams are analyzed, the analyst and the dreamer may be so delighted at answering the first question that they ignore the second. For example, if a dream contains a snake, a sword, or a cucumber, that may symbolize a penis. But after you consider that a penis has been symbolized, you then take the "final" approach, and ask, "If a penis was symbolized, why was it symbolized by a snake, a sword, or a cucumber?" And then you consider the inherent properties of the symbol itself: a snake is alive and potentially poisonous; a sword is sharp, cruel, and destructive; a cucumber contains seeds and is blunt and edible. With each symbol you ask: "What are the properties of a penis that the symbol referred to?" Doing this will help you understand not only that the dream was about a penis, but how the dreamer feels about penises, and this additional information will expand your understanding of the dream.

Freudian dream symbols: rationale and modification

Why do so many standard symbols described by Freud and other psychoanalysts relate to bodies and body parts? Is there a scientific rationale for this emphasis?

The answer is that when we were children, bodies were extremely important. We were acutely aware of our bodies and their functions, and the bodies of our parents. Our mother's breasts, our ability to take in nutrition and excrete waste products, were primary preoccupations for us, and that stays with us throughout our lives.

There is neurological evidence that body parts have special representation in the brain. For example, Orlov *et al.* (2010) found evidence that different body parts activate different areas in the occipitotemporal cortex (OTC). They did not find any analogous mapping of parts of inanimate objects and their parts, like cars and cellos. The implication is that human body parts receive special mapping in perception; and it is possible, via the hypothesis of perception/dream-creation relatedness[5] (Blechner, 2001, pp. 260–261), that when constructing dream symbols, the mindbrain privileges body parts and their homoforms.

Therefore, I think that anyone who is interested in dreams should learn the basic symbols identified by Freud and his followers. Yet one should always be ready to find new, subtle modifications to the original Freudian symbols. For example, at a conference, Galit Atlas (2013) presented a series of dreams from one of her patients, Sophie, and I was asked to comment on them (Blechner, 2013). In the first dream, Sophie is riding on a motorcycle. "Things fall out of my bag on the way, and I realize I am losing all of my stuff." We know Freud thought that bags, pocketbooks, and objects with enclosed space can symbolize the female genitals or the womb. It occurred to me, "What does it mean that things are falling out of her bag, that she is losing all her stuff? What has come out of her vagina or womb?" I wondered if the dreamer had had an abortion or a miscarriage.

As with all hypotheses about dreams, however inspired they feel, one must consider them only as hypotheses and check them out with the dreamer (French and Fromm, 1964). However, there was data that might support my hypothesis in Sophie's subsequent dreams. In Dream 2, the dreamer was kidnapped (isn't one meaning of kidnapping "the forcible stealing of a child?") in Bolivia and taken hostage. She considered sending her brother a text message to get help, but she did not know whether her family already knew about the kidnapping and she did not want to worry them. In waking life, this would be insane. You won't text your family for help when you are kidnapped because you don't want to worry them? Would they rather not hear about it and have you suffer? This then reminded me of someone I once knew who had an abortion. After the procedure, she returned to her boyfriend's apartment alone, where she felt terrible cramps. She was so ashamed of the abortion that she did not tell anyone, friends or family, and suffered alone. Granted this was my association, but I would use it in clinical work to generate a possible hypothesis about how the irrational behavior in the dream, of suffering in self-isolation and not using helpful resources, could make sense.

In Dreams 3 and 4, there is cooking occurring in an unseen location. We know that there are several common expressions that equate cooking with pregnancy, such as "She has a bun in the oven." Also, in Dream 4, Sophie meets a man. "He touches my hand and consoles me for all of the things I have lost while riding the motorcycle with my brother" (in Dream 1) (Atlas, 2013, p. 245). The day after discussing the dream in therapy, Sophie meets a man whom she will marry. How will the new man console her for what she lost from her bag in Dream 1? Will he provide her with children to console her for children she has already lost through abortion or miscarriage? Again, I recognize this is my association, not the dreamer's. I would use my association to formulate questions about the dreamer, not answers, to help guide my inquiry into the dreams and the dreamer's experiences. In this case, Atlas confirmed that the dreamer had had an abortion, that it was a significant event in her life, and that the new husband indeed fathered children with her subsequently.

Can emotions be symbolized in dreams?

Dreams are characterized by their emotionality. Yet for some dreamers, emotions are not experienced, but rather are symbolized. Freud changed his mind several times about whether emotions are ever changed in a dream. Sometimes he argued that emotions represent themselves, and the dreamwork leaves them intact. For example, Freud (1900a, p. 248) writes: "It will be noticed that the affect felt in the dream belongs to the latent content and not to its manifest content, and the dream's affective content has remained untouched by the distortion which has overtaken its ideational content" (cf. also p. 323).

At other times (e.g., p. 467), he raised the question of whether emotions could be transformed by the dreamwork. He felt it more likely that sometimes the dreamwork hides emotions. I would like to amplify that theory, and note that sometimes the emotions are suppressed experientially in the dream but are nevertheless symbolized in the manifest content.

For example, one of my patients was a woman who was very successful in her career. She had been raised in a very traditional manner. Her mother was a housewife, and her father seemed to enjoy being the main financial support and the clear leader in a patriarchal family. My patient did not consciously experience guilt about her success. But she kept having dreams in which she was punished. Her first such dream went as follows:

> *I was being prepared for execution. I was wearing an orange jumpsuit, like the one worn by the Unabomber.*[6] *There were people I know around. My husband was helping prepare me to be electrocuted. I was thinking about how embarrassing it would be to lose control of bladder and bowels in the chair.*

She felt no conscious guilt, but the figure of the Unabomber allowed her to symbolize and condense guilt and a psychopathic denial of it; the dreamer felt that the Unabomber was definitely guilty of premeditated murder, although she noted that he did not feel guilty. In this way, she opened up a discussion of the standards of society as prescribed by her parents and how she felt about deviating from them. She noted that in the dream, she was worried about looking right, not losing control of her bodily functions, when she was being killed. She connected this to a diversion of her main emotions by a concern for looking right, which she eventually shifted in a way that seemed more attentive to her most serious emotions.

How big is a symbol?

By this question, I am not asking about the physical size of a symbol. I am not asking, is an elephant as a symbol bigger than a mouse as a symbol? I am asking instead about the scope of what is considered a symbol. Dream scholars tend to think of symbols as circumscribed objects or actions. But a larger perspective would consider whether the whole story of the dream can be a symbol, and in that sense symbol translation of the global dream story requires considering how one story can stand for, i.e., symbolize, something else. In waking life, we sometimes refer to such a symbol as an allegory. Freud (1900a) discussed such symbols in his chapter on "typical dreams," dreams in which the story line tends to appear often in the general population. For example, dreams in which the dreamer is naked, feels shame, but is inhibited from moving – Freud argued that these dreams were a portrayal of our underlying desire to exhibit ourselves, which we all felt when we were children, but which was masked and suppressed by the prohibitions of elders, who shamed us. Freud saw the story of the Garden of Eden as an allegory of this common trend in human development. "In the beginning" humans wore no clothes and did not feel self-conscious about it. That was paradise. But then Eve ate the apple and received the blessing or the curse of knowledge of good and evil; nakedness was no longer acceptable, shame about nakedness came on the scene, and we all put on clothes. But we all yearn for the Eden-like time of shame-free nakedness.

Notes

1 Readers interested in the intricacies of this question should consult Lakoff (1988) about whether Tuesdays have an external reality, and then consider Fodor's (1998) counterargument.
2 For an expanded interpretation of this dream, which takes the political situation more into account, see Szaluta (1980).
3 This example is also discussed on p. 90.
4 Freud wrote in the *Introductory Lectures on Psychoanalysis* (1916, p. 153): "The very great majority of symbols in dreams are sexual symbols."

5   In dreams, different levels of perceptual processing can provide *input* to the final 'percept' of the dream. They can all do so separately, and without the usual coordination of waking consciousness. If this is so, then *the specifics of bizarre dream experiences may be a source of data about the different levels of perceptual processing. By careful examination of the experiences in dreams, we may gain insight into the workings of our mind/brains.*

(Blechner, 2001, pp. 260–261)

6 The Unabomber was a man who had sent letter-bombs to various people around the United States, killing or seriously maiming them. He had been recently found and received much attention in the news.

Chapter 10

Dreams and the mindbrain's structuring of experience

Many people mistakenly believe that Freud made no significant changes to his dream theory after 1933. This overlooks the radical reformulation that Freud suggested in the *Outline of Psycho-Analysis* (Freud, 1938/1940). In it, Freud developed his theory of "dreams from above" and "dreams from below." He proposed that the formation of a dream could be provoked in *two* different ways. Either, on the one hand,

> an instinctual impulse which is ordinarily suppressed (an unconscious wish) finds enough strength during sleep to make itself felt by the ego, or, on the other hand, an urge left over from waking life, a preconscious train of thought with all the conflicting impulses attached to it, finds reinforcement during sleep from an unconscious element. In short, dreams may arise either from the id or from the ego. The mechanism of dream-formation is in both cases the same and so also is the necessary dynamic precondition. The ego gives evidence of its original derivation from the id by occasionally ceasing its functions and allowing a reversion to an earlier state of things.
> (Freud, 1938/1940, p. 166)

This description is very terse, as is most of the *Outline*, and somewhat enigmatic, but it opened the way for psychoanalysts to consider the role of the mindbrain in dreams and how much the characteristic structure of each person's mindbrain makes itself visible in a dream. This line of thought was elaborated by Erik Erikson, in his great paper of 1954, "The dream specimen of psychoanalysis," which laid down a pathway for looking closely at how the mindbrain structures experience in dreams. Erikson proposed that in dream analysis, we do a sentence-by-sentence analysis of the manifest dream with the four "W questions": Who is there at that moment (the dreamer and other people)? What is the emotion? Where is the dream taking place? What is the time – past, present, or future, or some mixed tense? Using this kind of analysis, one obtains a startling picture of the dreamer's mindbrain and interpersonal world. Erikson wrote:

> Any segment of overt behavior reflects, as it were, the whole store. One might say that psychoanalysis has given new depth to the surface, thus building the basis for a more inclusive general psychology of man.... Officially, we hurry at every confrontation with a dream to crack its manifest appearance as if it were a useless shell and to hasten to discard this shell in favor of what seems to be the more worthwhile core.
>
> (1954, pp. 16–17)

Erikson showed us how to chart a dream: divide it into segments, more or less equivalent to sentences, and then analyze each segment according to the five dimensions (see Table 10.1). By charting out a dream in this way, we can see the dreamer's characteristic ways of dealing with the inner and outer worlds. This method of analysis can reveal how consistent or changeable is the dreamer's experience of other people, what role

Table 10.1 This is what Erikson's chart looks like before being filled in

I. Interpersonal		II.	III.	IV.
(a) The dreamer	(b) The population	Affective	Spatial	Temporal

Note
Derived from Erikson (1954, pp. 27–31).

they play in the dreamer's life, and how this interacts with the dreamer's emotions and psychological defenses.

The pattern of interpersonal configurations in a dream may tell us something significant about the dreamer, especially in relation to the affects in the dream. Does the dreamer, for example, become anxious when the interpersonal situation gets more intimate, or does the dreamer feel pleasant feelings when intimacy is increased?

By doing this kind of analysis, one can see how the dreamer's mindbrain is portrayed in the dream and how that representation interacts with emotions and other aspects of experience. It could be called the dreamer's "mindbrain style," especially if the pattern repeats, more or less, in other dreams.

Erikson first applied his chart to Freud's "Irma" dream. Here is Freud's dream, in the Brill translation used by Erikson:

A great hall – a number of guests, whom we are receiving – among them Irma, whom I immediately take aside, as though to answer her letter, and to reproach her for not yet accepting the "solution". I say to her: "If you still have pains, it is really only your own fault." – She answers: "If you only knew what pains I have now in the throat, stomach, and abdomen – I am choked by them." I am startled, and look at her. She looks pale and puffy. I think that after all I must be overlooking some organic affection. I take her to the window and look into her throat. She offers some resistance to this, like a woman who has a set of false teeth. I think, surely, she doesn't need them. – The mouth then opens wide, and I find a large white spot on the right, and elsewhere I see extensive greyish-white scabs adhering to curiously curled formations, which are evidently shaped like the turbinal bones of the nose. – I quickly call Dr M., who repeats the examination and confirms it.... Dr M. looks quite unlike his usual self; he is very pale, he limps, and his chin is clean-shaven.... Now my friend Otto, too, is standing beside her, and my friend Leopold percusses her covered chest, and says: "She has a dullness below, on the left," and also calls attention to an infiltrated portion of skin on the left shoulder (which I can feel, in spite of the dress).... M. says: "There's no doubt that it's an infection, but it doesn't matter; dysentery will follow and the poison will be eliminated."... We know, too, precisely how the infection originated. My friend Otto, not long ago, gave her,

Table 10.2 How Erikson filled in the chart for Freud's "Irma" dream

	I. Interpersonal		II. Affective	III. Spatial	IV. Temporal
	The dreamer	The population			
1.	WE are receiving	WIFE receives with him	Festive mood?	Spacious hall	Present
2.	I take Irma aside	IRMA has not accepted the solution	Sense of urgency	Constricted to a "space for two"	Present
3.	I reproach her	Complains, feels choked	Sense of reproach		Past reaches into Present, painful
4.	I look at her	Looks pale and puffy	Startle	Close to window	"
5.	I think		Worry		"
6.	I take her to window	Offers resistance	Impatience		"
7.		THE MOUTH opens		Constricted to parts of persons	
8.	I find, I see organic symptoms		Horror		
9.	I quickly call Dr. M	Dr. M confirms symptoms	Dependence on authority		Present co-operative effort
10.		Looks pale, limps, is beardless			"
11.		OTTO, LEOPOLD, join examination			"
12.		LEOPOLD points to infiltration			"
13.	I "feel" infiltration		Fusion with patient. Pain?		
14.		Dr. M gives nonsensical reassurance	Sense of reassurance		Future brighter
15.	WE know cause of infection		Conviction, faith		"
16.		OTTO gave IRMA injection			Past guilt displaced
17.					
18.	I see formula				
19.	(judges)		Sense of righteousness		Present, satisfactory
20.		THE SYRINGE was not clean			Past, guilt localized

Note
Erikson (1954, pp. 28–29)

when she was feeling unwell, an injection of a preparation of propyl ... propyls ... propionic acid ... trimethylamin (the formula of which I see before me, printed in heavy type).... One doesn't give such injections so rashly.... Probably, too, the syringe was not clean.
(Freud, 1900b, p. 89)

There is something very important about the time dimension of this dream; nearly all of the dream is in the present tense, except for the sentence at the end about Otto's injection and the conclusion that the syringe was not clean. Erikson's analysis makes this time dimension clear, and it is important.[1] Yet the version of Freud's *Interpretation of Dreams* that most English speakers read is the translation by James Strachey, which is part of the so-called "Standard Edition." Strachey transposes the dream into the past tense, with the sentence about Otto's injection and the final sentence in the past perfect (Otto had given ... Probably the syringe had not been clean). In the original German text of *The Interpretation of Dreams*, almost all of Freud's own dreams are in the present, and Strachey transposes nearly all of them into the past (Mahony, 1977).

A second serious change made by Strachey is the sentence which Brill translates as "The mouth then opens wide." This is quite different (and closer to the original German) than Strachey's "She then opened her mouth properly" which is less dreamlike. It softens the focus on the body part opening independently and being separated from the patient's volition.

If one thought that the manifest dream was not so important, then the tenses of the dream might not seem to matter. But as Erikson shows, they do matter. The present tense keeps the dream feeling most specifically in the immediate present of the dreamer. Both times that the dream moves into the past, it has the effect of creating psychological distance from what may be the most painful part of the dream. The parts in the past tense refer to Otto's bad medical practice; Max Schur (1972) revealed that the events in the "Irma" dream were almost identical to the bad medical practice of Freud's friend Fliess in Berlin. Freud referred his patient to Fliess for a nasal operation to treat her hysteria. During the surgery, Fliess left a piece of gauze in the wound, which led to serious postoperative complications that almost killed Irma. Thus the acts of medical malpractice in the dream are located in the past – they refer to actual past events that Freud would prefer to repress. Indeed, on the day after Freud had the Irma dream, he wrote to Fliess, saying he missed him and yearned to hear from him. He made no mention of his dream or of Fliess' disastrous operation on Freud's patient.[2]

With Erikson's method of charting dreams, we can analyze the ways that the five dimensions change or remain consistent within a dream, and also between different dreams of the same dreamer. We can notice things like: Do the emotions differ when there are more or fewer people? What are the time zones that the dreamer uses, and what does this tell us about the dreamer's sense of self in different eras of his life and in the present? How is the location of the dream represented, and what is the dreamer's sense of space in the world? We can ask similar questions about any interaction between the five parameters of the dream.

For example, the Irma dream starts with a crowd, along with festive emotions. It then shifts to a close two-person intimacy, with emotions of urgency, worry, impatience, and horror. The dream then brings in other doctors, making the situation less private, and the emotions switch to reassurance, conviction, and righteousness. (I would see guilt at #5 where Erikson sees only worry; there is subjectivity to judging the emotions of the dream without the cooperation of the dreamer.)

Erikson's approach makes us acutely aware of the precise time dimension in dreams and how grammatical tenses are subtly variegated. The grammatical tense of dreaming even matters when dreams are spoken about in songs and public life. We know the song from *The King and I* – "I have dreamed that your arms are lovely" (Rodgers and Hammerstein, 1953), which is located in the continual past tense. It makes the song much more vivid than if the words were "I dreamt that your arms are lovely"; it lets us know it is an ongoing state, and more such dreams will come until they can be made real. And there is Stephen Foster's "I dream of Jeanie with the light brown hair" which is cast in the continual present, implying that I dream of Jeanie often and habitually. (We would probably not care for the song: "I am dreaming of Jeanie with the light brown hair.") "I have a dream" is a statement in the continual present tense, an ongoing experience that continues into the future. But also, to say "I have a dream," makes the dream an object that is continually alive, not a memory of a past experience (which is what most, perhaps all, of our night dreaming seems like). Martin Luther King's famous "I have a dream" speech subtly shifted the metaphoric connotations of dreaming. It combined the fantasy and wish fulfillment of night dreams with the purposiveness of wakefulness, the dream as a plan for the future.

It is less common for the future tense to appear in a dream account, but it happens. A woman whose brother had died in combat had a repeated dream.

I am walking down the street. I meet him [my brother]. He is with a group of people whom I know now. I feel that I will be so happy to see him. I say to him, "I'm glad you're alive," but he'll deny that he is my brother and he'll say so, and I'll wake up crying and trying to convince him.

(Epstein and Ervin, 1956, p. 45)

Let us apply Erikson's approach to a dream of Allan Hobson:[3]

I am in Williamstown, Massachusetts, talking to a colleague, Van, who is wearing a white shirt (he usually wears blue) open at the neck (he is normally neck-tied, and even collar-clipped) and khakis (he usually sports flannels). Casual. Van says, as if by the way, that he attended the committee meeting that had yesterday considered my candidacy for an invited lecture series. (I know from his tone that he is going to deliver bad news.) The committee has decided against it because "They don't feel that psychoanalysis should be confronted with laboratory data."

I allowed as to how bad an idea that was. "It's the wrong reason," I said. "And their timing is off, because Adolf Grünbaum is just about to publish his important new book in which he insists that this is precisely what psychoanalysis must do." Van ignores this statement, appearing never to have heard of A. G.

Van then begins a gentle pirouette and tosses me a piece of hardware, something like the lock of a door or perhaps a pair of paint-frozen hinges. It is as if to say, "Here, take this as recompense." Despite my scavenger nature, I think I should refuse this "gift," and so I toss it back to Van on his next choreographic spin. He insists that it is meant for me, and the scene changes without clear resolution of whether or not I will keep it.

We go out a door (which is on the corner of the building) to behold the beautiful Williams campus. A red-brick walk extends down a green lawn to the classic white Puritan buildings.

Van says, "They chose Mary" (or seems to say that), "reflecting their priorities, to attract a speaker who might help them with their fundraising efforts."

"That is why you have such beautiful buildings," I note, "and why there is nothing in them."

(1988, pp. 232–233)

Let us chart this dream, using Erikson's approach (see Table 10.3). The population in this dream is constant from beginning to end – always two people, Hobson and Van, which suggests constancy, perhaps rigidity. The spatial dimension is quite static, with only one change, moving from indoors on the Williams campus to outdoors (where there is "a breath of fresh air" but the dream soon reverts to nastiness.) The temporal dimension is very static – always locked in the present, except moving strangely into the past at #4, where Hobson "allowed as to how bad an idea that was," perhaps indicating that this is a view he has held in the past, or perhaps a defensive distancing of his categorical dismissal.[4] While the population, time, and place stay relatively constant, the variability for Hobson is mainly emotional. The emotions are intense and rapidly changing: from casual friendliness to dread, anger, defensive, playful, graceful, propitiating, self-righteously rigid, persistent, wonder, pleasure, definitive, with the ending being nasty and sarcastic. From this dream, one could surmise that Hobson's "mindbrain style" is stability bordering on rigidity, with a great affective lability.

Let us now consider the dream of Judith, a college student in psychoanalytic treatment:

I was in my college dorm that was being used for prostitution. An equal number of let's say ten men and ten women were signing up for sex. But when the women came out of the room they were crying because they felt abused in a brutal way. I felt guilty because I set up the situation for these people to sign up. I put the sign-up sheet on my dorm door. Although I felt guilty I had to do it because I was threatened or felt threatened to do it. Then I woke up feeling anxious.

Table 10.4 shows the dream charted in Erikson's method.[5]

The "population" goes from the dreamer being with others to the dreamer being totally by herself; and the affect goes from very

Table 10.3 Charting Hobson's dream using Erikson's framework

I. Interpersonal		II.	III.	IV.
The dreamer	The population	Affective	Spatial	Temporal
1. I am talking	To Van	Casual	Williamstown, MA	Present
2. To me	Van says he attended committee meeting	"By the way" but ominous	"	Present
3.	"The committee decided against it."	Bad news, disappointed	"	"
4. I allowed as to how bad an idea that was …	To Van	Angry	"	Past
5.	Van ignores this statement	Defensive	"	Present
6. To me	Van begins pirouette and tosses hardware	Playful? Feminine? Flirtatious?	"	Present
7. To me	As if to say, "Here, take this as recompense"	Propitiating, trying to make up	"	Present
8. I toss it back	To Van	Self-righteous, rigid, competitive	"	Present
9.	He insists it is meant for me	Persistent	"	Present
10.		Lacking resolution Wonder	Scene changes	Present
11. We go out a door	We go out a door to behold beautiful Williams campus	Pleasant, exploratory	Williams campus, red brick wall to lawn and buildings	Present
12.	Van says, "They chose Mary"	Definitive, explanatory	"	Present
13. I note, "that is why …"	To Van	Nasty, retaliatory, sarcastic	"	Present

Table 10.4 Judith's dream charted using Erikson's framework

I. Interpersonal		II.	III.	IV.
The dreamer	The population	Affective	Spatial	Temporal
1. I was in college dorm		Neutral	College dorm that was being used for prostitution	Past
2.	Ten men and ten women signing up for sex	Neutral – eager?	Dorm	Past ongoing
3.	The women came out of the room they were crying because they felt abused in a brutal way	Pain sadness	The room	Past ongoing
4. I felt guilty because I set up the situation for these people to sign up		Guilt	Unclear	Past
5. I put the sign-up sheet on my dorm door		Guilt	Dorm door	Past
6. Although I felt guilty I had to do it because I was threatened or felt threatened to do it	Unknown other person	Guilt, exoneration, being threatened or feeling threatened	Unclear	Past
7. Then I woke up feeling anxious		Anxiety	Unclear	Past

business-like to angry, guilty, and then anxious. Note that the dreamer seems to have no agency until after the crisis has happened. Then, she seems to feel total agency and responsibility. Does this progression delineate her personality style? As long as others are around, she is able to maintain a cool, business-like detachment, even when something terrible is happening. But when she is alone, she feels horror and enormous responsibility. The dream may indicate that a goal in psychotherapy might be to moderate the splitting between Judith's detachment and her sense of total responsibility and guilt.

If we do enough Erikson-model dream analyses, we can start to ask, "What is the role of psychological defenses in dreams?" Each dream seems to delineate certain psychological defenses. In Freud's Irma dream, the defenses are projection, denial, and intellectualization. In Hobson's dream, the defenses are reversal of affect and sarcasm. In Judith's dream, the defenses are isolation of affect, intellectualization, and projection "(I had to do it because I was threatened") or disavowal ("or felt I had to do it"). It all ends in undifferentiated anxiety.

We will consider the question of dreams and psychological defenses in more depth in the next chapter.

Notes

1 Erikson, in his paper, uses the translation by Brill (Freud, 1900b), not Strachey. The Brill translation retains the present tense of the German original, as does the later translation by Joyce Crick (Freud, 1900c). If one used the Strachey translation, with its distortion of tenses, the charting of the time dimension would be wrong.
2 On the day after the dream, Freud wrote to Fliess:

> Daimonie [Demon], why don't you write? How are you? Don't you care at all any more about what I am doing? What is happening to the nose, menstruation, labor pains, neuroses, your dear wife, and the budding little one? True, this year I am ill and must come to you; what will happen if by chance both of us remain healthy for a whole year? Are we friends only in misfortune? Or do we want to share the experiences of calm times with each other?
>
> (Masson, 1985, p. 134)

There is no mention in this letter of Freud's dream, his interpretation of it, nor the disastrous operation by Fliess on Freud's patient.
3 See Blechner (1997) for a different analysis of Hobson's dream.

4 It may seem that such a shift in tense may not be meaningful, just carelessness in the dreamer's description of the dream, but usually they are significant.
5 Erikson's dream-charting method is improved when done by a group, which allows for a greater range of responses and a correction for any one person's bias. The charting of Judith's dream was done at a conference, with the participation of over 50 people.

Chapter 11
Psychological defenses and dreams

On September 11, 2001, terrorists crashed airplanes into the twin towers of the World Trade Center in New York City. The event was traumatic for all New Yorkers. Shortly after the event, three different people told me dreams which they related directly to the terrorist attacks.

1. One person dreamt: "*I was sleeping in my apartment, and a plane crashed through the window of my bedroom. I awoke suddenly, terrified and unsure if the attack had really happened.*"
2. Another person dreamt:

   I am on a train. I am looking at the Upper West Side skyline. I watched a plane going into a building. Then one went into a building in Queens, where my niece lives. Then one went into Harlem where Bill Clinton's office was.

3. A third person dreamt:

   I am a prisoner of war in a German camp during World War II. Single-handedly, I escape to another camp, which I liberate by tying a bungee cord around it. I see Hogan from Hogan's Heroes, except that Hogan is a German officer, and I must evade him, since Hogan knows all of my tricks.

None of the three dreamers had been at the site of the World Trade Center buildings during the attack. None had lost anyone they knew in the attacks or had been physically harmed. And yet one can see in each dream a different style of relating to the world and a different set of psychological defenses against trauma, conflict, unacceptable desires, and unpleasant experience.

Each of the three people who reported dreams after 9/11 employed a different pattern of psychological defenses that showed up in his dream. The first dreamer was generally anxious and fearful even before the World Trade Center attacks and often braced himself for the worst to happen. After the attacks, he modified his life in New York. He refused to fly, and he would not take the subway or trains. He had always led an avoidant and schizoid existence, and believed, after the terrorist attacks, that he needed to change his life toward even greater cautiousness and constriction than before. His defenses were not very effective, primarily being an attempt to control danger and unpleasant affects by obsessional attempts at total control of his environment. The manifest content of the dream shows the lack of any defense at all. He is completely vulnerable, in his own bedroom, to the very attack that he fears. His obsessional defense is seen in his reaction to the dream; he awakens in a panic, "terrified and unsure if the attack really happened." This combination of terror and uncertainty, great fear and obsessional doubting, were essentials of his psychological functioning. He lived out that combination is his real life. After the attacks, he immediately worked out a plan for moving to a safer place; yet he did not put this plan into action. That is an essential trait of obsessional living: panic, rumination, resolve, and then inaction. One can see that living style in his dream.

The second dreamer spent most of his life detached from his emotions. In therapy, it was often hard for him to acknowledge any feelings, even about very important things that had happened to him. He had been subjected to so much shame and prejudice throughout his childhood that he learned to distance himself from feelings. His way of handling the World Trade Center disaster in real life was to live exactly as he had done before, making no changes and presuming that he would not be affected by trouble in the world. He occasionally had moments when he thought he should be more afraid, but he quickly dismissed those feelings. He relied on the defense of "isolation of affect"; he separated his emotions from his reactions. One can see that defense in his manifest dream. He observes the three planes crash, but always from a distance and in the safety of a train.

The third dreamer was a man who coped with danger situations through action. He liked to take charge of situations and fancied having a kind of omnipotence. He also was a thrill-seeker and had gone bungee-jumping. After the attacks of 9/11, he wanted to take action to make

America safer. Had he not been too old, he might have joined the Marines and gone to Afghanistan to hunt down terrorists. His prominent defenses were denial (of vulnerability), a sense of omnipotence, and reversal of roles. One could also describe this man as courageous; a virtue can be related to a psychological defense. What made his courage more of a defense was that it was extreme and unrealistic. One man could not wrap a bungee cord around an entire prison camp, nor is it clear what that would solve. In the dream, he changes his role from prisoner to captor, yet in the role of the captor, he knows the tricks of his true self.

One can see the defensive style of each person in the narrative of his dream. The first dreamer uses obsessional defenses; the second dreamer uses isolation of affect; and the third dreamer uses denial of vulnerability, omnipotence, and reversal of roles.

Psychological defenses are processes by which our mindbrains change reality, suppress or transform drives and emotions, misattribute personality characteristics from ourselves to others or from others to ourselves, or leave out aspects of reality to lessen anxiety (S. Freud, 1937; A. Freud, 1936; McWilliams, 1994, 2011). Defenses enable our mindbrains to distort who is doing what to whom, who feels what, what we are feeling in the moment, or what has happened or is happening. Defenses also can divert emotions to bodily processes, such as in the defense of somatization.[1] It is my view that many, perhaps all, psychological defenses[2] can appear in dreams, and a study of their operation in dreams will help us understand defenses better, give us increased understanding of how the mindbrain transforms the world, and give us new ways to approach defenses in clinical work.

In order to explore these questions further, I will trace briefly the history of psychological defenses in psychoanalysis and their interaction with the theory of dreams. I will then move to an examination of three ways that we can see evidence of psychological defenses in dreams. Then, I will explore 11 psychological defenses; I will define each defense and then examine how the defense can appear in dreams.

Basic questions about dreams and defenses

One of the basic questions about dreams is whether and how psychological defenses are involved in dream formation, and how we may see evidence of defenses in dreams. Nearly half a century after Anna Freud (1936) wrote her book on the psychological defenses, Joseph Sandler interviewed her extensively about how her views had evolved and changed. He published their conversations in a wonderful book, *The Analysis of Defense: The Ego and the Mechanisms of Defense Revisited* (Sandler and Freud, 1985). Sandler suggested at one point that characteristic waking defenses would appear in the dream, so that, for instance, a patient who used projection in his waking life would also do so in his dreams. Anna Freud said she doubted it. Faithful to her father's original views of dream formation, Anna Freud replied that perhaps defenses show up in the recounting of the dream, but probably not in the dream itself.

I think Anna Freud was wrong; there is merit in Sandler's hypothesis that many or all of the psychological defenses appear in dreams. I have been collecting data on this question for more than three decades, from the dreams of my patients and those of my students' patients, from members of my dreams groups, as well as from my own dreams. I now believe we can find most psychological defenses in dreams. This is a work in progress; I am still collecting data, and would like my colleagues to understand the project I am undertaking and collaborate with me in finding evidence of psychological defenses in dreams.[3,4]

There are three primary ways that we can observe psychological defenses in dreams:

1 The dream image may represent the defense itself.
2 The dream's story line, rather than the imagery itself, shows the operation of the defense.
3 The dreamer may also show the operation of a defense in the way the dream is told and experienced, including glosses.

I will now consider each of these three ways psychological defenses can appear in dreams and provide some examples.

1 **The dream image may represent the defense itself.**
   A patient of Peter Fonagy had the following dream: "*The dream was of a bureau with many drawers. He spent a long time finding the key. He knew that the drawers should be full but when he opened each in turn they were empty*" (Fonagy, 1989, 1991).

   This is a remarkable imagistic representation of repression. The dreamer knows that the drawers should be full, but when he opens

them, they are empty – a vivid pictorialization of the experience that one has some kind of knowledge, but one cannot get access to it.
2 **The dream's story line, rather than the imagery itself, shows the operation of the defense.**
The third 9/11 dream shows the dreamer's omnipotence (single-handedly wrapping an entire prison camp in a bungee cord) and reversal of roles (switching from prisoner to captor).
3 **The dreamer may show the operation of a defense in the way the dream is told and experienced, including glosses, comments, associations and the forgetting of certain parts.**[5]
Let us go back to the dreams after 9/11; in the first one, the dreamer was sleeping in his apartment and a plane crashed through the window. The dreamer awoke and was unsure if the dream really happened. He treated his dream with obsessional defenses of doubting and rumination.

The dreamer may also introduce the telling of a dream with characteristically defensive comments, such as: "I had a dream, but it's not significant" (denial); "I had a dream, but I only remember a fragment of it" (partial repression); "I had a dream but it was short and uninteresting" or "Don't get your notebook out; this dream isn't worth it" (dismissal). All of these statements preceding the actual dream are attempts to dismiss the significance of the dream or the possibility of finding any meaning in it.

The defense may also affect the time in a psychoanalytic session in which a dream is told. For example, a dreamer reported a very negative dream at the beginning of a session, and then a second, very positive dream at the end of the session, demonstrating the defense of splitting. (See pp. 168–171 on splitting for more detail.)

I have identified three ways that psychological defenses can appear in dreams: (1) pictorialization of the defense in a visual image; (2) portrayal of the defense in the dream storyline; and (3) glosses and commentaries before, during, or after the telling of the dream. Can all of the psychological defenses appear in dreams? And if so, in all three ways?[6]

There is no universal agreement about how many defenses there are and what their definitions are. Anna Freud (1936) listed ten defense mechanisms. Laughlin (1970) described 22 major and 26 minor defense mechanisms, Vaillant (1992) named 18. McWilliams (2011) elaborated ten primary defensive processes and 14 secondary defensive processes. I am choosing 11 defenses to discuss. I will briefly describe the defense and then consider the data of how that defense appears in working with dreams.

Repression

Repression is the defense in which an unpleasant thought, memory, or feeling is actively kept from awareness, by forgetting or ignoring.[7]

As mentioned above, Peter Fonagy (1989, 1991) reported a dream of a patient who had repressed memories of sexual abuse as a child, in which there is a bureau of many drawers. The dreamer knows the drawers should be full, but when he opens them, they are empty.

What a precise portrayal of repression! The dreamer knows there is something there, but he sees nothing. As it later turned out, this man had repressed childhood memories of anal rape by his father as well as many other kinds of abuse. Here we are seeing the portrayal of repression by the dream image.[8]

I have discussed how working with dreams can be like the game show *Jeopardy!* in which one is provided the answer, and the task is to find the question that fits the answer (Blechner, 2001). If one applies this model of dreaming to the dream reported by Fonagy, the question might be: "What is your conscious memory like?" The answer provided by the dream is: "My conscious memory is like a bureau with many drawers. I know that there is a lot there, but when I open the drawers, they are empty."

One should also note the rebus: "drawers" is another word for underpants, and "bureau" also has the meaning of an official organization, so the "Bureau of Drawers" could be an official organization charged with investigating what happens in someone's underpants; in this dream, they find nothing, which could symbolize the lack of awareness by official agencies of the abuse.

Here is another dream that describes repression. It does not portray repression with an image, but rather the actual experience of forgetting a dream which the dreamer knew he had:

I dreamed that I had a dream, and I wanted to tell you about it. I was looking for a piece of paper to write it down. There was a dream that I was dreaming but I couldn't remember it.

The dreamer then told me a second dream about a man who had been in elementary school with him and was jailed as an adult for child molestation. The material was disturbing. It was hard to tell, at the time, if the first dream which had felt forgotten was indeed the second disturbing dream, or whether the forgotten dream was of an actual experience of sexual molestation as a child. Later in the analysis, it turned out that the patient had been sexually molested as a child. The first dream, forgotten, was a portrayal of the repression, while the second dream alluded to the repressed material, but projected[9] it onto his school classmate, who was a sexual abuser.

Repression also can happen in the telling or forgetting of dreams, so that it becomes an interpersonal event. Such repression can occur in varying degrees. In clinical work, I may remind patients of a dream they had in the past. Sometimes, they have trouble remembering the dream, but after I have mentioned the beginning of the dream, they will recall the rest of the dream, so it is not repressed. Sometimes they will acknowledge that they had the dream, but not remember the rest until I tell it to them, which seems to be partial repression. And sometimes – and this I consider the strongest dream repression – they will say: "I never had that dream. You must be mixing me up with someone else." That is a statement that will strike fear in any psychoanalyst. But since I keep written records of my patients' dreams, I can look it up. So far, I have always been right; the patient had the dream, but it is now completely repressed. I can even remind the patient of the day the dream occurred, the context of the person's life at the time, and how we interpreted the dream, and still they have no memory of it. That is major repression.

Sometimes, a dreamer will remember most of a dream, but completely repress just a part of it. For example, one of my patients, Lucy, had the following dream, which she wrote down herself and sent me by email before discussing it with me:

A woman was walking along the shore and met a man who was scooping shellfish back into the sea. The shellfish were in a jar. When he was down to the last one, he invited the woman to put the last one in. When she took the ladle, he jumped into the ocean and swam out to the deep. She had invited a friend to hear the story as it was happening. When she feared for the stranger's life, she jumped in to save him. When she reached him, he grabbed her and tried to drown her.

Her friend, who was originally a man, was now a woman. She dove in to save her friend. When she reached her, she knocks out the man with a jar and saves the woman.

A few months later, I referred to her dream in which she "knocked out a man with a jar." She said she didn't know what I was talking about. I then recounted the first few sentences of the dream to her, which she recognized, and she filled in the rest of the dream. But for her, the dream ended where she jumped in to save the swimmer. She had no memory of the rest of the dream. But since she had written it down, she looked it up and was startled to see how the dream ended with her knocking the man out with a jar. She said, "I have the record so it must be true, but even now, I don't feel like I remember that part." Her forgetting the end of the dream acted out the denial of her aggression that went on in her waking life and was often targeted at me in the transference. Also, her father had died when she was a young child; perhaps the dream ending expressed a fantasy of having killed her father (turning passive into active). The forgotten end of the dream also may have represented her bigendered identification (Blechner, 2015), symbolized by the man who turned into a woman. The fact that even when she looked at her written record of the dream, she did not recognize the ending, indicated that powerful repression was going on.

Repression is usually meant to indicate an unconscious process. If a dreamer consciously and deliberately leaves out a part of a dream, it is usually not considered to be repression. And yet, at times, the person who suppresses parts of a dream may not fully be aware of doing it or why – I call that "secondary pruning" (Blechner, 2001, p. 127) which, like "secondary elaboration," can be done unconsciously.

For example, one of my patients in analysis, Wayne, had a first dream in which he was portrayed as a physical cripple, which captured many aspects of his self-representation, as well as actual experiences in his life.[10] The dream was so rich, we continued to work on it throughout the analysis. After nine years of treatment, we started to plan termination. I said, "Let's set a date a few months from now and see. But be sure, during that time, to bring up anything that occurs to you that you might have left out."

Wayne came to a subsequent session and said, "I was going through my papers, and I came across some notes that I made to myself during our first week of analysis. Would you be interested in looking at them?" He handed me five sheets of paper, typed in single space. The pages included the text of his first dream, and I thought it would be interesting to compare it to my records. Actually, his text and mine were quite similar, except the dream ended on a much more upbeat note than the way he originally told it to me. It also turned out that the dream had started with a section that he completely left out, and which would have helped explain the part of the dream that he did tell me. The notes also had statements about how he consciously wanted to control me, what I thought and did. Only now, at the end of the analysis, when we had worked through this need to control other people, could he reveal to me how he had controlled me by keeping parts of his dream secret for nine years.

Dissociation

Dissociation has been defined in a number of ways. Extreme dissociation is a global disconnection with reality. Dissociation is a reaction to a traumatic event that basically allows us to not "be there" during the event. This leads to the complete obliteration of the event from consciousness.[11]

Here is a dream that portrays extreme dissociation:

> *I was holding my nephew. He wasn't a person. He was a circle with a hole in the middle. A dangerous, devouring circle. The more open and open this hole, the more I was afraid it would get me. Someone said, "You can't drop your nephew like that." It was devouring and unpleasant.*

The dreamer had been born prematurely and had nearly starved to death during the first two weeks of life. You can see the representation of the experience of near-annihilation in the graphic representation of his nephew as a circle with a hole in it – there is no memory, just a bare shape and a void, which is terrifying. Lewin's (1973) concept of the "dream screen" drew our attention to the backdrop and textural qualities of a dream. This dream exemplifies the "negative dream screen" (Blechner, 2001) in which the dream image is one of ever-increasing emptiness and nothingness.

More "moderate dissociation" keeps different areas of awareness separate (Janet, 1887). The person holds two groups of information and feelings in mind, but keeps the connection between the groups separate.[12] Freud (1900a, 1909a) considered this type of dissociation a subspecies of repression – in ordinary repression, a thought is kept out of awareness; in moderate dissociation, the two thoughts are not kept out of awareness, but the connection between them is repressed, or the connection between a thought and an emotion are repressed. Hilgard (1977) extended this view; he considered the repressive barrier "horizontal" and the dissociative barrier "vertical." The metaphorical "vertical" barrier of dissociation may have a literal anatomical example in "split-brain" patients, who have had a cerebral commissurotomy, in which the nerve fibers connecting the two brain hemispheres have been severed vertically (Gazzaniga *et al.*, 1962; Gazzaniga, 1989). In such cases, there are separate, independent awarenesses in each half of the brain. Laughlin (1970, p. 97) described "affect dissociation" as the "splitting-off of emotional feeing or affect from an idea, situation, object, or relationship."[13]

Goldberger describes a dream which pictorially portrays dissociation:

I was in a place that had an upstairs with two rooms. In each lives a family, and I'm watching both rooms. The father in one room has chopped up every member of the family, drowned the puppy, and chopped himself up too ... I knock on the door of the other room, and they don't know what happened.

(1989, p. 400)

Goldberger tells us:

One association was to the previous session, in which she had spoken of cutting things off from each other – for example, her experiencing her analyst and herself as being in two separate cubicles. In that hour she had also spoken of her tendency to "side-step" issues, just as her father did. The patient herself had no real sense that walling off was an active defensive process in her mental life. Because of the clarity of the pictorial representation of this defense in a number of dreams over two years, I was able to help the patient become aware of this defense in her dreams as a habitual mechanism for dealing with certain anxieties.... This example illustrates that a defense can remain so ephemeral in daily life as to be unusable in analytic interpretation, but may be more easily comprehended in a dream because of its plastic representation.

(1989, p. 400)

Another dissociation of experience was portrayed pictorially in the following dream:

I was in my apartment and there were two fish tanks, aquariums, side by side, against the wall, in my living room. They were identical. The same tank, with the same kinds of fish inside each of them. One of them had the two kinds of fish that the aquarium in my house has, these big ugly looking fish, and these small other cute fish. These fish typically don't get along, they aren't usually the kind of fish that live together, but they lived in the same tank for a long time without any problems. The big ones didn't eat the small ones. The water was clean, the tank was clean. The other tank was the same one, with the same fish in them, but the water was a bit dirtier, murkier, and had this big dead, black thing lying on the bottom of it. It was like a big black eel-looking thing.

The dreamer had a steady boyfriend who was white-skinned, but she was also having an affair with a black-skinned man. She was not honest with anyone but her analyst about what she was doing. The dream portrayed two aquariums, two versions of her life that were almost identical, except that one aquarium symbolized a sanitized version of her life where everything was fine and all the creatures got along, and the other aquarium symbolized a different version of her life. It included the black eel-looking thing (her lover's penis?) that made things murky. An aquarium is a container made of glass, into which one can see the live creatures inside. In this dream, her life can be seen in two split versions.[14]

A final dream may portray dissociation or perhaps a different defense. Bill dreamt that *there was a piece of Plexiglas in his brain.*[15] *It kept things dissociated, but he thought that if he looked through the Plexiglas in the right way, he could see what was being dissociated.*

Bill had an intense transference reaction to me. When he rang my doorbell, he imagined I cringed at the thought of having to see him again. I was not feeling this way, and consciously found Bill to be both likable and interesting. Yet Bill's fantasy persisted for years. He had been born to a very young mother, so I proposed an interpretation about whether his mother had resented him when he came to her door so early in life. He thought the interpretation plausible, but not affecting. Later in the analysis, after his mother died, a relative revealed that Bill's father was not his biological father. His mother had the child by a man in college, briefly her first husband. Bill spent the first six months of his life in transit between his mother's chaotic home situation and the care of his grandparents, and so he was unwanted for much of his early life. His mother then started an affair with another man whom she married. She hid the situation of Bill's early months and his true parentage throughout his life. The Plexiglas therefore may have represented an insight (an "endopsychic perception" – see p. 174) that there was something to be seen and known, but he could not get access to it. He had no conscious declarative memory of this time of life, but he seemed to have affective memory of it.

Reaction formation

> The human organism is capable of turning something into its polar opposite in order to render it less threatening. The traditional definition of reaction formation involves this conversion of a negative into a positive affect or vice versa. The transformation of hatred into love, or longing into contempt, or envy into attraction, for example, can be inferred from many common transactions.
>
> (McWilliams, 2011, p. 140)

In reaction formation, the person shows an attitude that belies the underlying emotion or character structure by expressing its opposite in an exaggerated way. For example, an actress may say about her enemy, "Oh, I just love her!"; people who are closeted homosexuals may express hatred and hostility toward homosexuals; or an authoritarian person may try to act especially open-minded and easy-going. Longing and desire can be transformed into contempt.

Freud described dreams with reaction formations, where something is represented by its opposite. A fear of being arrested for something can hide a wish to have the life situation that would allow one to commit the crime. For example, a man dreams that he is to be heavily fined by tax commissioners (Freud, 1900a, p. 157). His manifest fear of arrest in the dream hides his desire to have a high income that would allow him to "qualify" for the crime of tax evasion. He hides his ambition and greed with a stance in the dream of guilt and remorse.

In reaction formation, the mindbrain masks the true emotion by a display of its opposite. And here we come up against another very thorny but fundamental issue – whether emotions in a dream are always true, or whether emotions themselves can be subject to transformations by the dreamwork. Freud changed his mind about this and expressed differing viewpoints about it in different parts of *The Interpretation of Dreams*. At times he argued that affects are primary and are not subject to distortion by the dreamwork: "It will be noticed that the affect felt in the dream belongs to its latent and not to its manifest content, and that the dream's *affective* content has remained untouched by the distortion which has overtaken its *ideational* content" (Freud, 1900a, p. 248, cf. also p. 323, n.1). Elsewhere he proposed that affects can be inhibited by the dreamwork, if not actually changed (p. 467), and then went on to say that the dreamwork can turn an affect into its opposite. "There is yet another way in which the dreamwork can deal with affects in the dream-thoughts, in addition to allowing them through or reducing them to nothing. It can *turn them into their opposite*" (p. 471). Freud cites his dream in which hidden slander is turned into manifest affection: "In the dream of 'my uncle with the yellow beard' [Freud, 1900a, pp. 137ff.] I felt the greatest affection for my friend R, whereas ... the dream-thoughts called him a simpleton."

Ferenczi relates a similar example of a dream's reversal of affect:

I was lying in my bed; an acquaintance came in; I wanted to turn up the light, but could not do it. I tried again and again – in vain. Thereupon my wife got up out of bed to help me, but she could not manage it either; but because she was embarrassed before the gentleman at being in her negligée she finally gave it up and went back to bed again; all this was so comical that I had to laugh exceedingly at it. My wife said, "Why do you laugh, why do you laugh?" but I only went on laughing – till I awakened. The following day he was depressed and had a headache – "from laughing so much that I was exhausted," he thought.

(1913, p. 345)

Ferenczi tells us that the man has serious arteriosclerosis and had reason the day before to worry about dying. He had wanted to copulate with his wife, but failed despite her negligée. The dreamwork transformed the impotence and fear of death into a comic scene. We might say that the dream exemplified the adage: "Eat, drink, and be merry, for tomorrow you may die." The realization that the laughter was inappropriate is projected, in his dream, to the character of his wife – and she may have thought it no laughing matter that he failed in his lovemaking nor that he was in such poor health.

Identification with the aggressor

In identification with the aggressor, the person who is a victim of aggression identifies with the aggressor and mimics the aggression of his or her persecutor. Thus, people who were prisoners of war sometimes act in their later lives like prison wardens toward their family members.[16]

Children often show "identification with the aggressor" after being hurt. Anna Freud gave this clinical example:

> A six-year-old boy came to his analysis after having been to the dentist who had hurt him. He attacked various objects in the room, cut a piece of string into pieces, and went on to sharpen and re-sharpen pencils. He broke off the points and sharpened them again.
> (Sandler and Freud, 1985, p. 380)

Identification with the aggressor shows up in dreams, in which the dreamer mistreats someone in the manner that he has been mistreated. Freud dreamt (1900a, p. 137):

> I ... *My friend R. was my uncle. – I had a great feeling of affection for him.*
> II *I saw before me his face, somewhat changed. It was as though it had been drawn out lengthways. A yellow beard that surrounded it stood out especially clearly.*

Through his associations, Freud connected the composite image of Freud's friend R. and Freud's uncle with two of his Jewish colleagues. The dream revolved around the anti-Semitism of the time, which was preventing Freud and many of his Jewish colleagues from becoming professors at the university. Freud[17] thought that the dream involved identification with the aggressor. He observed that in his thoughts about the dream, he identified with the anti-Semitism of which he was a victim:

> In mishandling my two learned and eminent colleagues because they were Jews, and in treating one as a simpleton and the other as a criminal, I was behaving as though I were the Minister, I had put myself in the Minister's place.
>
> (1900a, p. 193)

The dream also showed the defense of "reversal of affect." In the dream, Freud had great affection for his uncle, which, he tells us, was not true. He did, however, have great affection for his friend, R., but in the dream, this affection is reversed into contempt (by means of Freud's identification with the anti-Semitic aggressor). We may ask: How much does reversal of affect come into play whenever there is identification with the aggressor?

Although Anna Freud, as we noted above, doubted that higher-level psychological defenses appeared in dreams, there is evidence for identification with the aggressor in one of her own dreams. At the time that her father, Sigmund Freud, was undergoing multiple surgeries for cancer of the mouth, she was upset by their aggression. At that time, she dreamt,

> "Tonight I dreamt that I killed our cook Anna. I cut off her head and cut her to pieces and had no feelings of guilt, which was very peculiar. Now I know why: because her name is Anna, and that means me." She identified with the aggressiveness of the surgeons and then turned it on herself – or at least refused to acknowledge that there might be any other "Anna" than herself.
> (Young-Bruehl, 1988, p. 211; the dream is quoted from a letter from Anna Freud to Eva Rosenfeld, August 27, 1931)

One could say that in this dream, Anna Freud is both aggressor and victim, both the person who chops people up, but also the victim, since the cook who is chopped up is named Anna. She is identified both with the aggressor and the victim.[18]

Identification with the aggressor can be a by-product of the interpreter's approach to dreams. The notion that everyone in the dream is an aspect of the dreamer (what Jung called the "subjective approach to dreams") *produces* this defense. That is, if one assumes that everyone in the dream is an aspect of the dreamer, then every aggressor portrayed in the dream can be interpreted as an internalized aspect of the dreamer. It is questionable whether this should be included in examples of identification with the aggressor. One could also argue that dreams tend to project the dreamer's aggression onto other people, so that they often employ a defense of "projection of the aggressor."

Projection

In projection, the mindbrain takes one of its own characteristics, emotions, or attitudes, and projects it onto someone else; a person who is a habitual liar may regularly accuse other people of lying. A person who hates a colleague may feel that the colleague hates him. A person who is a rabid nationalist may accuse other countries of their nationalism.

Projection is a common defense in dreams. Jung's idea of "the subjective viewpoint," in which everyone in the dream is an aspect of the dreamer, encourages us to consider that in dreams, we often project our feelings and thoughts onto other people. However, Jung also proposed the objective viewpoint, in which everyone in the dream is who they are (Jung, 1948/1974). Taking the objective viewpoint, we can still see projection in the manifest content. Consider the following example:

> A young woman was terrified of therapy and of any sense of intimacy with me. We met once a week, on Mondays. Since national holidays often fall on Mondays in the United States, there were several missed appointments that always brought up a great deal of feeling. One year, we missed two sessions in a row. The first missed session was for President's Day, and the patient had to miss her next session because of a work obligation. So, after not having a session during a three-week period, the patient came in and said that she had woken up angry each morning, and she did not know why. She said she was especially angry the previous Tuesday morning. Uncharacteristically, she acknowledged that she wished she had had a session. She also noticed that she has been feeling a kind of generalized anger lately. She said, "You name it, I can tell you why I am angry at it." Since she did not connect her anger with the missed sessions, I did. I suggested that she missed

me, and that although such feelings make her uncomfortable, they exist, alongside her dread of the treatment.

She then told me a dream:[19]

> *I was here, in this chair. We were having some really difficult conversation. You said something to me. I was just sitting here, trying to decide, am I going to leave or stay? For some reason the hassock was bigger. If I put my head down, you couldn't see me anymore. I decided to leave. I get to the door. There is a bookcase here. (She points to the right of the door; in reality the bookcase is to the left of the door.) I tried to open the door, I couldn't get it open. I felt my face get red. I was flushed and embarrassed. I said to you (it seemed to take forever), "What's the matter with the door? Why can't I get it open?" You say, "There is nothing the matter with the door." I still can't get it open. I asked, "Did you put a new lock on it?" You replied, "No." I was leaning against the bookcase, trying and trying the doorknob. I woke up so angry, sad, and embarrassed.*

One can see her conflict between wanting to escape from the session and wanting to stay in the session (the dream's story line portrays the defense). She cannot acknowledge her wanting to stay and instead projects the pressure to stay in my office on me: "Did *you* put a new lock on the door?" she asks me in the dream. I tell her no, and she is embarrassed that she cannot leave. She has experienced the psychotherapy as increasingly helpful, and so the long gap since the last session has made her angry. Yet she is terrified of dependency and has often wanted to leave sessions early.

Isolation

Isolation is the separation of affect from cognition. For example, an event may remain in memory, but it is devoid of how the person felt about it. "In isolation, the affect is usually displaced, warded off, changed into the opposite, or denied. The important thing is that the result is that the affect isn't connected with the original source, with the original idea" (Sandler and Freud, 1985, p. 125).

Psychological defenses and dreams 163

Isolation of affect can be considered a subset or a recombination of other defenses. The affect and the idea are separated, in a form of dissociation. The affect is then denied, repressed, or reversed.

We already saw (p. 147) how isolation of affect operated in the dream of a man after the attacks on the World Trade Center in New York. He watched the planes going into buildings but felt no emotion as he watched it. He was not threatened himself, but people he admired or loved were threatened.

Another patient had a dream that exhibited both the defense of isolation and the emotion that was being isolated. *The emotion and the defense were portrayed by two different characters in the dream.* In this way, the dream could pictorialize the defense by the separation and interrelationship of the two characters. The dream was:

> *I was sitting with my father – I think it was my father, though he was somehow foreign or alien to me – and we were on a cliff. My brother was there too. He wanted to hike down the cliff. Then he disappeared. My father and I were still sitting there and I started to panic. My father said he thought he fell. We called his name but there was no response. Then the dream ended, and I was feeling, "Oh my God, my brother is dead." I was trying to look down, but I couldn't see anything. That's it.*

In the dream, there is a situation that would arouse intense emotion in most people, and the dreamer says that she feels panic. The figure of the father, who says he thought the brother fell, seems bland and unemotional. The fact that the father seems foreign or alien could indicate that his defensive emotional blandness in the dream seems foreign to the dreamer yet is also closely related to her. Of course, there is also projection involved, namely, that the isolation of affect is projected onto the father.[20]

Sometimes, instead of expressing the isolation of affect, dreams undo the defense of isolation by bringing together the idea and the affect that are kept separate during waking life. I have found this to occur in patients who are having panic attacks; their dreams allow one to quickly and powerfully reconnect affect that is disconnected in waking life. For example, during the worst years of the AIDS epidemic, when there were no effective treatments, a gay man in his 30s, John, consulted me about his severe panic attacks. During the day he would feel as if he was having a heart attack, and he would wake up in the middle of the night in terror. I asked if he was dreaming when he awoke, and he said that at times he was dreaming that he had AIDS. He was involved in a relationship of two years' standing with a man, Leo. A brief inquiry revealed that Leo's prior lover had died of AIDS, yet he never told John, who found out three months into the relationship from someone else. He mentioned it to Leo who had a lame excuse for keeping it secret. John rationalized away his immediate suspicion and then forgot about it (except in his dreams). Leo himself had not been tested for the HIV virus; in fact, he refused to be tested. I commented to John that anyone in a gay relationship at that time would be concerned about AIDS, that anyone would be especially concerned if their partner had had a long-standing relationship with someone who died of the disease, even more so if the partner had concealed this fact, even more so if their partner had not been tested, and even more so if the partner refused to be tested. John seemed startled by these thoughts; but the panic attacks ceased. The patient's idea, that he was at risk for AIDS, came together with the affect of panic only in his dreams, and then woke him up (Blechner, 1997, 2007a). In my view of panic disorder, the main mechanism is dissociation of affect and idea, which need to be brought together. Dreams sometimes offer an excellent path for this reintegration of affect and idea.

Intellectualization

> Intellectualization is the name given to a higher-order version of the isolation of affect from intellect. The person using isolation typically reports that he or she has no feelings, whereas the one who intellectualizes talks about feelings in a way that strikes the listener as emotionless. For example, the comment, "Well, naturally I have some anger about that," delivered in a casual, detached tone, suggests that while the idea of feeling anger is theoretically acceptable to the person, the actual expression of it is still inhibited.
>
> (McWilliams, 2011, p. 132)

There has been some question about how much intellectual work can be done in dreams.[21] In the following clinical example, the dreamer ponders an intellectual problem within her dream. This part of the dream is both an example of the defense of intellectualization within a dream, while also being a condensation of meaning.

A woman, Rosa, came from a very dysfunctional family, in which she was the "identified patient." When Rosa complained or tried to stand up for herself, both her mother and sister would tell her that she was being unreasonable and the dispute was all her fault. She came to believe this, which led to severe depression. While she was in psychotherapy, there was an incident in which the family was clearly abusive and cruel to her. Rosa's family members would not acknowledge that they had wronged her, so she stopped seeing them and talking to them. But she heard from other relatives that, as usual, her parents spoke of the rift as "Rosa causing trouble again and Rosa failing to make peace with the family." During this time, she had the following dream:

> *I'm in a garden party. It is at the front part of our house, but it's different. It's the 60s. Everyone is a hippy. I'm wearing a caftan and a headband. I have long blond hair. Mamma Cass was at the party. I'm talking to a young man who is a serious hippy. Several of the people are standing around. Some are in other groups. I start to hear a noise in a distance. It seems like some kid has a playing card taped to his bicycle. It slowly starts to get louder. I see an airborne something. I think about the Doppler effect.[22] I'm aware that this thing is not good. I realize it's something flying. It's a man in a contraption that flies. The man I am talking to says, "Oh, shit, look who it is! It's Mr. Gill Tee." Nothing good happens. Everyone is annoyed that he showed up. We decided that one of the groups would distract him, while the rest of us would try to get rid of him.*

The dreamer feels something ominous coming at her and intellectualizes the problem by considering the physics of her experience and whether the sound or the sight will get to her first. But while there is intellectualization on the manifest level, the Doppler effect also condenses the traumatic experience of hearing about how the members of her family are talking about her and blaming her. Usually with the Doppler effect, the sound changes based on the observer's physical relation to the source of the sound. Now that the dreamer is not seeing her family and she is more distanced from them, the guilt-inducing information about what they are saying sounds different.

The dream also applies intellectualization to the dreamer's guilt. The man in the flying contraption is "Mr. Gill Tee (Mr. Guilty)." He is distanced from the dreamer by being a male, and everyone is annoyed by him. The group will try to get rid of him. The dream shows the dreamer (the group perhaps symbolizing all parts of her) recognizing that someone is guilty and trying to get the guilt to go away.

Undoing

Undoing is an effort to counterbalance an unpleasant affect with a behavior or attitude that will magically erase it. Many religious rituals (confession, penance, etc.) have an aspect of undoing.

As an adult, Freud dreamt:

A hill, on which there was something like an open-air closet: a very long seat with a large hole at the end of it. Its back edge was thickly covered with small heaps of faeces of all sizes and degrees of freshness. There were bushes behind the seat. I micturated on the seat; a long stream of urine washed everything clean; the lumps of faeces came away easily and fell into the opening. It was as though at the end there was still some left.

(1900a, pp. 468–469)

He associates the dream to great acts, such as Gulliver's extinguishing the fire in Lilliput and the cleansing of the Augean stables by Hercules. But we also know that one of the great shaming experiences of Freud's youth was when he urinated on his parents' bed and his father said, "This boy will never amount to anything." In light of this, Freud's dream seems very much a case of undoing: The urination, once a source of shame, is turned into an act of greatness and constructive cleanliness.

Turning aggression against the self

In this defense, the person cannot tolerate feeling aggression toward other people, because of moral or other reasons. She can, instead, defend against her aggression by turning it against herself. This may be a subset of introjection, in which the person cannot bear to deal with the aggression intrinsic in the other person, so he or she feels that the problem comes from the self. McWilliams (2011, p. 113) writes: "Children in destructive families prefer to believe there is something wrong with them (preserving hope that by changing they can improve their lot), than to take in the terrifying fact that they are dependent on negligent or abusive caregivers."

Anna Freud describes a nine-year-old girl who could not tolerate her hatred against her sister and other members of her family. She would break into tears saying, "I'm a total failure. I'm no good, no one loves me. I'm bad." She became her own victim, the victim of her own aggression (Sandler and Freud, 1985, p. 201).

This defense mechanism can turn up in dreams. One of my patients was raised in a strict religious home in which anger was considered sinful. Yet there was much aggression in the home, both against the patient and between other members of the family. She was frequently hit and verbally abused by her mother, and her alcoholic father could be rageful, especially when he was drunk. In her current life, she often became panicked when a situation would arouse her aggression, such as when she discovered that her husband had been having an affair for several years. She tended to deny her own anger, instead attacking herself verbally, such as by saying, "I am so pathetic."

The defense was especially well illustrated by one of her dreams:

Alfred (my husband) and I are in our house, although it seemed different from our house. A grizzly bear is in the neighborhood and it was coming our way. The house wasn't secure enough and I wanted to get out of the house. There is an impending crisis and I am trying to get Alfred to do something. I said, "We have to get into the car." (The car was a small truck that Alfred owned in the 80s.) He said, "Let me be sure that all the candles are out." Suddenly, the bear is there, breaking down the front door. Alfred and the cat are in the truck. The dog and I are in the basement. I am trying to get the dog into the truck. I had to pick her up. She is heavy, but somehow I managed. I picked her up. The bear has come out of the kitchen. The dog and I are under the deck. There is a person on the deck with the bear. The bear is tearing the person apart. I see an arm go flying. I manage to get the dog into the truck. We have to back out of the driveway. The bear is coming. He is carrying just a torso under his arm. There is blood everywhere. The blood splatters on the truck and windshield. I say, "Let's GO!" But he is not going.[23]

The dreamer associates to a story she recently read, about a grizzly bear that attacked a family, killing a girl in her sleeping bag. I suggest to her that the grizzly bear may represent her own anger at Alfred and her wish to tear off his limbs. Yet Alfred is strangely safe in the manifest dream. He is in the truck, and the bear is in the house with her. The dream brings the grizzly's destructiveness closer to her than to Alfred, just as the dreamer often turns her destructive wishes back onto herself. However, the dreamer keeps changing her location; and the bear tears up "the person on the deck."

Splitting

Splitting is dichotomized thinking taken to an extreme. Either something is good or bad; there can be no middle ground. Splitting can be applied to the self or to other people. Splitting of the self was portrayed by Oscar Wilde (1891) in his novel *The Picture of Dorian Gray*, in which a handsome man retains his good looks, while an oil painting of him shows him becoming uglier and uglier, reflecting the evil of his actions.

Splitting of the self in a dream is reported by Fonagy (1989, p. 103):

A man is walking along the street and sees himself coming the other way. But the figure is not really his, it's older, greyer, and very ugly. He slips, and they bump into each other. He feels terrified and says, "Excuse me, it was my fault."

The dream portrays the dreamer in the future, looking in very bad shape, and the dreamer apologizes to himself. Can the dreamer excuse himself for what he has done, or will he do so in the future? Does he feel terror at the rebus interpretation of the dream – having the negative side of himself collide with his better self-image?[24]

Sometimes a dream will portray splitting not of the self but of another person into all good/all bad, all-loving/all-hating, or some other polarity. For example, Martin, a man in his mid-30s, dreamt the following:

I was in the garden of my family's house, standing on the big step of the staircase that leads to my parents' apartment. The garden was in bloom, especially the jasmine which is near that staircase. I was dressed in a lush housecoat – peacock green, made of silk and longer that my height. Laura (my former fiancée) appeared and shared the step with me. She was dressed in an equivalent gown – burgundy red. Suddenly another female person was present and identical to the first one, another Laura. Even if there were two Lauras, I could only see one face at a time. When I was talking with one of them, the other one was facing in a way that I could see her rear – but I had the sensation that the one I could not see, she was Laura, too. They were alternating in dialogue with me, as if they were one person taking different stances. I cannot remember what she – they – told me, but I had the feeling that it was sarcastic and judgmental. Toward the end of the dream I am looking at her – them – from a level below that step and some distance.

There are two Lauras, and Martin cannot see them both simultaneously. That is splitting. He has two images of Laura, past and present – the woman who loved him so much, who pursued him so intently, and whom he rejected; and now, the Laura who does not answer his emails and who seems indifferent to him, and whose love he misses and yearns for. He cannot yet mourn her loss, so he keeps two images of her, the one facing him, and the one who has "turned her back on him."

Here is another example of splitting of the self:

I dreamt I was interviewing someone younger about giving her a job. We had lunch. Then we were in bed. The interview continued. I suddenly emitted a big round shit out of my ass. I caught it with my hand. I acted like she didn't notice, and she seemed not to notice. I said to her that I needed to take a shower. I went into the bathroom. I guess there was another door into the bathroom, and she came in. She was discouraging me from taking a shower, but I insisted. I said she could, too. Then she told me there had been a funny smell about me, all the time. It was even at the restaurant. I put my forearm under her nose and said, "Did it smell like this?" She said, "No." We were then going to go out to dinner.

The dreamer was self-righteous and moralistic, and spoke contemptuously about colleagues who use "the casting couch" to seduce attractive young women. Yet in the dream, he is doing just that. The dream has an obvious rebus: "My shit doesn't stink! Or does it?" When I behave badly, mixing my professional standing and sexual conquest, it doesn't smell, or I wish it didn't. Because even though the woman doesn't smell the obvious shit, she did notice that there is a funny smell about me. My moral hypocrisy cannot be totally hidden, even if I try to hide my obvious shit.

In another case, a patient who was discussing termination showed splitting over the span of two sessions. In the first session, the dreamer told me the dream and then continued speaking only of positive feelings in the dream and positive associations to it. In the next session, the dreamer told me about completely different, very negative feelings in the dream and hostile associations to it. Here is the dream:

> *I had a dream about you Saturday night. It was our last session. I am in a hotel room. You gave me a goodbye present. A nightgown. I was pleased by it a lot. It was more like a housecoat. It had an opening in the front, buttons. Very short sleeves. It was bluish-green. It had little flower patterns, chintz. I took it, said "Thank you, let me try it on." I had lots of clothes to get out of. I tried it on and really liked it. I came out of the room to model it. The front was flying open. The chintz pattern was quite translucent. There was a lot of affection in the room. Feeling very close. I was trying to do everything without doing anything bad. I'm on the bed, on my stomach. You lay next to me, on your back. We are not touching. I looked at your hands, they looked quite small. We compared hands. My fingers were longer than yours. I look over at you and see you have an erection. I can see through the button fly the skin of your penis.*

The dreamer spoke about her affection for me, both tender and erotic. In the next session, she told me that in the dream, the nightgown I gave her was not the kind of thing she would like. She does not like to wear nightgowns at all, and she would not in any case like something made of that cheap fabric and in that style. It was a dream whose content was acted out in the dream interpretation process; in the first session when she told me the dream, her interpretation focused only on the positive aspects of my gift and her feelings. She split off the critical and hostile aspects, as if to say, in the next session:

You are cheap and you don't really know what I want. I act as if it is what I want and I don't show my bad feelings. Perhaps that is the problematic aspect of me that we still must focus on.

Denial

Denial is a defense in which a person handles unpleasant experiences by refusing to accept that they are happening. It is a common defense in the face of hearing very bad news, such as the death of a loved one, to which one responds: "It can't be true; I don't believe it." Some denial is more detailed – an emphatic or unnecessary statement that something is not the case makes us paradoxically aware that it is the case.

Denial is a rather common defense in dreams. People often deny the importance of something in their dreams. Consider the following excerpt from a dream told to one of my supervisees by her patient: "There were lots of people chasing me. They weren't male or female – not black or white – just people." This is a curious dream formation. It draws attention to something by denying it. The dream denies the sex and race of the people chasing the dreamer. In hearing such a dream, I would want to get closer to the dream experience. What do people who are neither men nor women, black nor white, look like? In this case, the dreamer was a black lesbian having an affair with an Hispanic, heterosexually-married woman – so the importance of sex and race were *simultaneously highlighted and eliminated* in the dream. This may have corresponded to a wish that prejudices about race and sexual orientation did not exist.

Here is another example of the attempt to hide a meaning of the dream actually drawing our attention to it, thus creating an attempt at denial and a failure to achieve it. A woman dreamt of being addicted to heroin.[25] She felt the meaning of the dream was that she was addicted to being a heroine, but she didn't consciously want to admit that. She found such wishes for grandeur more embarrassing than a drug addiction would be. And so, in discussing the dream, she mispronounced the word "heroine" with a long "I" sound, as "herro eye n," hoping I would not notice that heroin is a homonym of heroine. Actually, the mispronunciation *directed* my attention exactly to what she consciously hoped I would not notice.

Neurobiology of psychological defense

One of the pathways to our eventually understanding the neurobiology of psychological defenses is to compare particular kinds of brain damage which produce symptoms that are like certain defenses. For example, people who have had a stroke in the right hemisphere sometimes develop anosognosia, the unawareness and denial of illness (Babinski, 1914; Prigatano, 2010). The patient's left arm may be completely paralyzed, yet she may deny it. You can ask her: "Mrs. Smith, how is your left arm today?" "Fine," she replies. "Please lift your left arm, Mrs. Smith." The left arm remains stationary. "Can you lift your left arm?" "I just did it for you," she replies.

Anosognosia may be analogous to denial, and the analysis of the neurobiology of anosognosia may clarify the neurobiology of denial in people without brain injury. Ramachandran (1996) has proposed that people with anosognosia would show an awareness of their symptoms in their dreams that they deny in their waking life. He reports a single case of a woman with anterograde amnesia whose dreams seem to show memory for events that she cannot remember in her waking life. It would be useful to collect much more data on this question. Neurologists would need to ask their patients about dreams more often.

Postscripts on psychological defenses

Heterogeneity of psychological defenses

As I mentioned in note 2 to this chapter, the psychoanalytic literature has often referred to psychological defenses as "ego defenses," but I have substituted the term "psychological defenses." There are a number of problems with the concept of "ego defenses." One is that the defenses are assembled into a single group, when it is not at all clear that they form a unity, either with respect to their purpose or the psychological and neurological means that they use to achieve their purpose. As already noted, defenses change the perception and processing of internal reality and external reality, to avoid anxiety or for some other purpose. But how do they do so? Whether all these transformations are accomplished by a unitary ego (or a unitary part of the mindbrain) seems questionable. For example, it seems unlikely that denial involves the same mindbrain processes as reaction formation. Both might be seen as distortions. But denial involves the outright nullification of something factual, whereas reaction formation is a transformation of one emotion into its opposite.

One of the most thoroughly studied fields involving defensive operations is prejudice (Greenwald and Banaji, 1995) using the Implicit Association Test (IAT). It has been shown by the IAT that individuals who believe themselves not to harbor prejudice unconsciously show such prejudice in their responses to various stimuli. Some deny these feelings, even when faced with objective data, saying, "I have never felt racial prejudice toward any group." Some go much further, masking or transforming their prejudice into its opposite (reaction formation), an expression of special affection for the group toward whom they are prejudiced, as in the "some of my best friends are..." phenomenon.

Somatization is another defense that seems to operate quite differently from other defenses. It involves the transformation of psychological experience into bodily experience. The neural systems required to perform this transformation have yet to be specified, but they clearly are not just involved in expressing knowledge or whether to attribute a characteristic to oneself or another person.[26]

One notes the heterogeneity of psychological defenses especially when trying to account for them neurologically, an endeavor that is still in its infancy (Berlin, 2011), with some notable studies of suppression and repression (Anderson *et al.*, 2004), dissociation (Reinders *et al.*, 2006), and catatonic regression (Northoff *et al.*, 2007). If we are to study defenses neurobiologically, it seems useful to first parse out the psychological transformations involved in each defense. We may also look to localization studies to find the involvement of neurological structures that may help us find commonalities and differences between defenses.

For example, is reaction formation a cortical or limbic process, or both? Is there one process in the mindbrain for generating affect, and another for registering and classifying the affect? Such a model of defenses would fit into the model of consciousness in which the mindbrain registers and intuits its own processes much as it intuits the workings of another person's mindbrain (e.g., Graziano and Kastner, 2011). According to this model, consciousness itself is an approximation of brain activity; it registers a mere subset of the kinds of thinking, perceiving, information processing, and feeling that the mindbrain achieves. This model seems counterintuitive to many people. We assume we know consciously what happens in our own mindbrains better than we know about other people's mindbrains, but that may not be true. As Emily Dickinson (1862, p. 301) wrote: "The Mind is so near itself – it cannot see, distinctly – and I have none to ask" with the implication that others may know about our mental processes *better* than we do.[27]

Our dreams may give us "a second look" at all that is going on in our mindbrains, filling in much of the content that is unavailable to waking consciousness. This separation of mindbrain processes into separate phenomena of generation and experiencing, whether of affect or information, would help account for the operation of many defenses. It would allow for misreading of affect (as in reaction formation), reading no affect when there is affect (as in isolation), registering only good or bad affect when both are present (as in splitting), and other defensive processes involved with affect. It would allow misreading of information, too, reading no information when there is information (repression and denial) or separating related information (dissociation). Many defensive processes, perhaps all, involve combinations of information and affect.[28] To be sure, repression, denial, and dissociation all have an emotional underpinning. To spell this out further, it would help to have further neuropsychoanalytic studies, in which each defense is aligned with its respective neurological processes and phenomenology.

Endopsychic perception and defenses in dreams

In *The Dream Frontier* (Blechner, 2001), I discussed how dreams could involve either endopsychic perception or endoneuropsychic perception. With the term "endopsychic perception," Freud meant that psychopathological symptoms like hallucinations and delusions also have a positive value for researchers, in that they suggest how the human mindbrain is organized and structured. For example, delusions of being watched may be considered a projected "endopsychic perception" of the superego. Freud wrote:

> [Psychotics] have turned away from external reality, but for that very reason they know more about internal, psychical reality and can reveal a number of things to us that would otherwise be inaccessible to us.

We describe one group of these patients as suffering from **delusions of being observed**. They complain to us that perpetually, and down to their most intimate actions, they are being molested by the observation of unknown powers – presumably persons – and that in hallucinations they hear these persons reporting the outcome of their observation: "now he's going to say this, now he's dressing to go out" and so on. Observation of this sort is not yet the same thing as persecution, but it is not far from it; it presupposes that people distrust them, and expect to catch them carrying out forbidden actions for which they would be punished. How would it be if these insane people were right, if in each of us there is present in his ego an agency like this which observes and threatens to punish, and *which in them has merely become sharply divided from their ego and mistakenly displaced into external reality*?

(1933, p. 59, italics mine)

In this fascinating discussion, Freud is suggesting that psychotic delusions can reflect an insight into the organization of the mind. The delusion of being judged is an "endopsychic perception" of the morally judging aspect of the personality; the internal psychic agency, the punitive superego, is perceived as being outside the self. But the delusion itself may be evidence of the existence of the internal agency.

When a dream portrays a psychological defense, it may be another example of endopsychic perception. That is, the dream shows the mindbrain seeing itself, being aware of its own psychological defenses and portraying them, either in a pictorial symbol or in the dream narrative. The dream may register and portray defenses that the person is not aware of in waking consciousness.

I proposed (Blechner, 2001, Chapter 22) that we expand "endopsychic perception" into an area called "endoneuropsychic perception": Certain psychological phenomena may represent an insight into the neurological organization of the mindbrain. We are extending Freud's principle from metapsychology to neuropsychology, a focus that Freud himself originally adopted in the "Project for a Scientific Psychology" and which he would probably not have abandoned had he lived a century later. For example, it is a common experience in dreams that one attempts to move and yet nothing happens. This may be an example of endoneuropsychic perception, an oneiric registration of the fact that during sleep, voluntary muscular movement is for the most part inhibited (Jouvet, 1967, 1969; Brooks and Peever, 2012).[29] Hobson (1988) observed this, but used it as evidence that such dream events are not meaningful. I do not agree; I wish to stress that the connection of the dream experience with the reorganization of the mindbrain during sleep does not invalidate the psychological meaning of the dream. The dream may reflect mindbrain organization, and the dreamwork may still use those correlated mindbrain phenomena as tools to express meaning. Another intriguing possibility is that the dream content can *cause* some of the changes in mindbrain activation.

The psychological defense can be the latent content of the dream, which may function as both endopsychic and endoneuropsychic perception. The dream shows: This is how my mindbrain works; this is how my mindbrain registers the world, blocks out aspects of the world, adjusts and transforms the world, and defends against the world. The "world" is both the external environment and the person's internal world, including emotional and bodily experience.

A patient may not consciously be able to describe his or her primary defenses when the dream can. If the patient can come to appreciate the defense that the dream portrays with a vivid, sensory image, it may never be forgotten.

A note on Bion

Wilfred Bion (1962/1977) proposed that waking thinking involves the transformation of raw sensory data, which he called beta elements, into symbolized thoughts, which he called alpha elements. His theory raises significant questions, parallel to those I am exploring in this book, about the substrate of thought and the place of dreaming in relation to the substrates of thought. Bion referred to alpha function as an "as yet unknown set of mental operations that, together, transform raw sense impressions (beta elements) into elements of experience (alpha elements)" (1962, p. 17) His idea, much debated, seems to me to be a transformation by the mindbrain of sense impressions into more abstract and symbolized material, which becomes what I call "the substrate of thought."

The mental transformations that I have outlined in the first part of this book may comprise some of the operations Bion was expecting to find. However, many of the transformations I have described are not transformations of raw sensory data, but transformations of one set of mental representations (which I would consider alpha elements) into another set of alpha elements.

Whereas Bion talks of psychosis as a failure of symbolization, I and others have noted that in psychosis, the symptoms (including hallucination and delusions) contain symbolization of psychological conflicts.[30] And when the symptoms abate, the symbolization of their symptoms can be incorporated into their dreams (Arieti, 1963; Blechner, 1983; Marcus, 1992; Quinodoz, 1999).

Ogden (2003) has reconsidered Bion's ideas and proposed that some people, even though they report having dreams, may be incapable of what he calls "true dreaming," where "true dreaming" involves alpha elements. Ogden's proposal has led to some chaos, where a clinician who cannot make sense of a patient's dream may take flight in the notion that the dream is not a true dream (e.g., Sands, 2010; Blechner, 2010).

Ogden gives as an example the Borges story "Funes the memorious" (1941/1962) in which a man remembers every detail and is incapable of normal forgetting. In my opinion, Funes is an example of a mnemonist, an individual with an extraordinary memory for detail. Mnemonists highlight the importance in human thinking of forgetting to allow concept formation, illustrated most vividly in nonfiction by Luria (1987) in *The Mind of the Mnemonist*. It would be useful to find out how savants experience falling asleep, what their dreams are like if they can dream at all, and how they remember them (Blechner, 2003).

It would also be useful to discover how savant syndrome is related to a biological operation in sleep known as "synaptic scaling," a process of altering the structure and molecular machinery of synapses (Acsády and Harris, 2017; de Vivo *et al.*, 2017; Diering *et al.*, 2017). Studies suggest that this neurological shrinkage of dendritic spines might be connected with computational processes such as memory consolidation and informational transformation during sleep. Much of our thinking involves selective forgetting and filtering, so that the gist and essence may be seen more clearly. Perhaps in the future it will be possible to study whether the neurological transformations of synaptic scaling have a linkage with thinking processes, the nature of dreams, and the informational transformations described in this book.

Notes

1   Freud's patient who presented with ataxia (problems with balance on walking) was expressing her sense of being off-balance in a social situation. She didn't have a leg to stand on. The image-schema having to do with balance was imaginatively extended to metaphorically express the patient's emotional state. These ways of thinking and symbolizing are so viscerally understandable to us that we hardly even think about them, yet it is with precisely these transformed bodily understandings that we do actually think and reason.

（Barry, 2001, p. 63）

2 In the psychoanalytic literature, psychological defenses were often called "ego defenses." I avoid that terminology for a number of reasons. The term "ego" is vague. When we discuss the neurological basis of defense mechanisms (see p. 172), it becomes apparent that different parts of the mindbrain may be involved in different defenses, and so the global term "ego defense" does not accurately portray the multiplicity of psychological processes involved, nor whether all of them really involve only the ego.

3 Erikson's paper on dreams leads directly to an exploration of how the psychological defenses, analyzed in detail by Anna Freud, may make their appearance in dreams. Yet we know that Anna Freud, who was Erikson's analyst, became hostile to Erikson's work and especially to Erikson's paper on her father's dream (Brenman-Gibson, 1997; Burston, 2007).

4 The best exploration of defense in dreams was published by Goldberger (1989). She did not attempt an exhaustive exploration of the defenses, but showed how some of them can be portrayed in dreams and how the dream defenses can be interpreted. I draw extensively on her excellent work in this chapter.

5 This is the one way that Anna Freud thought defenses could be seen in dreams. She said they could appear in the recounting of the dream, but was doubtful that they could be seen in the dream itself (Sandler and Freud, 1985, p. 85).

6 As will be seen, I have examples of all three methods of defenses operating in dreams for repression. For most of the other defenses, I do not have illustrations of all three methods, but that does not mean that they do not occur.

7 Freud (1915d, p. 147) wrote: "the essence of repression lies simply in turning something away, and keeping it at a distance, from the conscious." McWilliams (2011, p. 127) wrote that repression is "motivated forgetting or ignoring." (The inclusion of "ignoring" makes repression closer to what Sullivan (1953, p. 170) called "selective inattention.")

8 There are certain parallels between the statements of dreamers and those with brain damage. Solms (2000, p. 135) reports a patient G, with an anterior communicating artery subarachnoid hemorrhage, who was asked questions about events for which he had no recollection, G did not say "I cannot

remember anything about that time"; instead he said, "We will have to consult my hospital notes about those events but I am not sure we will find what you are looking for because some of the files seem to be missing."
9 Note that dreams can combine two or more defenses; this dream combines repression, projection, and reversal of roles.
10 This dream is discussed in more detail on p. 53.
11 Pierre Janet defined dissociation as "unconscious compartmentalization of normally integrated mental functions" (Van der Hart and Horst, 1989). Meissner defined dissociation as "temporary but drastic modification of character or sense of personal identity to avoid emotional distress; it involves fugue states and hysterical conversion reactions" (Laughlin, 1970. p. 241). Sullivan (1956, p. 166) wrote:

> To account for the phenomena of dissociation, it was necessary to add to our conceptions that which is related to the personified self in the sense of its contradictory, the not-me, a phase of the organization of experience personal acquaintance with which must be at best (1) marginal, unelaborated observations of particular other people – real or more or less mythological – which show this personal reference by attendant experience of awe, dread, loathing, horror, horror (with arrest of referential process within awareness), or (2) starkly terrifying events in the deeper levels of sleep.

In all these definitions, there is a global alteration in consciousness and functioning. In recent years, more circumscribed areas of separation of mental contents have also been called dissociation, as will be described later in this section in the discussion of moderate dissociation.
12 Brown (2006) suggested that two kinds of dissociation should be differentiated according to process rather than degree and that they be called "detachment" and "compartmentalization."
13 Affect dissociation is closely related, perhaps identical, to isolation of affect. The dissociation of mental contents is also seen in splitting, where two emotions and valuations, good and bad, are separated.
14 It could be argued that this dream illustrates splitting rather than dissociation. Splitting can be a subset of dissociation, in which good and bad feelings are dissociated (compartmentalized).
15 All defenses, as all mental processes, must have a biological underpinning in the mindbrain. This dream portrayed this awareness, with a metaphor of inhibition and connection between various parts of the mindbrain. We will consider the issue of neurobiology and defenses later in this chapter, in a discussion of the connection of the psychology of defenses and certain kinds of brain injuries. There is much to discover in this area.
16 Identification with the aggressor has an overlap with two other psychological processes that may serve defensive purposes: (1) Identification in general, which can also include a positive identification with an admired

person; (2) Displacement, which is "the redirection of a drive, emotion, preoccupation, or behavior from its initial or natural object to another because its original direction is for some reason anxiety ridden" (McWilliams, 2011, p. 139).

17 Note that while Anna Freud doubted that the higher defenses could be seen in the dream content, Sigmund Freud thought they could.
18 "Identification with the victim" was suggested as an additional defense by Orgel (1974). It was illustrated in dreams discussed by Goldberger (1989).
19 I have noted elsewhere (see Chapter 13) the significance of when an analyst makes an interpretation, and the patient, in response to the interpretation, remembers a dream. In those cases, the meaning of the dream may be the analyst's interpretation, although the patient often is not aware of the connection. In this case, I could have spelled it out more:

> I suggested that you feel ambivalence toward me and that your anger might have been due to our missing sessions, which you partially like. You remembered this dream right after I made the comment, so perhaps the meaning of the dream is connected with my comment. In the dream, you don't leave the office, but you can't understand why. Instead of considering that you feel close to me and don't want to leave the office, you suspect that I have locked the door, forcing you to stay. Your wish to be close to another person is "locked in" and you project the source of the lock onto me.

20 A psychoanalyst might also wonder whether the dream portrays a way that the analyst reacted blandly to something that the dreamer thought was a crisis.
21 See p. 270 about the experiment with OTTFF, that shows that intellectual work can be accomplished in dreams, but that the dreamer may not recognize the solution when awake.
22 In physics the Doppler effect changes the pitch of a sound depending on where it is relative to the listener. It is the reason that as an ambulance speeds by, its perceived pitch changes as it passes.
23 This dream is also interesting from the perspective of the time dimension, which was integral to the way Erikson charted dreams. The dream shifts continually from past to present, even within the same sentence. Perhaps this shows a defensive struggle to handle a currently traumatic situation by relegating it to the past, but the defense is unsuccessful. By the end of the dream, when the bear attacks, it is all in the present tense.
24 Splitting of the self is also portrayed in the film *Mia Madre* (Moretti, 2015). In the film, a film director, Margherita, wanders past moviegoers standing in line outside a movie theater and encounters in the line her younger self.
25 This case was mentioned in Chapter 3, on Condensation (p. 28).
26 One theory of somatization is that it is not a transformation, but a retransformation. In this theory, all experience is primarily bodily, and our language

and representational processes derive, in evolution and in development, from our primal bodily experience. Hence, somatization reverses that developmental process, taking our psychological and emotional experiences back to their bodily roots (Barry, 2001).
27 Baumeister *et al.* (1998) have differentiated psychological defenses based on the results of social psychology experiments.
28 There may indeed be no cognition of any kind without affect (Zajonc, 1980; Damasio, 1994).
29 See Blechner (2001, Chapter 22) for other examples of endoneuropsychic perception.
30 Aulagnier (1975/2001) describes the "pictogram" as a pre-language representation of early traumatic interpersonal interactions. While her work is brilliant and useful clinically, she also tends to view the imagistic as early in development, to be superseded by language.

Part II
Working with dreams clinically

Learn the rules so you know how to break them properly.
Dalai Lama, *18 Rules for Living*

Chapter 12

New ways of conceptualizing and working with dreams

The most fundamental change in psychoanalytic thinking about dreams has to do with their place in mental life. Freud thought of dreams as minipathological events that occurred relatively rarely, about once or twice a night, when a wish arose that would disturb sleep. This viewpoint had to be revised when Aserinsky, Dement, and Kleitman discovered that we dream regularly throughout the night, at least every 90 minutes, and much more often than we consciously realize (Aserinsky and Kleitman, 1953; Dement and Kleitman, 1957a, 1957b). Today, we recognize that a dream is a mental event that occurs regularly throughout the night.

Since dreams are such a regular occurrence during the night, it seems less sensible to look for a single cause of dreaming. If we keep asking "Why do we dream?" then we shall have to ask also "Why do we think?" In neither case can we expect a single answer. Both thinking and dreaming are regularly occurring mental activities, both take many different forms, and both probably occur for many reasons.

Freud believed that a dream was instigated when an unacceptable impulse or wish was activated during the night. In order to protect our sleep, censorship processes are activated. The mindbrain disguises the wish, using all the mechanisms of the dreamwork, including condensation, displacement, and pictorial representation.

Was Freud correct that dreams are disguised and censored? I do not think so. We know that disguise occurs in some waking thought, through psychological defenses (A. Freud, 1936; McWilliams, 1994) and security operations (Sullivan, 1953), but we do not assume a high level of disguise and censorship in all waking thoughts. The same may well be true of dreams. There may be more than one process in the instigation and construction of dreams, just as there may be varied processes in the generation of waking thought.

Many of us who work with dreams regularly are surprised by how *undisguised* most dreams are; sometimes they are not disguised at all. There are several sets of data that show this. In my book *The Dream Frontier* (Blechner, 2001), I proposed that before engaging in elaborate processes of interpreting a dream, the analyst instead ask the dreamer, "Have you ever experienced what happened in the dream or something like it?" The phrase "or something like it" is important, since dreams rarely reproduce life experiences without some modification (Fosse *et al.*, 2003; Schwartz, 2003). I had asked dreamers this question for years, and it did not seem to me to be something radical. If you really believed Freud's approach to the dream, such a question would be senseless. You probably would not ask it, and most psychoanalysts did not. But of course if you never asked a patient this question, you might never find out how often the answer yielded something essential to understanding the dream. People who read and reviewed *The Dream Frontier* (e.g., Young-Eisendrath, 2003) singled out that recommendation, saying things like, "I was skeptical, but I tried it, and I was surprised how often that question yielded something significant." The question may not yield something immediately; often, the patient will answer at first, "No, nothing in the dream is like anything I have actually experienced." The thing for the analyst to do in that circumstance is just wait. Sometimes, only after some time has passed – an hour, a day, a week – the dreamer may recall an actual experience that was the source of the dream (Blechner, 2008).

That dreams are not very disguised has been observed by several psychoanalysts (e.g., Schur, 1966; Spanjaard, 1969; Greenberg and Pearlman, 1978; Levenson, 1983; Blechner, 2006). If a dream censor is operating, it is not doing a very good job. In some cases, an interpretation of latent dream thoughts, a leap from surface to depth, may skip the most essential, anxiety-provoking meaning of the dream that is right there on the surface. While psychoanalysis is known as a "depth psychology," psychoanalysts often do their best work looking not *below* the surface, but looking as deeply as possible *at* the surface. As Margaret Millar (1985, p. 216) has written: "Some people become so expert at reading between the lines they don't read the lines."

Freud (1933) said that without the dreamer's associations, you cannot interpret the dream, and some contemporary Freudians adhere to that rule.[1] I have been to psychoanalytic conferences at which a dream was presented. If the dreamer's associations were not available, the psychoanalysts would not consider trying to understand the dream.[2]

This approach to dreams is still taught today. It makes many psychoanalytic students feel terrible pressure, with a kind of performance anxiety. If the patient tells a dream with associations, and the analyst does not come up with the latent dream thought, he may panic and start to avoid working with dreams. Patients pick up this anxiety and may unconsciously learn not to report their dreams.

There are many other ways of working with dreams that do not raise so much anxiety; they allow more collaboration, freedom, and creativity in understanding dreams, and the result will often be more rewarding and insightful. The analyst can, for example, use a dream to indicate significant emotions, defenses, or past experiences of the dreamer, which may lead to an inquiry into an aspect of the dreamer's life not attended to before. The psychoanalyst can also use the patient's dream as supervision, as a way for the psychoanalyst to understand his countertransference and to correct his way of working with the patient (Blechner, 1995).

Vectors of interpretation

Since so many kinds of information about the dreamer are compressed into each dream, the clinician and the dreamer have many choices about which aspect of the dream to consider. I call these "vectors of interpretation." By vectors of interpretation, I mean an approach to looking at a dream from a number of particular perspectives, with each perspective yielding a different kind of information about the dream. Vectors can include an unconscious wish of the dreamer, which is what Freud suggested we find in a dream. Some other possible vectors of interpretation are:

- what is the most prominent issue and the area of greatest conflict for the dreamer at the present time?
- what is the dreamer's personality like?
- what was the dreamer's childhood development like, down to some very specific facts of his or her history?
- what does the dreamer want?
- how does the dreamer experience himself or herself in the physical world?

- how does the dreamer see his or her body?
- how does the dreamer see himself or herself in relation to other people?
- what were some significant traumas in the dreamer's history?
- if the dreamer is in psychoanalytic treatment, what is the nature of the transference and countertransference?
- what are the prominent emotional patterns of the dreamer?

The dream may have many kinds of information about the dreamer condensed in the dream. Depending on the question you ask, you will discover different information about the dreamer.

Are associations necessary for dream interpretation?

A major modification in contemporary psychoanalytic work with dreams is that we do not need the dreamer's associations to understand most dreams. This is not just a theoretical assertion; we can show it empirically. When I teach a course on dreams, I always start by having the students present a dream – either a patient's dream or the student's own dream – without any of the dreamer's associations, in fact, without any information about the dreamer at all, except for the manifest dream. I then ask the students to think freely about the possible meaning of the dream. Usually, within ten or 15 minutes of this exercise, the meaning of the dream has become apparent. Only then do we consider the dreamer's associations. Occasionally, the associations may clarify one or two details, but usually they do not significantly alter the meaning of the dream that had already been proposed.

I strongly recommend that students learning about dreams have experience considering a dream without the dreamer's associations. It allows them to learn for themselves how much information is encoded in the manifest content itself. One could even argue that in some cases, knowing the dreamer's associations, as well as biographical facts about the dreamer, interferes with optimal understanding of a dream. One often observes in clinical conferences that the dream is used to confirm or tie into facts already known about the dreamer. This may feel satisfying, but it may divert one from learning things about the dreamer that are new and fresh.

This was noted by Jung. Free associations, Jung believed,

> always lead to a complex, but we can never be certain whether it is precisely this one that constitutes the meaning of the dream.... We can, of course, always get to our complexes somehow, for they are the attraction that draws everything to itself.
>
> (Jacobi, 1973, p. 84)

Jung felt that Freud's procedure of relying primarily on the patient's associations led to a *reduction* of the dream. We will get to a reflection of the patient's complexes, but that is not the most essential meaning of the dream.

Secondary and tertiary revision

Freud introduced the concept of secondary revision to address the process by which we fill in gaps in the dream narrative to have it be more coherent and make more sense. Secondary revision can be like waking confabulation in psychotic and neurologically damaged patients (Blechner, 2007b). The patient makes up material to fill in the gaps.

Sometimes Freud thought that secondary revision is only a kind of patchwork; it fills in the holes in the narrative structure, cleaning it up and making it more coherent. At other times he thought that *most* of the narrative structure of the dream came from secondary revision. If we see dream meaning as something that is constantly evolving, we can combine both of Freud's views about secondary revision. Part of the complexity of secondary revision is that it is not a one-time process. Secondary revision may go on as a sub-process of dream formation, and it can continue after the dream experience. Each time we recollect or tell a dream, there is more secondary revision. Freud was aware of this tendency to alter dreams with each telling and argued that when a dream is told twice, the altered sections are especially important areas of repression and may be key to the interpretation.

The process of dream revision does not stop with the dreamer. When we tell our dream to a psychoanalyst or any other person, that person also will revise the dream as he or she recalls it or tells it. When such revision is done by someone other than the dreamer, I call it "tertiary revision."

Secondary and tertiary revision are not fundamentally different processes, but whereas secondary revision involves an intrapsychic elaboration of the dream, tertiary revision is more interpersonal. The process of dream revision does not stop even with tertiary revision. Dreams can continually be told and retold to as many people as will listen. One theory of myth formation is that myths start with one person's dream. As the dream is retold by one person to the next, it changes, as in the child's game of "telephone." With each successive telling, a few idiosyncratic and personal details are stripped away, and the core elements that are relevant to the larger group are retained or amplified. In the end, we have a revised dream story that functions as a parable for all the members of a society.

Psychoanalysis cuts off its right arm

In 1967, the members of the Kris Study Group on dreams, led by Charles Brenner at the New York Psychoanalytic Institute, published a monograph entitled *The Place of the Dream in Clinical Psychoanalysis*. They came to the conclusion that dreams have no special significance in clinical psychoanalysis (Waldhorn, 1967). They felt that the psychodynamics that can be understood from dream analysis can also be understood from analysis of a patient's free associations. When Freud wrote *The Interpretation of Dreams*, he had not yet discovered the basic technique of free association, and much of Freud's self-analysis was devoted to the analysis of his own dreams. But, they argued, today's analysts who understand how to use free association have no special need of dream analysis.

When one reads the monograph, one is shocked not just by the wrongness of the reasoning, but by the terrible work done with dreams. The idea that the way to work with dreams is by getting associations to them has taken a bizarre turn and has come to serve the defensiveness of the analyst, allowing the analyst to remain distanced from the primary experience of the dream. For example, a woman reports (Waldhorn, 1967, p. 61):

> *I had a very bad dream. I had a cancer of the breast. A doctor, a woman, said it would have to be removed. She said that there would be aftereffects which I would feel in my neck. My friend R. had this operation. I was scared and I panicked, and I wondered how I could get away, run away, and not have to have this done.*

She went back to sleep and continued to dream:

> *It was at my sister's wedding. All our relatives were seated in rows of chairs. My aunt was there. There was a big cupboard filled with watches and chains or something like that. She had received it from my uncle. There were watches and rings and jewels repeated in rows and rows. Hundreds of them. She took one out and showed it around to everyone, and told them how expensive it was. My uncle said it was not so expensive, but she went on exaggerating what it cost, exaggerating its value. There were aunts and uncles I do not like, that I am sort of ashamed of. They are my mother's family and I didn't like my friends to see them. My sister was supposed to go away, and the next day she would come back. Then there was a drawing done by my friend N. and then I can't remember.*

The analyst says first, "About your dream: What do you associate to the business about the doctor?" It is hard to imagine a more distant, emotionally isolated response to the patient's dream.[3] It captures the core problem: the analyst is keeping himself disconnected from the dream's emotion, which is so intense – terror of bodily damage. This example shows the importance of a basic principle of working with dreams: the analyst must first and foremost register the primary emotion of the dream and must be sure that the patient also feels the emotion of the dream. This is the essence of the way Robert Bosnak (2003) works with dreams. He focuses primarily on the three or four primary affects in the dream and takes the patient back into the dream to reexperience them and integrate them. Even if one does not work like Bosnak, one should make contact with the dreamer's emotion. Who among us would not be terrified by cancer and by disfiguring surgeries (which in 1967, in the era of radical mastectomies, were much more damaging than such surgeries usually are today)?

The second principle essential to clinical work with dreams is that one should consider the dream's implication for the transference and countertransference (Blechner, 1995) (but only after making connection with the main emotions of the dream). How might this dream refer to the treatment? Is the patient terrified about the experience of the analysis and its aftereffects? Will it be terribly painful, and might she end up disfigured by the analysis, with pains in her neck?

The analyst instead focuses on aspects of the patient's conscious experience of awkwardness. This is not wrong; she does feel awkward. But it avoids the primary emotion of terror expressed in the dream. If the analyst relates everything in the dream to what the patient already knows, the analyst will not learn anything new from the dream. And then one will conclude that there is nothing special to learn from the dream. On the contrary, if the analyst stays close to the experience of the dream and is eager to find what the dream communicates that is new, then the dream will be invaluable to psychotherapy.

The attitude toward dreams, expressed in the report of the Kris Study Group, is generally one of fitting the dream into what one already knows about the patient, rather than looking to the dream to find out something about the patient that you do not already know. We can see this problem in an article written by Brenner (1969) following up on the main themes of the Kris Study Group. Brenner presents material from one of his own patients, who dreams:

He was on a toboggan, rushing swiftly downhill on an icy slide. At first the ride was exciting and enjoyable. Soon, however, he grew frightened. He was going too fast. An accident seemed inevitable. He did not awaken, but the dream, or his memory of it, ended.

Brenner fits the dream into what he knows about the patient: disowned homosexual and feminine feelings, which the patient has fought against counterphobically with extreme athletic pursuits. This is not wrong, but it is distanced from the immediate affect and the communication about the analysis: "This has been exciting and enjoyable, but now we are going too fast, and I am frightened. If we don't slow down, there will be a crash." This is a new and immediate communication. It does not require associations, and it does not require interpretation. If we apply the *Jeopardy!* approach to this dream, the question is: How is the analysis feeling to you? And the answer is the dream itself: Out of control and terrified of disaster.

The report of the Kris Study Group sent a shudder through the psychoanalytic world that can still be felt. Psychoanalytic training institutes cut back the amount of teaching on dreams. In 2013, Otto Kernberg was invited to comment on the White Institute's curriculum. He accepted, and one of his comments was, "You have two courses on dreams. Why is that?"

When I attended conferences of the Association for the Study of Dreams, I was one of the only psychoanalysts there. Psychoanalysts were distanced from dreams, and scholars of dreaming were distanced from psychoanalysis.

In 2017, I was invited to participate in a discussion group about dreams at the annual conference of the American Psychoanalytic Association. It was the first such meeting about dreams in many years. This hiatus was a tragic sign. Psychoanalysis, which started the modern study of dreams, had cut off its right arm.

It was an error. The belief of the Kris Study Group, that you cannot get anything from the dream that cannot be gotten from free association, can be disproven. One source of significant data comes from examples of "second analysis" or "reanalysis" (Wagner, 1963; Szalita, 1968, 1982), in which a person has had an extensive treatment but then seeks further analysis from a different analyst. For example, a man came to me for a consultation. He had previously been in what sounded like a very good treatment. The first analysis was extensive and conducted by a well-trained and respected analyst. The analysis reached what seemed like a good termination, yet the patient came to me for further treatment. I asked, "It sounds like your analyst was good. Why are you not returning to him for further treatment?" His response was vague. In the next session, the patient reported a dream, in which he is at a restaurant and goes into the bathroom. He dives into the toilet and is swimming around. The water is very clear, but there are turds floating in it. I thought of water being a symbol of sexuality. The separation of its purity and defilement led me to ask the patient: Is there something secret or embarrassing to you about your sex life? He looked startled, then responded that he had been doing something sexually since his adolescence that made him deeply ashamed. He had never discussed it in his previous treatment (for more than a decade) and might not have done so with me, had I not picked up the clues from his dream.

In another example, a woman seeking reanalysis reported a dream in which a body part appeared defective and she tried to cover it over. It led me to inquire about body dysmorphic disorder, which turned out to be a major concern, which she found distasteful and embarrassing to discuss, but which, fortunately, was indicated by her dream.

In the 1967 monograph on dreams, which concluded that dreams do not bring to analysis anything that could not be discovered through free association, there are several examples of dreams in reanalysis that bring up issues never before raised in treatment. One of them ("Clinical Illustration VI," p. 77) is the case of a woman who has been in multiple treatments, always finding the analyst inadequate and leaving treatment. In her previous analysis, some questions came up which she refused to answer, leading her to fire that analyst, too. She has also had a number of boyfriends whom she has summarily dismissed, and divorced her first husband after just a few months. In her latest analysis, she has the following dream:

> *I am walking with another woman on a street like Park Avenue. We pass a hotel (near the analyst's office) where there is an outdoor café. A woman is seated at the table and beckons us to come sit down and join her. I don't want to, but my companion prevails on me. I have absolutely no money. Everybody says it doesn't matter. I don't really care, either. The woman orders dinner for us. This will cost us a quarter each, which I don't have. I throw a nickel down on the table. The seated woman looks at me pityingly and then I feel her knee and leg pressing against mine (long pause, great effort). I know she is inviting me to have a Lesbian affair with her. She says she will pay for me, but that is her price.*

In a patient who has been secretive with all her analysts, who has had constantly tumultuous relations with men, and who has abruptly ended treatments when something unspeakable seemed to be emerging, this dream seems quite a breakthrough. The patient had avoided speaking about lesbianism in many treatments, yet her dream brings the issue into focus. The lesbian seductress is the other woman in the dream, but as Jung showed us, from the subjective point of view, everyone in the dream is an aspect of the dreamer, so the woman with lesbian feelings is also the dreamer. The analyst asks the dreamer, "What is it about lesbianism that makes you uncomfortable?" She replies that she has extreme aversion, yet she starts to speak about which women appeal to her and then says: "This dream feels very queer." She bursts into tears, for the first time in the treatment (Waldhorn, 1967, pp. 77–78).

Through tendentious reasoning, the discussion of the Kris Study Group dismissed the special significance of the dream, although Leonard Altman disagreed:

Analytic material communicated in dreams has a greater impact on the patient than material with similar latent content arrived at from the analysis of other communications or behavior ... in certain patients the topographic regression in dreams gives access to psychic contents not available in any other way.

(Waldhorn, 1967, pp. 79–80)

Altman's view applies to this clinical example; the woman's dream has allowed the emergence of an issue that seems not to have been addressed with her many previous analysts.

The theory that all unconscious issues can be arrived at via the patient's free associations did not hold up in these examples. The patients brought up issues in their dreams that had not emerged in their free associations in their current or previous analyses or at least had not been registered by their analysts. The data show that dreams are enormously valuable in communicating things that cannot be communicated otherwise. The dream is, as Freud said (1900a, p. 608), "the royal road to a knowledge of the unconscious activities of the mind"; it is also sometimes the only road to aspects of psychopathology that the patient cannot or will not speak about.

Shame is like a giant vault. Its thick walls keep our secrets hidden, and we do everything in our power to bar others from seeing what we have hidden there. Analysts can spend years trying to peek into another person's cache of shame. For many people, the quickest and most effective pathway into that vault is through their dreams.

Notes

1 In 1933, in the *New Introductory Lectures on Psychoanalysis*, more than three decades after he published the *Interpretation of Dreams*, Freud continued to assert that dream interpretation requires the dreamer's associations. And some psychoanalysts, loyal to Freud, have persisted in this point of view.

2 Erikson pointed out the duality between how many analysts work with the manifest content directly, while trying to adhere to Freud's doctrine:

Unofficially, we often interpret dreams entirely or in parts on the basis of their manifest appearance. Officially, we hurry at every confrontation with a dream to crack its manifest appearance as if it were a useless shell and ... discard this shell in favor of what seems to be the more worthwhile core.

(1954, p. 17)

3 This case has been critically reconsidered by Greenson (1970).

Chapter 13

The dream guides its own analysis
How to work with dreams over time

> The Dream is a law to itself; and as well quarrel with a rainbow for showing, or for not showing, a secondary arch.... The Dream knows best, and the Dream, I say again, is the responsible party.
> Thomas De Quincey, *Confessions of an English Opium-Eater*

Reading textbooks on dream interpretation, one can have the impression that psychoanalytic dream interpretation is a circumscribed process. The patient tells the dream, the patient associates to the dream, and an interpretation is developed by the analyst and patient. In actual clinical practice, however, dream interpretation is usually not so neat and circumscribed. Dream interpretations evolve, sometimes over the length of an entire analysis. And actions are as important as words. The patient may reveal meanings of the dream nonverbally, such as small gestures or tics, or grander, dramatic behaviors that extend over time (Schimel, 1969; Levenson, 1983; Joseph, 1985; Blechner, 1995).

Most dreams have a huge amount of material condensed in them, including the primary psychological concerns of the dreamer, facts of the dreamer's life history, and feelings of the dreamer toward other people. To understand and discuss all these aspects of every dream would be very time-consuming and not realistically possible. The clinician, with the dreamer's collaboration, must use judgment about what in the dream is most emotionally salient for the dreamer and also what in the dream is most new.

An exhaustive analysis of a dream is very useful as an exercise for training the psychotherapist. But in day-to-day practice, work with dreams is quite different. I will present some examples of dream interpretation as it is carried out in psychotherapy.

In the first example, I will contrast an academic, exhaustive analysis of a dream, and then I will contrast it with what I actually did with the dream. I will first analyze each element of the dream for at least one or two meanings. I will then go on to explain what actually happened with the dream, what I said to the patient about his dream, and what followed in the interaction between us.

Jim's dream – focus on emotional expression

Jim was a man who began psychoanalysis in his early 30s because of compulsive voyeurism.[1] His wife was pregnant with their first child, and he said he did not want his future child to grow up with a father who was a voyeur. I told him that I was not sure whether psychoanalysis could help him stop being a voyeur. He had already been in a four-times-a-week treatment that had not helped him. I told him that analysis might make clearer why he was a voyeur, what was appealing to him about it, and perhaps why other patterns of sexuality were not so compelling to him.

I also told him that analysis might help him with other problems. His mother had died recently, and on her deathbed had confided to Jim's mother-in-law that she had been having a long-term affair with Sam, a waiter at a vacation resort. Jim had long suspected the affair, but his mother had denied it. I told him that analysis might sort through his feelings about his mother and their effect on his current life. I also told him that analysis might help him with his career, which was going well but seemed to be limited by his personality issues.

An important fact of Jim's history is that when he was three, his father underwent an experimental brain surgery that he survived, but which left him essentially immobile for the rest of his life.

Jim had the following dream:

> *I'm in a hotel in Phoenix. I'm looking out the window at a parking lot. It's my car. Someone does something with one car and a bunch of them get rolling, including mine. It gets smashed in the front. I think, "Oh no, not again." I call down to the lobby. A woman answers. I yell, "One of your fucking guys just ruined my car." She is perturbed at my language. She says, "How do I know it was one of my guys?" There is a guy my age, talking about how much they will*

give me to fix my car. They ask me, do I want to get it all fixed? I want my car all fixed.

I will go through the elements of the dream and their significance. I wish to be clear that I did not tell Jim all these potential meanings of his dream, but I do so here, to illustrate how a single dream captures so much of the dreamer's current concerns, his history, and his hopes and wishes for the future:

I'm in a hotel in Phoenix.

Jim had been planning to eventually leave New York and move to a location in the U.S. that was more conducive to bringing up children. He was considering mostly small to midsize cities, one of which was Phoenix. The phoenix is also a mythological creature which used to burn up and then recreate itself. This was symbolic of Jim's wish to recreate himself.

I'm looking out the window at a parking lot.

A lot of Jim's voyeurism was done using cameras and long-distance lenses to watch people out of his window. New York provided ample opportunity for this technique of voyeurism, with its high-rise buildings with multiple windows. He was afraid that when he moved to a smaller town, he would not have comparable opportunities for voyeurism; the view out of his window might be just a parking lot, instead of other buildings. Also, in the dream, he hardly moves. This immobility is in part an identification with his disabled father.

It's my car.

A car is symbolic of a vehicle that allows us to get somewhere. "It's my car" means "it's my mobility" referring to several kinds of mobility:

1 Social mobility: Jim was ambitious, seeking upward mobility; his mother had been a professional, but her lover had been working-class.
2 Physical mobility: his father's immobility frightened him; also, a beloved relative had died of a heart attack after physical exertion, so Jim avoided most exercise.

3   Sexual mobility: how much could he physically go after a woman versus staying immobile and watching from his window? Also, there is the childhood joke, about a man asking a woman, "Can I park my car in your parking lot?" Jim was fond of jokes, especially those connected with sex and genital integrity. The car, as symbol of the penis, indicates that he has anxieties about his genitals and the dangers of female violence.

Someone does something with one car and a bunch of them get rolling, including mine. It gets smashed in the front.

Translation: When my sexuality or my life in general get rolling, I fear physical damage. When Jim was a child, he was pestering his mother. She threw a pair of scissors at him, which pierced his flesh and stayed stuck in his leg until it was removed. When recalling this trauma, he would feel actual pain in his leg. Is "smashed in front" a reference to this incident, and his general concern with genital damage or other bodily injury?

I think, "Oh no, not again."

He has been through bodily damage before, and he fears its repetition.

I call down to the lobby.

A lobby is an entryway, also a symbol for the entryway to the woman (Freud, 1900a). Jim calls down to it, but does not go there; this is similar to his voyeurism. He deals with women from afar, but fears interacting with them in person. The "call" also refers to an actual telephone call. He had recently identified the name of his favorite woman to watch, found her telephone number, and called her. By doing so, and by his voyeuristic looking, he could both approach the woman and stay safe from her.

A woman answers.

The woman may be a conglomerate of his mother, his wife, and the women that he watches.

> *I yell, "One of your fucking guys just ruined my car."*

"Fucking guys" (note the plural) may refer to Sam, the lover who fucked his mother. What was Sam's effect on Jim's car, that is, his life, his sexuality, and his mobility?

> *She is perturbed at my language.*

Jim's mother was a language expert. His own speech alternated between sophisticated English, which he learned from his mother, and a conglomerate of different kinds of bad English. The woman on the phone will be perturbed by the way he talks. "Perturbed" is a sophisticated word that can mean (1) to cause to be upset; or (2) to be aroused emotionally. Perhaps the second meaning of perturbed is also implied, since his mother had such passion for her working-class lover.

> *She says, "How do I know it was one of my guys?"*

Mother, with this sentence, is admitting in the dream that she had more than one guy, acknowledging the affair with Sam. Which of her guys, husband or lover, has damaged Jim's ability to live?

> *There is a guy my age, talking about how much they will give me to fix my car.*

Jim and the psychoanalyst were close in age. Money issues were prominent in the analysis. His character changes allowed him to make more money, so the analysis was financially costly but also rewarding. Jim is also concerned with how he will use or save his inheritance from his mother.

> *They ask me, do I want to get it all fixed? I want my car all fixed.*

What does Jim want from his analysis? To have everything all fixed? Yes.

I did not choose to interpret all these aspects of the dream. Some of the themes were already well established in the treatment. I wanted to focus on what was *new* in the dream and also the core emotions. I noted how much Jim wants himself all fixed. I also noted that he is much more assertive and angry in the dream than he has allowed himself to be in person with me. This unleashed much emotion. Jim spoke about how much the analysis cost him; he was concerned that it would cost as much as a new car, which he wanted. He said, "I coulda had a Taurus!" (A Taurus, besides being a brand of popular car, is a bull, symbol of animal power and determination.) In the end, would the analysis seem worth it?

The dream was at least in part about his anger and how he dealt with it. After being so pushy and assertive with the woman in the dream, he was able to be much more forceful with me. This, in itself, was therapeutic. His voyeurism expressed anger and aggression toward the women he watched, yet they rarely knew they were the object of his aggression. As he was able to integrate and use his aggression in a productive way, his career and life improved dramatically.

Wayne's dream – analyzed over nine years

In some treatments, a single dream will be constantly reexamined and reunderstood throughout the treatment. Sometimes, new parts of the dream are revealed long after the first telling of the dream. The case of Wayne, a gay man who was in psychoanalysis for nine years, illustrates this phenomenon vividly.

Wayne told me a dream early in his analysis:

> *I recall seeing two brightly colored roosters in the road, walking in tandem. They seemed to be moving in a certain determined synchronicity. Then I looked again, and rather than roosters were these figures crossing the road. It took me a while to conclude that they were indeed human, although severely deformed. They were short – perhaps half the size of "normal" humans – and very, very thin. Emaciated – almost like a Giacometti but smooth, skin-colored. They were accompanied by humans, I believe, of normal proportions. They were severely impaired, and had great difficulty walking. Their legs were relatively long, but they didn't seem to take them very far. I can't recall whether they needed help crossing the road – perhaps they were being supported by the "humans." They also were both male, I believe, and looked like each other – maybe brothers. I don't know if they were adult or not. They were tragic to look at.*

The other element was that they had large, webbed feet, which were shocking and disturbing. I wondered what made them so deformed. It was these feet that made it so difficult for them to walk.

It was painful to look at them. Finally, ultimately, with the help of their accompaniers I believe, they did make it to the other side of the street, at which point they entered into an open restaurant/bar. Again, they had great difficulty moving forward – I recall at one point one or both of them had to hold onto the mantle of a fireplace, a carved mahogany mantle like I had in my old apartment. At one point, one of them was holding on to it, to help him walk. But at the same time, or just after, he slid his hand across the top of the mantle, like he just wanted to touch it but didn't need it to hold onto – it was a gesture that I thought was strange, like it didn't fit in with the rest of it.

The dream, as first told to me, captured something essential about Wayne. He had worked in a high-powered business. He was a superstar at a young age and was given enormous responsibility. But he privately was terrified of the aggressive confrontations that he needed to address in his work. His business partners had no idea of his anxieties at first, but suddenly he had a breakdown, completely withdrew from his job, got a leave of several months, and never returned. It was like in the dream; he went suddenly from being a cocky rooster strutting his stuff to being a broken-down cripple. When he came to see me, he had embarked on a new career, which he thought would evade his problems with aggression. It did not, and our work zeroed in on those problems.

His developmental history was also reflected in the dream. There was a mutual idealization between him and his father. But his father, who was placid most of the time, beat him very harshly on two occasions. He had felt knocked down and damaged by these violent attacks, yet at other times he felt admired, even envied, by his father. These two versions of himself, the cocky, admired self and the beaten-down, crippled self were both represented in the dream.

The dream seemed to capture his core issues and we often referred to it during the subsequent years of analysis, constantly revising our view of it. Then, after nine years of analysis, we seemed to be almost done. He raised the issue of termination. I was unsure we were done, but I said, "Let's set a date a few months from now and see. But be sure, during that time, to bring up anything that occurs to you that you might have left out."

Wayne came to a subsequent session and said, "I was going through my papers, and I came across some notes that I made to myself during our first week of analysis. Would you be interested in looking at them?" He handed me five sheets of paper, typed in single space. It included the text of his first dream, and I thought it would be interesting to compare it to my records. Actually, his text and mine were quite similar. But as I read it, it turned out that in his diary, there were two parts of the dream that he had completely omitted in the first telling of it to me.

In his recorded version of the dream, it ended:

Then, he [the rooster] pulled up his zipper, which he noticed was down – and seemed to do this all by himself. I was surprised that he could do this without much problem – it seemed in contrast to how crippled he seemed otherwise.

Wayne left out this ending, which was optimistic and also showed how he turned out in the end to be less crippled than he originally appeared. He also had left out an earlier part of the dream:

In what I believe was a slightly earlier part of the dream, I was in the lobby of an apartment building, on line for something. Suddenly A. appeared – a woman with whom I had been close friends during my first big summer job, but then lost complete contact with over the five years I was at the big company. Neither one of us kept up the friendship. She had a very little dog with her. I remember wondering for a moment if she was black, since she looked dark-skinned to me. But somehow that struck me as incorrect.

I remember introducing her to my fiancée, a pregnant woman who was with me. A. was confused and congratulated the woman and the other man who was with us. I don't know who he was – but I was thinking he is gay. I also was ashamed – I wanted her to know that it was I who was marrying a woman and going to be a father. I said, "No, it's me!" But I wondered what she thought of what I was telling her – that I was going to be with a woman. I remember thinking she might judge me. She congratulated me and didn't seem ridiculing. But I still thought, what does she really think of me? It wasn't clear whether I was gay, or what my relationship with this pregnant woman was.

Note that this additional segment reveals a dramatic episode in which he is trying to mislead the woman from thinking he is gay. He is unsure of whether his ruse is succeeding. This parallels a frequent issue that came up during the treatment – he often adjusted his self-presentation to control the other person; altering his identity is some way to create an impression on the other person. Some of these deceptions were obviously untrue, but people did not always question them. He was more conscious of this strategy early in treatment than I realized. He wrote in his private notes: "I am competitive with Mark. I withhold information from Mark in order to control him. I want to decide what he thinks and feels. I want things my way, and I'll do anything to get it." His showing me these notes at the end of treatment may have signified that he had less need to try to manipulate me secretly.

The new "beginning" of the dream changed my view of the dream as a whole. It raised the issue for him: "How is my managing of what that woman thinks about my sexuality interacting with my sense of wholeness?" When he told his mother that he was gay, she "took it personally"; she felt it as a personal rejection. This left him with a degraded sense of two men together (crippled roosters).

The dream with two sections, as Freud (1900a) described, can have an if/then structure, with the two halves of the dream functioning as dependent clauses to one another. In other words, one underlying meaning of the dream could be:

> *Because I hurt my mother with the news that I was gay, I will try to deceive people about it. But the result of this deception is that I feel crippled. I need to "cross the street," find my own place in the world (my own apartment of which I was so proud), and thus regain my sense of wholeness and potency.*

Ralph's dreams at the start and end of psychoanalysis – change and continuity

It is interesting to compare dreams from the same patient at the beginning and end of treatment. How do the psychological changes during psychoanalysis show up in dreams? To what degree are the basic psychological issues retained throughout life? How much do the issues change, and how much is the change in how the person deals with those issues (Glover, 1955; Alexander, 1961; Saul, 1972; Blechner, 1983; Warner, 1983)?

The following case vignette shows the relationship between a dream that is reported at the beginning of treatment, and a dream many years later, when the treatment was close to its end.

When Ralph started treatment in his early 30s, he was very depressed and cautious. Yet he was also using cocaine, which was the only thing before beginning treatment that relieved his depression. He had had a repetitive dream, in which he was driving a car that was going extremely fast, and was about to crash into a concrete wall. At the time, he was suicidal and panicky. His life felt out of control. The dream showed how he felt quite plainly, although the dream used the common metaphor described by Lakoff and Johnson (1980): "life is a journey." In this dream, life is a car that is out of control and about to crash.

After many years of treatment, Ralph had the following dream:

> *I was driving at night somewhere in the suburbs, Westchester or Long Island. I was coming down an incline toward a traffic light. On the left, a policeman was standing there. The brake pedal went to the floor. I ran through the light. The cop was bug-eyed, and yelled, "Hey, what are you doing?" Later on, I attempted to stop and the brake worked fine. I kept going.*

He commented about the dream:

> I had done something risky, not something I chose to do. The cop was on foot, and couldn't chase me. It reminds me of my old repetitive dream, where I am driving at very high speed and hit a concrete wall.
>
> There was an article in the newspaper about an executive who was on a plane at LaGuardia Airport. There was ice on the runway. The plane started to skid. He thought he would die. But he didn't. Now he takes more care to monitor things. I thought I was going to die. A sense of inevitability.
>
> Also, I was reading a novel, *Canada*, by Richard Ford. A 15-year-old boy is in Montana because his father is in the Air Force. His parents were mismatched. They got married because the mother was pregnant. Things end badly for the parents. They rob a bank.

Years later, the same themes are there as in the original repetitive dream – driving a car, the dangers of it, trouble – but there are important differences. The car still loses control, but Ralph doesn't crash. He goes through the light, stays calm, perseveres, and then he regains control.

The policeman (his superego?) protests, but doesn't stop him. He used to be paralyzed by guilt, but now he hears the extreme superego protestations (of the "bug-eyed cop") and still can "move on." Getting someone pregnant, leading to disaster, which is the theme of the novel, has not happened to him, but it was always a significant fear for him.

One can see by comparing the two dreams how analysis can help someone: the basic psychological issues may remain but the patient can learn how to know them and master them. A punitive superego can be transformed into one that is less destructive and punishing. An ego can be strengthened to face the same basic problems with more calm and assurance, so that there is a good outcome when there are crises. These psychic changes are portrayed by the dreams.

Kevin's dream – nonverbal associations

Freud believed that we should hear the patient's associations to his dream to help us understand the latent meaning. Sometimes, it is not the patient's words that clarify a dream, but his nonverbal actions, as in the following two examples of Kevin and Fred:

> A patient, Kevin, came to see me for consultation.[2] He was severely depressed and was also lost in his career and personal life. He was refined, cultured, and mild-mannered, and showed a lively intellect despite his depression. We agreed to begin psychoanalysis.

The consultation was my last session of the day. After Kevin left, I straightened things out on my desk and walked out of my office into the waiting room. I suddenly thought, "Kevin is hiding in the utility closet, and as soon as I walk past it, he will spring out and hit me over the head with a baseball bat." This seemed a bizarre thought, but I could not shake it. Carefully, I opened the door of the utility closet. He was not there. I thought of what Kernberg (1975) calls "micro-paranoid reactions." (Theoretical concepts can soothe us in difficult clinical times.) I thought about how strong my reaction was, and I wondered about the details of it. Kevin had not mentioned any interest in baseball during the session, and it is not a particular interest of mine. My own thought was that beating people with bats was something that street kids do. They are too young to get guns (times have changed since then) and so they use what is available. Kevin's intellect was extremely well developed, but I wondered if my fantasy was a way of registering that he had another side to him, a violent, anti-intellectual side that reveled in physical violence or at least the idea of it. Also, since in the fantasy he was smashing me over the *head*, he would be destroying my brains. I wondered if this was also a projection of hating his own brains, because they were so highly cathected at the expense of his other bodily needs.

As the analysis progressed, my seizure of fear, as I tend to think of it, turned out to be meaningful. Kevin, who had seemed so civilized, expressed the most violent reactions during his sessions. When he told me that he wanted to stretch out his arm, make a fist, and swing it like a bat right into my mouth and smash in my teeth, I was quickly reminded of my fantasy after the first session of his hitting me with a baseball bat. Was there telepathy? There certainly was a very striking similarity between my fantasy and his.

As the analysis progressed, he felt stronger and able to pursue his professional goals. He applied to graduate school programs. We looked at his anxieties about interviews and examined some of the concrete ways that he had sabotaged himself in the past. With all this concrete work, he also would take a magical approach: He said, "If I can just get into my first-choice program, I will never want anything again."

This became a repetitive pattern. He would take this oath at each professional milestone – doing his dissertation, having his doctorate awarded, getting a good post-doctoral position, getting a regular job. I interpreted to him that he felt that his desire for professional success was unseemly, that it felt greedy to him, and so he would take these oaths to undo the guilt about his greed and to put a limit on it. He steadily progressed to a prestigious position within his field. At each landmark, he would make a similar bargain, which we analyzed in many different ways, such as a reassurance and protection against the envy of his mother for his strength and "masculine" achievement.

Around the time of his acceptance into graduate school, Kevin had a strange, brief dream. In it, he saw the words "Prestyl Dolby."[3] I thought of Dolby noise-reduction systems, but that didn't seem right to him. Ultimately, his associations led to the phrase, "Press the till; dough'll be yours." This connected with earlier dreams of gambling machines that could yield rich monetary rewards. We connected the dream to his having achieved some of his professional goals, with the hope of eventual financial rewards. He thought there might be more to the dream, but could not specify what.

A few years later, he was awarded his doctorate. Almost immediately after this achievement, he noticed some sores in his mouth and a coating on his tongue. He was convinced he had AIDS. This was at a time when fears of AIDS were prominent in the general culture, and there were no effective treatments. Kevin and I reviewed his few sexual experiences. None of them were likely to have transmitted HIV. Also, he had been celibate during the time that HIV transmission had become most common.

These reassurances did little to assuage his panic. He consulted an internist who believed that the symptoms were not serious but drew blood for an HIV-antibody test. The results would be known in two weeks. The interim period was terrorizing for Kevin. He continually examined his oral cavity, and he was convinced that his symptoms were not improving, which he took to be evidence of being immuno-compromised. He described canals, ridges, and protrusions around the underside of the tongue. He obtained an ENT consultation and was diagnosed as having "a normal tongue."

Still the anxiety persisted and even increased. Kevin telephoned in a panic. We had an emergency session, during which he reported a dream.

> *Some people had filled a bathtub with all kinds of groceries, including an open gallon-container of milk. I pissed into the tub, onto the groceries and even into the open container of milk. I was horrified at what I had done.*

He felt that the groceries may have been for the religious holidays.

Shortly after telling me the dream, Kevin felt an urgent need to urinate, and he wanted to know how much longer remained to the session. More than half an hour remained. He said he didn't want to urinate in my bathroom for fear of giving me AIDS. I told him that was not the way it was transmitted. When he returned from the bathroom, I interpreted to him that his comment before going to the bathroom had indicated that he thought of his urine as destructive, to me and to the "food" in the dream. Although he had felt horrified in the dream about what he had done, he had done it.

He lay silently on the couch, and then started to tap his fingers, as if he were playing the piano. I asked him about it. He said he wasn't sure, but "playing the piano" had an additional meaning to him. It meant: "stealing from the cash register." He then volunteered an important memory: His great aunt, with whom he was very close, had told him that she had stolen money from her father's cash register regularly, in order to collect money for her wedding. I was startled and said, "Oh, that was the original prestyl dolby!" (remembering his association, "Press the till, dough'll be yours.") Kevin looked confused at first, then sighed, and said that the interpretation had felt very strongly affecting; he relaxed, and almost fell asleep on the couch. The effect of clarifying and working through his dissociated identification with his great aunt's antisocial side was profound. The fear of AIDS disappeared, and we obtained new insight into his fantasies of robbery, shootouts, and domination. Gradually, these became more integrated into his idealized vision of his great aunt as a kindly, mothering figure. She was that, but she had other less saintly aspects, too. He had internalized both sides of her, but kept them apart with the defense of splitting, and needed to bring them together. (This also made sense of my early split countertransference puzzle – my impression of his gentleness in the first session contrasted with my fantasy after the session of his attacking me violently.)

The key to the "Prestyl Dolby" dream had been a physical gesture. When Kevin strummed his fingers on the couch, it was a nonverbal link to "playing the piano" and its meaning of stealing from the cash register. This clinical example shows how the analyst must pay attention not only to what the patient says but what he does. Nonverbal gestures and actions after the dream can intersect with dream content. The action helps you understand the dream, and the dream helps you understand the action.

Fred's dream – enactment of the dream

Sometimes, the nonverbal action that clarifies the dream is on a broader scale. The following vignette shows an extended and dramatic enactment of a dream:

> *Fred, a wealthy and successful man, dreamt that he was in a professional school, wearing rags. His wallet was empty, except for a credit card that, in his actual waking life, he used only for incidental*

expenses. He interpreted the dream as expressing a simple wish: "*I don't want my money or my career anymore.*" He felt his career was too pressured, and that the more money he made, the more expenses he incurred, which led to his needing even more money. He felt nostalgic for the days when he was a starving student.

Fred reported the dream in the last session we had before an extended summer break, and his interpretation, about not wanting his money or career, was virtually the last thing he said to me. I made a note to remember to bring up his dramatic statement when we resumed sessions after the summer.

Fred almost always arrived on time, but in our first session after the summer break, he was late. While still waiting for him to arrive, I suddenly noticed that he had left me the following voicemail: "I'm right in front of your office, but I forgot to bring my wallet and I have no money to pay the taxi driver, so I must go back home. I'm sorry, but I will miss the session." I heard the message and called him immediately. He was only a few blocks away, so I suggested he come back. I would lend him the money to pay the cab driver and then we could have the session.

He did come back to my office. I lent him $50. I noted that he had said in our last session before the summer break, "I don't want my money or career anymore." And now he had left his money at home!

There was a further meaning to the dream and the significance of money issues. His mother had a higher income than his father. She was contemptuous of the father and was openly seductive with Fred, who had a higher income than both of his parents. His wish not to have so much money may also have reflected his anxiety about the way his financial success fueled his mother's intense interest in him and may have humiliated his father.

He then told me a recent dream that spelled out further his anxiety about success. Fred is in a car with his parents. His father is driving, he is in the passenger seat, and his mother is in the back seat.

> *We are driving down a hill, past a spot where my father, in reality, had a car accident. In the dream, Dad is hunched over, drunk or dead. I'm supposed to hold the wheel, while my mother presses the gas. Or vice versa. I push Dad to the side, and get into the driver's seat. I pull the car to the side of the road. I had a really angry fight with my mom.*

Freud told us that, in the unconscious, a man wants to kill off his father and marry his mother. Yet in most cases, the oedipal pattern is shaped not just by the desires of the child, but by the needs and anxieties of the parents (Kohut, 1977, pp. 220–248). In this case, the mother was contemptuous of the father and seductive with her son. The dream portrays how chaotic and dangerous this was, and so Fred finally takes a firm stand in the dream and puts a limit on his mother's wishes. The oedipal danger, in this case, may not be from being overwhelmed by Fred's internal drives of aggression against the father and lust for the mother, but rather that the normal parental limits to the expression of those drives are missing and causing anxiety in the son.

Later in the analysis, Fred dreamt:

> *There was a Persian rug. It was infested with bright blue caterpillars. They were glassy, jewel-like. Like Lapis Lazuli. They were multiplying. They carried rice-sized eggs on them, which would fall off. They were multiplying, out of control. There was lots of junk and stuff, like my work table. Lots of unrelated objects.*

Fred told me that his mother collects valuable rugs. I said to him, "In the dream, your mother has bugs in her rug, and they are out of control." (This is a clear and simple rebus.) He replied, showing that he understood my meaning,

> In street slang, a rug is a hairy vagina. These bugs are both precious and destructive, and that is my trouble with my mother: I adore her and hate her. I stimulate her, and I try to keep her in control.

Bugs make one itch; do the mother's bugs in her rug signify her erotic itching for her son?

The bugs in her rug that look like jewels are a dream symbol of her erotic and financial desires. Fred is ambivalent; his mother is precious, but she is also dangerous. She can be arousing, but she can feel disturbing. In the dream, there is lots of "junk" (another sexual slang term that means "genitals") like the junk on his work table; his mother is both an inspiration and impediment to his work.

Ruth's dream – supervising the analyst[4]

Sometimes a patient in psychoanalysis will use a dream to tell the psychoanalyst about something problematic in the way he is conducting the treatment. Resistance to seeing one's own countertransference is quite common, so the analyst may not immediately understand the communication. There may then be a cycle of enactments until the dream is more fully understood.

For example, a woman, Ruth, engaged in ritualized sexual masochism. Although she never could play the sadistic role sexually, she had had outbursts of rage against her lover which frightened her and led her to seek psychoanalysis.

She had grown up with parents who were very concerned about her, but were unempathic with a child's ways of thinking. For example, at the age of six, when she was on her first cruise on an ocean liner, her father told her, laughing, about the *Titanic*. It was interesting and informative, but unempathic of the father not to realize that a six-year-old (not to mention an adult) might find that information terrifying while on a cruise ship.

Ruth told me the following dream about one year into the analysis:

> *The dream doesn't really take place in my parents' apartment. There is a bookcase there in what used to be my bedroom. What next occurs is a realization that the book that perfectly captures the situation is* As You Like It. *Then we are in the dining area, which used to be my parents' bedroom. Both my father and I end up sitting at the dining room table, which is oval. I sit at my father's place. My father is in my mother's place. My father also had the same thought, that* Macbeth *accurately reflects the situation. I think he must think of the correct play himself. He then says: It's not* Macbeth, *it's* As You Like It. *Then, in the dream, I told you the dream.*

She associated the dream to James Thurber's 1937 story, "The Macbeth murder mystery," which is hilarious and makes "Who committed the murder?" the central question.

Ruth was intelligent and witty but used intellectual games as a defense. The form of her participation in the dream interpretation was similar to the content of the dream itself. In the first session after she had the dream, she told me, "I had a strange dream, and in the dream I told you the dream. But now, I am not ready to tell it to you." In the next session, she made reference to the content of the dream: "Well, of course, it was about incest, as I told you." Actually, she had not told me (at least according to my memory), although she had done so in the dream. On one hand, this shows one function of the dream-telling within the dream – it allows a persistent avoidance of actually telling the dream. But it also indicates the parallel between the dreamtext and the process of dream analysis. Just as in the dream she expects or hopes that her father will realize what she is thinking without her having to say it, so too does she expect or hope that her analyst will know the content of her dream without her having to say it. This had been a continual event in the analysis. Ruth had actually stopped working with a prior therapist when she had concealed some very important information and the therapist failed to notice it. Ruth claimed that she continued working with me because she had not been able to fool me. (Of course, in telling me this, she did not tell me how she had tried to fool me and how I had seen through it. Probably, as in the dream, she hoped I would know this; and I certainly had my ideas, although, as always with her, I had some doubt.)

You can see from my description of the dream the nature of the transference and countertransference. (As I write this, I realize that I am talking to you, reader, as the patient talks to me in the dream and the sessions, as if, "Of course you know."[5]) By itself, the dream could be interpreted as indicating, on one hand, a romanticized transference within an oedipal constellation – mother is out of the picture, father sits in her chair, alone with his daughter, and the daughter wants him to think of romance and seductiveness (*As You Like It*), not violence and guilt (*Macbeth*). Intellectual games had been the favorite means of sexual seductiveness between her and her father. Moreover, the way they played them had a distinctly sadomasochistic cast. Her manner of reporting the dream, however, added several dimensions to this interpretation; she had a wish for me to have total empathy with her that bordered on mind-reading. At the same time, there was a dread of overt self-assertion and a kind of covert control that was achieved through these sorts of intellectual games, in which the rules alternatingly adhered to and broke stereotyped gender roles. (Note that in the dream Ruth sits in the father's chair and he in the mother's, reminiscent of the switches in gender roles, clearly in *As You Like It* and more subtly in *Macbeth*.)

I must admit that the dream itself succeeded in engaging me in a sort of mind game. I was intrigued by a startling coincidence that seemed like telepathy. Ruth spoke fluent French, and I remembered that during the session in which she told me that she had had the dream, without telling me the content of the dream, I had thought to myself, "*à votre guise*," which in French means "as you wish," or, one might say, "As You Like It!" But the experience that this was telepathy seemed to me to reflect the nature of the transference wishes, with which I was complying.

Then, in the next week, I discovered how my deep and convoluted attempts to understand the dream, as I have just described them, were in themselves part of the transference–countertransference matrix. Ruth told me at the start of a session that she was very angry with me. "Do you know why?" she asked. (I was already bracing for a new game in the Olympics of empathy.) I confessed that I did not. But instead of games, she told me, quite simply, that she was angry that I interpreted too much about her. Some things she told me were simple conversation, icebreakers, and she felt I was overinterpreting and overpathologizing her. I then realized that the dream had been a simple message about this complaint. It was a wish-fulfillment transference dream. In it, the father [the analyst] is thinking *Macbeth* (i.e., tragedy, corruption, murder, greed, etc.) while she is thinking *As You Like It* (i.e., comedy, lighthearted, good-natured). She hoped that her father would understand this without her saying so in the dream, and he eventually did. But I did not, and my attempts at depth interpretation of the dream continued the pattern. Even her association to "The Macbeth murder mystery," which makes a delicious joke of a tragedy, had not stopped me. And so she had to tell me explicitly that my continued interpretation was too disturbing. This action on her part was itself a therapeutic breakthrough, since she tended, when angry, either to suppress her anger until there was an outbreak of violence or to bind it in masochistic rituals. Of course, the grave, Macbeth-like issues of murderousness, deception, and conspiracy in crime were also potent issues in Ruth's psychology and received further attention as the analysis progressed, but the dream alerted me to the need to be more balanced and to temper the focus on somber issues.

The meanings of the dream continued to unfold. I took Ruth's request seriously and focused less on what I saw as her pathology and destructiveness. I realized that I had been guarded in dealing with her and wondered whether that was necessary. It turned out that my countertransference feeling with her was justified. In the ensuing months, Ruth played a practical joke on me (the details of which I cannot relate for reasons of confidentiality). She had played this joke on other people, but it had a more serious outcome with me because it seriously embarrassed and humiliated me. It was a practical joke that her father had played on her, as well as on a number of his relatives and acquaintances. But the essence of the practical joke had been reflected in the dream: is it a comedy or is it hostile? All practical jokes have this combination of motives: there is an aspect of fooling or humiliating the other person in the guise of humor and fun. The question raised by the dream of whether the play that describes the situation is *Macbeth* or *As You Like It* was very much to the point of Ruth's psychology and her experiences with her father. He was someone who did things that were supposedly in good cheer but often conveyed an underlying hostility, of which the practical joke was only one example. Ruth was frequently the victim of these games from early childhood, when she was even less well-equipped to handle them. They left her with the unconscious questions, "Is what has happened with my father destructive or fun? Is this a destructive murderous tragedy (*Macbeth*) or a comedy (*As You Like It*)?"

Her association to Thurber's "The Macbeth murder mystery" set up the same dialectic – can you make a comedy out of something that is full of underlying destructiveness? And the question of who did it, in the Thurber satire, was also relevant. When I was hurt by Ruth's practical joke, her first reaction was a complete lack of empathy, as if it was my doing and my problem that I got burned. After a great deal of analytic reflection on this, we were able to elaborate how this was her own experience of her father's destructiveness. If he claimed no destructive intent, but she was hurt by him, then "Who done it?" The tension of this conflict lay at the root of her own masochistic sexual practice, with its rituals of domination and control. The title of the play *As You Like It* contains within it the essence of her masochism, as if she were saying, "Do with me as you like it, with no concern for my well-being, and I will act as a smiling, willing participant, but know that underneath this veneer of pleasure, there is great hurt to me."

Thus, the actions that followed the dream helped clarify the dream. Laughter and comedy are good, but not when they mask real cruelty and suffering. Ruth was able, through watching my pain and humiliation caused by her practical joke, to realize how her father's sense of humor could be cruel and hurtful to her. When I first heard how he told her about the *Titanic*, I interpreted to her that he might have been cruel to her under the guise of humor, and that her masochism might have been a way to try to master that cruelty. But, as in most psychoanalyses, verbal interpretations, however precise and correct, can be relatively ineffective; real, substantial change occurs only when the patient experiences the psychological issues, in the relationship with the therapist, in a vivid and emotional way.

When the patient tells only scant information about a dream

Sometimes a person will relate just scant information about a dream, something like, "I had a dream, but I can hardly remember anything about it." The analyst may wonder, "Is there anything I can do with that? Should I just ignore it until more material is remembered by the patient?"

The analyst need not simply wait passively. I usually encourage the dreamer to tell me whatever he or she remembers about the dream, however inconsequential it may seem. Sometimes I ask a general question, like, "What was the feeling in the dream?" or "Was it pleasant or unpleasant?" Whatever the patient tells you may be significant. Also, as you start to talk about the dream, other details may be remembered.

Alternatively, you can work productively with the scant details that are remembered. For example, early in treatment a gay man, Andrew, told me he hardly ever remembered his dreams. In one session, he said, "I had a dream over the weekend, but I can hardly remember any of it. It took place in my house. My mother was there. Somehow, there was something sexual about the dream." That is all he remembered. This sliver of a dream suggested a hypothesis: Andrew's mother has something to do with his sexuality. I noted this hypothesis quietly and listened to what material followed. He recounted that he was exploring sexual sadomasochism. He had made contact with a couple, who engaged him in a three-way interaction in which he was primarily submissive. He then also added that in one of his favorite masturbation fantasies, he enters someone's home. The host has many guests and instructs Andrew to have sex with the different guests, telling him exactly what to do with each person. He wasn't sure why this fantasy was so exciting. He had never actually lived it out. I noted that this fantasy might not be so unusual. In *The Story of O* (Réage, 1954), the heroine is instructed by Sir Stephen to have sex with other men.

Andrew then started speaking about his mother. He mentioned that his mother always wanted him to be a great athlete. He didn't have much athletic talent, so when he was in high school, she arranged with a coach for her son to be assigned to helping the football players get dressed. I noted (thinking that the connection was obvious to him) that this might reflect the meaning of the dream, that his mother was connected with his primary sexual fantasy. Just as his mother instructed him to minister to the football players (which was erotic for him), now he found the scenario of being instructed to tend sexually to other men to be very erotic. Andrew was startled by the connection, but found it valid.

When the interpretation precedes the dream

Psychoanalysts usually expect that understanding of a dream will be worked out after a patient tells a dream in treatment and adds associations. However, sometimes the reverse occurs. A session will be moving along, the analyst may make a comment or interpretation of something about the patient, and the patient will suddenly say, "I just remembered a dream." Often, the dream that suddenly is remembered is about the very theme of the analyst's comment. In these situations, the interpretation precedes the dream.

This is a sequence that is common in psychoanalysis, especially when the analyst and patient are well attuned to one another. As the analyst inquires into a certain area, or interprets about a particular theme, the patient may respond by telling a dream. In the moment, the patient may not be aware of why the dream answers the analyst's question, or corresponds to the interpretation, although it usually does. We could say there is an unconscious meta-knowledge of the connection between the dream and the interpretation, or merely that the patient has learned to trust "free association" enough to report the dream when it arises in his awareness seemingly unbidden. An alternative explanation (not mutually exclusive) is that when the analyst makes his interpretation, if it is on target, it may dissolve some of the patient's resistance, leading to memory of the dream.

In the following example, a patient told me a dream. I commented on the dream, which reminded him of a different dream, whose meaning corresponded to my comment. A middle-aged gay man, Michael, was living in a long-term relationship with Bruce. They were very devoted to one another, but the relationship had become routine, predictable, and, for Michael, lacking in passion. He had started an affair with a man named Rob. It was meant to be primarily a sexual dalliance, although as it proceeded, there were danger signals that the relationship with Rob might become more emotionally significant and threaten Michael's relationship with Bruce.

Michael dreamt:

I had made the decision, because I was being mistreated or harassed, to disappear. I did, for 12 years, or 15, or 17. No one knew where I was. I was watching myself in the dream. The person I was watching was a female. Then I was trying to locate Bruce. I was upset I hadn't seen him in so long. His telephone number had changed. I couldn't locate him.

I asked Michael what is happening with Rob. He asks why, and I mention that he enjoyed sex with him and raised questions about his relationship with Bruce, so I wondered if this was connected with the failed attempt to locate Bruce in the dream. Then, Michael suddenly remembers another dream: "Last night, I dreamt that I told Bruce I was leaving him. I was going to get my own apartment. I was thinking, how was that going to be?"

Remembering the dream was his way of opening up the issue of his ambivalence and acknowledging much more directly that the relationship with Rob is seriously threatening his relationship with Bruce; in his dreams, he is considering leaving Bruce, something he would not entertain in his conscious waking life.

The two dreams together capture the conflict, "Should I try to find Bruce and stay with him, or should I move out?" When I interpreted the first dream in terms of his looking for Bruce, he remembered the second dream, which portrayed the wish to leave Bruce more blatantly, bringing more balance to the picture. Jung proposed the idea that dreams portray the unconscious stance, which is a compensation – i.e., a balancing out and counterpoint of the conscious attitude. In this case, however, the two dreams are compensations of each other.

Conclusion

There are many ways of working with dreams that depart from the model of dream-telling, associations, and interpretation. Work on a single dream may extend over several sessions, even years. The analyst and patient must always be ready to hear new meanings. Sometimes, the meaning comes in the form of a nonverbal gesture. Sometimes, there is an extended enactment, where action in the psychotherapy clarifies the dream content, and the dream content clarifies the action. Sometimes, the patient's dream clarifies the analyst's countertransference biases and blind spots, and this then leads to the analyst being more effective in clarifying the patient's transference and resistance. There is no single formula in working with dreams, and each dream calls for a different approach. Each analyst and patient can find new ways to mine the dream for meaning and understanding, and for finding new solutions to old problems. In a sense, the dream guides its own analysis.

Notes

1 This case is discussed in more detail in Blechner (2016).
2 This case was mentioned in Chapter 3, on condensation.
3 This is reminiscent of the dream described by Erikson (1954) in which a single word appeared with some of the letters bracketed.
4 This case was also discussed in Blechner (1995).
5 This may be an example of parallel process different from that usually discussed in the literature. Searles (1955), Ekstein and Wallerstein (1958), Caligor (1981), and others have discussed parallel processes that occur in psychoanalytic supervision. Perhaps parallel processes can occur, too, in a psychoanalytic paper, where the relationship between the writer and the reader parallels the relationship between analyst and patient described in the paper.

Chapter 14

Group dream interpretation

The interpretation of dreams has been practiced mostly in two-person situations. In ancient Babylon, Gilgamesh told his dream to his mother, and she interpreted it. In the Old Testament, Pharaoh had his dream about the seven lean cows eating the seven fat cows, and Joseph interpreted it as a prediction of seven years of plenty followed by seven years of famine. In the New Testament, Pilate's wife had a dream that Jesus should be let go; she told the dream to her husband, but Pilate did not heed her dream.

In modern times, in psychoanalysis and psychotherapy, the most typical situation is for a patient to tell a dream in a session, along with associations, and for the dream then to be interpreted by the clinician and patient. Nevertheless, there are other formats for interpreting dreams. In some cultures, for example, family members report dreams at breakfast, and the family, often guided by an elder, consider the meaning of the dream (Pick and Roper, 2004; Blechner, 2001). There also have been various attempts to analyze dreams in group contexts. In this chapter, I would like to report on my own research, using a group approach for dream exploration. I will describe the process used, its relationship to traditional clinical work with dreams, and its potential to modify both psychoanalytic training and psychoanalytic technique.

In 1998, I attended a conference of the Association for the Study of Dreaming. There was a demonstration of the Experiential Dream Group approach of Montague Ullman. The group leader, Wendy Pannier, brought together seven people who were mostly strangers to one another; a single person presented a dream; and in just an hour and a half, the group helped the dreamer reach a profound understanding of her dream.

In order to learn this approach to group dream analysis, I attended several of Ullman's weekend training seminars. Ullman (1994) believed that group dream analysis should be part of the basic psychoanalytic training, yet, while I had been a student in a psychoanalytic institute, I had never been exposed to his approach. I informally surveyed several colleagues who had been trained in other institutes, and none of them had been exposed to the Ullman approach during their training, either.[1]

By that time (20 years ago), I had been teaching dream interpretation at three psychoanalytic institutes. I decided to try teaching the Ullman approach and give the students in every course at least one taste of the group dream experience. At my first attempt, I asked for one volunteer to present his or her own dream; no one volunteered. I assumed that they were too anxious about self-exposure, so I volunteered to present one of my own dreams. They were thrilled with the experience, and then they all wanted to try it with their own dreams. Unfortunately, we had other things scheduled for the rest of the classes.

Since then, I have devoted at least one class in every course I teach on dreams to the Ullman approach. There has never again been a lack of volunteers. I think that the lack of volunteers that first time may have been due to my own anxiety, since I had never before run a dream group with psychoanalytic candidates; as I became more self-assured as a dream-group leader and more convinced about the enormous benefits of the process, the students felt more safe and eager to participate.

Before my experience with the Ullman approach, I had participated in groups in which I had presented my own dreams on occasion, without any particular structure. I learned from those experiences how problematic that can be. Group members may volunteer interpretations of the dream that feel intrusive or shocking. They may also press the dreamer to explore aspects of the dream without regard for the defenses of the dreamer. This can be enormously anxiety-provoking, even traumatic for the dreamer, without a firm structure to protect the dreamer.

The genius of the Ullman approach to group dream interpretation is that it guarantees the safety of the dream presenter. The dreamer is protected against major spikes of intolerable anxiety, and this protection makes deep exploration of the dream possible. The dreamer is in control of the process. The dreamer is never required to speak, to produce associations, or to respond to questions. Whatever the dreamer says is voluntary. In addition, before moving from one stage of the dream interpretation process to the next, the dreamer is asked for permission to proceed. Usually, permission is granted, but sometimes, it is not. It is the dreamer's prerogative to stop the process at any time. Usually, just the knowledge that the dreamer can stop the process if desired makes the dreamer feel safer.

The dream-group leader is responsible for enforcing the rules to keep the dreamer feeling safe. This usually requires small interventions. Most of the time, the group leader wants to take part in the group interpretation process; he asserts his supervisory and didactic role only when he senses that a group process is getting out of control or the dreamer's safety is being threatened.

I would like to describe Ullman's original approach here and also some of the modifications that I have worked out over many years of running dream groups. Interested readers may get a more comprehensive description of Ullman's ideas from his own writing (e.g., Ullman, 1987, 1996). I will try not only to describe the basic process of each stage, but also some of the ways that the process can commonly go awry, requiring the group leader to intervene. I would also like to show how this approach can yield profound insights, using a method that differs from traditional dream interpretation in psychoanalytic treatment.

The process

The dream group starts with a volunteer reciting his dream to the group. All the other group members write down the dream on paper. While this can be very valuable (it is often revealing how we write down someone else's dream – where we insert punctuation, where we produce new paragraphs, etc.), it is also quite time-consuming. In my own dream groups, I have usually had the dreamer bring in a printed transcript of the dream and distribute it to the group members. The dreamer then reads the dream, and the group members follow along in the written text. This procedure takes much less time than having everyone transcribe the dream-text themselves.[2]

During this stage, no one speaks except the dreamer. If the group members have any comments or questions about the text, they may not raise them at this point. They only listen, as carefully as possible.

In the second stage, the group members are allowed to ask the dreamer questions that clarify the manifest dreamtext. They can ask about words that are unclear. They can ask about the identity of people who are merely mentioned by name, although they may not ask the dreamer for associations to that person or detailed descriptions. If the dreamer says, for example, "I felt in the dream the way I felt the night before the dream," the group may ask what the dreamer felt the night before, but only to clarify the statement. But if the dreamer does not mention how he felt during the dream, the group members may not ask about feeling. The purpose of this stage is to allow the group members to be sure they understand the manifest dreamtext as presented.[3]

In the next stage, with the dreamer's permission, the dream is turned over to the group; the dreamer must remain silent during this stage and only listen. During this stage, the group members associate to the dream as if it were their own dream. In fact, they introduce each of their comments with the phrase, "If it were my dream..." They can say anything during this stage, as long as they speak in the first person. A comment can reflect empathy with the general situation of the dreamer; it can also be a totally personal association of the group member. The group member can say, for example, "If it were my dream, I would be feeling hatred for my mother in the dream for what she did." The group member may not say, "If it were my dream, you must have felt hatred for your mother." The group member may say: "If it were my dream, I would be reminded of a TV show about penguins I saw last month..." The group member may not say, "Did you see the TV show about penguins last month?" Also, the group members do not look at the dreamer during this stage. They address their comments to each other; the dreamer fades back. This is important; it is common for group members to want to look at the dreamer, to seek affirmation from facial reactions of the dreamer. This defeats the purpose of the process, which is to allow the group members to associate on their own to the dream, without being tied to the dreamer's reactions. The dreamer also feels much safer listening to the group's associations if no eye contact (and hence implicit communication) is required. If any of the group members break either of these rules (a fairly common occurrence), the group leader must interrupt them and remind them to speak always in the first person and not to look at the dreamer when speaking.

When the group is finished associating to the dream, they can, with the dreamer's permission, proceed to the next stage. In this stage, the dream is given back to the dreamer. The dreamer may say anything during this stage: reactions to other people's associations, recollections about the dream details, past waking experiences, or anything else that comes to mind. Only the dreamer may speak during this stage. The other group members must remain completely silent, even if they feel the impulse to ask the dreamer questions. The dreamer may also choose to remain completely silent during this stage. This may happen for a number of reasons – most commonly, when something was evoked in the previous stage that was very anxiety-provoking. The dreamer should never be prodded to speak, if he or she is reticent. The wish for silence must be respected. It should be remembered that just because the dreamer is silent, it does not mean that there are no thoughts there. But the dreamer must be guaranteed the right to have strong reactions to the dream and keep them to himself. However, if the dreamer decides to remain silent during this stage, it does not mean that the group process must stop. On the contrary, the dreamer should be asked if he or she wants to proceed to the next stage. If he says "yes," proceed. If "no," stop, with no further questions asked.

In the next stage, the dream group is allowed to ask questions of the dreamer that contextualize the dream. These may include questions about what happened in the day or days preceding the dream. It may include questions that relate the characters in the dream to people in the dreamer's life. The procedure during this stage is most open to difference, depending on the group and the group leader. I have participated in dream groups in which one or several group members start to pry into the dreamer's thoughts about the dream, sometimes trying to break though obvious resistance of the dreamer. In my view, this can be productive, but it also can be problematic. It may nudge the dreamer to explore resistances to certain aspects of the dream, but it can also feel threatening. It is here that the clinical judgment of the group leader is crucial. The dreamer must feel safe from being excessively pressured; the dreamer must always feel safe to keep thoughts private. The group leader must be attentive to the balance between encouraging the dreamer to explore and pressuring the dreamer unduly. The dreamer should feel free to say, "I don't want to answer that," and the group leader, always attentive to the dreamer's anxiety level, should feel free to interrupt a "pushy" group member, or say, "Let's leave that question to our own imagination."

The next stage is the playback; if the dreamer agrees to proceed with this stage, someone from the group volunteers to read the dream back out loud to the dreamer, pausing for a substantial amount of time after every one or two sentences, and allowing the dreamer to tell the group of any thoughts that crop up while hearing his own dream. As in the previous stage, the dreamer may remain silent during any pause, or even remain silent during the entire stage. Also, while the choice of who will read back the dream is left open to the group, occasionally the dreamer will say that he does not want that particular person to read the dream back, or that he would rather prefer another individual to be the reader. In either case, the group must respect the dreamer's wishes. During the playback, the group can draw the dreamer's attention to an aspect of the dream that has not yet been addressed. As always, the dreamer can choose to respond or not to such questions. Sometimes, especially when the manifest dream is very long and it looks like we may run out of time, I or the dreamer has asked to skip the playback stage.

The penultimate stage is the "Orchestrating Projections." With the dreamer's permission, the dream is once more returned to the group; the dreamer is completely silent. The group members take everything they have heard – the initial manifest dreamtext, the group's associations, and the dreamer's comments – and put it all together into a more or less comprehensive view of the dream. This stage is called Orchestrating Projections because the group members orchestrate, i.e., put together into a coherent whole all the voices, external and internal, that they have been hearing. It is called a projection, because it is acknowledged that the group member's synthesis is still essentially a projection, which may or may not have much to do with the dreamer's psychology. Thus, in this stage, the group members again begin their comments with the phrase "If it were my dream..." and refrain from looking at the dreamer. Often, after so much back and forth, the group members feel like breaking those rules; the group leader must use his or her judgment, but in my experience, it is often best for the dreamer if these rules are followed without exception. The dreamer, of course, should have a prominent voice in how the group proceeds.

The final stage occurs during the next meeting of the dream group, which is usually one week or month later. In this stage, after having time to digest all that has happened, the dreamer may share with the group any reactions to anything that happened during the dream group. As may be expected, the dreamer is free not to say anything at all in this stage. Sometimes, if it is known that the group will not meet again, soon or ever, this final stage can be placed at the end of the original dream group. However, at that point, the dreamer is usually quite overwhelmed by all the material that has been raised, so that it is hard to respond to it all. The passage of time allows the dreamer to "metabolize" the feedback.

The group process can make not only the dreamer, but all of the dream-group members vulnerable. In sharing their own associations, especially if they do it freely, they will be exposing their own thoughts. Often, the most personal, idiosyncratic associations of the group members, which may feel to them as wholly private and probably irrelevant to the dreamer, may turn out to be illuminating about the dreamer and worthwhile to him. The whole process works best when all the group members are freest with their associations. As Marie-Louise von Franz has written (Boas, 1994, p. 16): "The trouble with interpreting your own dreams is that you can't see your own back. If you show it to another person, he can see it, but you can't."

Ogden has described a clinical teaching group that encourages "group dreaming": "A group unconscious is constructed which is larger than the sum of the unconscious minds of each participant, while, at the same time, each participant retains his own separate subjectivity and his own personal unconscious life" (Ogden, 2006, p. 1074). The dream group does something similar, but it works primarily with manifest dream material. The group members, in effect, all dream the dreamer's dream. While dreams are a person's most private mental processes, the sharing of dreams with a group, in a safe and structured environment, can be one of the most illuminating ways of getting perspective on one's unconscious. It also yields important insights into dream analysis. When the dreamer is listening to other people associate to the dream, he not only learns much from the content of their thoughts. He also can monitor, in himself, the spikes and dips in anxiety. This experience, in itself, teaches student psychoanalysts important lessons about the importance of monitoring the dreamer's anxiety level during dream interpretation and the value of seemingly "stray" thoughts about someone else's dream to be relevant to unconscious dynamics.

Experimentation

As a dream group continues to meet over a long period, the group members at times become restless with the standard Ullman structure and express wishes to experiment with different procedures. These forays into uncharted territory can be exhilarating. I will describe only a few of the alternatives:

1 A group member presented two dreams, one from 20 years before and one from the preceding week. It was fascinating to observe how the same core psychological issues were present in both dreams, yet the way the dreamer dealt with those same issues had evolved and matured over time.
2 A dreamer presented a repeated childhood dream that she had never understood, even after discussing it at length in her personal analysis. She felt the group process clarified an essential aspect of her early experience that continued to resonate in her current life.
3 A group member presented a recent dream, which followed on her attending a memorial service for the relative of one of the other group members. The dream exploration thus involved an unusual "group within the group" process. The person whose relative had died could not dream the dreamer's dream as "If it were my dream…" without having very personal feelings, not only about the death, but about the other person's empathy with the loss. The dream evoked a profound outpouring of recent and impending losses experienced by all the group members.
4 A group member presented a dream and did not tell the group whose dream it was. The group associated to race relations in the United States, fear for the safety from assassination of Barack Obama (who was then president), and many other meanings. We found out in the end that the dream was President Obama's, drawn from his book *Dreams from My Father* (Obama, 1995).

There can be many other forms of experimentation. In one instance, a group member brought in a drawing, to clarify a visual aspect of her dream. The visual image was puzzling, but one of the group members turned the image upside down, whereupon the meaning of the image was startlingly clear (a woman giving birth) and spelled out the meaning of the dream. It was as if a new operation of the dreamwork had been discovered – "figurative transposition."

In another dream group that was conducted as part of a dream course at a psychoanalytic institute, the dreamer stated outright that the dream was "about the group" – about the members of the psychoanalytic class, their interactions with each other, and with the training institute. In that case, we modified the procedure to focus primarily on what the dream said about the group, borrowing from the technique of "the social dreaming matrix" (Lawrence, 2003).[4] I instructed the group, when associating to the dreamer's dream as if it were their own dream, to limit their associations to what the dream might say about the group. They did so, and there were trenchant insights into their group dynamics, their experience of psychoanalytic training, and the relationship of the psychoanalytic students to the training institute.

Group process

When a dream group meets regularly for several years, inevitably certain group dynamics evolve. While the main task of the group is the clarification of dreams and not, strictly speaking, group therapy, it has been my experience that it is perilous to ignore group dynamics in an ongoing group. The departure of a group member, for example, can have a strong impact on the remaining group members. The group members may wonder: Why did the person leave? Was it something I said that offended the person without my being aware of it? How did the group feel about the group member? Is he or she missed? Is the departure experienced as an aggressive act against the group, or as a result of aggression from some or all of the group members? Has the group had a chance to mourn the departure?

In addition, group members may have feelings about other aspects of group participation. These issues may not be resolved, but I have found that it is useful periodically (one or two meetings a year, or as needed) to devote some time to the airing and exploration of these groups reactions. If not aired, they may fester and eventually be destructive to group functioning (Bion, 1961).

Group processes and psychoanalysis

Psychoanalysis has tended to focus on dyads. The psychoanalytic process usually involves one analyst and one patient. Developmental models tend to give special emphasis on the mother–child dyad. While attention is paid to expansions of this dyad – the triadic oedipal constellation, the triadic interaction of supervisor, analyst, and patient – the interactions of larger groups have received less attention.

And yet, several analysts have observed pitfalls in focusing on the dyad. There are times in the psychoanalytic encounter when the transference of the patient and the countertransference of the analyst interact in a way that can delimit or even paralyze the therapeutic process. These situations have been called interlocks (Wolstein, 1959; Bonovitz, 2009), unconscious collusions (Jacobs, 2001), bastions of jointly constructed resistance (Ferro, 1999), impasses (Rosenfeld, 1987), or deadlocks (Blechner, 1995). Analysts have pondered how best to handle such situations and suggested multiple solutions, including:

1 self-analysis to free the psychoanalyst from a stuck pattern of responding to the patient (McDougall, 1993);
2 a supervisory consultation for the psychoanalyst (Rosenfeld, 1987);
3 a consultation by the patient with a different psychoanalyst (Pizer, 1998);
4 a verbal description by the analyst of the apparent impasse, with an invitation to the patient to comment or analyze the situation (Schafer, 1995);
5 a foray into mutual analysis, whereby the patient and analyst temporarily shift roles, and the patient analyzes the analyst's psychodynamics, which may be interfering with the psychoanalyst (Ferenczi, 1933/1988; Blechner, 1992); and
6 a consultation by the analyst with a supervisory group (Wolstein, 1984; Ogden, 2006).

The latter – consultation with a group – has the advantage of enabling the therapist to hear multiple perspectives about his unconscious involvement with the patient. Each group member may resonate with a different aspect of the dynamics of both the patient and the analyst. In addition, in one-on-one supervision, the supervisor cannot go further than the supervisee's resistance will allow; in a group, on the other hand, the discussion of the case need not be limited by the supervisee's response in the moment. The group members can take the discussion of the psychodynamics of the treatment as far as they want. The supervisee may eavesdrop on this discussion, taking in as much as is possible in the moment and recording parts for reconsideration in the future, without having to accept or even respond to anyone's input.

Groups tend to neutralize specific biases that may distort dyadic consultations. Groups also tend to hear more detail, leading to a more complete picture, not only of the transference, but of the transference–countertransference interaction. In supervision groups, Ogden calls this "dreaming the patient" – each group member allows his or her unconscious to resonate with the unconscious processes of both analyst and patient, amplifying and distilling the most important psychic elements in a manner analogous to the dream (Ogden, 2006).

I have described, in this chapter, a structured method whereby a group can help a dreamer clarify the meaning of a dream. A group can not only "dream the patient" as Ogden describes. It can "dream the dreamer," paying close attention to private reveries that may seem idiosyncratic to the self, but that ultimately may be revealing about the other.

What can we learn from group dreamwork about working one-on-one with patients' dreams?

One of my colleagues asked me: How has your work with dream groups affected your work with dreams in one-on-one psychotherapy? It was a good question, and I did not have a ready answer. But after some consideration, I realized that the answer is: "Enormously." After over 20 years of working with dream groups, the Ullman approach has penetrated almost all my work with dreams, even if I don't follow all the stages in order. For example, when anyone tells me a dream, I always try to envision how the dream was dreamt. Thanks to Ullman, I feel freer to ask questions about the manifest content of the dream, making sure I know, as well as possible, what the experience of dreaming the dream was like. I want to make sure I know who everyone in the dream was, if it is not clear, and that any vague word usages are clarified as much as possible. I want to know the feelings in the dream at each point. All of these things have been done to some degree by clinicians in the past, but work with dream groups empowers one to ask questions more freely, not being so worried about contaminating the dream.

When I hear the patient's dream and associations, I listen carefully, externally and internally. By that I mean that I listen to what the patient is saying and also to any of my own associations; the patient's associations get priority, but I am freer about revealing my own associations. I am careful to spell out that this is my association, and may not have much to do with the dream. The authority of the clinician may give his own associations extra importance (see Freud, 1900a, "The Lovely Dream"; Meltzer, 1978; Blechner, 2001). I also feel freer to press the patient about the specificity of the dream images. If the dream has a married couple and two children, and the patient associates to a married couple with one child, I may feel freer to press the patient about a married couple with two children (see dream, p. 58).

In general, then, work with dream groups allows me to work with dreams in individual psychotherapy with more freedom, more lively interaction, and more attention to specificity. If done right, this kind of active engagement can inspire the patient to work harder and more spontaneously on his own dreams. It requires a sensitive awareness of the sharp spikes of anxiety that working on dreams can elicit. When the dreamer's anxiety zooms up suddenly, the analyst needs to recognize it and pull back, at least for the time being. Too little anxiety can lead to stasis, but too high anxiety can lead to paralysis. There are no formulas about this, but the experienced clinician must be expert at keeping anxiety at the optimal level (Sullivan, 1954), recognizing the ups and downs of the patient's anxiety, and also the clinician's own anxiety.

A modified version of a dream group when presenting the dream of a dreamer who is not present

I have produced another modification of Ullman's way of working with dreams in groups. Sometimes, especially in clinical conferences, I have had a clinician present the dream of a patient without the patient being present (though after obtaining consent from the patient). In this case, we cannot receive the reactions of the dreamer to the group process, nor do we have the powerful back and forth of the regular dream group. Nevertheless, it is possible to have the dream presented and then the group does just the third stage of the classic Ullman dream group – in which the group members associate to the dream as if it were their own dream. This modification allows the group to work with the dream and at least recognize the power of the group to intuit many meanings of the dream. I call this modified approach the "third-person dream group" format.

Who can take part in dream groups?

People sometimes assume that the members of a dream group need to be professionals in mental health or at least have some expertise in working with dreams. However, the members of a dream group can be individuals with no special training in psychology or dreams. Sometimes the most inspired contributions to a dream group come from people with no special training.

However, the age or demographics of the members of a dream group can sometimes make a difference. In one instance, I was asked by a journalist who wrote about dreams to run a one-time dream group. She organized a group of young women, all in their 20s and 30s, while I was in my 60s. I don't have the entire dream recorded, but I remember it started with Hillary Clinton doing a line dance. This was in the middle of the 2016 presidential campaign. All of the members of the group talked about how preposterously Hillary was behaving, trying to act young and cool. They all connected her to their mothers and saw the dream as a political condemnation. My own associations to Clinton were more positive, and I recognized how the dream captured the broad division between age groups to the Clinton candidacy.

In another instance, I lectured to a group of 120 psychoanalysts. Many of them were middle-aged or older, but at least half were quite young, in their 20s. After my lecture, a trainee presented a patient's dream, and the group of 120 psychoanalysts worked with the dream in the modified "third-person dream group" format.[5]

The dream contained an image of a beautiful place with jewels and crystals. The dreamer was told by her mother that she would meet her later at this special place.

Many of the older members of the group associated to the place with jewels and crystals as an idealized mother–daughter relationship. But then one young woman in the audience said that the dream made her very uncomfortable. If it were her dream, the mother telling her daughter that she would meet her in their special place sounded seductive and a wish for the mother to have incest with her daughter. Many of the young women in the audience echoed that point of view and became quite alarmed about the dream. It turned out that the young people intuited something important; the dreamer was involved in an incestuous relationship with the mother.

Notes

1 In 2017, I conducted a modified dream group at the meeting of the American Psychoanalytic Association. Of the 90 people who attended, only two had previously experienced the dream-group process before.
2 I usually run dream groups for either 90 minutes or 110 minutes. When Ullman ran his dream groups for training purposes, he tried to have the duration

of the group be open-ended, which was useful for training purposes and was workable when the group members had committed an entire weekend to the process.
3 This stage is associated with my recommendation to individual dream interpreters (Blechner, 2001, p. 126): "The first stage of dream analysis is careful listening. The analyst should *re-imagine* the dream, inquiring about anything that is vague or unclear. You must try to get as close as possible to the dreamer's experience of the dream."
4 In the social dreaming matrix, one person tells a dream and the dream group associates to the dream, but only with respect to how the dream reflects something about society or the world at large. Some social dreaming matrices occur online, which allows people from around the world to participate.
5 To work effectively with such a large dream group, it helps to have several wireless microphones, which are moved around the room by assistants, to ensure that every person can be heard.

Part III
Dreams, knowledge, memory, emotion, and the mindbrain

Ever tried. Ever failed. No matter. Try again. Fail again. Fail better.
Samuel Beckett, *Worstward Ho*

Chapter 15

How neuropsychoanalysis and clinical psychoanalysis can learn from each other

Many clinical psychoanalysts, when they think of neuropsychoanalysis, become anxious. They anticipate having to absorb difficult data from PET scans and the like, and they wonder, "Is that effort going to make any difference in my clinical work? Will it, for example, change what I do when I hear a patient's dream?" While neuropsychoanalytic findings are consequential for a reassessment of psychoanalytic theory (Solms, 1995, 1999; Blechner, 2006), it is not always obvious whether such data are relevant to how clinicians work. Some analysts are also intimidated or made anxious by the prospect of learning about data collected by methods with which they are not familiar. As a consequence, they may reject the whole enterprise of integrating modern neuroscience and psychoanalysis. Some do this privately; some do it publicly and in print, e.g., Pulver (2003); Blass and Carmeli (2007). This wish not to know is unfortunate. Surely, if a psychoanalytic patient said categorically, "What you have to offer is of no interest to me," we might suspect resistance and defensiveness.

Even if one were to accept the spurious arguments that findings in neuroscience have no bearing on clinical work, there is the reciprocal possibility that findings from clinical psychoanalysis could be of use to further neuroscience research (Pugh, 2007; Mancia, 2007). The clinician can do research in the consulting room, finding unique data that would be useful to neuroscientists in guiding their research. In doing so, the clinician would be following a plan anticipated by Freud.

The rejection of neuroscientific data was not Freud's attitude. On the contrary, Freud began his work studying neuroanatomy and his first publications were in that field (Gray, 1948; Triarhou and del Cerro, 1985). He continued to value neuroscientific findings and suggested that the whole edifice of psychoanalysis might one day require complete revision, based on neuroscience research:

> The deficiencies in our description would probably vanish if we were already in a position to replace the psychological terms by physiological or chemical ones.... Biology is truly a land of unlimited possibilities. We may expect it to give us the most surprising information and we cannot guess what answers it will return in a few dozen years to the questions we have put to it. They may be of a kind which will blow away the whole of our artificial structure of hypotheses.
>
> (Freud, 1920, p. 60)

Note the phrase "the questions we have put to it [biology]." Freud foresaw a collaboration between psychoanalysis and neuroscience, with an emphasis on psychoanalysts formulating significant questions for biologists to answer. It is this direction of inquiry that I wish to stress in this chapter.

The reciprocal flow of information between psychoanalysis and neuroscience already has several precedents. For example, in 2007, after the Neuro-Psychoanalysis conference in Vienna, robot scientists from the Siemens Company scheduled a second conference. The scientists of robotics in Vienna wanted to hear from the neuropsychoanalysts what were the essential aspects of being human that had been studied by psychoanalysis and affective neuroscience, in order to build robots that most resembled humans. This was a rare interchange between engineers, scientists, and psychoanalysts. It addressed important questions, many of which have been explored in this book, such as: how much is all of our experience involved with emotion, even the most computer-like calculations? What is the domain of bodily experience which informs our every action, although mostly out of our awareness? The psychoanalysts were encouraged to formulate knowledge of human nature in a precise way that could be modeled by the scientists of robotics.

Psychoanalysts tend to become defensive about whether they are scientists and whether they have anything to offer to the world of neuroscience. The area of dreams is one in which psychoanalysts have the potential to make major discoveries of use to neuroscientists. In this chapter, I would like to highlight how clinical psychoanalysts can contribute unique and crucial data to the scientific understanding of dreams. A rigorous approach to data collection from psychoanalytic consulting rooms may also lead to a reconsideration of which aspects of dreams are most significant clinically.

After all, psychoanalytic clinicians collect data unlike any other scientists. Psychoanalysts hear more dreams every day and in greater detail than anyone else in our society. Also, psychoanalysts hear dreams that come from people's natural experience, which we know are different from dreams collected in a laboratory; dreams collected at home contain more verbal aggression and sexual elements than dreams collected in the laboratory (Weisz and Foulkes, 1970; Okuma *et al.*, 1976; Urbina, 1981). Psychoanalysts also immerse themselves in uncanny, intense affective situations, which they then try to understand rationally. From these data, psychoanalysts can suggest many important questions that can be taken up by those doing laboratory research.

Psychoanalysts can analyze the dream in many new ways. Besides their usual efforts to decipher what the dream means, they can also analyze how the manifest content is structured, what forms of irrationality are present, and how that irrationality is experienced by the dreamer. If they pool their data and systematize their observations, psychoanalysts may discover things about the operation of the brain that are quite different from what laboratory neuroscientists are discovering and just as important.

If psychoanalysts listen to dreams, not just for psychodynamic meaning, but also with neurobiological questions in mind, they may be able to outline some neurological processes based on the phenomenology of dreaming. Psychoanalysts sometimes say, "Anything can happen in the unconscious," but this is not true. There are constraints on what can and cannot happen in dreams. I call this the "grammar of irrationality" (Blechner, 2005). For example, the German physicist Hermann von Helmholtz noted how frequently in dreams, when we start an action, we usually continue it according to the way things happen in the natural world. For example, we can dream that "we are stepping onto a boat pushing off from the shore, gliding out on the water, and seeing how the surrounding objects change their positions" (Helmholtz, 1863/1968, p. 223). We do not particularly notice in dreams when the rationally expectable thing happens, but I believe that this is important. Psychoanalysts can systematically observe which kinds of irrationality are common, rare, or impossible in dreams, and how these trends differ from waking experience. Then, they can take these observations and formulate proposals about how people process information and emotion differently when dreaming and awake. Such proposals could then help guide neurophysiologists in organizing their research, by outlining which mental functions may be functionally and neurologically separable from one another, and how, in sleep, these mental functions are reorganized.

As examples of such observations, I will outline two kinds of dream phenomena – "disjunctive cognitions" and "interobjects" – that are special forms of irrationality in dreams (Blechner, 2001). Both of these phenomena involve irrationality that does not surprise most dreamers. We seem to have certain inner guidelines for judging "acceptable reality in dreams." Some kinds of irrationality strike most dreamers as bizarre, but some seem perfectly acceptable and not very surprising in dreams.

Disjunctive cognitions

A dreamer says, "I knew she was my mother, although she didn't look like her." Any clinician who hears dreams regularly knows that such statements are not uncommon. It surprises me that this is not usually surprising to people. Many people, when reporting a bizarre experience in a dream, will prepare the listener by saying "It was the strangest thing..." or "I don't really understand how this could happen, and yet..." But when people in a dream see someone whose identity doesn't match his or her appearance, they usually don't use a qualifying preface to describe the experience. They take it for granted that I will know what they mean. It is what I call "a commonplace bizarreness (or irrationality) of dreamlife."[1] The dreamer recognizes a character's identity, even though the person's appearance does not match the identity. There is a disjunction between appearance and identity. In waking life, most sane people would assume that they mis-saw or misidentified the person, and correct for it; but not necessarily in dreams.

This is just one example of what I call "disjunctive cognitions." Two aspects of cognition do not match each other; the dreamer is aware of the disjunction, yet that does not prevent it from remaining. In our waking lives, we would not normally say "She didn't look like her, but I knew it was my mother." Somehow we feel comfortable reporting such experiences when they occur in a dream. Yet when communicating about waking experiences, we tend to avoid, or at least qualify, statements that are logically impossible, lest we be thought insane.

That is one of the main things that distinguishes the schizophrenic from the nonschizophrenic. Arieti (1974) gave the example of a schizophrenic man who said "My mother is Switzerland." He felt his mother was like Switzerland, in that she was independent and free. But if he had said "My mother is like Switzerland," that statement would have seemed more poetic than mad.

In dreams, we usually cannot make that choice. In dreams, there are usually no qualifiers. We can dream "She didn't look like her, but I knew it was my mother." We don't tend to dream "She didn't look like her, but I felt that in some way she was like my mother." That is the language of waking thinking. Dreamers are like Hamlet (I.ii.76), when he said to his mother, "Seems, madam! Nay, it *is*. I know not 'seems.'" And when we are awake and speak about our dreams, we continue to accept the disjunctive cognition without qualifiers.

What disjunctive cognitions can tell us about the mindbrain

Disjunctive cognitions may have important implications for understanding the organization of the mindbrain. The larger working hypothesis that I suggest we explore is as follows: Wherever disjunctive cognitions occur, the two aspects of cognition that are disjunctive are handled in different mindbrain systems whose mutual integration is suppressed or shifted during sleep. Thus, in the example of the dream with the mother who doesn't look like mother, perceiving how a person looks and identifying who the person is would be processed in different systems of the mindbrain. The specifics of bizarre dream experiences may help identify the different components of perceptual processing. As these are clarified, we can update Freud's regression model and spell out how different modules of mental processing can interact and provide input to create the dream.

We also will want to pay attention to which disjunctive cognitions do not occur. For example, although it is common to dream, "I knew it was my mother even though it did not look like her," the converse dream is not common: "I knew it was not my mother, even though it looked like her." In fact, in all of my records of my patients' dreams and my own over 25 years, I don't have a single dream like that. Of course, that is not the most systematic research; we would like a much larger sample, collected not only from clinicians, but also from experimental dream researchers, to state definitively that such a dream does not occur or occurs only very rarely. If, however, this tendency is true for the general population of dreamers, it is a significant fact. It may mean that not all contradictions are tolerated unconsciously; something more constrained and systematic than Freud (1915b) described may be involved.

Another disjunctive cognition has to do with time. It is quite common to dream that as an adult, one goes back to a time and place of one's childhood. In this case, the perceived age of the dreamer is disjunctive with the setting of the dream.

The disjunctive cognition of time seems also to have important constraints. Judging by my own experience and that of other psychoanalysts, it is much more uncommon to dream the opposite – that is, someone dreaming of himself as a child, but where the time and place are the present (Kaplan-Solms and Solms, 2000; Blechner, 2001). It is common, however, to dream of others at an earlier age appearing in the present. For example, Appelfeld reported:

A few days after my return [from Prague], I dreamed about my parents. They had not aged since we were together sixty-three years ago in Prague, and their faces expressed amazement that I had grown older. We were briefly united in mutual astonishment, and I knew that I had something important to tell them. But, as in every profound dream, I could not get the words out.

(2001, p. 41)

In the above dream, the dreamer is his current age, while the other characters in the dream are their ages in the past. This is especially common in dreams of people who have lost close relatives (Blechner, 2001, p. 287).

If the possible disjunction of time between the setting of a dream and the age of the dreamer is, in fact, asymmetric, that will be significant for the theory of the unconscious. It might indicate a division in the mindbrain between our sense of the time of our self-representation as separate from our sense of time about other aspects of our experience, and an asymmetry in how these can be combined. Whereas Freud (1915b) described the timelessness of the unconscious, there may be more specific constraints on how time can be altered and distorted unconsciously (Blechner, 2000, 2004; Schwartz and Maquet, 2002). We need to move away from a model of the unconscious in which "anything can happen" to one that specifies which things can happen under which psychological and neurological conditions.

The neurobiology of object representation and transference

Usually, clinicians think of disjunctive cognitions in terms of their psychodynamic meaning. In Fosshage and Loew's (1987) book on dream interpretation, they present one patient's dreams to six clinicians from different schools of thought for interpretation. The first dream included the following disjunctive cognition: "My mother was in there going through my purse. She didn't look like my mother."

Most of the clinicians, regardless of their school of thought, agreed that the person who does not look like who she is represents, not the person herself, but the internal object, the internalized mother. The focus among these analysts was not the division of the mindbrain function, but the division between actual people in the outer world and internalized "people," the internal object representations, that we all carry in us.

But here we face an intriguing possibility. The division of our internal and external object representations must have a mechanism in the mindbrain. What is the mindbrain basis for internal object representations and for the projection of those object representations in transference? Is the neural anatomy that allows internal object representations related to the separate mindbrain areas involved in feature perception and identity perception? For anyone interested in a neurally grounded psychoanalytic science, this seems to be an essential question, even though we may not yet have definitive answers, given our current neurological knowledge.

We may ask, isn't it odd to feel so certain about the identity of the person in the face of contradictory physical evidence? What does this division tell us? It suggests that the processes of seeing the physical attributes of a person are not identical, perhaps not even isomorphic, with the recognition of the identity of that person. But is there any other evidence that those processes are separate in our mindbrains?

Indeed, there is. Let us first look to the field of neuropsychology. We find that some people who have suffered strokes or other mindbrain damage have a syndrome known as "prosopagnosia." A prosopagnosic man may look at his wife of 50 years, see all of her features clearly, and yet not recognize who she is. In such people, the process of seeing is intact, but the process of facial identity recognition is not (Bodamer, 1947).

We also have the phenomenon of Capgras syndrome, in which a person may feel that a close relative is actually an impostor. The features are recognizable, but the person's identity is not. And there is also Frégoli syndrome, in which a person may mistakenly identify strangers as people that he actually knows. Frégoli syndrome is connected with damage to ventral temporal areas, mostly in the right hemisphere, and to the prefrontal cortex (Young *et al.*, 1990; Hudson and Grace, 2000).

We also can find relevant data from research on visual perception in animals and humans. Scientists are identifying the parts of the mindbrain that are responsible for different aspects of face recognition (see Mesulam, 1998). Gorno-Tempini *et al.* (1998) found that in humans, identifying unfamiliar faces activates unimodal visual association areas in the fusiform region, whereas the recognition of familiar faces also activates an area in the lateral midtemporal cortex. Also, a similar division of function was found by Perrett and colleagues (1982) in macaque monkeys. From such findings, we have come to recognize that the process of facial recognition is indeed very complex and may be achieved by parts of the mindbrain that are different from the mindbrain areas involved in the preliminary analysis of visual features.

We have, thus, a case of several kinds of data converging on a single phenomenon; we have data from human neuropathology, from experimental brain research with humans and animals, and from psychoanalytic observation of dreams, all showing that the processes of feature perception and identity recognition are separated. In normal waking consciousness, the two work in tandem. That may be one of the reasons why it is hard in analysis for people to become aware of their "internal objects." But perhaps the person-recognizing module of the mindbrain can see mother even when the physical features show "not mother." In dreams, psychosis, neuropathological syndromes, and very intense transference states, this division shows up more clearly than in normal waking consciousness.

Psychoanalysts should be excited by this. It suggests a manifestation in dreams of two fundamental concepts of psychoanalysis – namely, transference and object representations – and holds out the possibility of identifying the neurobiological mechanisms of these phenomena (Schwartz and Maquet, 2002).

Interobjects

I would like to turn our attention to another strange form of dream thinking, which I call "interobjects."[2] Interobjects are a kind of dream condensation in which the dream thoughts converge and create a new object that does not occur in waking life and could not occur in waking life. It may have a vague structure that is described as "something between an X and a Y." Allan Hobson (1988) dreamt of "a piece of hardware, something like the lock of a door or perhaps a pair of paint-frozen hinges." Bert States (1995) dreamt of "something between a swimming pool and an aqueduct." In dreams we accept these sorts of intermediate structures. Hobson calls them "incomplete cognitions" and Freud calls them "intermediate and composite structures." I prefer to call them "interobjects." Rather than focus on what they are not (not complete condensations), I would prefer to focus on what they are (new creations derived from blends of other objects).

It is remarkable that in our waking reports of dreams, we readily report these interobjects. As with disjunctive cognitions, the dreamer usually does not qualify his report by noting how strange it was to have perceived the interobject in his dream. He usually just reports it. Interobjects, like disjunctive cognitions, are a commonplace irrationality of dreamlife. In waking life, such a percept would be considered bizarre. But an interobject that could be judged irrational in the waking world is nevertheless not experienced as bizarre in the dream world.

These intermediate and compromise structures, these interobjects, may have an elementary function in human thought that has barely been explored. By violating our usual category boundaries, they can, via "Oneiric Darwinism" (Blechner, 2001) be crucial in the formation of really new ideas that would be harder to come by using only fully formed, secondary process formations. An interobject dream, for example, may have been the source of the composite figures of mythology that cross species, like the Minotaur, griffin, and sphinx, as well as many artistic creations. Leonardo da Vinci considered imagination to be based on *fantasia*, which is the ability to recombine images or parts of images into entirely new compounds or ideas.

Interobjects suggest something else about cognitive processing. We humans tend to categorize items into discrete categories. But, at least in our dreams and perhaps in our unconscious waking life, we may find commonalities between objects that are normally kept in separate categories. The interobject reported by Meltzer that I mentioned before (p. 31) – "something between a phonograph and a balance" – suggests a category of objects that have circular metal platters and straight metal bars. This is not a category of objects of which most of us are aware. It is an open question whether the dream of this interobject suggests something undiscovered about mental feature detectors and unconscious category formation – an important part of the "unrepressed unconscious" (Freud, 1923; Matte-Blanco, 1975, 1988; Lombardi, 2011).[3]

In this way, the interobjects produced in dreams may tell us something about the way the mindbrain organizes information. In dreams, when the mindbrain is generating stimuli rather than perceiving them, these internal organizational factors, of which we are usually unaware, can make their existence known. When the mindbrain is producing percepts during dreaming, while serotonin activity is reduced, patterns of neural firing may bring together representations that are grouped together in psychical reality, which allows the creation of new objects. Although aqueducts have very different functions from swimming pools, we may ignore that in dreaming. Instead, the dreaming mindbrain "notices" the similarity of aqueducts and swimming pools – they are both man-made objects containing large amounts of water – and can condense them into "something between a swimming pool and an aqueduct," or an "aque-pool" (States, 1995). It may be worth our while to specify the constraints of possible interobjects, in the interest of further specifying the grammar of irrationality. Can the mindbrain combine any two things? Are night-time mental recombinations subject to total chaos? And if not, which rules apply?

So far, there is little data to answer these questions, although research aimed at other questions offers suggestions about what some of the rules of mental recombination might be. For example, Rakison and Butterworth (1998; see also Rakison and Cohen, 1999), found that infants aged 14–22 months can distinguish between the categories of animals and vehicles, such as a cow and a car. But they wanted to know, what was it about a cow or a car that was important to the distinction? And so they presented infants with what I would call interobjects: a cow with wheels instead of legs, and a car with legs instead of wheels. The infants either stopped being able to categorize the stimuli, or tended to categorize them according to legs versus wheels, which may have indicated that they attended most to the parts most involved in movement.[4] While these studies provide interesting information on how infants deal with interobjects created by adults, they do not answer our question about the grammar of object combinations that are permissible in dreams.

More relevant to our question, Rittenhouse *et al.* (1994) have provided data on a related phenomenon, the transformation of objects in adult dreams, such as "the car turned into a bike." In their study, which collected dreams from students in a continuing education class, they found that inanimate objects never turned into humans, nor vice versa. There were five cases, however, in which there was a transformation of either a person or an inanimate object into a *nonhuman* animate object. They also found that in most transformations, the new object shares formal associative properties with the prior object.

We can also look to the literature on mindbrain damage and the localization of capacities for different kinds of objects. Warrington and McCarthy (1983) showed that some aphasics lose the ability to name only a certain category of objects; they may, for example, lose the ability to name inanimate objects while still being able to name animals. They may also lose the ability to name just one category of things, such as animals, fruits and vegetables, or humans. (These different abilities are discussed in more detail in Chapter 2.) We may posit a continuum of categories – from inanimate objects, to fruits and vegetables, to animals, to humans – with each of these being processed in a different part of the mindbrain. It is possible that the mindbrain, in creating dream interobjects tends to combine things from within one category, or two things that are one category apart.

Exceptions to this rule may occur when something in one category is *experienced* as belonging to another category. For example, a cellphone is technically inanimate, but it has some animate and human characteristics. The interobject cellphone-baby looks like it has objects three categories apart, but they are closer experientially. They both belong to a class of small things that we hold close to the body and speak to, and they both emit loud noises unexpectedly.

In addition, there may be a difference between general inanimate objects and tools that humans can manipulate (Lewis, 2006). If we could amass a large catalogue of interobjects, we might be better able to generalize about these guidelines. It may be relevant, also, to consider the kinds of interobjects that have appeared in mythology, in modern fiction (such as children's cartoons), and in the products of computer "morphing" programs (e.g., Goldenberg *et al.*, 1999).

Let us go back for a moment to the child's dream of the seal/boat, which was discussed on p. 19:

They were crossing the channel, and for some reason needed another boat. They were frightened, but then a seal swam up to them. They thought it was just a seal, but then they looked and under the water it was a whole boat, it was huge, so they climbed onto the seal/boat, and it brought them to the shore of mainland.

The child puts together a seal and a boat; both are objects that can navigate through water. That is an aspect that they share; but one is animate and the other inanimate. We know that children don't place as much store by the animate/inanimate distinction as adults. Children like to imagine that the inanimate world can come to life. Teacups dance; books speak. Read any child's book and you will find many examples of this. Children say, "Goodnight moon" (Brown and Hurd, 1947). As the child develops, he or she learns to suppress this tendency, although as adults, when we say things to our children like "Here comes Mr. Wind!" we may be rediscovering our capacity for blurring the animate/inanimate distinction.

There may also be certain kinds of perception that are shaped genetically. Polk *et al.* (2007) compared neural responses to faces, houses, pseudowords, and chairs in monozygotic and dizygotic twins and in unrelated people. They found that face- and place-related items were more similar for monozygotic than dizygotic twins, but there was no difference for written words. We might expect that face recognition is an evolutionarily older process than word recognition, so this result may not be a surprise. But it opens up the question of whether there are similarities in dreaming, as well, in monozygotic twins that are not there in dizygotic twins.

These data help us approach larger questions: How is the world organized in the mindbrain? How does this organization shape the kinds of phenomena that appear in dreams?

By collecting more data on dreamt interobjects, psychoanalysts could be at the forefront of such research. It would be an enormous contribution to neuroscience, which is very concerned with processes of categorization (Rosch, 1977; Edelman, 1987).

Psychoanalysis of patients with neurological syndromes

Another path of research that could be undertaken by psychoanalysts is to study the dreams of patients in psychotherapy with neurological illnesses, those that are relatively common as well as rare syndromes. For example, there has been a theory that dreamlike experiences while we are awake (sometimes referred to as hallucinosis) are connected in content and structure to dreams while we are asleep. Do all dream materials partake of the same unconscious themes, or are there special characteristics to night dreams that differentiate them from other fantasy dreamlike productions caused by illness or mindbrain damage, as in Parkinson disease (Arnulf *et al.*, 2000)? Feve and Hart (2006) looked into this question, with a single patient following a stroke, and found similar content and latent themes in the patient's waking hallucinations and night dreams. Epstein (1995), studying people with seizure disorders, found similar content in the imagery of their seizures and dreams.

There is much research that could be done by clinical psychoanalysts to explore the relationship of other dreamlike experiences to night dreams. For example, in Charles Bonnet syndrome, people with deteriorated vision start to have hallucinations. Bonnet syndrome is much more common than once was thought; it occurs among more than 10 percent of elderly people with visual disturbances such as macular degeneration. Many people with it try to hide the fact that they are hallucinating for fear of being thought psychotic. Yet most patients with Bonnet syndrome show no signs of psychosis besides their hallucinations, and they benefit from being told that such hallucinations are normal.

An important question is: to what degree are Charles Bonnet hallucinations similar to dreams in the same patient? One woman said, "In my dreams I experience things which affect me, which are related to my life. These hallucinations, however, have nothing to do with me" (Teunisse *et al.*, 1996, p. 796). But some patients thought their visions could have psychological significance. "One elderly childless man was intrigued by recurrent hallucinations of a little girl and boy and wondered whether these hallucinations reflected his unfulfilled wish to be a father. One widow hallucinated her recently deceased husband three times a week" (ibid.) In these two examples, the visions fulfill a wish, much as some dreams do. It would be useful to collect the dreams of patients with such neurological syndromes and to compare them systematically with the hallucinations. Such a study might further clarify the relationship between waking visual nonpsychotic hallucination and dream hallucination.

Do neuroscience findings guide clinical work?

Can findings in neuroscience improve the way one works clinically? This is an issue too large to discuss thoroughly in this chapter (see Brockman, 1998). There is an emerging consensus that with some kinds of psychopathology – specifically, post-traumatic stress disorder (PTSD) and borderline personality disorder (BPD) – "correct interpretations" may not be effective, and may actually cause disruption. The clinician needs to be aware of the biological limitations of the patient who is under extreme stress and whose mindbrain has been changed by traumatic experience. Interpretations of splitting, however correct, can be useless or even destructive when a borderline patient's biological state precludes hearing clearly and thinking. As Brockman (2002, p. 97) has written:

> Is [the borderline patient's] problem at the level of hierarchical organization, and the failure of the integration of self and object images within the neocortex, and thus to be treated cognitively from above? Or is her problem the failure of cognition and the inability to think because hidden biological systems, the underlying regulators of behavior, have changed? We need to know whether the neurotransmitters of attachment are operating around basic set points of safety or set points of fear. It makes a difference in what we do, in what we say, in how we help. And knowing how to help and at what level to help is important.

Anyone who has offered interpretations to a borderline patient along the lines recommended by Kernberg (1975), only to find the patient storming out of the consulting room and engaging in self-destructive behavior, can appreciate the need to stay attuned to the biological tuning of a patient's nervous system.

Similarly, with PTSD patients, knowledge of neurobiology can change how one intervenes. Most significant is the finding that sexual and violent trauma during childhood may be literally "unrememberable" because of the effects of trauma on memory encoding and the development of the hippocampus (Jacobs *et al.*, 1996). The result is that *the person's emotional system reacts very strongly to reminders of the original trauma while the actual experience of trauma cannot be remembered.* Interestingly, however, traces of the events may be discovered in dreams, and we do not yet know how that happens.

Yovell (2000) has outlined four basic precepts for the psychotherapist treating someone with early sexual trauma:

1 Do not make interpretations that aim to recover early traumatic memories, when such recovery is impossible and may lead to unnecessary frustration and anger in the patient.
2 In patients with early trauma, do not "go for the affect" and "strike while the iron is hot" in one's interventions. This may overwhelm the patient and render the intervention useless, while "striking while the iron is cold" may be more effective.
3 Consider administering SSRIs (selective serotonin reuptake inhibitors), not just for their antidepressant effects, but for their potential to enhance neuronal regeneration in a compromised memory system.
4 Use neurological findings to explain to the patient how he or she might continue to react to a trauma that is not remembered – in fact, may be incapable of being remembered.

The clinical recommendations of Brockman and Yovell are subject to confirmation. Clinicians may test them out in the consulting room and observe if they are helpful to the clinical interaction. In this way, clinicians may improve the effectiveness of their clinical interventions and perhaps formulate new questions for researchers to investigate.

Notes

1 It may be helpful to distinguish between "irrationality" and "bizarreness" in dreams. Most bizarreness is irrational, but not all irrationally is experienced as bizarre. Bizarreness in dreams might be defined as surprising, illogical aspects that engender a feeling of strangeness in the dreamer, which nonbizarre irrationality does not. This distinction is another important dimension of the grammar of irrationality.
2 Interobjects were also discussed in Chapter 3. The reader may wish to reread pp. 30–33 at this point.
3 Freud (1923) acknowledged the existence of the unrepressed unconscious and saw it as a potentially enormous segment of mental functioning.
4 Hence, in a presentation of their work prior to publication, Rakison and Cohen gave their paper the more catchy title "You've got to roll with it, baby: The effect of functional parts on infants' categorization."

Chapter 16

Elusive illusions

Reality judgment and reality assignment in dreams and waking life

> HAMLET: Was't Hamlet wronged Laertes? Never Hamlet.
> If Hamlet from himself be ta'en away,
> And when he's not himself does wrong Laertes,
> Then Hamlet does it not, Hamlet denies it.
> Who does it then? His madness.
> William Shakespeare, *The Tragedy of Hamlet,
> Prince of Denmark*

I am a clinical psychoanalyst. While I used to do laboratory research in cognitive psychology, these days my laboratory is my office. I have been collecting data from the clinical psychoanalytic situation, not only from brain-injured patients, but also from patients who have no known brain injury. I then try to formulate, from that data, some hypotheses about how the mindbrain is organized, and to look in the cognitive neuroscience literature for studies that might shed light on these questions. I also make comparisons with the phenomenology of neurologically injured patients, and I try to propose experiments that might test the hypotheses generated by my clinical data (Blechner, 2000, 2001, 2014).

Practicing psychoanalysts have access to a kind of data that no one else does in our society. We hear more dreams and look at them more carefully than anyone else in today's world. We also immerse ourselves in uncanny, intense affective situations which we then try to understand rationally. From these data, we can suggest many important questions that can be taken up by those doing laboratory research.

The study of dreams brings us to some central questions of modern cognitive neuroscience which I would like to explore, namely: What do we know, and how do we know that we know it? How can we tell whether something really happened to us or whether we imagined or dreamt it, which is known as "reality monitoring" (Johnson and Raye, 1981; Johnson et al., 1984)? Mostly, we are quite good at making such discriminations, but there are ways that so-called normal people make reality-monitoring mistakes. This was the case with Harry Stack Sullivan's spider dream (Sullivan, 1953, p. 335), from which he woke up and continued to see his dream spider on the bed for a while; many people know first-hand the experience of an intense dream that carries over into the waking state for a bit.

I would also like to explore the degree to which the reality-monitoring systems of dreaming and waking are unitary or separate. There is a Chinese tale in the *Chuang Tzu*:

> *Once Chuang Chou dreamed that he was a butterfly. He fluttered about happily, quite pleased with the state he was in, and knew nothing about Chuang Chou. Presently he awoke and found that he was very much Chuang Chou again. Now, did Chou dream that he was a butterfly or was the butterfly now dreaming that he was Chou?*
> (Parsifal-Charles, 1986, p. 65)

And to these questions, we can add: Could Chou, while asleep, compare his judgment that he was a butterfly with his waking belief that he was a human and decide during his dream which was more real? And is this determination during sleep different, functionally and neurologically, from the determination Chou would have made during the waking state? (Chuang Tzu, 1997; see Metzinger, 2003, for a more recent philosophical analysis of these questions.)

The process of how we can tell whether an experience is a perception of the environment or an internally generated image is not fully understood. Kosslyn outlines several cues may help us distinguish imagery from perception, but notes that this capacity may be diminished during dreaming:

> First, the stimulus-based attention-shifting subsystem operates only during perception; thus, if our attention is suddenly grabbed by an object or event, we are not engaged in imagery. This may not be true during dreams, however: During waking imagery, one always knows the identity of the objects one is imaging; during dreaming, this apparently is not always true. Moreover, the "rules" of dreaming allow objects to appear in unusual contexts, so it is conceivable that

one's mental attention is "grabbed" during dreaming in a way that is reminiscent of the way it is captured during perception. I have no evidence one way or the other that the same subsystem is used when attention is shifted by stimulus properties during perception and during dreaming, but I tend to doubt it: The connections from the eye to the superior colliculus, which appear critical for the attention-shifting subsystem, are unlikely to be evoked during imagery.

(1994, pp. 102–103)

Kosslyn proposes here that reality judgments may be carried out by different neurological subsystems during waking and sleeping. He does not address the comparison of reality judgments between the two states. He also does not consider the additional role of strong wishes and affects in shaping our judgments of reality during waking and sleeping, which is more frequently studied in the psychoanalytic consulting room than in the laboratory.

I have evidence from clinical material suggesting that there is a complicated interrelationship between reality judgments made during dreaming and waking states. This complicated interrelationship was vividly illustrated by the dream of one of my patients, Robert, which went as follows:

My mother and I are on a bus, going to do an errand. Waiting for the bus, there is a line of people with my father in it. He has been dead 20–25 years. He is looking well. He is in his 40s. (He actually died in his 50s.) I see him and he sees us. It seemed unbelievable that, seeing us, he'd get on the bus. The line shortened. Dad got on. I had fantasized that my father was alive, but this was real.

Dad, while not oblivious to my mother and me, was as interested in his acquaintances sitting in front of us. After reaching our destination, we all got off the bus. Dad went his way, unconcerned, leaving Mother and me to do the business we had set out to do. I was tremendously upset by the fact, and matter-of-factness, of the situation. Mother was controlled.

Mother's explanation revealed an elaborate plan, involving the collusion of the undertaker, in which a double was substituted for my father at the time of his supposed death. He, of course, had not died; he had just wanted to remove himself from Mother and the family, and with Mother's help, had devised this complex scheme. Now he

> *was living, going about his business – I think he was working for a hotel as a kind of upper-class servant – essentially unconcerned about the family he left behind.*

It was striking to me that, in the dream, Robert was comparing his dream experience with a waking fantasy and deciding that the dream experience was *more real*. As he said: "I had fantasized that my father was alive, but this was real." In daytime reality, Robert seems convinced that his father died. When Robert was 12, he saw his father suffer from chronic illness and waste away for many months. Nevertheless, he has at times imagined that his father is still alive. And in this dream, he compares the dream with his waking fantasy, and judges that his father is *really* alive.

Clinically, I felt that this dream showed that Robert's belief that his father was dead was coexisting with the belief that his father was alive. I got support for this conclusion when, as part of Robert's associations, he told me another dream, in which he and his father are in a long hall, and the hall keeps getting longer and shorter. He said it reminded him of a scene in Alfred Hitchcock's *Vertigo*.

The critical point in the film *Vertigo* is that it shows a woman killing herself by jumping off a bell tower. Later, we discover that this was a hoax; the woman we had seen climbing the bell tower turns out to still be alive; after she had climbed the bell tower, a man at the top threw his already murdered wife from the bell tower. Everyone was fooled – which proves that just because you see someone die doesn't mean that they really died. That, at least, was the unconscious lesson that I think Robert learned from the movie; *Vertigo* fit Robert's unconscious fantasy that his father was still alive, and that his death was a ruse.

The idea that his father was alive was not really unconscious for Robert. He had often fantasized it, so we cannot even say that it was repressed. Instead, it was dissociated, segmented off from the bulk of his conscious thinking.

I said to Robert,

> Part of your mind believes your father is dead. But another part of your mind believes that your father is still alive, still walking among us. He is hiding out from the family that he wanted to get away from, working as you say as a high-class servant. As you note in your dream, this idea is real to you.

He said, "But it was just a dream!" He felt I was making this up, although, he acknowledged in the next session that when reading over his record of the dream, he could see how I could take it that way. He imagined telling his mother, "My analyst thinks that Father is still alive and working in a hotel," and her saying, "Your analyst is crazy." (Of course, given what she had done in the dream, she *would* say I was crazy, rather than admit it.)

I felt unsure about my interpretation, but I felt very clear that it was derived from Robert's experience of the dream. If the interpretation was wrong, he at least needed to think through what he meant by, "This was real."

He protested against my view and struggled with it, but it made sense out of things that had been happening in his life and in our sessions. His transference tended to become too real, and I think that was part of the trouble in his previous analyses. Once in our work together, when he was talking about how his father had abused him, he became overwhelmed with fear, rage, and grief, in a way that seemed like he was actually reexperiencing the early trauma in the moment, in abreaction. He jumped up from the couch and ran out of my office. He had had the same experience a few times before in prior treatments and had wondered then if he was going crazy. I think the recognition of simultaneous beliefs, of his father being dead and alive, made the vividness of those rages more understandable.

Also, the more he spoke about the hoax carried out by his parents in the dream, the less farfetched it seemed to him. He said, he didn't think they had really done it, but they could have, given their personalities. Mother was quite secretive and very good at maintaining her composure. He thought she was capable of pulling off the scheme portrayed in the dream if she wanted to.

So gradually he explored more calmly and explicitly the idea of his father not having died when Robert was 12. It allowed his mindbrain to work through and integrate what was mostly a split-off idea. He said that even if the dream was real, by today his father would be very old and almost certainly would have died anyway. This was in itself useful; it allowed him to work through his feelings about his father's death, now.

I think that Robert's dream and the whole clinical interchange show how complex the mindbrain's appraisal of reality can be, and how it may be altered by strong wishes and affects. It is not very unusual for us to judge, wrongly, that what is happening in our dreams is real.[1] It is more unusual for us, during a dream, to do what Robert did – to compare the dream with a waking fantasy, and to judge, during the dream, that the fantasy is not real, but that the dream is real.

We can get a better perspective on the significance of Robert's dream by comparing it with findings in mindbrain-injured patients and experimental studies with normal subjects. For example, some patients with mindbrain damage may have experiences that are analogous to Robert's dream experience. Karen Kaplan-Solms and Mark Solms (2000), in their book *Clinical Studies in Psychoanalysis*, describe a patient with damage in the frontal limbic region, who dreams excessively but loses the ability to distinguish between dreams and real experiences, while Whitty and Lewin (1957) describe a similar phenomenon in patients who have undergone right cingulectomies. The blurring in these patients between reality, fantasy, and dreaming seems similar to Robert's situation, although much more severe.

It suggests that Robert might even have a "shadow syndrome" version of a patient with clear frontal limbic damage. Interestingly, he felt a great deal of anxiety at the blurring of fantasy and reality in others. Sometime after reporting this dream, he expressed great annoyance: a friend's dog had died, and the friend had written a fantasy-obituary in the first-person voice of the dog. Some people had found the obituary creative and moving, but Robert felt quite distressed about the blurring of fantasy and reality, as well as the possible misrepresentation of the friend's experience as the dog's. One would like to investigate, along these lines, how the patients with frontal limbic damage described by Kaplan-Solms and Solms (2000) can experience fantasy, not only their own but that of other people, and to what degree they find confusions of fantasy and reality to be frightening, as they are to Robert.

Reality testing and reality assignment

Robert's dream raises some other questions that have not been addressed in depth by cognitive neuroscientists so far: What does it mean to judge, in a dream, "This is real"? Think about the phrase "a real experience in a dream." Is that an oxymoron? It raises the question: How much are our judgments of reality based on mental conclusions about the situation perceived in the world around us? Or, alternatively, *how much is reality just a quality that our mindbrains can apply to an experience?* It could be that we should study not only "reality testing" but also "reality assignment."

In our waking life, we usually presume that the real world is our waking world, and the dream world is not real, but imagined. But what do we presume when we are asleep and dreaming?

There is no single answer. There are many kinds of awareness of sleeping and dreaming. The most common state of dreaming is a kind of agnosia. We don't realize that we are dreaming. Most dreaming is "non-reflective" (Rechtschaffen, 1978). As the dream is going on, we think it is really happening. Thus, in "normal" dreaming, our reality monitoring is faulty.

By contrast, there is also the phenomenon known as "lucid dreaming," in which the dreamer is aware that he or she is dreaming. Lucid dreamers seem to have more accurate reality monitoring than regular dreamers, at least in their dreams. Some lucid dreamers also claim to be able to direct the outcome of the dream during the dream (Gackenbach and LaBerge, 1988).

But even that is not the whole story. There are many ways in which the experience of sleep and dreaming can be weirdly nested. For instance, one person told me: "In my dream I got tired, so I lay down and took a nap." Another person had a dream within a dream. He told me: "In the dream, I fell asleep and then I dreamt that such and such happened...." Another person told me, "I had a dream.... And then in the dream, I told you the dream." People also have the experience during a dream of waking up from their sleep. In fact, they are still dreaming.

These phenomena raise many questions about consciousness: What does it mean to "know" that one is asleep or to know that one is dreaming, especially since we can be wrong? How does the sleeping mindbrain create the illusion of going to sleep or of waking up, while asleep? And there are more fundamental questions: How does reality monitoring occur when we are asleep? Is it the same as, related to, or completely different than our waking reality monitoring? Might there be two relatively independent reality-monitoring systems, one for waking and one for dreaming, as suggested by Rechtschaffen (1978) and Kosslyn (1994)? And if so, is there cross-talk between the two systems, what Purcell *et al.* (1986) called "cross-phase transference?"

Studies of these questions so far have not been conclusive. There has been some research comparing waking and dreaming states that concludes that they are quite different and relatively isolated from one another (Rechtschaffen, 1978; Hobson, 1988). Other researchers, especially those interested in lucid dreaming, argue that the differences and isolation between waking and sleeping are exaggerated (Kahan and LaBerge, 1994, 1996; Kahan et al., 1997). Bradley et al. (1992) found that dreaming is not as "single-minded" as Rechtschaffen (1978) argued. They found that eight out of ten subjects reported having experiences of "dream reflection," in which subjects gave "reports of having reflected, during the dream, on the plausibility of the events experienced" (p. 162). Yet they do not report anyone comparing the reality of the dream events to waking fantasy, as Robert did. In fact, their subjects did not report comparisons, while sleeping, between the dream experience and any episodic memory.

Nevertheless, lucid dreamers report that while dreaming, they are sometimes able to remember the circumstances of waking life (Green, 1968; LaBerge, 1985). And some can even assess that they must be dreaming by analyzing, during the dream, the scientific plausibility of the experienced situation, as in this example reported by Moers-Messmer (LaBerge, 1985, pp. 38–39):

From the top of a rather low and unfamiliar hill, I look out across a wide plain towards the horizon. It crosses my mind that I have no idea what time of year it is. I check the sun's position. It appears almost straight above me with its usual brightness. This is surprising, as it occurs to me that it is now autumn, and the sun was much lower only a short time ago. I think it over: The sun is now perpendicular to the equator, so here it has to appear at an angle of approximately 45 degrees. So if my own shadow does not correspond to my own height, I must be dreaming. I examine it: It is about 30 centimeters long. It takes considerable effort for me to believe this almost blindingly bright landscape and all of its features to be only an illusion.

It is interesting that many of these studies of self-reflectiveness during dreaming cite examples of dreamers who correctly judge reality during the dream. In Robert's dream, by contrast, he compares the waking fantasy and dreaming situation, and incorrectly concludes that the dream experience is real.

Wishes and reality judgments

We can come to appreciate psychic reality in our dreams. When we awaken, we may question the reality of something that felt real in a dream. When we sleep, we may question the reality of things that felt real in our waking life. As Robert's dream shows us, such judgments may be swayed by strong wishes and affects (De Masi et al., 2015).

Robert's dream led me to consider that the wish to deny death could be especially powerful in shifting our reality judgments during dreaming and waking, producing self-reflections that are factually faulty but with a high level of conviction. When I discussed Robert's dream with one of my colleagues, he told me that he had had a similar dream experience. He said,

> *The night after my mother died I had a dream in which she appeared, dressed as she was at my wedding, walking toward me and smiling. I started to cry in the dream, tears of relief, and thought, "Oh! She is alive! That was just a dream that she died!"*

I have been keeping records of my patients' and my own dreams for 30 years. In all those recorded dreams, I have found only one other example of a patient making the judgment that something happening in a dream was "really happening," more real than waking reality.[2] This was the dream of Mr. P (Blechner, 1983, p. 493), in which he sees a gravestone of his late grandmother turn into a statue of her. The statue starts to deflate and inflate, and then it really becomes his grandmother. He thinks during the dream that this proves there is an afterlife.[3]

Interestingly, Mr. P was someone who had psychotic-like experiences during his waking life that felt to him like dreams. After one such experience, he said: "What happened? I thought I was a reality-testing individual. The whole thing took me over. I hate it when it happens. It's like having a dream."

In addition, Rechtschaffen reports a similar experience:

> *I recently dreamed that my father, who has been dead for many years, engaged me in conversation. My "understanding" in the dream was that he had returned from a place where dead souls rest to discuss a matter with me. In the dream, I was, for a passing*

moment, puzzled that he had been able to return from the dead, but I had no doubt that it had happened.

(1978, p. 100)

Thus, all the dreams that I have found (admittedly very few) – in which a person judges that the dream is real and compares it, during the dream, to waking reality – involve someone who is dead. Moreover, the patient described by Kaplan-Solms and Solms with damage to the frontal limbic region, who loses the ability to distinguish between dreams and real experience, is a widow, and her confused perceptions involve her late husband.

This is not a very large sample, nor is my data systematic and controlled, so it can only be suggestive, but I think there is something to look into here. It is also a fact that when a close relative dies, it is very common for the survivor to hallucinate the deceased person. Two studies – one in England and one in Japan – both found that approximately 50 percent of widows hallucinate their late husbands (Rees, 1975; Marris, 1958; Yamamoto *et al.*, 1969). That is a rather robust statistic, which has not been accounted for adequately by neuroscience nor neuropsychoanalysis.

Does the wish to have a dead person still alive have a special and widespread power to alter our reality testing and reality assignment? And, if so, how does that wish exert its effect neurologically? We wish that death did not exist, and we can see evidence of this wish everywhere. We can see it in the concept of an afterlife, which can be found in most religions and offers us a great deal of comfort. We can see it in the popular television show that featured a psychic who communicated with people's dead relatives. And we can see it in many movies on the same subject, such as *Ghost*, where dead people see what we are doing, even though we don't see them, and they intervene in our lives. The movie *The Sixth Sense* played on our sense of reality even more by having us see the world through the eyes of a dead man who thinks he is still alive. We do not discover that he is really dead until he does. And then we have to rethink the puzzling things that happened before and now make sense – much like Robert had to do in his analysis.

Psychoanalysts have observed how persistent is the belief in an afterlife, whether one is religious or not. Freud wrote, in "Thoughts for the times on war and death":

> It is indeed impossible to imagine our own death; and whenever we attempt to do so we can perceive that we are in fact still present as spectators ... in the unconscious every one of us is convinced of his own immortality.
>
> (1915c, p. 289)

Freud attributes our sense of immortality to our need to retain the love objects lost to death. "[Man] devised a compromise: he conceded the fact of his own death, but denied it the significance of annihilation.... It was beside the dead body of someone he loved that he invented spirits" (2015c, p. 294).

Arlow (1982, p. 192) wrote:

> In our work with patients, we observe again and again the persistent appeal of the notion of an afterlife, even in people who are non-believers. For people who have lost loved ones early in life or who have suffered bitterly from the injustices of the world, the belief in a future world after death, in which all wishes will be fulfilled, is hard to shake. Often it persists at an unconscious level in sharp contradistinction to the individual's ordinary, scientific outlook.

Can all dead people live on in our unconscious? We celebrate the 200th anniversary of Mozart's birth. The sane version of this commemoration is: if Mozart had lived, he would be 200 years old. The psychotic version is: Mozart is 200 years old.

A schizophrenic man continued to believe that his dead father was still alive and reported "experiences" of contact with the dead father; in these delusions, the father continued to age in a calendar-appropriate way.

Perhaps the most striking – and moving – example of this type of delusion (about the dead) was provided by a patient with an anterior communicating artery subarachnoid hemorrhage (Solms, 2000, Case G) who stated that his son (who had died at the age of three, 20 years before) was currently 23 years old.

If the wish to retain the beloved and to deny the reality of death is behind the hallucinations of the bereaved, how does that wish operate neurologically to produce a dream like Robert's or the "normal" hallucinations of widows and widowers? That is a question for further research.

I have been able to find some PET-scan data concerning hallucinations, but nothing particular to the hallucinations of the bereaved. For example, Szechtman *et al.* (1998) found that different parts of the mindbrain are involved in hallucinating an object and imagining an object. They propose that inappropriate activation of the right anterior cingulate (Brodmann area 32) may lead self-generated thoughts to be experienced as external, producing spontaneous auditory hallucinations. Interestingly, a study of dissociation in PTSD (Lanius *et al.*, 2002) also revealed higher levels of activation of the right anterior cingulate in patients who dissociated than those who did not, suggesting a possible role of the anterior cingulate in shifting consciousness of reality toward a pattern in which external input is downplayed in favor of internally driven, defensive, and need-based awareness.

Silbersweig *et al.* (1995), studying hallucinations in schizophrenics, also found activation of the right anterior cingulate, along with other areas (the bilateral thalamus, hippocampus/parahippocampal gyrus, right ventral striatum, and left orbitofrontal cortex). However, schizophrenics when hallucinating frequently feel frightened and persecuted. Thus, schizophrenic hallucinations are subjectively quite different from widows' hallucinations, which usually are comforting, rather than anxiety-inducing, and therefore might be expected to have somewhat different patterns of mindbrain activity.

Finally, some of the most prolific theorizing about hallucinations in the bereaved has come from parapsychologists. They do not use the word "hallucinations," which obviously stacks the epistemological deck. They use the word "apparition," which leaves open the question of whether the visual experience is fabricated by the mindbrain or results from an actual spiritual presence. And, indeed, most of the world's people see the frequent hallucination of the dead as evidence that the dead person's spirit really does survive and returns to visit the survivors.

In summary, I think Robert's dream identifies several properties of the human mindbrain and raises several questions, as well. The dream illustrates the human capacity to make judgments of reality *during* dreaming and to compare them with judgments made while awake. It suggests the possibility of a reality-monitoring system during sleep that is to some degree independent of waking reality-monitoring. It also demonstrates that the experience that something is real may not be based simply on perception of the outer world. On the contrary, reality may be *a quality* that the mindbrain can assign to *any* mental experience. We can even judge, in a dream, that the dream is more real than a waking fantasy or a waking perception. Finally, Robert's dream illustrates how the wish for someone to be alive, which we know causes waking hallucinations of the dead, can also modify our reality judgment during dreaming. We need more systematic data to determine whether our strong wish for the dead to be alive has a *special* capacity for altering our judgment of reality and, if so, what are the neural underpinnings of such a modification of reality monitoring.

Notes

1 Chuang Tzu (1997, p. 30) wrote: "In the midst of a dream, we can't know it's a dream." This is usually true, but not for lucid dreamers (Kahan and LaBerge, 1994).
2 It would be useful for dream researchers who analyze dream records from large nonclinical populations to determine how frequently dreams like Robert's are reported.
3 Daniel Kozloff (personal communication) notes how similar this dream is to the end of Shakespeare's play *The Winter's Tale* in which the statue of the dead queen, Hermione, comes back to life. Mr. P did not connect this dream to Shakespeare's play when we were working together, nor did I. However, if I had, it might have allowed an "amplification" of the dream in the way Jung did with myths. Mr. P shared a cultural heritage with the characters in Shakespeare's play, so he might have been brought up with similar underlying beliefs about afterlife and resurrection.

Chapter 17

When your mindbrain knows things that you don't

Please note: For a complete list of hyperlinks to the relevant musical examples featured in this chapter, please visit the author's website at the following dedicated webpage when prompted to listen: www.markblechner.com/mindbrain/music

It started with laughter. I was listening to a new recording of the *Piano Quintet* by British composer Thomas Adès. During the first movement there is a passage (listen to Musical Example #30 for 15 seconds) that sounds like the repeated cadence at the end of the first movement of Beethoven's Piano Sonata in E-flat, Op. 81a (listen to Musical Example #29 for seven seconds). When I heard it, I started laughing heartily. The resemblance between the two pieces is striking, but why, I wondered, was it funny? I listened to the piece again and again, trying to figure it out. More connections with Beethoven's Sonata jumped out at me. The first movement of the Adès has an opening theme of three rising notes; it could be an upside-down version of the opening theme of Beethoven's Sonata, which is three descending notes. Later in the Adès piece, the theme is reinverted so that it sounds even closer to the Beethoven. But from where did my laughter come? Suddenly it hit me; the Beethoven Sonata is called "Les Adieux" ("The farewell"). "Farewell" can translate into the German word *Adè*, and *Adè*, pluralized, is – Adès! I don't know whether Thomas Adès consciously calculated this play on his name, but I was shocked that my mindbrain figured it out unconsciously and caused my laughter, which my conscious mindbrain then had to figure out.

   A subject of much research in cognitive neuroscience is exactly about how the mindbrain can perform such complicated processing completely unconsciously. Modern science prefers to call it "implicit" processing instead of "unconscious," hoping thereby to avoid the implications of repressed sexuality and other basic drives that have accrued around Freud's thinking about the unconscious. However, in *The Ego and the Id* (1923), Freud discussed a part of the "third unconscious," which is not repressed, but which involves functions that are nevertheless out of awareness and not accessible to consciousness. This latter part of unconscious ego functions, about which Freud commented "and Heaven knows how important a part," has become the increasing focus of attention by cognitive neuroscientists (Kihlstrom, 1986; Libet, 1993; Eysenck and Keane, 2015). And here was my mindbrain responding with laughter to a new piece of music, without being able to spell out consciously what the "joke" was. That was something I had to work out slowly and laboriously.

I have had other experiences in which my mindbrain figured something out before I could. When I was a student in a college musicology class, I was assigned to write a paper, analyzing the opening movement of the Second Sonata for Clarinet and Piano, Op. 120 #2, by Brahms. I had not heard the work before. While listening to it, the thought occurred to me that "The first and second themes of the piece are the same." This thought felt completely convincing, yet, at least on the surface, it was false. As I examined the first and second themes of the piece, I could see that they were two different melodies with quite different characters, the first being very tender and serene, the second being quite forceful and distressed. What was the meaning of this thought that the two themes were the same?

For two weeks, I studied the musical score, struggling over this question. Finally, I wrote out the two themes, one above the other, and compared them. Eureka! I noticed that if you removed some notes from the first theme, what was left was the pitch progression of the first nine notes of the second theme. In a sense, they *were* the same; or, more literally, the melody of the second theme was embedded in the first theme (listen to Musical Example #31 and Musical Example #32).

(For those who do not read music, think of the word "apprentice." If you remove the first, second, fifth, sixth, and seventh letters, what do you get? You get "price." The word "price" is thus embedded in the word "apprentice." This is something like the relation of the two musical themes in the Brahms Sonata.)

My music professor, Ann Besser Scott, congratulated me on my insight into the Brahms Sonata, yet I felt a bit awkward taking credit for

Figure 17.1a Brahms Clarinet Sonata, Op. 120, #2, first movement, clarinet part, theme 1 (notes with an X beneath them occur in Theme 2, in order). Transcribed by Conrad Cummings.

Figure 17.1b Theme 2. Transcribed by Conrad Cummings.

it. I was not sure that "I" had discovered the relationship between the two themes; and if I did, I did not know how. I somehow "knew" that the two themes were the same before I understood how that was, in some sense, true. I then had to do a lot of work to achieve the understanding of the insight that had seemed to come mysteriously into my mindbrain.

This insight into the connection between the two Brahms themes seems to be what we mean when we speak of "intuition." It is a sense that we know something, although we don't know how we know it. It is knowledge of something basic without explanatory details and tempered with doubt; we are not sure it is true, and, true or not, we do not know how we arrived at the knowledge. It is knowledge without metaknowledge; we feel we know something without knowing how or why we know it. Albert Einstein, in a 1932 letter to Erika Fromm (Fromm, 1998), described his experience of developing the theory of relativity as looking for a solution that he felt his mindbrain had already worked out: "the creator of the problem possesses the solution."

Similarly, the mathematician Jacques Hadamard (1945) reported having the solutions to difficult problems leap to his awareness, even though his thoughts were elsewhere.

Freud, in *The Ego and the Id*, wrote:

> On the one hand, we have evidence that even subtle and difficult intellectual operations which ordinarily require strenuous reflection can equally be carried out preconsciously and without coming into consciousness. Instances of this are quite incontestable; they may occur, for example, during the state of sleep, as is shown when someone finds, immediately after waking, that he knows the solution to a difficult mathematical or other problem with which he had been wrestling in vain the day before.
>
> (1923, p. 26)

Is it correct to say that I *had* the thought about the relation of the two Brahms themes before I *understood* the thought? It raises the fundamental question of what it means "to have a thought." Having the thought is itself metaphoric. Have it where? Can you have it, without being able to spell it out?

Do composers always know what they are doing? Do they sometimes feel like they must write music in a certain way without knowing why? Shostakovich, for example, described the experience of feeling compelled to quote other composers in his Symphony No. 15 (discussed on p. 69), without knowing why. He told Isaak Glikman: "I don't myself quite know why the quotations are there, but I could *not*, could *not*, *not* include them." Glikman commented, "I offered the thought that since the creative process was not always accompanied by logic, it was possible that he [Shostakovich] had been guided by pure intuition" (Shostakovich and Glikman, 2001, p. 315).

I do not know if Brahms himself consciously knew of the relation of the two themes of his clarinet sonata. It is possible that he did and did not write or speak about it. It is also possible that in his composing, the second theme occurred to him as going well with the first theme, without his consciously being aware that the second theme was based on the notes of the first theme with some notes deleted.[1]

There are many instances in music history when composers have used musical techniques that were ahead of their time, and we do not know how aware they were of what they were doing or if it just sounded right to them – even if it sounded wrong or shocking to their contemporaries. The "octatonic mode" described by the composer Olivier Messiaen and used extensively by Shostakovich and other twentieth-century composers can be found more than 100 years earlier in the music of Beethoven, such as in his "Hammerklavier" Sonata (Blechner, 1989). But did Beethoven "know" he was using the octatonic mode at the time? Similarly, did Bach "know" he was using something close to a 12-tone row in his theme for the F-minor fugue of the *Well-Tempered-Clavier* (Book 1), and did Mozart know he was using a tone row when he wrote the finale of his 40th Symphony? More recently, a musicologist pointed out how the composer Ned Rorem has been using 12-tone rows; Rorem (2000) claimed not to be aware of it.

It seems to me that the relation of my intuition to conscious and communicable thought may be parallel to the relation of the manifest dream to the interpreted and understood dream. The manifest dream often shows knowledge of which we are not aware in waking life. It often "makes connections in a safe place" as Ernest Hartmann (1995) so felicitously put it; but the connections that the dream makes may not be verbalizable (Perogamvros *et al.*, 2013). Sometimes it takes hard, waking, conscious work to get oneself (the "I") to know what one's mindbrain (the "It") already seems to know. The understanding of dreams, like the understanding of intuitions, requires first an assumption that something true is there. If you start with that assumption, then analysis of dreams or intuition asks: Not, *is* this true? But rather, *how* is this true?

This was the case of chemist August Kekulé, who discovered the structure of the benzene ring in a dream. He dreamt of dancing atoms that fell into a snakelike pattern. As Kekulé wrote in his diary (Benfey, 1958, p. 22),

> *one of the snakes seized hold of its own tail, and the form whirled mockingly before my eyes. As if by a flash of lightning I awoke; and this time also I spent the rest of the night in working out the consequences of the hypothesis.*

The working out of the hypothesis apparently took much conscious effort on his part. He knew the dream image was meaningful, but working out what that meaning was in a conscious and communicable way took much effort on his part. He did not know immediately how the image was useful, but he clearly had the feeling that it was.

There are times when people know things in their dreams that they don't know in their waking life. One of my patients had a dream in which someone utters the sentence, "Your action was very probative." He then said, "What does probative mean?" I asked him to tell me what he thought it means, and he said he was not sure. He said, "Is it assertive? Effective?" These were both wrong. We looked it up in the dictionary, and the correct meaning, according to the dictionary, is:

1   Serving to test, try, or prove.
2   Furnishing evidence or proof.

In the dream, he used the word correctly, although in his waking life he came up with the wrong meaning.

This raises the interesting question: Can one be smarter in one's dreamlife than in one's waking life? Can we know things in our dreamlife that we don't know in our waking life, or at least don't know we know?

William Dement conducted an experiment that addresses these questions. Dement (1972) told his undergraduate class of 500 students that he wanted them to think about an infinite series, whose first elements were OTTFF, to see if they could deduce the principle behind it and to say what the next elements of the series would be. He asked them to think about this problem every night for 15 minutes before going to sleep and to write down any dreams that they then had. They were instructed to think about the problem again for 15 minutes when they awakened in the morning.

The sequence OTTFF is the first letters of the numbers: one, two, three, four, five. The next five elements of the series are SSENT (six, seven, eight, nine, ten). Some of the students solved the puzzle by reflecting on their dreams. One example was a student who reported the following dream:

> *I was standing in an art gallery, looking at the paintings on the wall. As I walked down the hall, I began to count the paintings: one, two, three, four, five. As I came to the sixth and seventh, the paintings had been ripped from their frames. I stared at the empty frames with a peculiar feeling that some mystery was about to be solved. Suddenly I realized that the sixth and seventh spaces were the solution to the problem!*

With more than 500 undergraduate students, 87 dreams were judged to be related to the problems students were assigned (53 directly related and

34 indirectly related). Yet of the people who had dreams that apparently solved the problem, only seven were actually able to consciously know the solution. The rest (46 out of 53) thought they did not know the solution.

I have conducted this experiment for many years with my dream classes.[2] My results are similar to Dement. While trying to solve the problem, people have dreams in which the solution appears to be obvious from the dream. *But it is rare for the dreamers to realize how their dreams have solved the puzzle*. No amount of coaxing or hints on my part gets them to realize it, although once I tell them the solution, they recognize how their dream solved it.

For example, one student dreamt:

> *There is a big clock. You can see the movement. The big hand of the clock was on the number six. You could see it move up, number by number, six, seven, eight, nine, ten, eleven, twelve. The dream focused on the small parts of the machinery. You could see the gears inside.*

Note that in the dream, he actually counts out the next elements of the series – six, seven, eight, nine, ten, eleven, twelve. Yet he does not realize that this is the solution of the puzzle. In such cases, we might propose that his dreaming mindbrain is smarter than he is. The mindbrain has solved the problem, but his conscious mindbrain is not aware how.[3]

The segmentation of the mindbrain

It seems that our mindbrains are able to perceive things, process information, and solve problems without conscious awareness, including some rather high-level abstractions and insights. And our mindbrains do not always tell us the reasons for the perception. You may be thinking that this is a curious sentence: Our mindbrains don't always tell us the reasons for the perception. To whom is my mindbrain communicating when it doesn't tell *me* the reasons for the intuition? And does it (my mindbrain) *know* them (the reasons)? Such sentences capture the problem that psychology is in today, in that we do not have adequate knowledge of the intrapsychic workings of the mindbrain, nor do we have the terminology to describe those workings.[4] We are constantly faced with evidence that the mindbrain can be segmented, and those segments can operate with different levels of conscious awareness, but we do not have terminology to label those segments. We continue to refer to "I" and "me" and "my mind" and "my body"; occasionally, we may say "a part of me" was aware of something, but such language becomes fuzzy and imprecise.

My sentence – "And our mindbrains don't always tell us the reasons for the perception" – captures the problem. There may be a segment of the mindbrain that seems to have knowledge, but that knowledge is not available to the other segment of our mindbrains, the one that expresses our conscious, formulated, verbal experience.

The problem of describing those mental segments, how they operate, and how they interact is a great unsolved task of psychology and neurology. We do not even know what to call those segments. We might turn to the archaic terms "I" and "the mind." Psychoanalysis has at times used the terms "the unconscious" versus "the conscious mind."

While these terms have the advantage of giving names to the mental segments, they can also be misleading. Our intuition is partly conscious; we know that we have an intuition, we may know what it is about, but the details and sources of that knowledge may be unconscious. Does the unconscious mindbrain know the explanatory details of our intuitions?[5]

The answer is not at all obvious. With the Brahms Sonata, did my unconscious mindbrain know that if you remove some notes from the first theme, you get the pitch progression of the second theme? Or did it just hear some powerful but undefined resonance between the two themes?[6]

Psychoanalysis has developed another model of the segmentation of the mindbrain. Freud's structural model included the structures of id, ego, and superego, to refer to impulsive, logical, and moral-judgmental aspects of the mindbrain. Freud noted that there were both conscious and unconscious segments of these three agencies, and this view was further developed by Anna Freud and the ego psychologists who followed her.

There have since been a number of attempts to label the segments of the mindbrain. One strategy is to speak of multiple selves. Mesulam (1998) writes of the "commenting self," which is similar if not identical to the psychoanalytic "observing ego." And several observers have suggested a two-system theory of human thinking such as Epstein *et al.* (1996), Sloman (1996), Langer (2000), and Kahenman (2011), in which one system of thinking is more rational, logical, and reasoning based, and the other is more irrational, intuitive, and associative.

Instead of multiple selves, some writers have used the notion of multiple personalities, in a nonpathological sense. Ramachandran (Ramachandran *et al.*, 1996, p. 44) writes of having "two mutually amnesic personalities," in accounting for a dream in which someone was telling him a very funny joke that made him laugh heartily in the dream. The laughter is brought on by the surprise of the joke's punch line, but to be surprised means that the "personality" hearing the joke did not know what was coming, while the "personality" telling the joke knew the punch line.

Multiple personalities, multiple selves, and dissociation: those are means for speaking of the segmentation of the mindbrain. Unlike id, ego, and superego, they connote multiplicity without specifying the structure of that multiplicity. And it is an open question whether or to what degree the multiplicity is organized by neural prewiring or by experience, and how much that organization can vary over time and can be different for different people.

The models of multiple selves avoid the reification of naming those segments as universal psychological constructs. Should we, or can we, identify those psychological segments?[7]

Scientists continue to struggle with this issue, and they sometimes come up with rather strange locutions. For example, Damasio describes his patient David, who has damage to his hippocampus, amygdala, and both temporal lobes. David, who,

> has one of the most severe defects in learning and memory ever recorded, cannot learn any new fact at all. For instance, he cannot learn any new physical appearance or sound or place or word. As a consequence, he cannot learn to recognize any new person, from the face, from the voice, or from the name, nor can he remember anything whatsoever regarding where he has met a certain person or the events that transpired between him and that person.
>
> (1999, p. 43)

Damasio set up a good guy/bad guy experiment in which one person dealing with David consistently acted obnoxiously to him, one acted very nicely, and one acted neutrally. Although David could not remember any of these people's names or identities, when asked "Who do you think is your friend in the group?" he usually picked the picture of the good guy.

He could not explain why. He seemed to have unconscious emotional reactions to the different people, without knowing why or consciously remembering anything that had happened between them and him.[8]

Damasio gets into a linguistic quagmire in trying to describe the mental segments involved:

> I also have little doubt that were we to have carried out this task for weeks in a row rather than for one single week, David would have harnessed such negative and positive responses to produce the behavior that suited his organism best, i.e., prefer the good guy consistently and avoid the bad guy. But I am not suggesting that *he* himself would have chosen to do so deliberately, but rather that his organism, given its available design and dispositions, would have homed in on such behavior. He would have developed a tropism for the good guy as well as an antitropism for the bad guy, in much the same manner he had developed such preferences in the real-life setting.
>
> (1999, p. 46)

Note what Damasio has done here; first, he distinguishes between him (David) and his organism. But then in the next sentence Damasio talks about him (David) developing a tropism for the good guy. We have switched terminology, and he (David), a person, now has a tropism. Tropism is a term usually applied to living things that are incapable of consciousness. We speak, example, of the "phototropism" of plants, which is their tendency to grow toward the light.

We do not have an adequate terminology for the segments of mindbrain, and I would be hard-pressed to describe the segment of my mindbrain that provides instantaneous musical insights. Whatever it was in my mindbrain that perceived the similarity between the two Brahms themes, it probably was not what we usually think of as a discrete personality. Its thinking and interest were consonant with my own. Only its processes seemed to differ from my usual waking thought processes. "It" is smarter, in some ways, than I am. "It" could quickly perceive something not immediately apparent to most listeners. But "I" have the power of systematic analysis and communication, which "it" does not.[9] You see the trouble we are running into: I am calling the conscious self that has the power of systematic analysis and communication "I." I am calling the unwilled aspect of my mindbrain "it." Yet surely they are both part of my mindbrain.

My referring to that other, unwilled part of my mindbrain as "it" is not new. In *Beyond Good and Evil*, Nietzsche wrote: "A thought comes when 'it' wishes, and not when 'I' wish, so that it is a falsification of the facts of the case to say that the subject 'I' is the condition of the predicate 'think.' *It* thinks..." (Nietzsche, 1886/1989, p. 24). Georg Groddeck expanded this notion, arguing that most physical illness is the expression of mental conflict that is largely dissociated. Groddeck called the unwilled, unconscious aspect of the mindbrain the "It" and described it extensively in *The Book of the It* (1923/1976). Later psychoanalytic translation into English changed the "It" to the "Id," but the "It" is more accurate. It describes how the conscious self, the "I," experiences this other segment of the mindbrain. Also, psychoanalysts tend to identify the id exclusively with drives, which is more limited than Nietzsche's "it."[10]

As my experiences with the Adès Quintet and the Brahms Sonata show, the mindbrain is capable of global and very fast insights about the world. The conscious, analytic mindbrain receives these unformulated inputs which may seem instantaneous and mysterious, but nevertheless have the *feeling of truth*; the mindbrain may then try to explain and analyze that input systematically.

Encapsulated modules of the mindbrain

Some modern neuroscientists have come to use the word "module" to describe segments of the mindbrain. Fodor (1983) has provided the most tightly-argued account of mental modules, arguing that much of perception is modular. Such a module works very fast and is "informationally encapsulated," which means that it cannot be altered by cognitive knowledge. A good example of a module can be seen in the famous Müller-Lyer (1889) optical illusion with arrows (Figure 17.2).

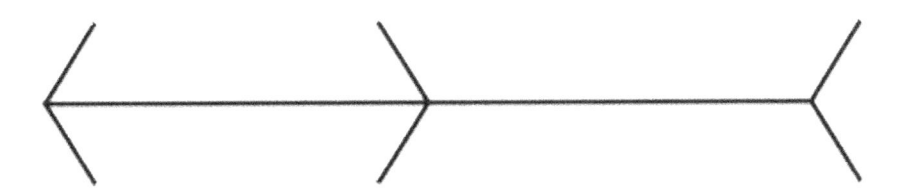

Figure 17.2 The Müller-Lyer optical illusion with arrows (1889).

The "shafts" of both arrows are exactly the same length, but the one on the left appears shorter than the one on the right. We can fully understand the illusion; we can measure the two arrow-shafts with a ruler; nevertheless, after all this, when we look at the image, the left arrow-shaft still appears shorter. The process of length perception is "encapsulated" (psychoanalysts might say "dissociated") from our cognitive knowledge (Fodor, 1983). In terms of information flow, the part of our mindbrain that knows what is "really" the case in an optical illusion has no effect on our visual experience of that illusion.

Encapsulation has been widely demonstrated in perceptual processes, especially vision. Neuroscientists and philosophers have questioned whether aspects of conceptual thinking and central processing can also be modular (Fodor, 1983). My perception of the similarity of the Brahms themes was so fast, it felt modular. It also was informationally encapsulated, encapsulated from my conscious knowledge that the two themes were apparently different melodies with different characters. I knew they were different, but I felt they were the same.

Here we have another rather popular way of describing the segmentation of the mindbrain – the distinction between "knowing" and "feeling." We can say, "Everything I know about him says he is a bad man, but I feel that he is good." The word "feel" in this situation combines an emotional sensing with unformulated knowledge. People sometimes satirize the tendency of psychotherapists to ask, "How do you feel about that?" But the question is very important. Feeling is not just a personal experience of emotion. The word "feeling" has spread its meaning; it still means experienced emotion, but it also means unformulated, nondeclarative knowledge, knowledge that we say, metaphorically, we have in our bones (Stern, 1997). Oatley and Johnson-Laird (1987) have proposed that it is precisely when our knowledge of a situation is imperfect or when we have conflicting goals that we rely on emotions to make decisions. It may be quite precise (rather than laughable) to describe such a situation of imperfect knowledge as "I feel."

With the Brahms Sonata, I knew, by simple facts, that the first and second themes were different. But I felt they were the same. This experience is quite similar to a common experience in dreams, what I have called disjunctive cognitions. Two aspects of cognition do not match each other; the dreamer is aware of the disjunction, yet that does not prevent it from remaining.

The most common disjunctive cognition in dreams has to do with appearance and identity. It is not uncommon to hear a dream with the statement: "She didn't look like my mother, but I knew it was my mother." Other kinds of disjunction are also possible: e.g., disjunction in time. Jaak Panksepp (1998, p. 126) in his book *Affective Neuroscience*, reported the following dream: "Somehow I knew that it is the Union and Confederate armies of the Civil War, although everything visual in the dream corresponds to our contemporary times." There can be disjunction of place: "The dream doesn't really take place in my parents' apartment. There is a bookcase there in what used to be my bedroom" (Blechner, 1995, p. 16). There are other disjunctions that appear more rarely, such as disjunction of sense of direction. One of my patients dreamt:

I am running across a flat open plain. I am heading west. On my left (south) was a railroad train, which was running at the same speed as I (or so it seemed. It might have been a distance away and really going faster). Behind it was a mountain range with a sunset or sunrise. I woke up really disoriented.

She knows she is heading west, even though the sun is rising or setting in the south. She is very aware of perspective (the relative speed of the train), but the direction makes no apparent sense (Blechner, 2001).

One of the important facts about disjunctive cognitions is that they are informationally encapsulated. I may know in waking life that if someone doesn't look like my mother, she almost certainly is not my mother, and if I say otherwise, people will think I am crazy. But that knowledge has no bearing on my dreaming experience, that the woman who does not look like my mother is, nevertheless, my mother. I may know in waking life that the sun doesn't set in the south, yet that does not stop it from happening in my dream.

This is an important aspect of psychology that is receiving more attention. Sloman (1996) argued that there are two kinds of reasoning, one rule-based and one association-based. (See also Kahneman, 2011; Evans and Stanovich, 2013.) The rule-based system captures the "logical, hierarchical, and causal-mechanical" structure of the environment. The associative system primarily reflects "similarity and contiguity." It operates reflexively and often provides "quick and dirty" answers. When we report a disjunctive cognition in waking life, we usually qualify it with something to soften it – she didn't look my mother, but there was something about her that reminded me of my mother. Sanity requires that; in our waking, interpersonal communications, we tend to avoid statements that are logically impossible. But in our dreams, that constraint gives way.

Notes

1 The issue of whether composers are sometimes or always aware of such thematic connections in their compositions is discussed further by Rudolph Reti (1951) in a chapter entitled, "Is the thematic process conscious or unconscious?"
2 The precise instructions are: The first five letters of a sequence are: O, T, T, F, F. This is part of an infinite sequence. Find a simple rule for determining any or all of the succeeding letters. According to your rule, what would be the next three letters in the sequence? If you are not sure or you don't know at all, think about it tonight for 15 minutes, just before you go to sleep. If you remember any dreams during the night, write them down, word for word, and think about them in the morning. Do they offer you any clues about the solution to the puzzle? Spend another 15 minutes thinking about the problem when you wake up in the morning.
3 For further data on problem solving and dreams, see Schatzman (1983), Barrett (1993), Wagner *et al.* (2004), and Maquet and Ruby (2004).
4 I discussed this issue previously in my book *The Dream Frontier*, especially in Chapter 4: "Who creates, has, remembers, tells, and interprets the dream?" I gave the following example of mental segmentation:

> If, following some stressful news, we have stomach cramps, how shall we most accurately describe the experience? We would find it awkward to say, "My brain decided to cause me to have stomach cramps," but that sentence may be close to the truth. If the brain is part of "I," then a paraphrase of that sentence is "I caused me to have stomach cramps," which sounds strange and awkward. The "I" refers to my brain [I would now say "mindbrain"], and the "me" refers to my total organism, including my stomach and my awareness through my brain of my stomach. We are accustomed to saying "I had stomach cramps," but the causation, if it is unconscious, is usually not linked with "I." It would perhaps be most precise to say, "Part of my brain caused my stomach to cramp, and part of my brain perceived those cramps."
>
> (Blechner, 2001, p. 41).

5 There has also been research on what is called "the feeling of knowing."

> In the feeling-of-knowing paradigm the participants were asked to predict the likelihood with which they would be able either to remember the answer to memory questions to which they could not immediately

provide the answers or to produce the solutions to problems that they could not immediately solve. Typically, there is a positive correlation between feeling-of-knowing judgments and later memory performance on a criterion task. One explanation of this positive correlation is that memory retrieval involves the gradual accrual of partial information, and that the judgments are based on this partial information.

(Metcalfe, 1998, p. 190)

See also Blechner (2001, "metacognition," pp. 245–246) and Schacter (1991).

6 The beginnings of an answer may be found in the theory of Lerdahl and Jackendoff (1983) *A Generative Theory of Tonal Music*. See also Jackendoff (1987) *Consciousness and the Computational Mind*, which proposes that listeners perceive and understand music through processes known as "prolongational reduction" and "time-span reduction."

7 Clinicians have grappled with this issue. The psychoanalyst Alberta Szalita (1958; Issacharoff, 1997) described the schizophrenic mind as being composed of "ego islands," and saw one of the tasks of the psychotherapist was to bring these different ego islands into communication with one another, so that they can operate cooperatively. She called this therapeutic process "psychointegration." Bromberg (1998) expanded this approach, seeing the mind as being composed of multiple self-states and advocating a therapeutic procedure akin to psychointegration.

8 The parallels should be apparent between David and Claparède's patient (see p. 282). Both have strong feelings toward people whose identity they seem not to remember. I once worked with an elderly (*c.*80-year-old) woman with short-term memory loss. I sent her to a neurologist for a consultation. She did not like what happened during the consultation. A year later, I suggested she go for a follow-up evaluation with the same neurologist. She claimed to have no memory of what happened during the previous consultation, but she was adamant that she would not return to her for a second consultation.

9 One should note that this is also the difference between the sleeping and waking mindbrain. Only in waking do we formulate thoughts in a way that is highly communicable.

10 Sartre attacked this aspect of psychoanalysis. He wrote:

By the distinction between the "id" and the "ego," Freud has cut the psychic whole in two. I am the ego but I am not the id. […] Thus psychoanalysis substitutes for the notion of bad faith, the idea of a lie without a liar; it allows me to understand how it is possible for me to be lied to without lying to myself since it places me in the same relation to myself that the Other is in respect of me; it replaces the duality of the deceiver and the deceived, the essential condition of the lie, by the "id" and the "ego." It introduces into my subjectivity the deepest intersubjective structure. […] Can this explanation satisfy us?

(1958, pp. 50–51)

Chapter 18
Memory, knowledge, and dreams

> Any person who has made observations on the state and progress of the human mind, by observing his own, cannot but have observed, that there are two distinct classes of what we call Thoughts: those that we produce in ourselves by reflection and the act of thinking, and those that bold into the mind of their own accord. I have always made it a rule to treat those voluntary visitors with civility, taking care to examine, as well as I was able, if they were worth entertaining; and it is from them I have acquired almost all the knowledge that I have.
>
> Thomas Paine, *The Age of Reason*

The study of dreams raises important questions about what it means to know something. If we know something, do we always know we know it? Are there times that we think we do not know something, but we actually do know it? And does the reverse happen: Are there times that we think we know something when we actually don't?

There are circumstances in which it seems that the mindbrain knows something that the person does not. This was the original idea of psychoanalysis, that there are unconscious psychological processes – including thoughts, memories, emotions, and intentions – of which we are unaware. Psychoanalysis posited the idea of "repression" in which the mindbrain's knowledge of some things is actively kept out of awareness because it causes anxiety or is taboo. Repressed mental contents can cause psychopathology, and it made sense for clinicians to study those phenomena. The theory was that "people suffer from reminiscences" (Breuer and Freud, 1895, p. 7) and if the person could get access to those troublesome bits of unconscious experience, clinical symptoms might be cured.

Repression due to anxiety has turned out to be only a small part of the process by which the mindbrain works unconsciously. Much psychic material and many psychic operations are unconscious. Our mindbrains are always working, calculating, and solving problems that face us. We often do not know about those calculations, but we "hear" about them after the fact. It is as if our mindbrains emit a message periodically to our conscious awareness with the result of its calculation; we may experience it as an intuition, or it may come to us in a dream, without an explanation of how the result was achieved. We often have to accept that message, without taking the time to figure out how our mindbrains came to that result. It allows us to get quick answers without the laborious task of understanding how we got to those answers.

The study of these non-repressed but unconscious psychological processes is now extensive and varied (see Westen, 1998; Bargh and Morsella, 2008). Cognitive neuroscientists often prefer the word "implicit" rather than "unconscious" (perhaps to avoid the connection to Freud's sexualized and aggressive unconscious), but implicit and unconscious are essentially the same. I will not summarize the literature here, but I would like to draw attention to the data on implicit or unconscious mindbrain functions that we obtain from the study of dreams.

The OTTFF experiment of William Dement gave an illustration of such "knowledge without knowing" when the issue is relatively intellectual and not emotionally problematic. As noted at p. 271, one dreamer actually counted out the next elements of the series – six, seven, eight, nine, ten, 11, 12. Yet he did not realize that this was the solution of the puzzle. In such cases, we might propose that his dreaming mindbrain is smarter than he is. The mindbrain has solved the problem, but he is not consciously aware how. This man might utter the following weird sentence: "I couldn't figure out the puzzle, but my dreaming mindbrain could. But then my waking mindbrain could not get access to what my dreaming mindbrain had already solved."[1]

It is possible that a good deal of what we call "thinking" or "working through a problem" involves our getting access to knowledge or a solution to a problem that our mindbrains have already worked out (in dreams, that we may or may not remember, or in waking unconscious thinking – we may never be able to know which). This puts an interesting slant on the theory of learning that Plato outlined in his dialogue *Meno*. In the *Meno*, Socrates argues that much knowledge is innate, and that learning involves bringing innate knowledge to consciousness.

Man cannot search either for what he knows or for what he does not know. He cannot search for what he knows – since he knows it, there is no need to search – nor for what he does not know, for he does not know what to look for.

(Hamilton and Cairns, 1961, p. 363)

Our data here suggest an alternative or an addition to Socrates' theory – not that knowledge is innate, but that much calculation and problem solving by our mindbrains goes on without our awareness; our job then in thinking and learning is to discover the solutions that our mindbrain has already worked out. We can see from examples, like the OTTFF experiment, that *man must search for the knowledge he (or his mindbrain) possesses*. This puts into question our very definitions of "knowledge" and our conceptualization of what it means to "possess" knowledge, as was illustrated in the previous chapter with regard to the Brahms Sonata.

We need, therefore, a word for the concept of owning knowledge that our mindbrains possess and having access to that knowledge. "Me-ness" is such a word. As discussed at p. 22, it was coined by the Swiss neurologist, Édouard Claparède (1911) ("me-ness" is *moïté* in French), although the word never caught on. Claparède described an experiment with a woman with alcohol-induced Korsakoff syndrome, who had lost most of her capacity for short-term memory. She did not recognize the doctors whom she saw every day. She said to her nurse, who had worked with her for six months, "With whom do I have the honor of speaking?" Her short-term memory seemed mostly gone, although her long-term memory was intact; she could name the capitals of Europe and make mental calculations. Claparède reports:

> I carried out the following curious experiment on her: to see whether she would better retain an intense impression involving affectivity, I stuck her hand with a pin hidden between my fingers. The light pain was as quickly forgotten as indifferent perceptions; a few minutes later she no longer remembered it. But when I again reached out for her hand, she pulled it back in a reflex fashion, not knowing why. When I asked for the reason, she said in a flurry, "Doesn't one have the right to withdraw her hand?" and when I insisted, she said, "Is there perhaps a pin hidden in your hand?" To

the question, "What makes you suspect me of wanting to stick you?" she would repeat her old statement, "That was an idea that went through my mind," or she would explain, "Sometimes pins are hidden in people's hands." But never would she recognize the idea of sticking as a "memory."

(1911, pp. 68–69)

To a third party observing this, it would seem that her speculation showed that some part of her mindbrain "knew" that Claparède had pricked her with a pin; it showed up in her speculation that he might have a pin in his hand. But consciously she had no memory of it. The knowledge may have been there in her mindbrain, but she could not own it. It did not have "me-ness." Perhaps a more precise (although wordy) term for "me-ness" would be "conscious awareness, control, and a feeling of ownership of one's mental contents and one's body."

That the mindbrain can solve a problem without the person being consciously aware of the solution is fascinating. We see this often in dream groups, where a dream that was first seen as innocuous by the dreamer is subsequently seen to explain a strong, but dissociated emotional experience. For example, a man dreamt:

I had a totally obsessional dream this morning. I was trying to find some papers. I didn't think I had them. And then I would see a big pile of papers. And then I would go through them. They were there. There was a big pile, not anything discrete. I kept doing it over. I would think that, and then I would do it over again, the same thing, and then I would be rediscovering that it wasn't what I thought.

The dreamer thought the dream was "the most boring dream in the world," and one of the group members agreed that, on the surface, the dream seemed quite boring. The dreamer associated the dream to several manuscripts that he had in his computer. He has gone over them many times; right before having the dream, he had realized that much of the material was finished and publishable, although the finished material was embedded in a "big pile" of unfinished material. He knew this, and didn't need to learn it from his dream.

When the group associated to his dream, one group member said that if it were his dream, looking for my papers and not being able to find them would remind me of scenes in wartime when officials would ask you to show your papers, and if you couldn't, or they weren't in order, you would be in trouble. It reminds me of a WWII movie about Nazis asking someone for his papers.

On hearing this, the dreamer realized a much more emotionally-charged meaning of the dream. The dreamer, born in the U.S., was the son of German-Jewish Holocaust survivors. Because of this lineage, he was entitled to apply for German citizenship. He had obsessed (as he did in the dream) for ten years about whether to take advantage of this possibility. A year before, he had finally decided to do so. He was granted German citizenship, and, shortly before having the dream, he had received his German passport, which listed his nationality as "Deutsch"; he felt strong waves of ambivalence at being identified as a German national.

In this case, two meanings were condensed in the word "papers": academic papers, which the dreamer was writing, and citizenship papers. During the discussion of the dream with the group, the dreamer connected part of the dream with his actual behavior: "In the dream, I kept doing it over. I would think that, and then I would do it over again, the same thing, and then I would be rediscovering that it wasn't what I thought." When awake, he kept looking at his German passport, which stated his nationality as German, and thought, "Am I comfortable with being identified as a German? Does this nullify my American nationality, which is not mentioned?" He did this over and over. While the dreamer was obsessional in general, he obsessed over his academic work steadily and methodically; the experience of the dream was fraught with emotion and conflict, which was like his concern over citizenship papers more than scholarly papers.

In dreams and in creative thinking, the mindbrain seems to emit enigmatic messages to our conscious awareness, without explaining all the processes of how it formulated those messages. We may benefit by accepting the messages from the mindbrain as true, even if they at first are hard to understand or seem factually false. We, conscious beings, then try to understand these messages through methodical thinking. Sometimes it takes hard, waking, conscious work to get oneself (the "I") to know what one's mindbrain (the "It") already seems to know.

There are times when people know things in their dreams that they don't know in their waking life such as the patient, described at p. 270, who used the word "probative" correctly in his dream even though he could not define the word correctly in his waking life. Does the fact that, when asked, he could not give the correct meaning of "probative" mean that *he* did not know it? Does the fact that he used the word correctly in his dream mean that he did know the correct meaning? One sees how complicated is the actual psychology behind the phrase "I know" or "I don't know." One could say that "he" did not know the correct meaning of probative, but his mindbrain did, when constructing the dream. The knowledge was encoded somewhere in his mindbrain, but it did not have "me-ness."

There are examples of people who feel during a dream that they have a certain intellectual ability, yet they cannot reproduce it on awakening. Does this show that their intellectual power in the dream was an illusory impression, or does it show that they cannot sustain the intellectual performance in waking, or transfer the ability from dreaming to waking? For example, a composer dreamt that if, in the song "Over the Rainbow" she changed one of the pitches, then she would have the power to influence Leonard, a man who attracted her, to become her lover. When she told me the dream, I asked her if she could say which pitch she changed, and she could not.[2]

The dream could be seen merely as a metaphor of her wish to use her compositional power to make a man love her. But one wonders, had she awakened right after the dream, would she have actually been able to identify the pitch change – whether or not it would have had the power indicated by the dream?

The area of foreign languages is another good example of meta-knowledge in dreams. People may feel that they are fluent in a foreign language, but when placed in a situation in a foreign country, they may perceive the limits of their ability to negotiate the language. I am not considering here the deliberate misrepresentation of one's knowledge, but rather the ability, in good faith, to be unaware of what one knows.

Vaschide (1911) remarks that it has often been observed that in dreams people speak foreign languages more fluently and correctly than in waking life. But do people actually speak those languages better in their dreams, or do they only have the impression that they are speaking better? Is there any way to test this? One piece of evidence would be if they would wake, and say something that they heard in the dream, which they do not understand while awake. Then, we would check if a native speaker of that foreign language confirms that the dream quotation was correctly formed in the foreign language.

Something analogous to this has been done in hypnosis. Erika Fromm worked in hypnoanalysis with a young man who was born in Japan but claimed not to know any Japanese. She did an age regression with him to age four, and he started to speak correct, although childlike, Japanese. Fortunately, she was tape-recording the session and so was able to confirm that his Japanese, spoken while in trance, was correct (Fromm and Nash, 1997).

The question of what "knowing" means can also be seen in people who have mindbrain damage. For example, there is evidence that different areas of the mindbrain process visual information for conscious "knowledge" and for object representations that control motor behavior. A patient known as D. F. had damage to the ventral visual areas of his mindbrain that resulted in severe agnosia, yet he could manipulate objects appropriately even if he could not consciously "see" them (Milner and Goodale, 1995). In another example, a patient with ventral damage was shown a picture of a clarinet. He said it was "perhaps a pencil," while his fingers clearly mimicked playing a clarinet. In these cases, our physical actions show evidence of "knowing" something, although we do not consciously know we know it.[3]

Daniel Schacter distinguishes between explicit and implicit knowledge, which, correspond, respectively, to conscious and unconscious knowledge. There have been several attempts to determine whether patients who show implicit knowledge "really" know what they do. One of the earliest studies of implicit knowledge in the dreams of neurologically normal people was conducted by Pötzl (1917/1960). He found that tachistoscopic images[4] that were not consciously perceived would show up in the drawings people made of their dreams. The study raised a profound philosophical question: if a dream shows a kind of knowledge, but the dreamer when awake has no idea of the source of the knowledge, then how are we to think of that knowledge? When we say "he knows" does his knowledge have to have me-ness? Is knowledge without me-ness really knowledge? We could describe the situation with the following strange sentence: "His mindbrain knows it, but he does not."

Metamemory

A similar division of mental processes and our awareness of them occurs with memory; we may remember something without knowing we remember it. Schacter (1991) has described a phenomenon known as "metamemory" or "memory monitoring," which is knowledge concerning the characteristics of one's own memory performance. You may not be able to remember the capital of Romania, but you may be able to predict accurately whether you would recognize that it is Bucharest if I told you.

People vary in their ability to estimate the accuracy of their own memory, but there are neuropathological syndromes in which people estimate their memory functioning especially inaccurately. Patients with the memory disorder known as Korsakoff syndrome, as well as patients with Alzheimer disease (McGlynn and Schacter, 1989), both of which involve frontal lobe damage (Kaszniak, 1986), tend to evaluate their memory incorrectly, whereas patients with other memory disorders, such as those with damage only to the temporal lobes but without frontal lobe damage, tend to be accurate (Parkin and Leng, 1993). This leads Schacter to propose that the frontal lobes are involved in memory monitoring.[5]

A patient told his psychoanalyst a dream, in which there was the phrase "Bodo Igesz" (he pronounced the last word "ee-gesh"). He could not figure it out, but had a feeling that it was something he had heard before. He thought it sounded Hungarian and he liked Hungary. The therapist told the patient that it sounded like a transformation of "Bogus Ego." The patient was impressed with this and went on to associate to this idea and to question its application to himself.

The therapist told me of the dream, and I noted that there was a person with exactly that name who was a director at the Metropolitan Opera. I had seen the name in programs of the opera, and I suspected the patient had, too. Since the patient worked in a music-related field, the significance of this name may have been quite different for him. If the analyst had dreamt of Bodo Igesz, it would likely have meant bogus ego. And clearly, the analyst thought that the patient did have a bogus ego, and used the dream interpretation as a vehicle to communicate this bad news. The patient could work with it, and one assumes that no terrible clinical harm was done, and that inevitably some insight into the patient's own dynamics may have occurred. But it points out how the dream thought can be constructed rather than deciphered. Of course, one could argue that Bodo Igesz was an overdetermined dream construction – that it was a condensation of "bogus ego" and the name of the person who worked at the Met. One could never prove that this is *not* so, but it would be more convincing if the concept of "Bogus Ego" had emerged from the patient's associations, rather than the analyst's.

This incident also highlights the fact that we can have a feeling that something that occurs to us is a memory, without being able to recall what it is a memory of. The dreamer had a feeling that he had heard the name Bodo Igesz before, but could not remember where. (This occurred in the days before Google; today he probably would have googled it and found out immediately who Bodo Igesz was.) This is another variation of metamemory – a "feeling of memory."

I had a vivid experience of metamemory in connection with one of my dreams: In it, *I was looking for a library whose address is "Le cercle d'Auteuil."* When I awoke, I had the distinct feeling that there was in fact such an address.

When I had the dream, I had not been in Paris for two years, but over my lifetime, I had been there many times. I thought that I might have once seen a reference to "Le cercle d'Auteuil" and then mostly forgotten it. I continued to ask about it. I wrote to a French friend who now lives in America, but who spent the first three decades of his life in Paris. He told me that Auteuil was a suburb of Paris; there used to be a series of trams around Paris, and that one of them might well have been called "Le cercle d'Auteuil."

Then I got out my guidebook of maps of Paris. It listed a rue d'Auteuil, a boulevard d'Auteuil, and a porte d'Auteuil. There was a restaurant named "Beaujolais d'Auteuil" and another named "Relais d'Auteuil." Still no "cercle!" It seemed that either there really is a cercle d'Auteuil which I was not able to find, or my mind, having witnessed the other versions of d'Auteuil, might have created it.

I did this research in the days before Google. Once Google was invented, I searched again for "cercle d'Auteuil" and found that it was a set of literary circles in eighteenth-century France, the most famous of which met at the salon of Catherine Helvétius. Since at the time I was working clinically with a French writer and since I myself write professionally, I suspect that my dream of the cercle d'Auteuil expressed a wish for collaboration or sharing writers' experiences with my patient or perhaps competition between us. I told the dream to my patient, but he showed no interest in it.[6]

We can see that knowing that one knows something is not an all-or-none phenomenon. One can have a feeling that one knows something, without knowing just what it is that one knows. This may just be a form of knowing with a low level of confidence. But it may tell us something more about the phenomenology of knowing and remembering.

In clinical work with dreams, we repeatedly encounter situations in which memory is better than metamemory; we know more than we think we know. This is experienced most dramatically with traumatic experiences, although dreams can illustrate memory for other kinds of material as well, as Pötzl (1917/1960) and others have shown. This has led to the question of the degree to which we can use dreams as reliable evidence of memories of which the dreamer is not conscious. We often see this in discussions by groups of clinicians, who see evidence in a dream of a traumatic experience. Sometimes the dreamer consciously remembers these experiences; sometimes not.

In dreams, a trauma may be represented, which others hearing the dream will notice, but the dreamer herself or himself does not identify. The difference is that in dreams, it is more common that when the dream interpreter points out the trace of trauma, the dreamer can recognize it and may sometimes recall a relevant memory. But in telling the dream, the dreamer does not notice how the dream re-represents the trauma.

Procedural knowledge in waking and dreaming

The rules of reality testing, which we struggled as children to learn, require us to dismiss as unreal that which we have learned *cannot* be as well as some things that *ought not* be. This is one message of Hans Christian Andersen's story of "The Emperor's New Clothes": If it ought not be that the emperor is parading naked through the streets, then it is not so. We learn to dismiss as a passing illusion many things that our sensorium registers but which do not follow our rules of how the world should work. Children, not having yet learned this, can often see what we adults cannot – except in our dreams, for there we find the survival of our early capacities for perception and thinking unfettered by reality testing.

One of the best-known examples of inattention to things that do not fit our expectations is the video of someone in a gorilla suit walking across a basketball court as the ball is being passed between the players.[7] Viewers are instructed to keep their eye on the ball. The majority of people seeing the video for the first time are blind to the gorilla, although it is in plain sight (Simons and Chabris, 1999; Chabris and Simons, 2010).[8]

The examination of mutual contradictions between what one knows can happen and what one perceives happening is part of what psychoanalysts call reality testing. It is something that develops over time; children may violate it without anxiety until a parent corrects them repeatedly. A young boy told his mother: "I just heard our dog speak." Mother said, "No, dear, that cannot be. You must have imagined it." The boy takes in his mother's lesson that dogs do not speak. But his perception had been that he heard the dog speak. He learns from this experience, not only that dogs do not speak, but that immediate sense impressions are not to be trusted if they violate knowledge of how the world works. Over time the boy learns to fine-tune this belief. Dogs and other animals may speak in stories and on television, but not in "real" life.

This knowledge is part of "common sense," which Marvin Minsky has defined as:

> knowing maybe 30 or 50 million things about the world and having them represented so that when something happens, you can make analogies with others ... you can push something with a stick but not pull it. You can pull something with a string, but you can't push it.
> (Dreifus, 1998)

In dreams the requirements of reality testing are lessened – though not entirely and not to the same degree in all dreams. When we are awake and recall our dreams, we tend to notice when the rules of reality testing were violated, but we do not notice when they were retained. While many strange and bizarre things may happen in our dreams, we do not usually notice how many normal facts of common sense and procedural knowledge, like those mentioned by Minsky, are retained in the action of our dreams. Helmholtz (as noted at p. 239), one of the great scientists of the nineteenth century, was impressed by this fact:

> The voluntary impulse for a specific movement is a psychic act which subsequently is also perceived as a change in sensation. Now

is it not possible that the first act causes the second by purely psychic means? It is not impossible. Something like this happens when we dream. While dreaming, we believe we are executing a movement and we then continue dreaming that what actually happens is a natural consequence of that movement, as would have occurred also during a waking state. We dream that we are stepping onto a boat pushing off from the shore, gliding out on the water and seeing how the surrounding objects change their positions, etc. *Here the expectation of the dreamer, that he is going to see the consequences of his activities, seems to produce the dreamed perception in a purely psychic way. Who can say how long and drawn out such a dream could become? If everything in a dream happened extremely regularly, according to the natural order, it would be no different than being awake except for the possibility of waking up, and the interruption of this dreamed sequence of images.*

(Helmholtz, 1863/1968, p. 223)

This is an important observation. Helmholtz is noting that in dreams much of our procedural knowledge still holds true (although, we must add, not all of it). Usually, we do not notice the extent of this – the fact, for example, that the laws of gravity apply in most of our dreams, although we notice when those laws are violated. This may lead us to wonder: what is the mindbrain mechanism by which procedural knowledge can be overridden? In clinical neurology, there are several syndromes in which prior knowledge fails to constrain our expectations and adjustments of action sequences that are necessary for goal-directed behavior. There are cortical versions of this problem, in which knowledge of categorical structure of object or action representations may be lost (as in the agnosias). There are also subcortical lesions (usually of the basal ganglia) in which overlearned/automatic action sequences (or habits) may be compromised (Mesulam, 1985; McCarthy and Warrington, 1990).

Shortly after his mother died, one of my patients dreamt that his mother came into his bedroom and asked him if he wanted the light on. She started looking through one of his drawers. She left the room, and suddenly, he saw the drawer moving along the floor toward the bed. He thought, "Maybe mom is under the bed." He looked, and she wasn't there. He picked up the drawer and walked toward the living room. As he walked past the kitchen, the burners were on with no pots. He asked his mother something, and she responded something.

Usually during the analysis of a dream, we especially notice the events that do not conform to common sense. This dream has a combination of natural events that conform to common sense and some strange ones that do not. The drawer moving along the floor by itself does not. In this case, the dreamer, *in the dream*, finds it strange and looks for evidence that his mother is secretly controlling the drawer's movement, but she is not. The dream captures the sense of his mother's presence and her absence, and the sense that she could have an uncanny influence on his life, even after her death.[9]

But the dream also has events that do conform to common sense. The first part in which mother enters the room could have happened in the natural world. The same is true of her looking through his drawers (a condensation of "chest of drawers" and "underpants"), which she might have done in real life, although probably not while he was present. The dream actually has a progression from expectable things, to slightly strange, to seemingly impossible, then back through strange, and back to normal. The dreamer was most struck by the uncanny part, the drawer moving by itself. In this instance, he has a meta-awareness, during the dream, of the break from reality and tries to solve the mystery.[10]

We have not paid enough attention to this: How is it that our procedural knowledge of the world is incorporated into the structure of a dream, and what determines when it is not (when violations of our procedural knowledge find their way into our dream)? Is there an orderliness to the determination of which rules of reality are retained or violated, or when? We do not know that. We notice some regularities. For example, flying in dreams is common, especially in children's dreams. And what determines whether the departures from reality strike us as odd *in the dream*?

Notes

1 When the dreamer says "The dream focused on the small parts of the machinery," it may be an endopsychic perception. The dreamer is focusing on the small machinery instead of on the dial and clock hands, which may be why he cannot see how his dream solves the puzzle.
2 There are anecdotal reports of compositions that originated in the composer's dreams, including Paul McCartney's "Yesterday," Tartini's "Devil Trill" Sonata, and Stravinsky's Octet. Uga *et al.* (2006) have systematically studied the generation of music in the dreams of musicians and nonmusicians.

3 Related data have also come from split-brain patients, in which the different brain hemispheres seem to "know" different things (Gazzaniga, 1989).
4 Tachistoscopic images are flashed onto a screen for such a brief time that we are not conscious of seeing them, but experiments show that our mindbrains do perceive them without consciousness.
5 This goes along with Mesulam's (1981) proposal that there are systems integrating various cortical and subcortical regions in both hemispheres in the working of one function.
6 As I stated in my chapter on the analyst's dreams about the patient (Blechner, 2001, Chapter 18), it is important, if the analyst tells a dream to his patient, that he be ready to discuss it openly, and also, if the patient wishes not to discuss it, that he be allowed not to do so without pressure.
7 You can watch video of this experiment at: www.theinvisiblegorilla.com/gorilla_experiment.html.
8 When I was doing my doctoral dissertation (Blechner, 1977), I discovered a special case of this in music perception. I found that professional musicians tended not to hear small differences in pitch that were not deemed harmonically relevant, whereas nonprofessionals heard those differences more reliably. Our perceptions are shaped by what we have learned is important.
9 Note that this experience of confused reality-testing occurred after the death of the dreamer's mother. Compare this to the case of Robert (Chapter 16), who also has a sense of confused reality-testing after the death of his father.
10 A traditional psychoanalytic explanation of this dream, using a rebus, might be that his mother "controls the movements of his drawers," i.e., she controls his sexuality. There are flames burning (he feels passion) but "nothing is cooking" (his passion is not going anywhere).

Chapter 19

The language of thought and the wakingwork

> I know that most men – not only those considered clever, but even those who are clever and capable of understanding the most difficult scientific, mathematical or philosophical problems – can seldom discern even the simplest and most obvious truth, if it be such as obliges them to admit the falsity of conclusions they have formed, perhaps with much difficulty – conclusions of which they are proud, which they have taught to others, and on which they have built their lives.
>
> Leo Tolstoy, *What Is Art?*

What is the language of thought? Is there a primary, primal language of thought? Does the mindbrain use something like the machine language that computers use? For computers, basically all language is reducible to a code of 1's and 0's. People who are not computer scientists may deal with computers for decades and never have direct contact with this system of binary code that underlies the most complex computer operation, but such a language exists. Similarly, there may be some underlying levels of mindbrain language to which we so far have no direct access. Might dreams give us insight into this underlying mindbrain language?

The question of the language of thought has been addressed by philosophers for centuries. Socrates, in Plato's *Theaetetus*, argues that thinking is no more than silent speech. Here are his own words (Hamilton and Cairns, 1961, p. 895):

SOCRATES: …And do you accept my description of the process of thinking?
THEAETETUS: How do you describe it?
SOCRATES: As a discourse that the mind carries on with itself about any subject it is considering. You must take this explanation as coming

from an ignoramus; but I have a notion that, when the mind is thinking, it is simply talking to itself, asking questions and answering them.... So I should describe thinking as a discourse, and judgment as a statement pronounced, not aloud to someone else, but silently to oneself.

Aristotle had a different view:

Spoken words are the symbols of mental experience and written words are the symbols of spoken words. Just as all men have not the same writing, so all men have not the same speech sounds, but the mental experiences, which these directly symbolize, are the same for all, as also are those things of which our experiences are the images.[1]
(McKeon, 1968, p. 40)

So here we have two basic views: (1) that thought is silent speech; and (2) that speech is a particular expression of thought, a translation of a basic underlying language in which all thoughts occur.

There are many reasons for each argument and the answer may ultimately not be entirely Aristotle's or Plato's view. The philosopher Gilbert Ryle made a small but significant adjustment to Plato's viewpoint, continuing to identify thought as silent speech, but also accompanied by visual imagery. He noted that:

much of our ordinary thinking is conducted in internal monologues or silent soliloquy, *usually accompanied by an internal cinematograph-show of visual imagery....* The trick of talking to oneself in silence is acquired neither quickly nor without effort; and it is a necessary condition of our acquiring it that we should have previously learned to talk intelligently aloud and have heard and understood other people doing so. Keeping our thoughts to ourselves is a sophisticated accomplishment.

(1949, p. 27, my emphasis)

I would expand Ryle's view even further. To the internal speech and internal cinematograph-show of visual imagery, I would add an ongoing stream of emotions that give vividness to our internal words and images.

Wittgenstein also added modifiers onto the idea of thought being based on language. He wrote, "Ask yourself whether our language is complete;

whether it was so before the symbolism of chemistry and the notation of the infinitesimal calculus were incorporated in it; for these are, so to speak, suburbs of our language..." (Wittgenstein, 1968, p. 18). As these suburbs multiply, perhaps they reflect more on the core metropolis of thought; we saw earlier that Wittgenstein (2001, frag. 527) wrote, "Understanding a sentence is much more akin to understanding a theme in music than one may think."

The experimental psychologist B. F. Skinner argued that thinking was nothing more than silent "verbal behavior." In the cognitive psychology revolution that succeeded behaviorism, thinking came to be seen as potentially independent of speech. In an essay entitled "Wordless thoughts," the philosopher Zeno Vendler (1977) argued that Socrates' view leads to preposterous conclusions. By contrast, at the most extreme end of the Aristotelian viewpoint, there are those who think that thought can be pure, unrelated to language, and that words distort thought. Thus Tiutchev said (Vygotsky, 1934/1986, p. 254): "A thought once uttered is a lie."

There are at least two possible points of view about the relation of dreams to the underlying language of thought: (1) that dreams, like waking speech, are a transformation of the underlying language of thought; (2) that dreams *are* the language of thought.

In this regard, I am reminded of a brief dream: "I have a manuscript. I need it translated. They don't translate it into English. They translate it into *meaning*." In this dream, there is a fundamental language called *meaning*. None of us speaks this language called "meaning." But do all of us understand it?

The question of what is the underlying language of thought is one of the most difficult in psychology. It was addressed directly by the great Russian psychologist, Lev Vygotsky. Vygotsky (1934/1986) studied the development of language and thinking in children and asked profound questions such as: What is the basic language of thought? How does this basic language interrelate with communicative speech? How does the basic language of thought develop from childhood into adulthood? Is it a given, or does it develop out of social interactions? What are the overt manifestations of this underlying language of thought? Are there thoughts that cannot be expressed in language? If so, what happens to them?

Vygotsky paid special attention to what he called "inner speech," which he argued develops out of "egocentric speech" in children. As

Piaget observed, young children in groups often speak in "collective monologues." Although very young children in groups may appear to be having a conversation, they are often speaking in a way that is not really communicative but expresses private thoughts that are not understandable to other people. As children learn that society expects them to speak in a way that is communicative (usually between the ages of three and seven), the language of collective monologues disappears from their overt speech with one another, but, according to Vygotsky, it does not actually disappear. Instead, such language goes inward, becoming "inner speech," which bears the meaning of thought, without taking into consideration communicability to others.

What are the characteristics of inner speech? Its primary characteristic is, according to Vygotsky, the omission of the subject while preserving the predicate – which I call "subjectless predicates." There are some situations in our everyday speech in which we also use subjectless predicates. Vygotsky (1934/1986, p. 236) writes:

> Pure predication occurs in external speech in two cases: either as an answer or when the subject of the sentence is known beforehand to all concerned. The answer to "Would you like a cup of tea?" is not usually "No, I don't want a cup of tea," but a simple "No." Obviously, such a sentence is possible only because its subject is tacitly understood by both parties.

If you merely hear someone saying "No," you will have no idea what he means, that is, what he is saying "No" about. But the situation is different if you hear the word "No" after hearing a preceding question. If the question is "Do you want a cup of tea?" "No" means "No, I don't want a cup of tea." If the question is "Have the Russians invaded Afghanistan?" "No" means "No, the Russians have not invaded Afghanistan." The same single word "No" can bear completely different meanings: "I don't want a cup of tea" versus "The Russians have not invaded Afghanistan."

Vygotsky distinguishes between the "grammatical predicate" and the "psychological predicate." The grammatical predicate, as we learned in grade school, is the part of the sentence that follows the grammatical subject and gives information about it. In the sentence "John went to school," the grammatical predicate "went to school" gives us information about the subject "John."

The psychological predicate, by contrast, is the part of the sentence that gives new information, while the psychological subject is the information that is shared by the speaker and listener. The psychological subject and predicate may be the same as the grammatical subject and predicate, but they do not have to be. Vygotsky gives the following example:

> Suppose I notice that the clock has stopped and ask how this happened. The answer is, "The clock fell." Grammatical and psychological subject coincide: "The clock" is the first idea in my consciousness; "fell" is what is said about the clock. But if I hear a crash in the next room and inquire what happened, and get the same answer, subject and predicate are psychologically reversed. I knew something had fallen – that is what we are talking about. "The clock" completes the idea. The sentence could be changed to "What has fallen is the clock"; then the grammatical and the psychological subjects would coincide.
>
> (1934/1986, p. 220)

The understanding of an implied subject is a very important aspect of communication. Two people who share certain kinds of knowledge can understand communications that would be incomprehensible to other people who do not share that knowledge. Couples in long relationships develop this sort of knowledge basis, so that their communications to each other can increasingly seem to resemble inner speech. I know a couple for whom it is normal to say, "Take the blue." To outside listeners, this is relatively meaningless. But if you know that they have two backpacks, one blue and one brown, the blue one has books in it, the brown one has food – then you know that "take the blue" means "bring the books" for this couple. (This example is also discussed on p. 112.)

Sentences that seem meaningless or psychotic can often become meaningful when we learn the underlying knowledge base that they presume (McCarthy-Jones and Fernyhough, 2011; Fernyhough, 2017). The example of "Please sit in the apple-juice seat" described by George Lakoff and Mark Johnson (discussed on p. 112), is an excellent example of this; it seems like nonsense, but it makes sense if you know that the table has four place settings, three with orange juice and one with apple juice. Kraepelin (1906, #247; see Heynick, 1993, p. 101) described a similar dream-sentence: "Mr. N was awarded the prize for an article on dentistry though he was not working at the notary office." This sentence is virtually incomprehensible, unless you know that Mr. N did not belong to the officially recognized group of researchers, and the notary office referred to an authorized dental office and to being officially notarized (recognized as valid).

Gertrude Stein was particularly fond of such compound sentences, in which the connection between the two parts was not immediately apparent, such as (Smith, 1999, p. E4): "It looked like a garden, but he had hurt himself by accident." Can you imagine a situation that would make this sentence understandable?

Another example is the quasi-telegraphic style that some people incorporate into letters. A letter from a friend may begin: "Glad to hear that you are well." While in English, that sentence is not grammatical, it is easy to understand the implied subject: "*I am* glad to hear that you are well." The "I am" is virtually certain. Who but "I" wrote the letter? However, consider a letter that begins: "I saw our mutual friend Bill yesterday. Glad to hear that you are well." In this case, the second sentence would be much less clear. Who is glad? The writer of the letter or Bill?

Vygotsky's analysis of inner speech is brilliant. I find it disappointing, though, that he did not integrate dreams into his discussion of inner speech. At one point, he wrote:

> Inner speech is to a large extent thinking in pure meanings. It is a dynamic, shifting, unstable thing, fluttering between word and thought, the two more or less stable, more or less firmly delineated components of verbal thought. Its pure nature and place can be understood only after examining the next plane of verbal thought, the one still more inward than inner speech.
>
> (Vygotsky, 1934/1986, p. 249)

When I read that last sentence, I felt sure where Vygotsky would go next – to dreams, of course, which are more inward than inner speech. But I was wrong. Vygotsky continued:

> That plane is thought itself. As we have said, every thought creates a connection, fulfills a function, solves a problem. The flow of thought

is not accompanied by a simultaneous unfolding of speech. The two processes are not identical, and there is no rigid correspondence between the units of thought and speech. This is especially obvious when a thought process miscarries – when, as Dostoyevsky put it, a thought "will not enter words."

(Vygotsky, 1934/1986, p. 249)

Vygotsky did not continue his argument about inner speech, applying it to dreams, nor do more recent researchers on inner speech (Alderson-Day et al., 2016), but I would like to do so here. In my opinion, the "realm of thoughts that are incompatible with words" is precisely the province of the dream. For dreams can represent totally wordless thoughts. "A thought that will not enter words" can find expression in an image, or an emotion – all of which are prominent constituents of dreams. Consider the dream that exemplifies the "negative dream screen" (Chapter 11b, on Dissociation, p. 154). No words can capture the terrifying emptiness of such dreams. For as soon as we use words, the void is already somewhat filled.

The wakingwork

Freud thought that behind the dream lay a "latent dream thought." The dream thought was conceived by Freud to be like a verbal sentence. The dreamwork transformed this latent dream thought into the dream by all manner of distortion: condensation, displacement, symbolization, pictorialization, etc. Calvin Hall (1953, p. 175) similarly wrote, "Dreaming is pictorialized thinking; the conceptual is made perceptual." Patricia Kilroe (2013, p. 233) wrote that in dreams, "verbal thoughts may be transformed into images."

I would like to propose instead that the verbal "latent dream thought" may not come first. I have suggested instead that we call it the "constructed dream thought" – it occurs after the fact. The mindbrain in creating the dream may not start with verbal, sentence-like thoughts. It may start with *the dream itself, a congeries of images, emotions, and words*. This assemblage may seem confusing to our waking selves, but it may be the essence of thought, when thought need not be communicable.

I would go further. Freud proposed that the latent dream thought is converted by all the operations of the dreamwork into the manifest dream. What if that is exactly the opposite of what is true? What if the dream, with its images and affects, and with very few words, represents the actual language of thought? What if our waking thought requires the transformation of affective-sensory-imagistic "dream thoughts" into grammatical, verbal waking thoughts? Instead of the mindbrain using the dreamwork to turn thought into dream, the truth may be that most of our thinking occurs in images and affects, and these affective/imagistic units are converted into conscious thought by what we could call the "wakingwork."

The wakingwork would operate on the sensory-emotional language of dreams and transform them into verbal sentences. When a dream solves an intellectual or emotional problem, it may do so only with images and affects, as we saw with the OTTFF example (p. 270), as well as Kekulé's dream about the benzene ring or Elias Howe's dream about the sewing machine.[2] The dream may then contain a solution to a problem, but the dreamer may not recognize the solution until he, or someone else, puts it into words (Kilroe, 2003).

Llinás and Paré (1991) anticipated the point of view that dreaming is primary and wakefulness is mental activity modulated by external sensory input. They wrote (p. 525), "Let us formally propose then that *wakefulness is nothing other than a dreamlike state modulated by the constraints produced by specific sensory inputs*."

I cannot prove that my model is correct, and it is possible that in the end the truth may combine both Freud's and my model, so that there is a continual reciprocal relation between dream thoughts and waking thoughts. However, the multilingual author Vladimir Nabokov would agree with my model. When asked: "What language do you think in?" Nabokov (1962) replied:

> I don't think in any language. I think in images. I don't believe that people think in language. They don't move their lips when they think. It is only a certain type of illiterate person who moves his lips as he reads or ruminates. No, I think in images, and now and then a Russian phrase or an English phrase will form with the foam of the brainwave, but that's about all.

Psychologist Edward Titchener also believed that images were the substrate of his thought. He wrote (1909, p. 16): "Is wordless imagery, under any circumstances, the mental representative of meaning? ... I have already answered, for my own case, in the affirmative."

Charles Brenner would disagree. He wrote:

> Since thinking and the use of language are so intimately associated, we may conveniently consider them together. There are numerous manifestations of the regressive alteration of these functions during dreaming. For example, a dreamer tends to think as a child does, in concrete sensory images, usually visual, rather than in words, as is characteristic for adult, waking thought.
>
> (1969, p. 126)

One can see in Brenner's statement the common identification of the non-linguistic and imagistic with mentation that is early, childish, and, in the adult, regressive.

In fairness, one could propose that both models of mental activity could be combined, with an interaction and back-and-forth commerce between the verbal and the nonverbal (Golding, 2015).[3] There may be individual differences in how much imagery forms the substrate of thought (Titchener, 1909), but it is also possible that some people are just more aware of the operation of imagery in thought.

Chinese philosophers noted the difference between knowledge encoded in words and images: Zhŭzĭ said, "That which can be gained through words is shallow; that which can be gained through images is deep" (Yuasa, 2008, p. 82). Cognitive scientists have considered this question (Pylyshyn, 1973; Anderson, 1978; Larkin and Simon, 1987; Richardson, 1999), debating whether abstract thought can be formulated in images at all. Those who study advertising see powerful ramifications of imagery and affect in consumer decision-making (MacInnis and Price, 1987).

Language is a great gift and an essential part of what makes us human. It allows us to formulate certain kinds of thought and communicate our thoughts to other people. Susan Schaller (1991) worked with a man, Ildefonso, who was profoundly deaf from birth and did not learn sign language as he was growing up. Although he seemed intelligent, responsive, and curious, Ildefonso's development was stunted until, at the age of 27, Schaller taught him that everything in the world has a name. It changed the way he could think, communicate, and live. We unfortunately do not know what Ildefonso's dreams were like before he acquired language.

Yet language can diminish our ability to perceive certain distinctions in the world or lose the ability completely. We know that five-month-old infants have the ability to appreciate conceptual and phonetic distinctions that are not indigenous to their culture and language, and that these abilities can be diminished or lost as language is acquired. Japanese infants, for example, can distinguish the liquid sounds /r/ and /l/, but lose this ability as they learn the Japanese language, which does not make this distinction (Miyawaki *et al.*, 1975; Eimas, 1975; Werker and Tees, 1984). In Korea, the distinction between "tight-fit" and "loose-fit" of one object to another is considered significant and there are special words, *kkita* – put together tightly and interlocked – and *nehta* – put in, around or together loosely – to describe this distinction. English does not have such words, but it does have "in" and "on," which indicate the spatial relationship without the tightness of fit. American adults tend not to process the Korean spatial relationship, yet five-month-old American infants perceive and distinguish it (McDonough *et al.*, 2003; Hespos and Spelke, 2004). From early on, before we learn the language of words, our infantile mindbrains have many capacities for appreciating perceptual and conceptual distinctions.

Dreams and the substrate of thought

In dreams, we see the fluidity of how the mindbrain represents ideas and feelings, and transforms them. In dreams, we see the mindbrain creating meaning in many forms and shifting meaning from one form to another. We see the intersection of words, images, sounds, tastes, smells, ideas, and emotions. We see the intersection of rebuses, symbols, metaphors, metonyms, categories, and other meaning transformations and encodings. While I have been asking the question about the language of thought in this chapter (a phrase that has a venerable history in works by Fodor and others), the term "language of thought" may be misleading. It implies language, which to most people involves words. It would be more accurate to ask about the "substrate of thought," that is, the underlying medium of thought, which may or may not involve words. The substrate of thought allows transformations that can break the bounds of language. As I have stated before, dreams allow us to think thoughts that are "extralinguistic," thoughts that can exist because they are not limited by representation in words. By being formulated in extralinguistic terms, some dreams allow us to transform mental contents without the constraints of language, leading to creative and generative thinking.

Notes

1 Some modern cognitive scientists refer to the underlying language of thought as "mentalese." Pinker (1995, p. 69) writes: "Do we use some other code for representing concepts and their relations in our heads, a language of thought or Mentalese that is not the same as any of the world's languages?"
2 Elias Howe, the inventor, learned from a dream how to perfect the sewing machine in 1846. He had been using a needle threaded through the middle of the shank. He dreamt that he was chased by a tribe of cannibals who captured him, tied him to a stake, and threatened him with spears. As they got closer to killing him, he noticed that the spears all had an "eye hole" near the point. He woke with a start, remembered his dream and eventually realized that the dream image would solve the problem he faced in trying to invent the sewing machine. The eye in the needle needed to be on the opposite end of a hand-held needle (Kaempffert, 1924).
3 Lyotard (1983, p. 25) wrote: "The *traumgedanken* [dream thoughts] are composites of text and figure. There are ready-made symbols in the depths of the dream, material designed to lead censorship astray, because it already contains elements of the unreadable and the figural."

List of dreams in *The Mindbrain and Dreams*

1	One last dance before death	10
2	Waterfall descent in a glass box	9
3	Drill bit	9
4	Squash-player doesn't show up	9
5	Cedar log with plastic bottom	9
6	Erotic kiss with unidentified woman	9
7	Disappearance for 12 years	12, 218
8	Finnish male in WW II	23
9	I was a dog or some other animal	23
10	Saddam Hussein and David or Bruce	30
11	Heroin – Heroine	28, 171
12	Bath in black water	28
13	Cantaloupe	41, 92, 121
14	Friend R. was my uncle	29, 158
15	A piece of hardware, lock or hinge	30, 66, 81, 140–142, 245
16	Between a phonograph and a balance	31, 32, 107, 245
17	A row of soldiers or gymnasts	31, 32, 41n3
18	S[E]INE	32, 118
19	Cellphone-baby	33, 39, 82, 247
20	Aqueduct-swimming pool	32, 40, 78–80, 245–246
21	Prestyl Dolby	35, 207–209
22	Wolf-Man's dream	37, 124
23	Giant bee buzzing around my head	52
24	Car smashed in front	53, 197–201
25	Two brightly colored roosters crossing the street	53, 201–204
26	Walking through an apartment and finding a new room	54
27	Short fuse	54, 91–92
28	Broken-down rocket ship that will not take off	54
29	Sinking to the bottom of the ocean	54
30	A door left open	55, 65–66

31	Evil teacher won't let me graduate	55–56
32	An ax fell from the sky	56–57
33	Standing by the Nile	57–58
34	Foreign-born couple and two children had gotten into house	230–231
35	Steward on an airplane offering to do laundry	59
36	South of France, fish flying in air	61–64
37	Gym locker, I didn't know combination	65
38	Had sex with daughter	117
39	Found $8 coin	117
40	Stab myself with a screwdriver	123
41	I need surgery	129
42	Crab-lizard	123
43	Riding on motorcycle, things fall out of my bag	130–131
44	Kidnapped in Bolivia	130–131
45	Being prepared for execution in an orange jumpsuit	132
46	A great hall, a number of guests whom we are receiving	136–139
47	Walking down the street. I meet him [my dead brother]	140
48	In Williamstown, Massachusetts, talking to a colleague Van	66, 140–142
49	In my college dorm that was being used for prostitution	141, 143–144
50	A bureau with many drawers	149–151
51	Dreamed I had a dream but couldn't remember it	151–152
52	A woman was walking along the shore and met a man	152–153
53	In my apartment and there were two fish tanks	156
54	A piece of Plexiglas in my brain	156–157
55	Am to be heavily fined by tax commissioners	157–158
56	Am lying in my bed; an acquaintance came in	158–159
57	I killed our cook Anna	160
58	I was here in this chair; we were having some difficult conversation	162
59	Sitting with my father; I think it was my father	163
60	I had AIDS	163–164
61	In a garden party. Mr. Gill Tee	101, 103, 122, 165–166
62	A hill, on which there was something like an open-air closet	166
63	Alfred and I are in our house. A grizzly bear	167–168

64	Walking along the street and see myself coming the other way	168
65	The garden of my family's house – two Lauras	168–169
66	Interviewing someone younger about giving her a job	169–170
67	In a hotel room. You gave me a goodbye present	170–171
68	Lots of people chasing me. They weren't male or female	171
69	I had a cancer of the breast	190–192
70	I was on a toboggan, rushing swiftly downhill	192
71	At a restaurant, and I go into the bathroom	193
72	Walking with another woman on a street like Park Avenue	194
73	In a hotel in Phoenix, looking out the window at the parking lot	197–201
74	Driving a car that was going extremely fast and about to crash	205–206
75	Driving at night somewhere in the suburbs	205–206
76	In car with parents. Father is driving	210–211
77	Persian rug, infested with bright blue caterpillars	211
78	Dream doesn't really take place in my parents' apartment	212–216
79	In my house, my mother was there, something sexual	216–217
80	Made the decision, because I was being mistreated, to disappear	23, 218
81	I told Bruce I was leaving him	218
82	Hillary Clinton doing a line dance	232
83	Mother would meet me at a special place with jewels and crystals	232
84	Parents had not aged since we were together 63 years ago	242
85	A seal swam up to me and my friends (seal-boat)	80–81, 247–248
86	Chuang Chou dreamed that he was a butterfly	253
87	Mother and I are on a bus, going to do an errand (dead father on bus)	254–264
88	From the top of a rather low and unfamiliar hill, I look out across a wide plain toward the horizon	259
89	The night after my mother died I had a dream in which she appeared	260
90	Statue starts to deflate and inflate, and then it really becomes my grandmother	260
91	My father, dead for many years, engaged me in conversation	260–261

92	Standing in an art gallery, looking at the paintings on the wall	270
93	A big clock. You can see the movement	271, 281
94	I knew that it is the Union and Confederate armies of the Civil War	277
95	I am running across a flat open plain. I am heading west	277
96	I was trying to find some papers. I didn't think I had them	283–284
97	Changing one of the pitches in *Somewhere Over the Rainbow*	285
98	Bodo Igesz	287–288
99	Looking for a library whose address is "Le cercle d'Auteuil"	288–289
100	Mother came into my bedroom and asked me if I wanted the light on	291–292
101	I have a manuscript. I need it translated. They translate it into meaning	296

References

Abraham, K. (1923). Contributions to the theory of the anal character. *International Journal of Psychoanalysis*, 4: 400–418.

Abraham, K. (1925). The influence of oral-eroticism on character formation. *International Journal of Psychoanalysis*, 6: 247–258.

Abraham, K. (1949). Psychoanalytic contributions to character formation. In: *Selected Papers*. New York: Basic Books, 370–418.

Acsády, L. and Harris, K. (2017). Synaptic scaling in sleep. *Science*, 355: 457.

Albee, G. (1968). *Who's Afraid of Virginia Woolf?* New York: Cardinal/Pocket Books.

Alderson-Day, B., Weis, S., McCarthy-Jones, S., Moseley, P., Smailes, D., and Fernyhough, C. (2016). The brain's conversation with itself: Neural substrates of dialogic inner speech. *Social Cognitive and Affective Neuroscience*, 11: 110–120.

Alexander, F. (1961). *The Scope of Psychoanalysis*. New York: Basic Books.

Anderson, J. R. (1978). Arguments concerning representations for mental imagery. *Psychological Review*, 85: 249–277.

Anderson, M., Ochsner, K., Kuhl, B., Cooper, J., Robertson, E., Gabrieli, S., Glover, G., and Gabrieli, J. (2004). Neural systems underlying the suppression of unwanted memories. *Science*, 303: 232–235.

Anzieu-Premmereur, C. (2016). Peter, the child who could not dream. *Psychoanalytic Inquiry*, 36: 231–238.

Appelfeld, A. (2001). The Kafka connection. *The New Yorker*, July 23.

Arieti, S. (1963). *The Psychotherapy of Schizophrenia in Theory and Practice*. Psychiatric Research Report No. 17. Washington, DC: American Psychiatric Association.

Arieti, S. (1974). *Interpretation of Schizophrenia*, 2nd edn. New York: Basic Books.

Aristotle (350 BCE/2000) On rhetoric. Rhys Roberts, W., trans. *The Internet Classics Archive*. Online at: http://classics.mit.edu//Aristotle/rhetoric.html.

Arlow, J. (1982). Scientific cosmogony, mythology, and immortality. *Psychoanalytic Quarterly*, 51: 177–195.

Arlow, J. (1993). Two discussions of "The Mind of the Analyst" and a response from Madeleine Baranger. *International Journal of Psychoanalysis*, 74: 1147–1155.

Arnulf, I., Bonnet, A. M., Damier, P., Bejjani, B. P., Seilhean, D., Derenne, J. P., and Agid, Y. (2000). Hallucinations, REM sleep and Parkinson's disease: A medical hypothesis. *Neurology*, 55: 281–287.

Aserinsky, E. and Kleitman, N. (1953). Regularly occurring periods of eye motility and concurrent phenomena during sleep. *Science*, 118: 273–274.

Atlas, G. (2013). Eat, pray, dream: Contemporary use of dreams in psychoanalysis. *Contemporary Psychoanalysis*, 49: 239–246.

Aulagnier, P. (1975/2001). *The Violence of Interpretation: From Pictogram to Statement*. Sheridan, A. trans. New York: Routledge.

Babinski, M. (1914). Contribution à l'étude des troubles mentaux dans l'hémiplégie organique cérébrale (anosognosie). *Revue Neurologique*, 1: 845–848.

Bargh, J. and Morsella, E. (2008). The unconscious mind. *Perspectives on Psychological Science*, 3: 73–79.

Barrett, D. (1993). The committee of sleep: A study of dream incubation for problem solving. *Dreaming*, 3: 115–122.

Barry, V. (2001). Freud and symbolism: Or how a cigar became more than just a cigar. *Annual of Psychoanalysis*, 29: 51–65.

Bartlett, F. (1932). *Remembering: A Study in Experimental and Social Psychology*. Cambridge, UK: Cambridge University Press.

Baumeister, R., Dale, K., and Sommer, K. (1998). Freudian defense mechanisms and empirical findings in modern social psychology: Reaction formation, projection, displacement, undoing, isolation, sublimation, and denial. *Journal of Personality*, 66: 1081–1095.

Belvin, F. (2015). No bell. Posting on "A Word a Day." Online at: www.wordsmith.org, December 27.

Benfey, O. (1958). Kekulé and the birth of the structural theory of organic chemistry in 1858. *Journal of Chemical Education*, 35: 21–23.

Berg, A. (1952). *Wozzeck*. Blackall, E. and Harford, V., trans. Vienna: Universal Edition.

Berlin, H. (2011). The neural basis of the dynamic unconscious. *Neuropsychoanalysis*, 2011, 13: 5–31.

Berlin, I. (1978). *Russian Thinkers*. New York: Penguin.

Berman, M. (1975). Erik Erikson, the man who invented himself. *New York Times*, March 30.

Bion, W. (1961). *Experiences in Groups and Other Papers*. London: Tavistock.

Bion, W. (1962/1977). Learning from experience. In: *Seven Servants*. New York: Jason Aronson, 1–105.

Blass, R. and Carmeli, Z. (2007). The case against neuropsychoanalysis: On fallacies underlying psychoanalysis' latest scientific trend and its negative impact on psychoanalytic discourse. *International Journal of Psychoanalysis*, 88: 19–40.
Blatt, S. and Ford, R. (1994). *Therapeutic Change: An Object-Relations Perspective*. New York: Springer.
Blechner, M. (1977). Musical skill and the categorical perception of harmonic mode. *Haskins Laboratories Status Report on Speech Research*, 52: 139–174.
Blechner, M. (1983). Changes in the dreams of borderline patients. *Contemporary Psychoanalysis*, 19: 485–498.
Blechner, M. (1989). The octatonic mode. *The Musical Times*, June, 322.
Blechner, M. (1992). Working in the countertransference. *Psychoanalytic Dialogues*, 2: 161–179.
Blechner, M. (1995). The patient's dreams and the countertransference. *Psychoanalytic Dialogues*, 5: 1–25.
Blechner, M., ed. (1997). *Hope and Mortality*. New York: Routledge.
Blechner, M. (2000). Confabulation in dreaming, psychosis, and brain injury. *Neuropsychoanalysis*, 2(1): 23–28.
Blechner, M. (2001). *The Dream Frontier*. New York: Routledge.
Blechner, M. (2003). Savant syndrome and dreams. *International Journal of Psychoanalysis*, 84: 1061–1062.
Blechner, M. (2004). Pleasantness is relative: Commentary on "The pleasantness of false beliefs." *Neuro-Psychoanalysis*, 6: 16–20.
Blechner, M. (2005). The grammar of irrationality: What psychoanalytic dream study can tell us about the brain. *Contemporary Psychoanalysis*, 41: 203–221.
Blechner, M. (2006). A post-Freudian psychoanalytic model of dreaming. *Neuropsychoanalysis*, 8: 17–20.
Blechner, M. (2007a). Approaches to panic attacks. *Neuropsychoanalysis*, 9: 93–102.
Blechner, M. (2007b). Interpersonal and affective factors in confabulation: Commentary on "Confabulation in Dementia." *Neuropsychoanalysis*, 9: 18–22.
Blechner, M. (2008). Proposals for the next century of psychoanalytic dream studies. In: Lansky, M., ed., *The Dream After a Century: Symposium 2000 on Dreams*. Madison, CT: International Universities Press, 29–44.
Blechner, M. (2010). Interpersonal and uniquely personal factors in dream analysis. *Psychoanalytic Dialogues*, 20: 374–381.
Blechner, M. (2011). Listening to the body and feeling the mind. *Contemporary Psychoanalysis*, 47: 25–34.
Blechner, M. (2013). New ways of conceptualizing and working with dreams. *Contemporary Psychoanalysis*, 49: 259–275.
Blechner, M. (2014). Understanding dreams: How neuropsychoanalysis and

clinical psychoanalysis can learn from each other. *Annual of Psychoanalysis*, 38/39: 142–155.

Blechner, M. (2015). Bigenderism and bisexuality. *Contemporary Psychoanalysis*, 3: 503–522.

Blechner, M. (2016). Psychoanalysis and sexual issues. *Contemporary Psychoanalysis*, 52: 1–45.

Blechner, M. (in press). Collateral damage in the battle to change sexual orientation. In: Feit, A. and Slomowitz, A., eds., *Unthinkable Orthodoxies*. New York: Routledge.

Blechner, M., Day, R., and Cutting, J. (1976). Processing two dimensions of nonspeech: The auditory-phonetic distinction reconsidered. *Journal of Experimental Psychology: Human Perception and Performance*, 2: 257–266.

Blundo, C., Ricci, M., and Miller, L. (2006). Category-specific knowledge deficit for animals in a patient with herpes simplex encephalitis. *Cognitive Neuropsychology*, 23: 1248–1268.

Boas, F. (1994). *The Way of the Dream: Conversations on Jungian Dream Interpretation with Marie-Louise von Franz*. Boston, MA: Shambala.

Bodamer, J. (1947). Die Prosopagnosie. *Archiv für Psychiatrie und Nervenkrankheiten*, 179: 6–54.

Bonovitz, C. (2009). Looking back, looking forward: A reexamination of Benjamin Wolstein's interlock and the emergence of intersubjectivity. *International Journal of Psychoanalysis*, 90: 463–485.

Borges, J. (1941/1962). Funes the memorious. In: Yates, D. and Irby, J., eds., *Labyrinths: Selected Stories and Other Writings*, New York: New Directions, 59–66.

Boring, E. (1930). A new ambiguous figure, *American Journal of Psychology*, 42: 444–445.

Bosnak, R. (2003). Embodied imagination. *Contemporary Psychoanalysis*, 39: 683–695.

Bostridge, I. (2015). *Schubert's Winter Journey: Anatomy of an Obsession*. New York: Knopf.

Bradley, L., Hollifield, M., and Foulkes, D. (1992). Reflection during REM dreaming. *Dreaming*, 2: 161–166.

Brenman-Gibson, M. (1997). The legacy of Erik Homburger Erikson. *Psychoanalytic Review*, 84: 329–335.

Brenner, C. (1969). Dreams in clinical psychoanalytic practice. *Journal of Nervous and Mental Disease*, 149(2): 122–132.

Breuer, J. and Freud, S. (1895). Studies on hysteria. In: Strachey, J., ed., *The Standard Edition of the Complete Psychological Works of Sigmund Freud (vol. 2)*. and trans. London: Hogarth Press, 1–306.

Brockman, R. (1998). *A Map of the Mind: Toward a Science of Psychotherapy*. Madison, CT: Psychosocial Press, 1998.

Brockman, R. (2002). Self, object, neurobiology. *Neuropsychoanalysis*, 4: 87–99.
Bromberg, P. (1998). *Standing in the Spaces*. Hillsdale, NJ: The Analytic Press.
Brooks, P. and Peever, J. (2012). Identification of the transmitter and receptor mechanisms responsible for REM sleep paralysis. *The Journal of Neuroscience*, 32(29): 9785–9795.
Brown, M. and Hurd, C. (1947). *Goodnight Moon*. New York: Harper.
Brown, R. (2006). Different types of "dissociation" have different psychological mechanisms. *Journal of Trauma and Dissociation*, 7: 7–28.
Burston, D. (2007). *Erik Erikson and the American Psyche: Ego, Ethics, and Evolution*. New York: Jason Aronson.
Caligor, L. (1981). Parallel and reciprocal processes in psychoanalytic supervision. *Contemporary Psychoanalysis*, 17: 1–27.
Caligor, L. and May, R. (1968). *Dreams and Symbols*. New York: Basic Books.
Carroll, L. (1865). *Alice's Adventures in Wonderland*. London: Macmillan.
Casasanto, D. (2017). Relationships between language and cognition. In: Dancygier, B., ed., *Cambridge Handbook of Cognitive Linguistics*. Cambridge, UK: Cambridge University Press, 19–37.
Chabris, C. and Simons, D. (2010). *The Invisible Gorilla and Other Ways Our Intuitions Deceive Us*. New York: Crown.
Chomsky, N. (1957). *Syntactic Structures*. The Hague: Mouton.
Chuang Tzu. (1997). *Chuang Tzu: The Inner Chapters*, Hinton, D., trans. New York: Counterpoint. (Original work dates from *c.*300 BC.)
Claparède, E. (1911). Recognition et moïté. *Archives de Psychologie*, 11: 79–90. English translation in: Rapaport, D. ed. and trans. (1951), *Organization and Pathology of Thought*. New York: Columbia University Press, 58–73.
Cleland, J. (1749). *Memoirs of Fanny Hill*. Paris: Liseux. Online at: www.gutenberg.org/files/25305/25305-h/25305-h.htm.
Cohen Kadosh, R., Cohen Kadosh, K., and Henik, A. (2007). The neuronal correlate of bidirectional synesthesia: a combined event-related potential and functional magnetic resonance imaging study. *Cognitive Neuroscience*, 19: 2050–2059.
Colace, C. (2010). *Children's Dreams: From Freud's Observations to Modern Dream Research*. London: Karnac.
Cook, G. and Glaspell, S. (1917). *Suppressed Desires*. New York: Frank Shay.
Damasio, A. (1994). *Descartes' Error: Emotion, Reason, and the Human Brain*. New York: Putnam.
Damasio, A. (1999). *The Feeling of What Happens*. New York: Harcourt Brace.
Darwin, C. (1872). *The Expression of the Emotions in Man and Animals*. London: J. Murray.
Darwin, C. (1902). *The Descent of Man*. New York: American Home Library.

Daston, L. and Mitman, G., eds. (2005). *Thinking with Animals: New Perspectives on Anthropomorphism*. New York: Columbia University Press.

De Masi, F., Davalli, C., Giustino, G., and Pergami, A. (2015). Hallucinations in the psychotic state: Psychoanalysis and the neurosciences compared. *International Journal of Psychoanalysis*, 96: 293–318.

de Vivo, L., Bellesi, M., Marshall, W., Bushong, E., Ellisman, M., Tononi, G., and Cirelli, C. (2017). Ultrastructural evidence for synaptic scaling across the wake/sleep cycle. *Science*, 355: 507–510.

Dement, W. (1972). *Some Must Watch While Some Just Sleep*. New York: Freeman.

Dement, W. and Kleitman, N. (1957a). Cyclic variations in EEG during sleep and their relation to eye movements, body mobility and dreaming. *Electroencephalography and Clinical Neurophysiology*, 9: 673–690.

Dement, W. and Kleitman, N. (1957b). The relation of eye movements during sleep to dream activity: An objective method for the study of dreaming. *Journal of Experimental Psychology*, 53: 89–97.

Devlin, J., Moore, C., Mummery, C., Gorno-Tempini, M., Phillips, J., Noppeney, U., Frackowiak, R., Friston, K., and Price, C. (2002). Anatomic constraints on cognitive theories of category specificity. *NeuroImage*, 15: 675–685.

Dickinson, E. (1862). Letter 260 (April 15, 1862) to T. W. Higginson. In: Todd, M. ed., *The Letters of Emily Dickinson 1845–1886*. Boston, MA: Little, Brown, 403.

Diering, G., Nirujogi, R., Roth, R., Worley, P., Pandey, A., and Huganir, R. (2017). Homer1a drives homeostatic scaling-down of excitatory synapses during sleep. *Science*, 355: 511–515.

Dixon, M. J., Smilek, D., and Merikle, P. M. (2004). Not all synaesthetes are created equal: Projector versus associator synaesthetes. *Cognitive, Affective, and Behavioral Neuroscience*, 4: 335–343.

Dreifus, C. (1998). A conversation with Dr. Marvin Minsky: Why isn't artificial intelligence more like the real thing? *New York Times*, July 28.

Dror, I. E. (2005). Perception is far from perfection: The role of the brain and mind in constructing realities. *Behavioral and Brain Sciences*, 28: 763.

Edelman, G. (1987). *Neural Darwinism*. New York: Basic Books.

Eimas, P. (1975). Auditory and phonetic coding of the cues for speech: Discrimination of the (R-L) distinction by young infants. *Perception & Psychophysics*, 18: 341–347.

Ekstein, R. and Wallerstein, R. (1958). *The Teaching and Learning of Psychotherapy*. New York: International Universities Press.

Ellman, S. J. and Antrobus, J. S., eds. (1991). *The Mind in Sleep: Psychology and Psychophysiology*. New York: Wiley.

Epstein, A. (1994). Searching for the neural correlates of associative structures. *Perspectives in Biology and Medicine*, 37: 339–346.

Epstein, A. (1995). *Dreaming and other Involuntary Mentation*. Madison, CT: International Universities Press.

Epstein, A. and Ervin, F. (1956). Psychodynamic significance of seizure content in psycho-motor epilepsy. *Psychosomatic Medicine*, 18: 43–55.

Epstein, S., Lipson, A., Holstein, C., and Huh, E. (1996). Irrational reactions to negative outcomes: Evidence for two conceptual systems. *Journal of Personality and Social Psychology*, 62: 328–339.

Erikson, E. (1954). The dream specimen of psychoanalysis. *Journal of the American Psychoanalytic Association*, 2: 5–56.

Evans, J. and Stanovich, K. (2013). Dual-process theories of higher cognition: Advancing the debate. *Perspectives on Psychological Science*, 8: 223–241.

Eysenck, M. and Keane, M. (2015). *Cognitive Psychology*, 7th edn. New York: Psychology Press (Taylor and Francis).

Fauconnier, G. (1985). *Mental Spaces: Aspects of Meaning Construction in Natural Language*. Cambridge, UK: Cambridge University Press.

Fauconnier, G. and Turner, M. (2002). *The Way We Think: Conceptual Blending and the Mind's Hidden Complexities*. New York: Basic Books.

Fechner, T. (1871). *Vorschule der Aesthetik*. Leipzig: Breitkopf und Härtel.

Ferenczi, S. (1913). Interchange of affect in dreams. In: *Further Contributions to the Theory and Technique of Psychoanalysis*. New York: Brunner/Mazel, 345.

Ferenczi, S. (1933/1988). *The Clinical Diary of Sándor Ferenczi*, Dupont, J., ed. Cambridge, MA: Harvard University Press.

Fernyhough, C. (2017). Talking to ourselves. *Scientific American*, 317: 74–79.

Ferro, A. (1999). *The Bi-Personal Field: Experiences in Child Analysis*. New York: Routledge.

Feve, A. and Hart, G. (2006). Hallucinosis and dreams. *Neuropsychoanalysis*, 8: 167–173.

Fodor, J. (1975). *The Language of Thought*. Cambridge, MA: Harvard University Press.

Fodor, J. (1983). *The Modularity of Mind*. Cambridge, MA: MIT Press.

Fodor, J. (1998). *Concepts: Where Cognitive Science Went Wrong*. Oxford: Oxford University Press.

Fonagy, P. (1989). On tolerating mental states: Theory of mind in borderline personality. *Bulletin of the Anna Freud Centre*, 12: 91–115.

Fonagy, P. (1991). Thinking about thinking: Some clinical and theoretical considerations in the treatment of a borderline patient. *International Journal of Psycho-Analysis*, 72: 639–656.

Forceville, C. J. (2009). Non-verbal and multimodal metaphor in a cognitivist framework: agendas for research. In: Forceville, C. J. and Urios-Aparisi, E., eds., *Multimodal Metaphor*. Berlin: Mouton de Gruyter, 18–42.

Fosse, M., Fosse, R., Hobson, J., and Stickgold, R. (2003). Dreaming and episodic memory: A functional dissociation? *Journal of Cognitive Neuroscience*, 15(1): 1–9.
Fosshage, J. and Loew, C., eds. (1987). *Dream Interpretation: A Comparative Study*, revised edn. New York: PMA Publishing.
Foucault, M. (1972). *Power/Knowledge*. New York: Pantheon.
French, T. and Fromm, Erika. (1964). *Dream Interpretation: A New Approach*. New York: Basic Books.
Freud, A. (1936). *The Ego and the Mechanisms of Defense*. New York: International Universities Press.
Freud, S. (1900a). *The Interpretation of Dreams. Standard Edition*, Vols. 4 and 5.
Freud, S. (1900b). *The Interpretation of Dreams*. Brill, A., trans. Overland Park, KS: Digireads.com Publishing.
Freud, S. (1900c). *The Interpretation of Dreams*. Crick, J., trans. Oxford: Oxford University Press.
Freud, S. (1901). The psychopathology of everyday life. *Standard Edition*, 6: 1–296.
Freud, S. (1905a). Jokes and their relation to the unconscious. *Standard Edition*, 7: 1–247.
Freud, S. (1905b). Fragment of an analysis of a case of hysteria. *Standard Edition*, 7: 1–122.
Freud, S. (1908a). Character and anal eroticism. *Standard Edition*, 9: 167–176.
Freud, S. (1908b). Letter from Sigmund Freud to Karl Abraham, March 13. In: *The Complete Correspondence of Sigmund Freud and Karl Abraham 1907–1925*. Falzeder, E., ed., 2002, London/New York: Karnac, 33.
Freud, S. (1909a). Notes upon a case of obsessional neurosis. *Standard Edition*, 10: 151–318.
Freud, S. (1909b). Letter from Sigmund Freud to Karl Abraham, February 2. In: *The Complete Correspondence of Sigmund Freud and Karl Abraham 1907–1925*. Falzeder, E., ed., 2002, London/New York: Karnac, 79.
Freud, S. (1913). Totem and taboo: Some points of agreement between the mental lives of savages and neurotics. *Standard Edition*, 13: 1–162.
Freud, S. (1915a). Instincts and their vicissitudes. *Standard Edition*, 14: 109–140.
Freud, S. (1915b). The unconscious. *Standard Edition*, 14: 159–215.
Freud, S. (1915c). Thoughts for the times on war and death. *Standard Edition*, 14: 274–300.
Freud, S. (1915d). Repression. *Standard Edition*, 14: 141–158.
Freud, S. (1916). Introductory lectures on psychoanalysis. *Standard Edition*, 15: 1–240.

Freud, S. (1914/1918). From the history of an infantile neurosis. *Standard Edition*, 17: 7–122.
Freud, S. (1920). Beyond the pleasure principle. *Standard Edition*, 18: 1–64.
Freud, S. (1923). The ego and the id. *Standard Edition*, Vol. 19.
Freud, S. (1925). Some psychical consequences of the anatomical distinction between the sexes. *Standard Edition*, 19: 241–258.
Freud, S. (1927). The future of an illusion. *Standard Edition*, 21: 1–56.
Freud, S. (1931). Female sexuality. *Standard Edition*, 21: 221–244.
Freud, S. (1933). *New Introductory Lectures on Psycho-Analysis*. *Standard Edition*, 22: 1–182.
Freud, S. (1937). Analysis terminable and interminable. *Standard Edition*, 23: 209–254.
Freud, S. (1938/1940). Outline of psycho-analysis, Chapter 5: Dream interpretation as an illustration. *Standard Edition*, 23: 165–171.
Fromm, Erich (1951). *The Forgotten Language*. New York: Rinehart.
Fromm, Erika (1998). Lost and found half a century later: Letters by Freud and Einstein. *American Psychologist*, 53: 1195–1198.
Fromm, Erika and Nash, M. (1997). *Psychoanalysis and Hypnosis*. Madison, CT: International Universities Press.
Funk and Wagnalls' New Standard Dictionary of the English Language. (1928). New York: Funk and Wagnalls.
Gackenbach, J. and LaBerge, S., eds. (1988). *Conscious Mind, Sleeping Brain: Perspectives on Lucid Dreaming*. New York: Plenum.
Galton, F. (1880). Visualised numerals. *Nature*, 22, 494–495.
Gardner, H. (1975). *The Shattered Mind: The Person After Brain Damage*. New York: Random House.
Gardner, H. (1983). *Frames of Mind: The Theory of Multiple Intelligences*. New York: Basic Books.
Gardner, H. (1985). *The Mind's New Science*. New York: Basic Books.
Garma, Á. (1974). *Psychoanalysis of Dreams*. New York: Jason Aronson. (Originally published in Spanish in 1940.)
Gazzaniga, M. (1989). Organization of the human brain. *Science*, 245: 947–952.
Gazzaniga, M., Bogen, J., and Sperry, R. (1962). Some functional effects of sectioning the cerebral commissures in man. *Proceedings of the National Academy of Sciences*, 48: 1765–1769.
Gibson, J. J. (1966). *The Senses Considered as Perceptual Systems*. Boston, MA: Houghton Mifflin.
Gibson, J. J. (1979). *The Ecological Approach to Visual Perception*. Boston, MA: Houghton Mifflin.
Glover, E. (1955). *The Technique of Psychoanalysis*. New York: International Universities Press.

Glucksberg, S. (2008). How metaphors create categories – quickly. In: Gibbs, R., ed., *The Cambridge Handbook of Metaphor and Thought*. Cambridge, UK: Cambridge University Press, 67–83.

Goldberger, M. (1989). On analysis of defense in dreams. *Psychoanalytic Quarterly*, 58: 396–418.

Goldenberg, J., Mazursky, D., and Solomon, S. (1999). Creative sparks. *Science*, 285: 1495–1496.

Golding, A. (2015). Mental imagery and metaphor. *Letrônica*, 8: 20–32.

Goller, A., Otten, L., and Ward, J. (2009). Seeing sounds and hearing colors: An event-related potential study of auditory-visual synesthesia. *Journal of Cognitive Neuroscience*, 21: 1869–1881.

Gorno-Tempini, M., Price, C., Josephs, O., Vandenberghe, R., Cappa, C., Kapur, N., and Frackowiak, R. (1998). The neural systems sustaining face and proper-name processing. *Brain*, 121: 2103–2118.

Grandin, T. (2006). *Thinking in Pictures*. New York: Vintage.

Gray, H. (1948). Bibliography of Freud's pre-analytic period. *Psychoanalytic Review*, 35: 403–410.

Graziano, M. and Kastner, S. (2011). Human consciousness and its relationship to social neuroscience: A novel hypothesis. *Cognitive Neuroscience*, 2: 98–113.

Green, C. (1968). *Lucid Dreams*. London: Hamish Hamilton.

Greenberg, R. and Pearlman, C. (1978). If Freud only knew: A reconsideration of psychoanalytic dream theory. *International Review of Psycho-Analysis*, 5: 71–75.

Greenson, R. (1970). The exceptional place of the dream in psychoanalytic practice. *Psychoanalytic Quarterly*, 39: 519–549.

Greenwald, A. and Banaji, M. (1995). Implicit social cognition: Attitudes, self-esteem, and stereotypes. *Psychological Review*, 102: 4–27.

Gregor, T. (1981). "Far, far away my shadow wandered…": The dream symbolism and dream theories of the Mehinaku Indians of Brazil. *American Ethologist*, 8: 709–720.

Grimes, W. (2016). Michel Richard, acclaimed chef at Citronelle, dies at 68. *New York Times*, August 15.

Groddeck, G. (1923/1976). *The Book of the It*. New York: International Universities Press.

Gutheil, E. (1951/1966). *Handbook of Dream Analysis*. New York: Washington Square Press.

Hadamard, J. (1945). *The Psychology of Invention in the Mathematical Field*. Princeton, NJ: Princeton University Press.

Hall, C. (1953). A cognitive theory of dream symbols. *The Journal of General Psychology*, 48: 169–186.

Hamilton, E. and Cairns, H. (1961). *Plato: The Collected Dialogues*. Princeton, NJ: Princeton University Press.

Hart, J. Jr., Berndt, R., and Caramazza, A. (1985). Category-specific naming deficit following cerebral infarction. *Nature*, 316: 439–440.

Hartmann, E. (1995). Making connections in a safe place: Is dreaming psychotherapy? *Dreaming*, 5: 213–228.

Helmholtz, H. von (1863/1968). Sensations of tone. In: Warren, R. M. and Warren, R. P., eds., *Helmholtz on Perception: Its Physiology and Development*. New York: Wiley, 223.

Hespos, S. and Spelke, E. (2004). Conceptual precursors to language. *Nature*, 430: 453–456.

Heynick, F. (1993). *Language and Its Disturbances in Dreams*. New York: Wiley.

Hilgard, E. (1977). *Divided Consciousness: Multiple Controls in Human Thought and Action*. New York: Wiley Interscience.

Hill, W. E. (1915). My wife and my mother-in-law. *Puck*, November 6, 16: 11.

Hillman, J. (1979). *The Dream and the Underworld*. New York: Harper and Row.

Hitchcock, A., dir. (1958). *Vertigo*. Universal City, CA: Alfred J. Hitchcock Productions.

Hobbes, T. (1651/1996). *Leviathan*. New York: Cambridge University Press.

Hobson, J. A. (1988). *The Dreaming Brain*. New York: Basic Books.

Hobson, J. A. (2005). *Thirteen Dreams that Freud Never Had*. New York: Pi Press.

Hobson, J. A. and McCarley, R. W. (1977). The brain as a dream state generator: An activation-synthesis hypothesis of the dream process. *The American Journal of Psychiatry*, 134: 1335–1348.

Hofstadter, D. and Sander, E. (2013). *Surfaces and Essences: Analogy as the Fuel and Fire of Thinking*. New York: Basic Books.

Horikawa, T., Tamaki, M., Miyawaki, Y., and Kamitani, Y. (2013). Neural decoding of visual imagery during sleep. *Science*, 340: 639–642.

Horowitz, M. (1972). Modes of representation of thought. *Journal of the American Psychoanalytic Association*, 20: 793–819.

Hudson, A. and Grace, G. (2000). Misidentification syndromes related to face specific area of the fusiform gyrus. *Journal of Neurology, Neurosurgery, and Psychiatry*, 69: 645–648.

Hwang, I.-S., Wang, C.-H., Yi-Ching, C., Chiung-Yu, C., and Yeung, K.-T. (2006). Electromyographic analysis of joint-dependent global synkinesis in the upper limb of healthy adults: Laterality of intensity and symmetry of spatial representation. *Journal of Electromyography and Kinesiology*, 16: 313–323.

IJzerman, H. and Semin, G. R. (2009). The thermometer of social relations: Mapping social proximity on temperature. *Psychological Science*, 20: 1214–1220.

Issacharoff, A. (1997). A conversation with Alberta Szalita. *Contemporary Psychoanalysis*, 33: 615–632.

Jackendoff, R. (1987). *Consciousness and the Computational Mind*. Cambridge, MA: MIT Press.

Jacobi, J. J. (1973). *The Psychology of C. G. Jung*. New Haven, CT: Yale University Press.

Jacobs, T. (2001). On unconscious communications and covert enactments: Some reflections on their role in the analytic situation. *Psychoanalytic Inquiry*, 21: 4–23.

Jacobs, W., Laurance, H., Thomas, K., Luczak, S., and Nadel, L. (1996). On the veracity and variability of traumatic memory. *Traumatology*, 2: 1–5.

Jakobson, R. (1956/1995). Two aspects of language and two types of aphasic disturbances. In: *On Language*. Cambridge, MA: Harvard University Press, 115–133.

Jakobson, R. (1971). *Selected Writings: Word and Language, Vol 2*. The Hague: Mouton.

Jakobson, R. (1988). Two aspects of language and two types of aphasic disorders. In: Waugh, L. and Monville-Burston, M., eds., *On Language*. Cambridge, MA: Harvard University Press, 115–133.

Janet, P. (1887). L'Anesthésie systématisée et la dissociation des phénomènes psychologiques. *Revue de Philosophie*, 23: 449–472.

Jewanski, J. (1999). *Ist C = Rot? [Is C = Red?]* Sinzig: Studiopunkt.

Jewanski, J., Day, S., and Ward, J. (2009). A colorful Albino: The first documented case of synesthesia, by Georg Tobias Ludwig Sachs in 1812. *Journal of the History of the Neurosciences*, 18: 293–303.

Jitendra J. (2007). Marin-Amat syndrome: A rare facial synkinesis. *Indian Journal of Ophthalmology*, 55: 402–403.

Johnson, M. (1987). *The Body in the Mind: The Bodily Basis of Meaning, Imagination, and Reasoning*. Chicago, IL: University of Chicago Press.

Johnson, M. and Raye, C. (1981). Reality monitoring. *Psychological Review*, 88: 67–85.

Johnson, M., Kahan, T., and Raye, C. (1984). Dreams and reality monitoring. *Journal of Experimental Psychology: General*, 113: 329–344.

Jones, K. (2015). *Hitchcock/Truffaut* (DVD). New York: Cohen Media Group.

Joseph, B. (1985). Transference: The total situation. *International Journal of Psycho-Analysis*, 66: 447–454.

Jouvet, M. (1967). The states of sleep. *Scientific American*, 216: 62–68.

Jouvet, M. (1969). *The Paradox of Sleep*. Cambridge, MA: MIT Press.

Julesz, B. (1971). *Foundations of Cyclopean Perception*. Chicago, IL: University of Chicago Press.
Jung, C. (1916–1948) General aspects of dream psychology. In: *Dreams*. New York: MJF Books, 23–66.
Jung, C. (1948/1974). General aspects of dream psychology. In: *Dreams*, Princeton, NJ: Princeton University Press, 23–66.
Jung, C. (1960). *Analytical Psychology: Its Theory and Practice*. New York: Pantheon.
Kaempffert, W. (1924). *A Popular History of American Invention*. New York: Scribners.
Kahan, T. and LaBerge, S. (1994). Lucid dreaming as metacognition: Implications for cognitive science. *Consciousness and Cognition*, 3: 246–264.
Kahan, T. and LaBerge, S. (1996). Cognition and metacognition in dreaming and waking: Comparisons of first and third-person ratings. *Dreaming*, 6: 235–249.
Kahan, T., LaBerge, S., Levitan, L., and Zimbardo, P. (1997). Similarities and differences between dreaming and waking cognition: An exploratory study. *Consciousness and Cognition*, 6(1): 132–147.
Kahneman, D. (2011). *Thinking Fast and Slow*. New York: Farrar Straus and Giroux.
Kanzer, M. (1955). The communicative function of the dream. *International Journal of Psycho-Analysis*, 36: 260–266.
Kaplan-Solms, K. and Solms, M. (2000). *Clinical Studies in Neuro-Psychoanalysis*. London: Karnac.
Kaszniak, A. (1986). The neuropsychology of dementia. In: Grant, J. and Adams, K., eds., *Neuropsychological Assessment of Neuropsychiatric Disorders*. New York: Oxford University Press, 172–220.
Kekulé, A. (1890). Benzolfest-Rede. *Berichte der Deutschen Chemischen Gesellschaft*, 23: 1302–1311. Benfey, O., trans. (1958). Kekulé and the birth of the structural theory of organic chemistry in 1858. *Journal of Chemical Education*, 35: 21–23.
Kernberg, O. (1975). *Borderline Conditions and Pathological Narcissism*. New York: Jason Aronson.
Kihlstrom, D. (1986). The cognitive unconscious. *Science*, 237: 1445–1452.
Kilroe, P. (2003). Psychology at the edge: Exploring Mark Blechner's *The Dream Frontier*. Paper presented at the Association for the Study of Dreams, June 28, Berkeley, CA.
Kilroe, P. (2013). Inner speech in dreaming: A dialogic perspective. *Dreaming*, 23: 233–244.
Kleiger, J. (1999). *Disordered Thinking and the Rorschach*. Hillsdale, NJ: The Analytic Press.

Klein, M. (1946). Notes on some schizoid mechanisms. In: *Envy and Gratitude and Other Works, 1946–1963*. New York: Delacorte, 1–24.
Köhler, W. (1929). *Gestalt Psychology*. New York: Liveright.
Kohut, H. (1977). *The Restoration of the Self*. New York: International Universities Press.
Kosslyn, S. (1994). *Image and Brain*. Cambridge, MA: MIT Press.
Kraepelin, E. (1906). *Über Sprachstörungen im Traum*. Leipzig: Engelman.
Kubovy, M., Cutting, J., and McGuire, R. (1974). Hearing with the third ear: Dichotic perception of a melody without monaural familiarity cues. *Science*, 186: 272–274.
LaBerge, S. (1985). *Lucid Dreaming*. New York: Ballantine.
Lacan, J. (2006). *Écrits*. Fink, B., trans. New York: Norton.
Laiacona, M. and Capitani, E. (2001). A case of prevailing deficit on nonliving categories or a case of prevailing sparing of living categories? *Cognitive Neuropsychology*, 18: 39–70.
Lakoff, G. (1988). Cognitive semantics. In: Eco, U., Santambrogio, M., and Violi, P., eds., *Meaning and Mental Representation*. Bloomington, IN: University of Indiana Press, 119–154.
Lakoff, G. (1993). How metaphor structures dreams: The theory of conceptual metaphor applied to dream analysis. *Dreaming*, 3: 77–98.
Lakoff, G. (1997). How unconscious metaphorical thought shapes dreams. In: Stein, D., ed., *Cognitive Science and the Unconscious*. Washington, DC: American Psychiatric Press, 89–120.
Lakoff, G. and Johnson, M. (1980). *Metaphors We Live By*. Chicago, IL: University of Chicago Press.
Lakoff, G. and Johnson, M. (1999). *Philosophy in the Flesh: The Embodied Mind and Its Challenge to Western Thought*. New York: Basic Books.
Lakoff, G. and Turner, M. (1989). *More than Cool Reason: A Field Guide to Poetic Metaphor*. Chicago, IL: University of Chicago Press.
Langer, E. (2000). Mindful learning. *Current Directions in Psychological Science*, 9: 220–223.
Langer, S. (1967). *Problems of Art*. New York: Scribner.
Lanius, R., Williamson, P., Boksman, K., Densmore, M., Gupta, M., Neufeld, R., Gati, J., and Menon, R. (2002). Brain activation during script-driven imagery induced dissociative responses in PTSD: A functional magnetic resonance imaging investigation. *Biological Psychiatry*, 52: 305–311.
Larkin, J. and Simon, H. (1987). Why a diagram is (sometimes) worth ten thousand words. *Cognitive Science*, 11: 65–99.
Laughlin, H. P. (1970). *The Ego and Its Defenses*. New York: Jason Aronson.
Lawrence, W. G. (2003). *Experiences in Social Dreaming*. London: Karnac.

Lazar, Z. and Schwartz, F. (1982). The contaminated Rorschach response: Formal features. *Journal of Clinical Psychology*, 38: 415–419.

Lerdahl, F. and Jackendoff, R. (1983). *A Generative Theory of Tonal Music*. Cambridge, MA: MIT Press.

Levenson, E. (1983). *The Ambiguity of Change*. New York: Basic Books.

Levenson, E. (2000). An interpersonal perspective on dreams. *Psychoanalytic Dialogues*, 10: 119–125.

Lewin, B. (1973). Sleep, the mouth and the dream screen. In: Arlow, J., ed., *Selected Writings of Bertram Lewin*. New York: Psychoanalytic Quarterly, 87–100.

Lewis, J. (2006). Cortical networks related to human use of tools. *Neuroscientist*, 12: 211–231.

Libet, B. (1993). *Neurophysiology of Consciousness*. Boston, MA: Birkhäuser.

Libet, B., Gleason, C., Wright, E., and Pearl, D. (1983). Time of conscious intention to act in relation to onset of cerebral activity (readiness potential): The unconscious initiation of a freely voluntary act. *Brain*, 106: 623–642.

Lipps, T. (1903). *Grundlegung der Aesthetik*. Leipzig: Voss.

Lipps, T. (1913). *Zur Einfühlung*. Leipzig: Engelmann.

Llinás, R. and Paré, D. (1991). Of dreaming and wakefulness. *Neuroscience*, 44: 521–535.

Locke, J. (1690/1836). *An Essay Concerning Human Understanding*. London: T. Tegg.

Lombardi, R. (2011). The body, feelings, and the unheard music of the senses. *Contemporary Psychoanalysis*, 47: 3–24.

Lorand, S. (1957). Dream interpretation in the Talmud. *International Journal of Psychoanalysis*, 38: 92–97.

Luria, A. (1987). *The Mind of the Mnemonist*. Cambridge, MA: Harvard University Press.

Lyotard, F. (1983). The dream-work does not think. *Oxford Literary Review*, 6(1): 3–34.

Lyotard, F. (1989). *The Lyotard Reader*. Oxford: Blackwell.

MacInnis, D. and Price, L. (1987). The role of imagery in information processing: Review and extensions. *The Journal of Consumer Research*, 13: 473–491.

Mahling, F. (1926). Das Problem der "audition colorée": Eine historisch-kritische Untersuchung. *Archiv für die Gesamte Psychologie*, 57: 165–301.

Mahon, B. and Caramazza, A. (2009). Concepts and categories: A cognitive neuropsychological perspective. *Annual Review of Psychology*, 60: 27–51.

Malcolm, J. (1982). *Psychoanalysis: The Impossible Profession*. New York: Knopf.

Mancia, M. (2007). On: The case against neuropsychoanalysis. *International Journal of Psycho-Analysis*, 88: 1065–1067.

Maquet, P. and Ruby, P. (2004). Psychology: Insight and the sleep committee. *Nature*, 427: 304–305.
Marcus, E. (1992). *Psychosis and Near Psychosis*. New York: Springer Verlag.
Marks, L. (1975). On colored-hearing synesthesia: Cross-modal translations of sensory dimensions. *Psychological Bulletin*, 82(3): 303–331.
Marris, P. (1958). *Widows and Their Families*. London: Routledge and Kegan Paul.
Masson, J. (1985). *The Complete Letters of Sigmund Freud to Wilhelm Fliess 1887–1904*. Cambridge, MA: Harvard University Press.
Matte-Blanco, I. (1975). *The Unconscious as Infinite Sets*. London: Duckworth.
Matte-Blanco, I. (1988). *Thinking, Feeling and Being*. London: Routledge.
May, R. (1961). The significance of symbols. In: *Symbolism in Religion and Literature*. New York: George Braziller.
McCarthy, R. and Warrington, E. (1990). *Cognitive Neuropsychology*. New York: Academic Press.
McCarthy-Jones, S. and Fernyhough, C. (2011). The varieties of inner speech: Links between quality of inner speech and psychopathological variables in a sample of young adults. *Consciousness and Cognition*, 20: 1586–1593.
McClelland, J., Rumelhart, D., and the PDP Research Group (1986). *Parallel Distributed Processing: Explorations in the Microstructure of Cognition*. Cambridge, MA: MIT Press.
McDonough, L., Choi, S., and Mandler, J. (2003). Understanding spatial relations: Flexible infants, lexical adults. *Cognitive Psychology*, 46: 229–259.
McDougall, J. (1993). Of sleep and dream: A psychoanalytic essay. *International Forum of Psychoanalysis*, 2: 204–218.
McGlynn, S. and Schacter, D. (1989). Unawareness of deficits in neuropsychological syndromes. *Journal of Clinical and Experimental Neuropsychology*, 11: 143–205.
McKeon, R., ed. (1968). *The Basic Works of Aristotle*. New York: Random House.
McWilliams, N. (1994). *Psychoanalytic Diagnosis: Understanding Personality Structure in the Clinical Process*. New York: Guilford.
McWilliams, N. (2011). *Psychoanalytic Diagnosis*, 2nd edn. New York: Guilford.
Meltzer, D. (1978). Routine and inspired interpretations. In: Epstein, L. and Feiner, A., eds., *Countertransference*. New York: Jason Aronson, 129–146.
Meltzer, D. (1984). *Dream-Life*. Strathclyde, UK: Clunie Press.
Mesulam, M.-M. (1981). A cortical network for directed attention and unilateral neglect. *Annals of Neurology*, 10: 309–325.
Mesulam, M.-M. (1985). *Principles of Behavioral Neurology*. Philadelphia, PA: F. A. Davis.

Mesulam, M.-M. (1998). From sensation to cognition. *Brain*, 121: 1013–1052.
Metcalfe, J. (1998). Insight and metacognition. In: Mazzoni, G. and Nelson, T., eds., *Metacognition and Cognitive Neuropsychology*. Mahwah, NJ: Erlbaum, 181–198.
Metzinger, T. (2003). *Being No One: The Self-Model Theory of Subjectivity*. Cambridge, MA: MIT Press.
Miceli, G., Capasso, R., Daniele, A., Esposito, T., Magarelli, M., and Tomaiuolo, F. (2000). Selective deficit for people's names following left temporal damage: An impairment of domain-specific conceptual knowledge. *Cognitive Neuropsychology*, 17: 489–516.
Miles, L. K., Nind, L. K., and Macrae, C. N. (2010). Moving through time. *Psychological Science*, 21: 222–223.
Millar, M. (2015). *An Air that Kills*. New York: International Polygonics Limited.
Mills, A. (2002). Will-o'-the-wisp revisited. *Weather*, 55: 239–241.
Milner, A. and Goodale, M. (1995). *The Visual Brain in Action*. Oxford: Oxford University Press.
Miyawaki, K., Strange, W., Verbrugge, R., Liberman, A., Jenkins, J., and Fujimura, O. (1975). An effect of linguistic experience: The discrimination of [r] and [l] by native speakers of Japanese and English. *Perception & Psychophysics*, 18: 389–397.
Modell, A. (2009). Metaphor: The bridge between feelings and knowledge. *Psychoanalytic Inquiry*, 29: 6–11.
Moretti, N., dir. (2015). *Mia Madre*. Rome, Italy: 01 Distribution.
Müller-Lyer, F. (1889). Optische Urteilstäuschungen. *Archiv für Physiologie Supplement*, 263–270.
Nabokov, V. (1962). Nabokov's interview. (02) BBC Television [1962]. Retrieved December 5, 2015.
Neubauer, P. (1994). The role of displacement in psychoanalysis. *Psychoanalytic Study of the Child*, 49: 107–119.
Nietzsche, F. (1873/1976). On truth and lies in an extra-moral sense. In: *The Portable Nietzsche*. Kaufmann, W., ed. and trans. New York: Viking Press.
Nietzsche, F. (1886/1989). *Beyond Good and Evil*. New York: Vintage.
Northoff, G., Bermpohl, F., Schoeneich, F., and Boeker, H. (2007). How does our brain constitute defense mechanisms? First-person neuroscience and psychoanalysis. *Psychotherapy and Psychosomatics*, 76: 141–153.
Núñez, R. and Sweetser, E. (2006). With the future behind them: Convergent evidence from Aymara language and gesture in the crosslinguistic comparison of spatial construals of time. *Cognitive Science*, 30: 401–450.
Oatley, K. and Johnson-Laird, P. (1987). Towards a theory of emotions. *Cognition and Emotion*, 1: 29–50.
Obama, B. (1995). *Dreams from My Father*. New York: Times Books.

Ogden, T. (2003). On not being able to dream. *International Journal of Psychoanalysis*, 84: 17–30.
Ogden, T. (2006). On teaching psychoanalysis. *International Journal of Psychoanalysis*, 87: 1069–1085.
Okuma, T., Fukuma, E., and Kobayashi, K. (1976). "Dream detector" and comparison of laboratory and home dreams collected by REMP-awakening technique. In: *Advances in Sleep Research, Vol. 2*. E. Weitzman, ed. New York: Spectrum Publications, 223–231.
Oppenheim, A. (1956). The interpretation of dreams in the ancient Near East with a translation of an Assyrian dreambook. *Transactions of the American Philosophical Society*, 46(3): 179–373.
Orgel, S. (1974). Fusion with the victim and suicide. *International Journal of Psychoanalysis*, 55: 531–538.
Orlov, T., Makin, T. R., and Zohary, E. (2010). Topographic representation of the human body in the occipitotemporal cortex. *Neuron*, 68: 586–600.
Ortony, A., ed. (1993). *Metaphor and Thought*, 2nd edn. Oxford: Oxford University Press.
Panksepp, J. (1998). *Affective Neuroscience*. New York: Oxford University Press.
Parkin, A. and Leng, N. (1993). *Neuropsychology of the Amnesic Syndrome*. Hillsdale, NJ: Erlbaum.
Parsifal-Charles, N. (1986). *The Dream: 4,000 Years of Theory and Practice*. West Cornwall, CT: Locust Hill Press.
Perogamvros, L., Dang-Vu, T., Desseilles, M., and Schwartz, S. (2013). Sleep and dreaming are for important matters. *Frontiers in Psychology*, 4: 474.
Perrett, D., Rolls, E., and Caan, W. (1982). Visual neurones responsive to faces in the monkey temporal cortex. *Experimental Brain Research*, 47: 329–342.
Pick, D. and Roper, L. (2004). *Dreams and History*. London: Taylor and Francis.
Pinker, S. (1995). *The Language Instinct*. New York: Harper.
Pizer, S. (1998). *Building Bridges: The Negotiation of Paradox in Psychoanalysis*. Hillsdale, NJ: Analytic Press.
Polk, T., Park, J., Smith, M., and Park, D. (2007). Nature versus nurture in ventral visual cortex: A functional magnetic resonance imaging study of twins. *Journal of Neuroscience*, 27: 13921–13925.
Pötzl, O. (1917/1960). The relationship between experimentally induced dream images and indirect vision. *Psychological Issues*, 2: 41–120. (First published in: *Z. f. Neurol. Psychiat.*, 1917, 37: 278–349.)
Prigatano, G. (2010). *The Study of Anosognosia*. Oxford: Oxford University Press.
Pugh, G. (2007). On: The case against neuropsychoanalysis. *International Journal of Psycho-Analysis*, 88: 1067–1068.

Pulver, S. (2003). On the astonishing clinical irrelevance of neuroscience. *Journal of the American Psychoanalytic Association*, 51: 755–772.
Purcell, S. Mullington, J., Moffit, A., Hoffmann, R., and Pigeau, R. (1986). Dream self-reflectiveness as a learned cognitive skill. *Sleep*, 9: 423–437.
Pylyshyn, Z. (1973). What the mind's eye tells the mind's brain: A critique of mental imagery. *Psychological Bulletin*, 80: 1–22.
Quinodoz, J.-M. (1999). "Dreams that turn over a page": Integration dreams with paradoxical regressive content. *International Journal of Psychoanalysis*, 80: 225–238.
Rakison, D. and Butterworth, G. (1998). Infants' use of parts in early categorization. *Developmental Psychology*, 34: 49–62.
Rakison, D. and Cohen, I. (1999). Infants' use of functional parts in basic-like categorization. *Developmental Science*, 2: 423–431.
Ramachandran, V. (1996). The evolutionary biology of self-deception, laughter, dreaming and depression: Some clues from anosognosia. *Medical Hypotheses*, 47: 347–362.
Ramachandran, V. and Hubbard, E. (2001). Synaesthesia: A window into perception, thought and language. *Journal of Consciousness Studies*, 8(12): 3–34.
Ramachandran, V. and Hubbard, E. (2003). The phenomenology of synaesthesia. *Journal of Consciousness Studies*, 10: 49–57.
Ramachandran, V., Levi, L., Stone, L., Rogers-Ramachandran, D., McKinney, R., Stalcup, M., Arcila, G., Zweifler, R., Schatz, A., and Flippin, A. (1996). Illusions of body image: What they reveal about human nature. In: Llinás, R. and Churchland, P., eds., *The Mind-Brain Continuum: Sensory Processes*. Cambridge, MA: MIT Press, 29–60.
Réage, P. (1954). *The Story of O*. d'Estrée, S., trans. New York: Ballantine, 1973.
Rechtschaffen, A. (1978). The single-mindedness and isolation of dreams. *Sleep*, 1: 97–109.
Reece, W. (2004). *Dukes' Physiology of Domestic Animals*, 12th edn. Ithaca, NY: Cornell University Press.
Rees, W. D. (1975). The bereaved and their hallucinations. In: Schoenberg, B., Gerber, I., Wiener, A., Kutscher, A., Peretz, D., and Carr, A., eds., *Bereavement: Its Psychosocial Aspects*. New York: Columbia University Press, 66–71.
Reich, W. (1933). *Character Analysis*. New York: Orgone Institute Press.
Reinders, S., Nijenhuis, E., Quak, J., Korf, J., Haaksma, J., Paans, A., Willemsen, A., and den Boer, J. (2006). Psychobiological characteristics of dissociative identity disorder: A symptom provocation study. *Biological Psychiatry*, 60: 730–740.
Resnick, J., Stickgold, R., Rittenhouse, C., and Hobson, J. (1994). Self-representation and bizarreness in children's dreams collected in the home setting. *Consciousness and Cognition*, 3: 30–45.

Restak, R. (1991). *The Brain Has a Mind of Its Own*. New York: Crown.
Reti, R. (1951). *The Thematic Process in Music*. New York: Macmillan.
Revonsuo, A. (2005). The self in dreams. In: Feinberg, T. and Keenan, J., eds., *The Lost Self: Pathologies of the Brain and Identity*. Oxford: Oxford University Press, 206–219.
Richardson, J. (1999). *Imagery*. Hove, UK: Psychology Press.
Rittenhouse, C., Stickgold, R., and Hobson, J. (1994). Constraint on the transformation of characters, objects, and settings in dream reports. *Consciousness and Cognition*, 3: 100–113.
Rorem, N. (1994). *Knowing When to Stop*. New York: Simon and Schuster.
Rorem, N. (2000). *Lies: A Diary: 1986–1999*. Washington, DC: Counterpoint.
Rosch, E. (1977). Human categorization. In: Warren, N., ed., *Studies in Cross-Cultural Psychology*. London: Academic, 1–49.
Rosenfeld, H. (1987). *Impasse and Interpretation: Therapeutic and Antitherapeutic Factors in the Psychoanalytic Treatment of Psychotic, Borderline, and Neurotic Patients*. London: Tavistock.
Rowell, M. (1976). *Joan Miró: Peinture – Poésie*. Paris: Éditions de la différence.
Ryle, G. (1949). *The Concept of Mind*. New York: Barnes and Noble.
Sachs, H. (1913). Ein Traum Bismarcks [A Dream of Bismarck]. *Internationale Zeitschrift für Psychoanalyse*, 1: 80.
Sacks, O. (2002). The case of Anna H. *The New Yorker*, October 7, 63–73.
Samson, D. and Pillon, A. (2003). A case of impaired knowledge for fruit and vegetables. *Cognitive Neuropsychology*, 20: 373–400.
Sandler, J. and Freud, A. (1985). *The Analysis of Defense: The Ego and the Mechanisms of Defense Revisited*. New York: International Universities Press.
Sandor, P., Szakadat, S., and Bodizs, R. (2014). Ontogeny of dreaming: A review of empirical studies. *Sleep Medicine Reviews*, 18: 435–449.
Sands, S. (2010). On the royal road together: The analytic function of dreams in activating dissociative unconscious communication. *Psychoanalytic Dialogues*, 20: 357–373.
Sapir, E. (1929). A study in phonetic symbolism. *Journal of Experimental Psychology*, 12: 225–239.
Sartre, J.-P. (1958). *Being and Nothingness*. Barnes, H., trans. London: Methuen.
Saul, L. (1972). *Psychodynamically Based Psychotherapy*. New York: Science House.
Schacter, D. (1991). Unawareness of deficit and unawareness of knowledge in patients with memory disorders. In: Pritagano, G. and Schacter, D., eds., *Awareness of Deficit After Brain Injury*. New York: Oxford University Press, 127–151.

Schafer, R. (1995). Aloneness in the countertransference. *Psychoanalytic Quarterly*, 64: 496–516.
Schaller, S. (1991). *A Man Without Words*. Berkeley, CA: University of California Press.
Schatzman, M. (1983). Sleeping on problems can really solve them. *New Scientist*, August 11, 416–417.
Schimel, J. (1969). Dreams as transaction: An exercise in interpersonal theory. *Contemporary Psychoanalysis*, 6: 31–38.
Schinco, M. (2011). *The Composer's Dream: Essays on Dreams, Creativity, and Change*. Pari, Italy: Pari Publishing.
Schlauch, M. (1956). *Modern English and American Poetry: Techniques and Ideologies*. London: Watts.
Schneider, S. (2011). *The Language of Thought: A New Philosophical Direction*. Cambridge, MA: MIT Press.
Schur, M. (1966). Some additional "day residues" of the "specimen dream of psychoanalysis." In: Loewenstein, R., Newman, L., Schur, M., and Solnit, A., eds., *Psychoanalysis: A General Psychology*. New York: International Universities Press, 45–85.
Schur, M. (1972). *Freud: Living and Dying*. New York: International Universities Press.
Schwartz, F. and Lazar, Z. (1984). Contaminated thinking: A specimen of the primary process. *Psychoanalytic Psychology*, 1: 319–334.
Schwartz, S. (2003). Are life episodes replayed during dreaming? *Trends in Cognitive Sciences*, 7: 325–327.
Schwartz, S. and Maquet, P. (2002). Sleep imaging and the neuropsychological assessment of dreams. *Trends in Cognitive Sciences*, 6: 21–30.
Schweitzer, A. (1911). *J. S. Bach, Vol. 2*. New York: Dover (reprinted 1966).
Searles, H. (1955). The informational value of the supervisor's emotional experiences. *Psychiatry*, 18: 135–146.
Shakespeare, W. (1600/1). *The Tragedy of Hamlet, Prince of Denmark*. In: *William Shakespeare: The Complete Works*, Wells, S. and Taylor, G., gen. eds. Oxford: Clarendon Press, 2nd edn., 2005, 681–718.
Sharpe, E. F. (1937). *Dream Analysis*. New York: Norton.
Sharpe, E. F. (1940). Psycho-physical problems revealed in language: An examination of metaphor. *International Journal of Psycho-Analysis*, 21: 201–213.
Shostakovich, D. and Glikman, I. (2001). *Story of a Friendship: The Letters of Dmitry Shostakovich to Isaak Glikman*. Ithaca, NY: Cornell University Press.
Silberer, H. (1914). *Probleme der Mystik und ihrer Symbolik*. Vienna: Hugo Heller and Co.
Silbersweig, D., Stern, E., Frith, C., Cahill, C., Holmes, A., Grootoonk, S., Seaward, J., McKenna, P., Chua, S., Schnorr, L., Jones, T., and Frackowiak,

R. (1995). A functional neuroanatomy of hallucinations in schizophrenia. *Nature*, 378: 176–179.

Simner, J., Mulvenna, C., Sagiv, N., Tsakanikos, E., Witherby, S., Fraser, C., Scott, K., and Ward, J. (2006). Synaesthesia: The prevalence of atypical cross-modal experiences. *Perception*, 35: 1024–1033.

Simon, L., ed. (1944). *Gertrude Stein Remembered*. Lincoln, NE: University of Nebraska Press.

Simons, D. and Chabris, C. (1999). Gorillas in our midst: Sustained inattentional blindness for dynamic events. *Perception*, 28: 1059–1074.

Skelton, R. (1996). Is the unconscious structured like a language? *International Forum of Psychoanalysis*, 4: 168–178.

Sloman, S. (1996). The empirical case for two systems of reasoning. *Psychological Bulletin*, 119: 3–22.

Smart, J. J. C. (2017). The Mind/Brain Identity Theory. *The Stanford Encyclopedia of Philosophy*. Zalta, E. N., ed. Online at: https://plato.stanford.edu/archives/spr2017/entries/mind-identity/.

Smith, D. (1999). Fresh look at a syntax skewer. *New York Times*, June 9, E1–4.

Solms, M. (1995). New findings on the neurological organization of dreaming: Implications for psychoanalysis. *Psychoanalytic Quarterly*, 64: 43–67.

Solms, M. (1999). The new neuropsychology of sleep: Commentary by Mark Solms. *Neuropsychoanalysis*, 1: 183–195.

Solms, M. (2000). A psychoanalytic perspective on confabulation. *Neuropsychoanalysis*, 2: 133–138.

Spanjaard, J. (1969). The manifest dream content and its significance for the interpretation of dreams. *International Journal of Psycho-Analysis*, 50: 221–235.

States, B. (1995). Dreaming "accidentally" of Harold Pinter: The interplay of metaphor and metonymy in dreams. *Dreaming*, 5: 229–245.

Stekel, W. (1943/1967). *The Interpretation of Dreams*. New York: Washington Square Press.

Stern, D. (1997). *Unformulated Experience: From Dissociation to Imagination in Psychoanalysis*. Hillsdale, NJ: The Analytic Press.

Stevens, A. (1996). *Private Myths: Dreams and Dreaming*. Cambridge, MA: Harvard University Press.

Strathern, P. (2000). *Mendeleyev's Dream*. New York: St. Martin's.

Strauch, I. and Meier, B. (1996). *In Search of Dreams: Results of Experimental Dream Research*. Albany, NY: SUNY Press.

Sullivan, H. S. (1940). *Conceptions of Modern Psychiatry*. New York: Norton.

Sullivan, H. S. (1953). *The Interpersonal Theory of Psychiatry*. New York: Norton.

Sullivan, H. S. (1954). *The Psychiatric Interview*. New York: Norton.

Sullivan, H. S. (1956). *Clinical Studies in Psychiatry*. New York: Norton.
Sundar, S. (2015). *Handbook of the Psychology of Communication Technology*. New York: Wiley.
Swinney, D. (1979). Lexical access during sentence comprehension: (Re)consideration of content effects. *Journal of Verbal Learning and Verbal Behavior*, 18: 645–668.
Szalita, A. (1958). Regression and perception in psychotic states. *Psychiatry*, 21: 53–63.
Szalita, A. (1968). Reanalysis. *Contemporary Psychoanalysis*, 4: 83–102.
Szalita, A. (1982). Further thoughts on reanalysis. *Contemporary Psychoanalysis*, 18: 327–348.
Szaluta, J. (1980). Freud on Bismarck: Hanns Sachs' interpretation of a dream. *American Imago*, 37: 215–244.
Szechtman, H., Woody, E., Bowers, K., and Nahmias, C. (1998). Where the imaginal appears real: A positron emission tomography study of auditory hallucinations. *Proceedings of the National Academy of Science*, 95: 1956–1960.
Taylor, R. (1963). *Hoffmann*. London: Bowes and Bowes.
Teunisse, R., Zitman, F., Cruysberg, J., Hoefnagels, W., and Verbeek, A. (1996). Visual hallucinations in psychologically normal people: Charles Bonnet's syndrome. *The Lancet*, 347: 794–797.
Thompson, R. (1930). *The Epic of Gilgamesh*. Oxford: Oxford University Press.
Thurber, J. (1937). The Macbeth murder mystery. *The New Yorker*, October 2.
Titchener, E. (1909). *Experimental Psychology of the Thought Processes*. New York: Macmillan.
Triarhou, L. and del Cerro, M. (1985). Freud's contribution to neuroanatomy. *Archives of Neurology*, 42: 282–287.
Trilling, L. (1950). Freud and literature. In: *The Liberal Imagination*. New York: Viking Press, 34–57.
Uga, V., Lemut, M., Zampi, C., Zilli, I., and Salzarulo, P. (2006). Music in dreams. *Consciousness and Cognition*, 15: 351–357.
Ullman, M. (1969). Dreaming as metaphor in motion. *Archives of General Psychiatry*, 21: 696–703.
Ullman, M. (1987). The experiential dream group. In: Ullman, M. and Limmer, C., eds., *The Variety of Dream Experience*. New York: Continuum, 3–30.
Ullman, M. (1994). The experiential dream group: Its application in the training of therapists. *Dreaming*, 4: 223–229.
Ullman, M. (1996). *Appreciating Dreams: A Group Approach*. Thousand Oaks, CA; Sage.
Ullman, M. and Limmer, C. (1999). *The Variety of Dream Experience: Expanding our Ways of Working with Dreams*. Albany, NY: SUNY Press.

Urbina, S. (1981). Methodological issues in the quantitative analysis of dream content. *Journal of Personality Assessment*, 45: 71–78.

Vaillant, G., ed. (1992). *Ego Mechanisms of Defense*. Washington, DC: American Psychiatric Association.

Valéry, P. (1936). La philosophie de la danse. Online at: http://cache.media.education.gouv.fr/file/Daac/30/0/valery_philosophie_danse_344300.pdf.

van der Hart, O. and Horst, R. (1989). The dissociation theory of Pierre Janet. *Journal of Traumatic Stress*, 2: 1–11.

van Eeden, F. (1913). A study of dreams. *Proceedings of the Society for Psychical Research*, 26: 431–461.

Varela, F., Thompson, E., and Rosch, E. (1991). *Embodied Mind: Cognitive Science and Human Experience*. Cambridge, MA: MIT Press.

Vaschide, N. (1911). *Le sommeil et les rêves*. Paris: Ernest Flammarion.

Vendler, Z. (1977). Wordless thoughts. In: *Language and Thought: Anthropological Issues*. McCormack, W. and Wurm, S., eds. The Hague: Mouton Publishers, 29–44.

Vernon, M. (1937). *Visual Perception*. Cambridge, UK: Cambridge University Press.

Vico, G. (1744/2001). *New Science: Principles of the New Science Concerning the Common Nature of Nations*. London: Penguin.

Vischer, R. (1873). *Über das optische Formgefühl: Ein Beitrag zur Aesthetik*. Leipzig: Hermann Credner. (For an English translation of selections, see Wind, E. (1963). *Art and Anarchy*, London: Faber and Faber.)

von Bubnoff, A. (2005). Stroke patients shed light on metaphors. *Nature*, May 26. Online at: www.nature.com/news/2005/050523/full/news050523-9.html.

von Riesemann, Oskar (1934). *Rachmaninoff's Recollections, Told to Oskar von Riesemann*. New York: Macmillan.

Vygotsky, L. (1934/1986). *Thought and Language*. Kozulin, A., trans. Cambridge, MA: MIT Press.

Wagner, P. (1963). The second analysis. *International Journal of Psychoanalysis*, 44: 481–489.

Wagner, U., Gais, S., Haider, H., Verleger, R., and Born, J. (2004). Sleep inspires insight. *Nature*, 427: 352–355.

Waldhorn, H. (1967). *The Place of the Dream in Clinical Psychoanalysis*. New York: International Universities Press.

Warner, S. L. (1983). Can psychoanalytic treatment change dreams? *Journal of the American Academy of Psychoanalysis*, 11: 299–316.

Warrington, E. and McCarthy, R. (1983). Category specific access dysphasia. *Brain*, 106: 859–878.

Warrington, E. and McCarthy, R. (1987). Categories of knowledge: Further fractionation and an attempted integration. *Brain*, 110: 1273–1296.

Weisz, R. and Foulkes, D. (1970). Home and laboratory dreams collected under uniform sampling conditions. *Psychophysiology*, 6: 588–596.

Werker, J. and Tees, R. (1984). Cross-language speech perception: Evidence for perceptual reorganization during the first year of life. *Infant Behavior and Development*, 7: 49–63.

Werner, H. (1948/1980). *Comparative Psychology of Mental Development*, 3rd edn., 1980. New York: International Universities Press.

Westen, D. (1998). The scientific legacy of Sigmund Freud: Toward a psychodynamically informed psychological science. *Psychological Bulletin*, 124: 333–371.

Whitty, C. and Lewin, W. (1957). Vivid day-dreaming: An unusual form of confusion following anterior cingulectomy. *Brain*, 80: 72–76.

Wilde, O. (1891/1974). *The Picture of Dorian Gray*. New York: Oxford University Press.

Wittgenstein, L. (1968). *Philosophical Investigations*. Oxford: Basil Blackwell.

Wittgenstein, L. (2001). *Philosophical Investigations*, 3rd edn. Anscombe, G. E. M., trans. Oxford: Blackwell.

Wolstein, B. (1959). *Countertransference*. New York: Grune and Stratton. Republished 1995, Northvale, NJ: Jason Aronson.

Wolstein, B. (1984). A proposal to enlarge the individual model of psychoanalytic supervision. *Contemporary Psychoanalysis*, 20: 131–144.

Yamamoto, J., Okonogi, K., Iwasaki, T., and Yoshimura, S. (1969). Mourning in Japan. *American Journal of Psychiatry*, 125: 1660–1665.

Young, A., Ellis, H., and Szulecka, T. (1990). Face processing impairment and delusional misidentification. *Behavioral Neurology*, 3: 153–168.

Young-Bruehl, E. (1988). *Anna Freud: A Biography*. London: Macmillan.

Young-Eisendrath, P. (2003). Review of *The Dream Frontier*. *Psychologist-Psychoanalyst*, 23: 41–43.

Yovell, Y. (2000). From hysteria to post-traumatic stress disorder: Psychoanalysis and the neurobiology of traumatic memories. *Neuropsychoanalysis*, 2: 171–182.

Yuasa, Y. (2008). *Overcoming Modernity: Synchronicity and Image-Thinking*. Albany, NY: SUNY Press.

Zajonc, R. (1980). Feeling and thinking: Preferences need no inferences. *American Psychologist*, 35: 151–175.

Zhong, C. B. and Leonardelli, G. J. (2008). Cold and lonely: Does social exclusion literally feel cold? *Psychological Science*, 19: 838–842.

Index

Page numbers in **bold** denote tables, those in *italics* denote figures.

9/11 attacks 146–148

Abraham, K. 48, 49
Activation-Synthesis Hypothesis 8
Adès, Thomas 110, 265
advertising, and metaphor 70, *72*
afterlife 260–262
agnosia 258, 286, 291
AIDS 163–164, 208–209
Albee, G. 92, 308
allegory, dream as 56–59, 133
alpha elements 176–177
Altman, Leonard 194–195
Alzheimer disease 287
amygdala 273
Andersen, H. 289
animals: animal-human category transgressions 36–37; animal-human metaphors 52; dreamers as 23
anosognosia 172
anterior communicating artery 178n8, 262
anthropomorphism 52
anxiety 20, 50, 51, 143, 144, 148, 172, 180, 186, 187, 208, 210, 211, 221, 224, 226, 257, 263, 280, 290
aphasia 39, 247
apophasis 96n3
Appelfeld, A. 242
Arieti, S. 177, 240–241
Aristotle 61, 295
Arlow, J. 84, 262

art: category transgressions 35, *36*; and metaphor 69–70, *70–71*; and metonym 113–117, *114*; nonlinguistic puns 106
Aserinsky, E. 22, 185
associations: and condensation 27–29; and metonym 117–118; necessary for dream interpretation 186–187, 188–189, 190; nonverbal associations 206–211; and symbols 124–125; *see also* group dream interpretation
Atlas, G. 130, 131
attachment 50
Aulagnier, P. 181n30

Bach, J.S. 68, 97n20, 269
Banaji, M. 173
Bargh, J. 281
Beckett, S. 235
Beethoven, Ludwig van 35, 68, 103–104, 108–110, 116, 118n3, 265, 269, 277
Belvin, F. 95–96
Benfey, O. 269
Berg, Alban, *Wozzeck* 104
Berlin, I. 62
Berne, E. 51
Bible 57–58, 220
Bion, W. 176–177, 228
bistable images 104, *105*, 106
bizarreness 9, 17, 19, 59, 69, 133n5, 190, 206, 240, 241, 245, 251n1

Blatt, S. 83
Blechner, M.: bigenderism 153; combined metaphors 60–67; concrete approach to dreams 7, 12n4, 186; disjunctive cognitions 240–244, 276–278; dreams as supervision 56, 187, 191, 212–216, 219n4; endoneuropsychic perception 174–176; extralinguistic thoughts 6, 303; grammar of irrationality 239ff; interobjects 107–108, 240, 244–248; *Jeopardy!* approach to dreams 59, 151; musical puns 103–104; negative dream screen 154; nonlinguistic metaphor 67–72; Oneiric Darwinism 33, 245; oxymoronic speech acts 17, 47, 96n3; perception/dream-creation hypothesis 130, 133n5; psychoanalyst's dream about the patient 101–102, 293n6; psychosis and dreams 177, 260; secondary pruning 153; tertiary revision 189–190; vectors of interpretation 187–188
blending theory 77–82, 85
blindness 74, 290
Boas, F. 226
Bochner, M. 117
bodily displacements 43–44
bodily experiences/parts *see* human body
borderline personality disorder (BPD) 250
Borges, J., Funes the memorius 177
Bosnak, R. 11, 63, 191
Bostridge, I. 47
Bradley, L. 259
Brahms, Johannes 67, 109, 266–267, 268, 272, 274–276, 282
brain-damage: and disjunctive cognitions 243–244; and interobjects 39–40, 247; and knowledge 286; and metamemory 287; and psychological defenses 172, 178n8; and reality monitoring 257, 262; and the unconscious 273–274
Brenman-Gibson, M. 178n3
Brenner, C. 190, 192, 302
Breuer, J. 280
Brill, A.A. 136, 138, 144n1
Brockman, R. 250–251
Bromberg, P. 279n7
Brown, R. 179n12
Burston, D. 178n3
Butterworth, G. 246

Cairns, H. 282, 294
Caligor, L. 129, 219n5
Capgras Syndrome 243
Carroll, Lewis 100–101
castration anxiety 50–51
categorical perception 293n8
categories 15, 25–41, 48, 78, 80–82, 98n23, 245–248, 251n4, 291
Chabris, C. 290
Charles Bonnet syndrome 249
charting a dream 135–144
Chaucer, G. 125
children: and dreams 19, 37, 52, 80–81, 247–248; and inner speech 296–297; and psychological defences 159, 167; and reality testing 289–290
Chomsky, N. 106n2
Chuang-Tzu 253, 264n1
cingulate 257, 263
cingulectomy 257, 332
Claparède, E. 22, 282–283
cognitive metaphor theory 47, 50, 77–78
Colace, C. 97n9
combined metaphors 60–67
commenting self 272
concepts 115, 177, 206, 244, 261, 276, 288, 300, 303, 304n1

conceptualizing and working with dreams 185–195; and associations 186–187, 188–189, 190, 192, 193–194, 195; disguised or undisguised dreams 185–187; and Kris Study Group 190, 191, 193–195; and primary emotion of dream 191, 192; and reanalysis 193–194; and role of psychoanalysis 190–195; secondary and tertiary revision 189–190; and transference 191; vectors of interpretation 187–188
condensation 18, 25–41; category transgressions 34–40; classification of 25–33; and cognitive neuroscience 38–40; Condensation Game 33–34; creative 29–30; formal 26; ideational 26–27; lexical 25–26; limits of category transgression 37–40; partial 30–33; simple overdetermined 27–29
connectionism 39
consciousness 3, 4, 9, 10, 11, 15, 20, 21, 22, 30, 35, 37, 45, 64, 91, 110, 119, 132, 133n5, 134, 151, 153, 154, 156, 157, 171, 173–175, 176, 178n7, 185, 192, 204, 218, 244, 255, 258, 263, 265, 268, 269, 271, 272, 274, 275, 276, 278, 279n6, 281, 283, 284, 286, 289, 293n4, 298, 301
constructed dream thought 300
contamination (of metaphor) 83
creative condensation 29–30
Cutting, J. 5, 26, 311, 321

Da Vinci, Leonardo 35, 245
Damasio, A. 10, 181n28, 273–274
Darwin, C. 1, 5, 33, 62, 76, 245
Day, R.S. 5, 311
deafness 302
death 114, 124, 127, 154, 159, 171, 197, 227, 254–256, 260–262, 292, 293n9

defenses see psychological defenses
Dement, W. 185, 270–271, 281
denial 148, 171, 172–173
Descartes 1
Dickinson, E. 174
disjunctive cognitions 19, 240–244, 276–278
displacement 4, 5, 16, 18, 23n2, 42–44
dissociation 154–157, 209, 255, 263
Doctrine of Affects 68
dream charts 135–144
dream doubters 7–8
dream immersers 7
dream screen 154; negative dream screen 154
dream translators 7
dreams, of composers 5–6, 110
dreams, new ways of working with see conceptualizing and working with dreams
dreams over time see evolving dream interpretations
dreamthoughts, latent 42, 88, 94, 158, 187, 245, 287, 300–301, 304n3
dreamwork 4–7, 12, 18, 19, 26, 27, 34, 93, 124, 131–132, 158, 159, 176, 185, 227, 230, 300–301
Dreifus, C. 290
dualism 1–2
Duchamp, M. 117
Dukakis, M. 96n3

Edelman, G. 248
ego 4, 38, 134, 149, 172, 175, 178n2, 206, 266, 268, 272, 279n10, 287–288
ego defenses see psychological defenses
ego islands 279n7
ego, observing 272–273
Eimas, P. 303
Einstein, Albert 12, 267, 316
embodied imagination 63–64

emotions: displacement of 43; and dream metaphors 54; embodied imagination 63–64; interaction with bodily experience 76–77; and music 68; primary emotions of the dream 191–192; and symbols 131–132; *see also* psychological defenses
encapsulated modules 275–278
endoneuropsychic perception 175–176
endopsychic perception 157, 174–176, 292n1
Epstein, A. 140, 249
Erikson, E. 6–7, 32, 118–119, 134–144, 178n3, 195n1
Ervin, F. 140
evolving dream interpretations 196–219; at beginning and end of treatment 204–206; enactment of the dream 209–211; interpretation preceding dream 217–218; and nonverbal associations 206–211; over long time period 201–204; from scant information 216–217; and supervising the analyst 212–216

face recognition 243–244, 248
Fauconnier, G. 85, 112
Ferenczi, S. 31–32, 158–159
Feve, A. 249
Fiorina, C. 96n3
Fliess, W. 138–139, 144n2
Fodor, J. 12, 133n1, 275–276, 303
Fonagy, P. 149, 151, 168
Forceville, C.J. 48
formal condensation 26
Fosse, M. 65
Fosshage, J. 101, 243
Foucault, M. 2
Franz, M-L. von 226
free association 189, 190, 193, 195, 217
Frégoli Syndrome 244
Freud, A. 7, 148–149, 159, 160, 162, 167, 178n3

Freud, S.: and condensation 25, 29, 30, 32, 34–35, 37; and death 261–262; and displacement 42–44; and dream interpretation 186–187, 189; dream thoughts 19–20, 300–301; as dream translator 7; and endopsychic perception 174–175; and formation of dreams 8, 134; and homoforms 107; Irma dream 136–139; mechanisms of the dreamwork 4–5; and metaphor 50–51, 58, 59, 85, 88–89, 90, 95, 99n29; mindbrain transforming reality 18; neuropsychoanalysis and psychoanalysis 237–238; and psychological defenses 155, 157–158, 159–160, 166; and puns 100; purpose of dreams 185, 195; and rebus 85, 88–89, 90, 95, 99n29; and repression 280; and secondary revision of dreams 189; and symbols 107, 121, 123–124, 127, 130–132, 133; and the unconscious 266, 268
Friedrich, Caspar David 69, *70*
Fromm, Erich 127
Fromm, Erika 286
Futurama 61

Galton, F. 26, 29, 73
Gardner, H. 5, 16, 75
Garland, Judy 29
Gazzaniga, M. 155, 293n3
Get Smart and metaphor 58, 108n2
Gilgamesh, dream of 56–57
Glikman, I. 268
Glucksberg, S. 98n23
Goethe, J. 25
Goldberger, M. 155–156, 178n4
Gorno-Tempini, M. 244
Greenson, R. 97n13, 195n3
Groddeck, G. 275
group dream interpretation 220–233; and composition of group 231–232;

group dream interpretation *continued*
and experimentation 226–228; and
group dynamics 228; impact on
one-on-one analysis 230–231; the
process 222–226; and
psychoanalysis 228–230; and
Ullman, M. 220–222; without the
dreamer 231

Hadamard, J. 267
Haldeman, H. 60
Hall, C. 300
hallucinations 249, 261–264
Hamilton, E. 282, 294
Hart, G. 249
Hartmann, E. 269
Helmholtz, H, von 239, 290–291
Helmsley, L. 52
Heraclitus 38
Herzen, A. 62
Hilgard, E. 155
Hillman, J. 38
hippocampus 250, 263, 273
Hirst, W. 113
Hitchcock, A. 44n1; *Vertigo* 255
Hobbes, T. 46–47
Hobson, J.A. 7–10, 66, 81, 140–141, **142**, 176
Holocaust 18, 255, 284
Homer 125
Homer1a 177, 313
homoforms 16, 107–108, 121
homomelodies 108–110
Howe, Elias 304n2
Hubbard, E. 75, 101
human attachment 50
human body: and metaphor 47–53, 64, 76–77; and symbols 123–124, 130–131; and synkinesia 76
hypnagogic imagery (Silberer) 64
hypnosis 286

Ibsen, H. 25
ideational condensation 26

identification with the aggressor 159–161
Igesz, Bodo 287–288
imagistic thinking 300–302
immortality 262
Implicit Association Test 173
implicit processing of mindbrain *see* unconscious processing of mindbrain
incest 117, 118, 127, 232
inner speech 296–300
intellectualization 164–166
interobjects 30–33, 38, 39–40; and blending theory 78–82; and neuropsychoanalysis and psychoanalysis 244–248
interpersonal relationships, and dream metaphors 55–56
intuition 40, 60, 173, 231–232, 267–269, 271–272, 281
isolation 147, 162–164

Jackendoff, R. 279n6
Jacobi, J.J. 189
Jakobson, R. 113
Janet, P. 179n11
Jeopardy! approach to dream 7, 59, 151, 192
Johnson, M. 47, 50, 64, 112, 205
Johnson-Laird, P. 276
Jones, K. 44n1
Joyce, James 44n1
Julesz, B. 26
Jung, C. 7, 120, 122, 123, 126, 129, 161, 189, 218

Kafka, F. 52
Kahneman, D. 272, 277
Kaplan-Solms, K. 242, 257, 261
Kekulé, A. 269
Kernberg, O. 192, 206, 250
Kihlstrom, D. 266
kiki-bouba effect 74–75
Kilroe, P. 300
kinesthesia 64

Klein, M. 43, 50
Kleitman, N. 22, 185
Kohut, H. 51, 211
Korsakoff syndrome 282, 287
Kosslyn, S. 253–254, 258
Kozloff, D. 264n3
Kraepelin, E. 298–299
Kris Study Group 190–195
Kubovy, M. 26

LaBerge, S. 259
Lacan, J. 44
Lakoff, G. 47, 50, 64, 112, 115, 205
Langer, S. 34
language of thought 294–304; and dreams 296; dreams and substrate of thought 303–304; images 301–302; inner speech 296–300; and wakingwork 300–303
latent dream thought 3–4, 86, 88, 90, 1, 93–94, 104, 128–132, 158, 176, 186–187, 195, 206, 249, 300–301
Laughlin, H.P. 155
Lawrence, W. 228
Lazar, Z. 83
Lerdahl, F. 279n6
Levenson, E. 97n13, 118, 186, 196
Lewin, B. 154
Lewin, W. 257
Lewitt, S. 117
lexical condensation 25–26, 34
Libet, B. 22, 266
Lipps, T. 69
Llinás, R. 301
Locke, J. 74
Loew, C. 101, 243
Lombardi, R. 246
Lorand, S. 127
lucid dreaming 24n5, 258, 259, 264n1
Luria, A
Lyotard, F. 70, 304n3

Magritte, René 69, *71*, 78, 106, 113–114, *114*

Mahler, Gustav 109
Mahling, F. 73
manifest content, dreams 26, 27, 29, 30, 31, 65, 93–94, 128, 132, 134, 135, 138, 147, 157, 158, 161, 165, 168, 188, 195n2, 222–223, 225–226, 230, 239, 269, 300–301
Maquet, P. 242, 244, 278n3
Marin-Amat syndrome 76
May, R. 12, 129
McCarley, R.W. 7–8
McCarthy, R. 247
McClelland, J. 39
McClelland, S. 117
McKeon, R. 295
McWilliams, N. 157, 164, 167, 178n7, 180n16
me-ness 22–23, 282–286
Meltzer, D. 31, 107, 230, 245
memory: and conscious awareness 282–283; metamemory 287–289; mnemonists 177; and PTSD 250; and repression 151–153
mentalese 304n1
Messiaen, Olivier 268–269
Mesulam, M.-M. 272
meta-knowledge 217, 292
meta-memory 287–289
metaphor 45–96; animal-human 52; blending theory 77–82, 85; bodily 47–53, 64, 76–77; combined 60–67; compared to puns 100–101; concept of 45–48; contamination 83; and dream as allegory 56–59; and dream interpretation 52–56; everyday use of 45–47; mappings between concepts and bodies 76–77; mixed 60–61; nonlinguistic 67–72; pictorial portrayal in dreams 59; and rebus 85–96; synesthesia 73–75; synkinesia 76; and transference 83–85
metonymy 44, 111–119; common and idiosyncratic 112–114; and dreams

metonymy *continued*
   117–119; and synecdoche 111–112; words in paintings 115–117
Millar, M. 186
mindbrain: concept of 1–2
mindbrain and mentation in dreams 15–24; dreamwork or wakingwork 19–20; experiencing dreams 20–23; how reality is transformed 18–19; and transformation of the world in dreams 15–17
Minsky, M. 290
Miró, Joan 115, *115*
mixed metaphors 60–61
Modell, A. 83
modules, mental 241, 244, 275–279
Mozart, Wolfgang Amadeus 68, 104, 109, 262; *Don Giovanni* 104, 109; Piano Concerto #23, 68; Symphony #40, 269
Müller-Lyer optical illusion *275*, 275–276
multiple personalities/selves 21, 272–273
music: category transgressions 35–36; homomelodies 108–110; implicit processing of mindbrain 265–269; and metaphor 67–69; non-linguistic rebus 95–96; and puns 103–104; and synesthesia 73; and synkinesia 76
Mussorgsky, Modest Petrovich 68
myth 35–37, 40, 122, 179n11, 190, 198, 245, 247, 264n3
mythology, category transgressions in 36–37

Nabokov, V. 75, 301
Neubauer, P. 44
neurological syndromes, and psychoanalysis 248–249
neuropsychoanalysis and psychoanalysis 237–251; and disjunctive cognitions 240–244; impact on clinical work 250–251; and interobjects 244–248; and neurological syndromes 248–249; rejection of 237–238
Nietzsche, F. 42, 46, 96n1, 97n5, 275
Nixon, R. 60
nonlinguistic metaphor 67–72, 74, 76
nonlinguistic puns 103–106
nonlinguistic rebus 95–96
nonlinguistic thought 5–6
nonverbal associations 206–211

Oatley, K. 276
Obama, R., *Dreams from my Father* 227n4
observing ego 272
octatonic mode 268–269, 310
Ogden, T. 177, 226, 230
Oneiric Darwinism 33, 245
Orgel, S. 180n18
Orlov, T. 130
Ortony, A. 78
Orwell, G. 52
OTTFF experiment 180n2, 270–271, 281–282, 301
oxymoronic speech act 47

Paine, Thomas 280
Panksepp, J. 277
Parallel Distributed Processing 39
parapsychology 263
Paré, D. 301
Parkinson disease 249
Parsifal-Charles, N. 253
partial condensation 30–33
Perrett, D. 244
Pharaoh's dream 57–58, 220
philosophy i, ii, 2, 16, 45–47, 50, 113, 253, 276, 286, 294–296, 302
Piaget, J. 97n7, 297
Picasso, Pablo 35, *36*, 106, 113, 115, *116*
pictograms 181n30

pictorialization 4, 59, 62–67, 150, 163, 300
Pinker, S. 304n1
Plato: *Meno* 281; *Theaetetus* 294–295
Polk, T. 248
post-traumatic stress disorder (PTSD) 250–251, 263
Pötzl, O. 286, 289
predicate 275; subjectless 297–299
prejudice 43, 147, 171, 173
procedural knowledge 289–292
projection 161–162
Prokofiev, Sergei 109
prolepsis 969n3
prolongational reduction 279n6
prosopagnosia 243
psychological defenses 6–7, 146–181; and 9/11 attacks 146–148; appearance of in dreams 149–151; and Bion, Wilfred 176–177; concept of 148; denial 171; dissociation 154–157; and endoneuropsychic perception 175–176; and endopsychic perception 174–176; heterogeneity of 172–174; history of in psychoanalysis 148–151; identification with the aggressor 159–161; intellectualization 164–166; isolation 162–164; neurobiology of 172; projection 161–162; reaction formation 157–159, 173; repression 149–150, 151–154, 280; splitting 168–171; turning aggression against the self 166–168; undoing 166
psychosexual stages 43, 50, 48–49
psychosis 37, 83, 174–175, 177
puns 100–106; nonlinguistic 103–104; semantic 100–102; syntactic 102–103; visual 104–106
Purcell, S. 258

Rakison, D. 246

Ramachandran, V.S. 21, 46, 75, 101, 172, 273
reaction formation 44n3, 157–159, 172–174
Reagan, Ronald 96
Réage, P. 216
reality monitoring 252–264; brain-damaged people 257; process of 253–257; reality testing and assignment 257–259, 289–291; and wishes 260–264
reality testing and assignment 257–259, 289–291
rebus 5, 12n3, 16–17, 85–96, 97n8, 98n25, 98n26, 98n27, 98n28, 98n29, 100, 115, 119, 120, 123, 125, 151, 168, 170, 211, 293n10; interpretation of 85–93; nonlinguistic 95–96; and understanding dreams 94–95
Rechtschaffen, A. 258, 260–261
Reich, W. 48
REM (rapid eye movement) sleep 4, 8
repression 149–150, 151–154, 280
Restak, R. 22
Revonsuo, A. 23
Rimsky-Korsakov, N. 73, 98n21
Rittenhouse, C. 246–247
Rogers, C. 51
Rorem, N. 5–6, 269
Rosch, E. 35
Rousseau, J.-J. 62
Ruscha, E. 117
Ryle, G. 295

Sachs, H. 121
Sandler, J. 148–149, 159, 162, 167
Sapir, E. 75
Sartre, J.-P. 279n10
savant syndrome 117
Schacter, D. 286, 287
Schaller, S. 302
Schinco, M. 110
schizophrenia 240–241, 262, 263, 279n7

Schlauch, M. 49
Schönberg, Arnold 36
Schur, M. 138, 186
Schweitzer, A. 68
secondary revision of dreams 189–190
segmentation of mindbrain 271–276, 278n4
self-esteem 51
September 11 attacks 146–148
Shakespeare 45, 97n17, 100, 113, 252, 264n3
shame 59, 131, 133, 147, 166, 191, 193, 195
Sharpe, E.F. 49, 101
Shostakovich, D. 69, 106n1, 268, 269
Silberer, H. 64
Silbersweig, D. 263
Simon, L. 125
simple overdetermined condensation 27–29
Sixth Sense (film) 261
Skelton, R. 101
Skinner, B.F. 296
Sloman, S. 277
Smart, J.J.C. 2
social dreaming matrix 227–228, 233n4
Socrates 281, 294–295, 296
Solms, M. 178n8, 257
somatization 173
speech perception, Japanese infants 303
Spelke, E. 303
Sperry, R. 155
split-brain patients (commissurotomy) and dissociation 155, 293n3
splitting 168–171
SSRI 251
States, B. 245–246
Stein, G. 125, 299
Strachey, J. 138, 144n1
Strauss, R. 69
striatum, right ventral 263
structuring of experience in dreams 134–145

Sullivan, H.S. 179n11, 253
superego 54, 174–175, 206, 272–273
Swinney, D. 28, 107–108
Swinney effect 40n2, 107–108
symbols 16–17, 18, 120–133; causal approach to 129; cultural references 122; and emotions 131–132; final approach to 129; Freudian 130–131; and homoforms 121; idiosyncratic connections 122; interpretation of 123–129; linguistic connection 121; mythic references 122; relation between symbol and symbolized 121–122; scope of 132–133; sexual 121, 123, 124, 125–126, 127, 128; symbols as themselves 127–129; what constitutes a symbol 123–125
synaptic scaling 177
synecdoche 111–112
synesthesia 6, 17, 23n1, 73–75, 98n21
synkinesia 6, 17, 76
Szalita, A. 193, 279n7
Szechtman, H. 263

Tancred 124
TAT (thematic apperception test) 8
Taylor, Elizabeth 70, *72*
Taylor, R. 73
tertiary revision of dreams 118, 189–190
Teunisse, R. 249
thalamus, bilateral 263
Thomson, E. 48, 64
Thomson, R. 56
thought disorder 17, 83, 98n24
thought, language of *see* language of thought
time span reduction 279n6
Tiresias 36
Titchener, E. 301–302
Tolstoy, Leo 294
transference 83–85, 156, 191, 213–214, 243–244

trauma and dreams 53, 84, 114, 118–119, 129, 146, 154, 165, 180n23, 181n30, 188, 199, 221, 250–251, 256, 289
Trilling, L. 44n1
Tristan chord 69
Trump, D. 96n3
Turner, M. 47, 115
turning aggression against the self 166–168
twelve-tone row 269
typical dreams 133

Ullman, M. 34, 56, 220–222, 230
Unabomber 132, 133n6
unconscious 4, 12n,4, 15, 20, 22, 31, 61, 76, 84, 115, 119, 122, 124, 153, 157, 173, 176, 179, 187, 195, 211, 215, 217, 218, 226, 229, 230, 239, 242, 245, 246, 249, 255, 262, 265, 266, 272, 274, 275, 278, 279n6, 281, 283, 284, 286, 289, 293n4, 298, 301
unconscious categorization 245–246
unconscious, collective
unconscious, group 226
unconscious processing of mindbrain 265–293; being smarter in dreams 269–271, 285–286; disjunctive cognitions 276–278; and encapsulated modules 275–278; and knowledge 280–289; and me-ness 282–286; metamemory 287–289; multiple selves/personalities 272–273; and music 265–269; prejudice 173; procedural knowledge 289–292; and segmentation of mindbrain 271–275; solving problems in dreams 269–271, 281–282, 301

unconscious, unrepressed 246, 251n3, 266, 280–286
undoing 166

Valéry, P. 66–67
Varela, F. 48, 64
Vaschide, N. 285
vectors of interpretation 187–188
Vendler, Z. 296
Vico, G. 47–48
Vischer, R. 69
visual puns 104–106
von Franz, M.-L. 226
voyeurism 197–201
Vygotsky, L. 296–298, 299–300

Wagner, R. 15, 69, 111
wakingwork 19–20, 300–303
Waldhorn, H. 190–191, 194, 195
Walters, B. 52
Warrington, E. 247
Westen, D. 281
Whitty, C. 257
Wish-fulfilment 3, 4, 8–10, 18, 52, 84, 97n9, 118, 119n2, 122, 127, 129, 134, 139, 157, 161, 168, 170–171, 185, 187, 198, 210, 211, 213, 214, 218, 232, 249, 254, 256, 260–264, 285, 288
Wittgenstein, L. 110, 295–296
Wool, C. 117
words in paintings 115–117
World Trade Center attacks 146–148

Young-Eisendrath, P. 186
Yovell, Y. 251
Yuasa, Y. 302

Zeus 36
Zhŭzĭ 302